D1711117

LAOS: BEYOND THE REVOLUTION

Also by Joseph J. Zasloff

APPRENTICE REVOLUTIONARIES: The Communist
Movement in Laos, 1930–1985 (*with MacAlister Brown*)
COMMUNISM IN INDOCHINA: New Perspectives (*editor with
MacAlister Brown*)
COMMUNIST INDOCHINA AND US FOREIGN POLICY
(*with MacAlister Brown*)
INDOCHINA IN CONFLICT (*editor with Allan Goodman*)
NORTH VIETNAM AND THE PATHET LAO (*with Paul
Langer*)
POSTWAR INDOCHINA: Old Enemies and New Allies (*editor*)
THE PATHET LAO: Leadership and Organization

Laos: Beyond the Revolution

Edited by

Joseph J. Zasloff
Professor of Political Science, University of Pittsburgh

and

Leonard Unger
Professor, School of Advanced International Studies
Johns Hopkins University

St. Martin's Press   New York

First published in the United States of America in 1991

Printed in Hong Kong

ISBN 0–312–04486–0

Library of Congress Cataloging-in-Publication Data
Laos: beyond the revolution/edited by Joseph J. Zasloff and Leonard
Unger
p. cm.
ISBN 0–312–04486–0
1. Laos—History—1975– 1. Zasloff. Joseph J. II. Unger.
Leonard.
DS555.84.L62 1991
959.404—dc20   89–77794
                                                            CIP

Contents

PART IV   EXTERNAL RELATIONS

PART V   US POLICY TOWARDS LAOS IN
HISTORICAL PERSPECTIVE

List of Maps

Acknowledgements

The editors of this volume, who also served as co-chairmen of the conference from which it emerged, would like to express gratitude to a number of people. We thank Hans Binnendijk, former director of the Center for the Study of Foreign Affairs, and Joseph V. Montville, director of research of the Center at the time the conference was planned, for their support in convening the conference. We are specially grateful to Linda Lum, professional staff member of the Center, for her valuable assistance. The National Defense University generously provided funds to commission papers by the academic specialists represented in the volume. We wish to thank Ambassador G. McMurtrie Godley for his support to the conference. Finally, we express our thanks to all of the authors for their thoughtful and articulate contributions to the Conference and the book.

JOSEPH J. ZASLOFF
LEONARD UNGER

Notes on the Contributors

Wendy Batson has been a freelance consultant since 1988. Her previous positions include consultant to the United Nations Development Program in Vientiane, Lao PDR, and Co-director of the Indochina Project, Washington, DC (1986–7); consultant to the UNDP in Vientiane (1985); Co-Director of the American Friends Service Committee programs in Vientiane (1981–4); and research, writing, and administrative responsibilities with the United Farm Workers Union of America (AFL–CIO) in California (1973–7). Ms Batson holds a BA from the University of California/Berkeley.

MacAlister Brown has been Professor with the Department of Political Science, Williams College, since 1956. He has taught courses on the American presidency and Congress, American foreign policy, the US political economy, American political thought, international relations, diplomacy and negotiation, international law and organisation, and comparative politics; and has held various administrative positions with Williams. Dr Brown has been Visiting Fulbright Lecturer in International Relations at Chulalongkorn University in Bangkok, Thailand (1980–1, 1984–5); and Fulbright Lecturer in Public Administration at Tribhuwan University in Nepal. He has been a Congressional Fellow of the American Political Science Association (1962–3), and has taught at Dartmouth College (1953–5). He has written several books and dozens of articles. His writings include *Apprentice Revolutionaries: The Communist Movement in Laos, 1930–1985* (co-author with Joseph J. Zasloff, 1986); *Indochina and Problems of Security and Stability in Southeast Asia* (co-editor with Khien Theeravit, 1981); *Communist Indochina and U.S. Foreign Policy: Postwar Realities* (co-author with Joseph J. Zasloff, 1978); and *Communism in Indochina: New Perspectives* (co-editor with Joseph J. Zasloff, 1975). Dr Brown holds a PhD from Harvard University and a BA from Wesleyan University, and has studied at the University of Geneva.

Arthur John Dommen has been Economics Editor for the World Agriculture Division, US Department of Agriculture, since 1987. His

previous positions have been Research Section Leader for the
Agriculture Department's Africa and Middle East Branch, International Economics Division, Economic Research Service (1980–7);
Project Manager for the Agency for International Development's
Siliana Integrated Rural Development Project in Maktar, Tunisia
(1977–9); Senior Economist with Poynor International (1975–7);
writer with the *Los Angeles Times*, stationed in Saigon, Paris, New
Delhi, and Tokyo (1966–9); and writer with United Press International stationed in Hong Kong, Saigon, New York, and Pittsburgh
(1958–63). He has received fellowships from the Council on Foreign
Relations, NYC, and the US Information Agency. Dr Dommen
holds a PhD from the University of Maryland and a BS from Cornell
University.

Grant Evans is a lecturer in anthropology and sociology at LaTrobe
University, Australia. He has written widely on Indochina, including
The Yellow Rainmakers (1983), *Red Brotherhood at War* (with Kelvin
Rowley, 1984), and *Agrarian Change in Communist Laos* (1988).

G. McMurtrie Godley was the US Ambassador to Laos, 1969–73. He
and Jinny St Goar are collaborating on a book about the American
role in Laos, focusing on Godley's tenure.

Mr Saly Khamsy was Ambassador of the Lao People's Democratic
Republic to India in 1988.

David Floyd Lambertson has been Deputy Assistant Secretary for
East Asian and Pacific Affairs since April 1987. Mr Lambertson is a
career foreign service officer who joined the Department of State in
1963. His previous assignments have included Saigon (1965–8);
Medan, Indonesia(1969–71); the Paris Talks on Vietnam (1971–3);
the Office of East Asian Regional Affairs (1973–5); the Department's
Office of Japanese Affairs as Deputy Director (1975–7); Tokyo
(1977–80); the Department's Office of Korean Affairs as Director
(1982–84); Canberra as Deputy Chief of Mission (1984–86); and
Seoul as Deputy Chief of Mission (1986–7). He has received the
Department's Meritorious Honor Award (1974) and Superior Honor
Award (1980). Mr Lambertson holds a BA from the University of
Redlands, and has attended the Royal College of Defense Studies,
London.

Mr Pradap Pibulsonggram was Counsellor of the Royal Thai Embassy in Washington, DC, in 1988.

W. Courtland (Court) Robinson has been a writer and policy analyst for the US Committee for Refugees since 1986. He writes articles for the monthly *Refugee Reports* and the annual *World Refugee Survey;* monitors and assesses refugee situations in Asia; and is a resource to Congress, the Administration, the media, and private voluntary organisations. He served as Development Coordinator for the Indochina Resource Action Center (1985–6); Educational Program Coordinator for the Consortium of World Education, Save the Children, and Experiment in International Living (1983–5); Training Supervisor for the Consortium of World Education (1982–3); and Project Coordinator and Research Specialist for the Indochina Refugee Action Center (1979–82). He has taught English Literature at the Friends School in Baltimore, Maryland; and English Language at Tunghai University, Taichung, Taiwan. Mr Robinson holds a BA from Haverford College.

Jinny St Goar is a freelance journalist. *See also* G. McMurtrie Godley.

Dr Ng Shui Meng is a former Senior Fellow at the Institute of Southeast Asian Studies, Singapore. She is currently a staff member of the United Nations International Children's Emergency Fund (UNICEF) in Vientiane, Laos.

Martin Stuart-Fox was formerly a correspondent for United Press International in Laos and Vietnam. He is at present a member of the faculty in Asian History at the University of Queensland, Australia. He is the author of *Laos: Politics, Economics and Society* (1986), the editor of *Contemporary Laos: Studies in the Politics and Society of the Lao People's Democratic Republic* (1982), and the co-author (with Roderick S. Bucknell) of *The Twilight Language: Explorations in Buddhist Meditation and Symbolism* (1986). He has published numerous articles on Laos in such journals as *Asian Survey, World Review, Australian Outlook, Asia Quarterly, The Bulletin of Concerned Asian Scholars, Contemporary Southeast Asia, Asia Pacific Community, Journal of Contemporary Asia, Journal of Southeast Asian Studies,* and *Southeast Asian Affairs.*

Leonard Unger was Professor on Southeast Asia at the School of Advanced International Studies, Johns Hopkins University when he and Joseph J. Zasloff, of the University of Pittsburgh, organised the conference 'Current Developments in Laos' (4 May 1988). Until March 1987 Ambassador Unger was Professor at the Fletcher School of Law and Diplomacy, Tufts University. He was co-leader at Harvard's Institute of Politics of seminars on Indochina and China–Taiwan–US relations (1979–80). He is an Associate with Harvard University's Fairbank Center and an officer of Harvard University. His government positions include Deputy Chief of Mission to Bangkok, Thailand (1958–62); US Ambassador to Laos (1962–5); Deputy Assistant Secretary of State for East Asian and Pacific Affairs (1965–7); US Ambassador to Thailand (1967–73); and US Ambassador to the Republic of China (1974–9). Ambassador Unger holds a BA from Harvard University and an honorary PhD from Williams College.

Joseph J. Zasloff is Professor of Political Science at the University of Pittsburgh. He and Ambassador Leonard Unger were the organisers of the 4 May 1988 CSFA conference 'Current Developments in Laos'. From January to April 1987 he was Scholar-in-Residence at the Center for the Study of Foreign Affairs, US Department of State. He holds a PhD in International Relations from the Graduate Institute of International Studies, University of Geneva; and has been Visiting Professor at the University of Saigon, the University of the Philippines, and the University of Nice. He has served in instructional and consulting capacities for the Department of State, the Agency for International Development, the Peace Corps, and the RAND Corporation. Dr Zasloff's most recent books are *Apprentice Revolutionaries: The Communist Movement in Laos, 1930–1985* (co-author with MacAlister Brown), Hoover Institution, Stanford University, 1986; and *Postwar Indochina: Old Enemies and New Allies* (editor), Center for the Study of Foreign Affairs, US Department of State (published by the Government Printing Office, 1988).

Preface

The two editors of this volume, who have a long-term interest and affection for Laos that grew out of residence there and continued study, have been disquieted by the paucity of scholarly and governmental attention devoted to Laos in recent years. We noted that, by contrast, Lao's two Indochina neighbours, Vietnam and Cambodia, involved in a power struggle and military conflict, have been the focus of much greater concern.

Since the communist takeover in 1975, only a few books dealing with contemporary Laos have been published. Martin Stuart-Fox is responsible for two of them, as author of *Laos: Politics, Economics and Society*, published in 1986, and editor of *Contemporary Laos: Studies in the Politics and Society of the Lao People's Democratic Republic*, published in 1982, which treats the first 5 years of communist rule. MacAlister Brown and Joseph J. Zasloff co-authored *Apprentice Revolutionaries: The Communist Movement in Laos, 1930–1985*, published in 1986, which examines the first 10 years of the communist exercise of power. Arthur Dommen, in a brief historical overview, *Laos: Keystone of Indochina*, published in 1985, devotes a final section to Laos after the communist takeover. (Each of these authors is represented in the present volume.)

Believing it was time to examine current developments in Laos, the editors convened a conference, from which this volume has emerged. The conference, entitled 'Current Developments in Laos', met in Washington, DC, under the auspices of the Center for the Study of Foreign Affairs of the Foreign Service Institute, on 4 May 1988. We invited papers on Laos from scholars, diplomats, journalists and specialists in international and voluntary agencies with expertise on Laos. They represented a variety of nationalities, ideologies, and professional and academic disciplines. The conference was attended by more than 200 professionals with a special interest in Laos. We were particularly pleased that the Lao Government sent two members of its diplomatic corps – the Ambassador of Laos to India and the director of the international organization department of the Ministry of Foreign Affairs in Vientiane – to join the Acting Chargé d'Affaires at the Lao Embassy in Washington in contributing a paper and participating in the conference discussion. We interpreted their presence as a gesture of interest in a wider scholarly exchange with the non-communist world and as testimony to improving Lao–US relations. We also welcomed participation of a member of the Embassy of Thailand in Washington. Papers were revised for this volume in light of the discussion, and several additional contributions were invited from specialists who could not attend the conference.

The book addresses issues of politics, economics, society, and external relations of contemporary Laos, with a final section devoted to US policy toward Laos in historical perspective. In the opening section on politics Joseph J. Zasloff, an American professor of political science and co-editor of this volume, examines problems of development (Chapter 1), a topic addressed by a number of the papers in the volume. He deals with political constraints on development, pointing to a cluster of problems which limit the Lao economic absorptive capacity. Laos's problem is not the lack of capital for development – international donors have provided generous funding – but rather the capacity of the Lao government to put it to work.

MacAlister Brown, an American professor of political science, offers some propositions on the politics of coalition-building, based on the Lao experiments with coalition government in 1957–8, 1962–3, and 1974–5 (Chapter 2). Laos provides a fascinating laboratory for such an examination, currently relevant in view of the frequent proposals for political coalitions in Nicaragua, Afghanistan, Angola, and Cambodia. Brown addresses the question of whether communist domination inevitably follows any communist participation in a coalition government, often answered in the affirmative by analysts who cite the 'classic model' of Czechoslovakia in 1948, which fits Laos in some ways.

The economic section opens with an overview of the current Lao economy, provided by an aide-mémoire prepared by the United Nations Development Program for the Round Table Meeting of donors convening in Geneva in April 1989 (Chapter 3). This study describes the economic potential of Laos, analyses its principal limitations on development, and reviews Lao development strategies from 1975 to the present.

Grant Evans, an Australian lecturer in anthropology and sociology, focuses upon a theoretical economic question which faces underdeveloped countries everywhere – how to solve the problem of capital accumulation in order to create economic growth (Chapter 4). Evans makes a case study of Laos, assessing economic measures since

1975, including the 'Stalinist model' the Lao leaders copied from Vietnam and followed rigidly though 1979. He evaluates their subsequent efforts, begun in 1980, to create a system of 'market socialism' and discusses Kaysone's strategy, announced in 1988, of proceeding to a stage of 'state capitalism'.

Wendy Batson, an American co-director of a voluntary agency that supported development projects in Laos in the early 1980s, examines the extent to which the highland minorities have been integrated into the new Lao state (Chapter 5). Noting that the lowland Lao elite continues to dominate the central government and party apparatus, she offers evidence that cadres from these minorities are slowly but gradually being drawn into administrative structures at the district and even the province level. She holds out hope that the trend will increase in speed, permitting more substantial entry of minority cadres into the central power structure.

Ng Shui Meng, a Singaporean sociologist serving with an international organisation in Laos, examines the LPDR record in health, education and the status of women (Chapter 6). While recognising the government's efforts to expand access to education, she shows that the rapid expansion has been achieved at the cost of quality, which has plummeted at every level since 1975. She discusses the government's vigorous literacy campaign but notes that illiteracy remains about 56 per cent among the 15 to 45 age group, despite official claims that it has been eradicated. The government has made laudable efforts to expand health facilities, but, as in education, resources have been spread so thin that the delivery of health services has been ineffective. In her insightful observations about the role of women, a subject rarely treated in studies of Laos, Dr Shui Meng explores the contradictions between the communist rhetoric about equality for women and the deep-seated socio-cultural values of Lao traditional society.

In an overview of Lao foreign policy (Chapter 7) Australian historian Martin Stuart-Fox argues that the policy of the Lao leaders has been to ensure the security and economic development of Laos through the cultivation of friendly relations with all neighboring states and with potential aid-giving states, within the constraints imposed by the 'special relationship' with Vietnam. He discerns the recent emergence of a new phase in Lao foreign policy: Laos has been mending its ties with China; Lao–US relations have been improving, despite a setback following US decertification of Laos for humanitarian aid because of continuing narcotics production; Soviet influence in Vientiane has been growing and was, in 1988 he notes, perhaps more significant than that of Hanoi; and relations with Thailand in the second half of 1988 and in 1989 have been growing closer. As a consequence, while the relationship with Vietnam remains intact, its relative importance has been reduced. If these trends continue, Stuart-Fox suggests, Vietnam may find a Laos less inclined to bend to the Vietnamese will.

The tenor of Lao–Thai relations in the spring of 1988 is well portrayed by the statement of Saly Khamsy, Ambassador of Laos to India, and by the response of Pradap Pibulsonggram, Counsellor of the Embassy of Thailand in Washington (Chapter 8). Each side notes the close affinities of the Lao and Thai peoples in culture, language, customs, habits, and religion, and each asserts his government's strong desire for harmonious and cooperative relations. Yet, since 1975, tensions between the two countries have been more often the rule than the exception. Border incidents have been frequently magnified into major sources of tension – as in the case of the December 1987 Lao–Thai border clash referred to in this exchange.

Lao spokesmen have laid the blame for the tensions on Thai shoulders and, as in this chapter, have often alluded to the 'revival of a Pan-Thai policy being pursued by some elements within the Thai ruling circle'. Thailand, as the response shows, has rejected the Lao charge, and Thai spokesmen unfailingly allude to the domination of Laos by Vietnam, suggesting that the manipulation by this outside power is the hidden source of Lao–Thai tensions. The good news after the conference has been that Lao–Thai relations have been dramatically improving, as will be discussed below.

Court Robinson, an American specialist on refugee affairs serving with a voluntary agency, reviews the Lao refugee problem (Chapter 9), with special attention to Thai and US policies, which have affected the more than 375,000 (some 10 per cent of the population of Laos) who have fled between 1975 and 1988. Robinson concludes with a focus upon the 75,000 refugees from Laos remaining in Thailand in 1988, setting forth the options relevant to their future: (1) voluntary repatriation, which has attracted only 15,000 in the past 13 years; (2) integration within Thailand, which has been available to perhaps 50,000 who have unofficially settled there; and (3) resettlement in third countries, which has accommodated the bulk of past refugees, but is becoming increasingly difficult as the doors to refugee-receiving countries have been closing.

The volume concludes with a collection of papers on US policy toward Laos in historical perspective. Arthur Dommen, who served as a journalist covering Laos during the wartime period, has examined recently declassified US diplomatic correspondence of the 1954–9 period (Chapter 10). He criticises US policy for working at cross purposes with Lao nationalism, and asserts that 'American policy toward Souvanna Phouma's governments in 1954–9 virtually ensured the perpetuation of Hanoi's control over the whole of the NLHS front (the Lao Communist Front)'.

Leonard Unger, US Ambassador to Laos from 1962 to 1965 and co-editor of this volume, offers a brief memoir which explains some of the sources of American policy during that period (Chapter 11).

Jinny St Goar, and G. McMurtrie Godley, who served as US Ambassador to Laos from 1969 to 1973, provide an absorbing case study of the construction of the Chinese road in Northwest Laos from 1961 to 1973 (Chapter 12). They provide rich detail of the domestic politics and external forces pursuing their interests in Laos during this period.

Finally, David Lambertson, Deputy Assistant Secretary of State for Far Eastern Affairs, with responsibility for US policy toward Laos in 1988, summarises US interests in Laos (Chapter 13). He lists three prominent issues which concern the US in its relations with Laos; (1) the POW/MIA question, noting his satisfaction at Lao cooperation in the joint excavation of airplane crash sites; (2) narcotics, stating US displeasure that Laos continues as a major source of illicit opium and marijuana and claiming that there is evidence of involvement of Lao government officials and military in the narcotics traffic; and (3) refugees from Laos, a source of long-term US concern.

CURRENT DEVELOPMENTS, 1989

The postscript to Zasloff's chapter (Chapter 1), based on his visit to Laos in April 1989, indicates that Laos has been undergoing change at an even more rapid pace than anticipated by the articles in this volume. The principal influences for change have been the Soviet Union, Vietnam, and even China, until the recent Tiananmen Square debacle. In addition the new Thai Prime Minister, interested in converting Indochina 'from a battlefield to a marketplace', has provided Laos an incentive for rapprochement with Thailand. Simultaneously the Lao leaders have come to recognise the inadequacies of their policies and the malaise of their people.

The reforms in Laos have been initiated by veteran party Chief Kaysone Phomvihan, who announced that while achieving socialism remains the ruling party's ultimate goal, Laos must pass through a stage of 'state capitalism'. Implementation of these reforms has stimulated economic activity. New private shops and stalls have opened, and the markets of Vientiane and towns along the Mekong River are now brimming with produce. Small businesses have sprung up in lumber-processing, furniture-making, and textile production.

In Vientiane there is a clutch of new restaurants, movie theatres with foreign video films, and even a few new nightclubs and discos. Taxis and three-wheeled motor scooters are now available for hire, and hotel rooms are becoming scarce. Town dwellers are encouraged by these changes and hope that their meagre standard of living will rise. Peasants are relieved that the campaign for collectivisation has subsided and that the government recognises family farms as legitimate.

A smaller measure of political liberalisation has accompanied the more dramatic economic reforms. The most striking foreign policy change has been the improvement of relations with Thailand. The Lao and Thai military chiefs who, one year earlier, were ordering their soldiers to shoot at each other, were seen in Vientiane dancing the *lamvong* together. Thai businessmen, with official Lao encouragement, have proposed a variety of joint ventures in Laos, and Thai tourists have been arriving in bus loads. Thailand, whose rapidly expanding economy far outperforms Vietnam's, is now regarded as a model for economic development by many Lao government officials, quietly challenging the Vietnamese model that the Lao communist leadership has almost automatically followed since 1975.

The Vietnamese, who have guided the Lao communist movement from its origins, have not displayed concern about the Lao rapprochement with Thailand – indeed they seem to endorse it. The Soviets believe that Lao accommodation with Thailand will serve the development efforts of Laos, and they are not disturbed by the relative decline of Vietnamese influence – they may even be pleased by it as their own influence in the region increases.

Although landlocked Laos is the least populated and least developed of the three communist Indochina nations, it has suddenly emerged as the front runner in economic and political reform.

Perhaps its new orientation will focus more attention on contemporary Laos, which the editors of the present volume would roundly applaud.

J.J.Z.
L.U.

Part I
Politics

1 Political Constraints on Development in Laos
Joseph J. Zasloff

This chapter deals with politics in contemporary Laos, particularly as this activity relates to the development process. I shall draw from interviews conducted with Lao government officials, members of the diplomatic community, and officials in international agencies during my research visits to Laos in December 1985 and December 1987. The discussion begins with the current leadership of the Lao People's Democratic Republic (LPDR), the LPDR's constitutional development, the leaders' goals, and the resources available to them as they attempt to implement these goals. The focus will then shift to the capacity of Laos to absorb external capital critical to Lao development, identifying key political constraints on that absorptive capacity.

Preliminary to that discussion, four simple propositions help to describe the underpinnings of Lao politics and explain Lao political behaviour. The first two propositions summarise long-standing attributes of Laos; the second two are more recent.

1. LAOS IS POOR

Laos ranks among the poorest of the poor nations – a member of the Fourth World. The International Monetary Fund (IMF) estimated the annual per capita income of Laos in 1979 at $95. In 1985, according to Lao government statistics, per capita income was $135 (it may well be lower). Ninety percent of its $3\frac{1}{2}$ million inhabitants are widely dispersed in rural communities. Only about 3.4 percent (800,000 hectares) of its 236,800 square kilometres of territory are under cultivation. Laos does not suffer the grinding urban poverty of some of its larger urban neighbours. Those who know Laos recall how happily – indeed joyfully – the Lao peasant seems to adapt to his simple circumstances. Yet the low per capita income of Laos calls attention to the fact that it shares the classic attributes of underdeve-

3

lopment, similar in many ways to Honduras, Sierra Leone, or Sri Lanka. Laos has low levels not only of income but also health and literacy. It lacks domestic savings for investment. It is severely limited in administrative competence and technical expertise. Its population is only tenuously linked by a primitive system of roads and communications.

Further, Laos is mountainous and landlocked, with access to the sea for imports and exports subject to the goodwill of Thailand or Vietnam. Laos is almost wholly dependent upon external assistance for development resources.

2. LAOS IS A TRADITIONAL, ETHNICALLY PLURAL SOCIETY, DOMINATED BY A LOWLAND LAO BUDDHIST ELITE

As a traditional society Laos was, until 1975, a conservative monarchy, dominated by a small number of powerful families. Now it is a communist oligarchy, but its social make-up remains the same.

As an ethnically plural society Laos is composed of approximately 50 percent lowland Lao (Lao Loum) and 50 percent tribal minorities, including tribal Tai, the Mon-Khmer peoples who dwell on the mountain slopes (referred to collectively as Lao Theung), and the Tibeto-Burman-speaking peoples who live near the mountain tops, mostly Hmong and Yao (known collectively as Lao Soung). A primary challenge to the current regime, as it was to its predecessors, is to build a nation of these diverse peoples. The Lao Loum dominate the current regime, as they did the preceding one.

In a traditional monarchy lasting for some 600 years the Lao king ruled from Luang Prabang. In other regions there were families with royal pretentions rooted in the royal histories of Champassak, Vientiane, and Xieng Khouang. Around them were lesser aristocrats from prominent families who became patrons to clients of lower status, building a network of allegiances. The king reigned from Luang Prabang but did not rule over much of the outlying regions of the country.

In December 1975, with the declaration of the Lao People's Democratic Republic, the king was dethroned. Even though the aristocratic families have been shorn of their influence, many of the attributes of the old society remain. New families and clans, with privileged access to the communist roots of power, have emerged, and clients of lower status search them out as patrons. Indeed, even some of the old families, who had links to the new revolutionary elite, managed to survive and wield significant influence. Although Laos is now organised as a communist people's democracy, important vestiges of traditional political behaviour remain. Where newly dominant clans have replaced old ones, they demand a similar deference.

Dominant clans of the Lao Loum still wield the greatest influence. Despite the rhetoric of the revolutionary elite concerning ethnic equality, highland minorities are low in the scale of national influence, just as they were in pre-1975 society. Power of the central government over the outlying regions is still tenuous, and it must rely upon bargains with local chieftains to secure the loyalty of their peoples.

3.   LAOS IS A RECENTLY VICTORIOUS COMMUNIST REVOLUTIONARY STATE

After two decades of revolutionary struggle the Pathet Lao leaders came to power in 1975. As new revolutionaries guided by Marxist-Leninist ideology, they retain a zeal for creating a 'new socialist society and a new socialist man'. They have been propounding their revolutionary slogans for so long that they may have come to believe them. They blamed the backwardness of Laos on exploitation by the old feudal class and their imperialist and colonialist masters. They had asserted that upon their accession to power this exploitation would be replaced by economic and social progress. It is not surprising to find, in their thirteenth year of power, that they often claim accomplishments which they have not achieved.

Although their economic and social achievements have been limited, the new leaders have been successful in implanting a stable communist political system. Communist party cadres, who have emerged from semi-secrecy since 1975, are distributed throughout the critical institutions of the society – the ministries, the army, the schools, the youth and peasant associations – and transmit orders of the party leadership.

The newly-established LPDR embodies many unfortunate charac-teristics of other communist regimes. It has a similar heavy bureaucratic style, with emphasis given to political training, and to long sessions of criticism and self-criticism for its civil servants. It imported from its Vietnamese mentor the concept of 're–education' camps, where many of its former adversaries of the Royal Lao Government were incarcerated during the early years in power. Nevertheless the communist government of Laos is moderated by two important factors: Lao Buddhism, and the incompetence of the new government in implementing the socialist measure. Thus what emerges in Laos is a system Souvanna Phouma aptly labelled 'socialisme à la laotienne'.

4.   LAOS IS A WEAK STATE, DEPENDENT UPON ITS MORE POWERFUL SENIOR PARTNER, VIETNAM

Laos operates within Vietnam's orbit. The Lao communist leaders have worked in an apprentice relationship to Vietnamese mentors since the formation of the Lao communist movement in the late 1940s. Some have close family ties to Vietnamese, most speak Vietnamese, and they have reason to feel a debt of gratitude to their Vietnamese mentors for their own accession to power.

The concept of Indochinese solidarity has been so ingrained in the thinking of the Lao revolutionary leadership since the early days of their struggle that they may not distinguish a Lao national interest as distinct from a Vietnamese one. This linkage to Vietnamese mentors provides the key to important Lao policy inclinations, particularly in foreign and defence policy. In these fields the LPDR will strictly follow the Vietnamese policy line and take no action that could be judged inimical to Vietnam's interests. Since Vietnam is allied to the Soviet Union and the Eastern European bloc, Laos is linked to them too. When Vietnam's relations with China deteriorated into an outbreak of hostilities in early 1979, Laos felt compelled to align itself with Vietnam against China.

Although there is more latitude for divergence from Vietnamese practice in domestic policy decisions, these also show a strong imprint of the 'special relationship' of Laos with Vietnam. Large numbers of Lao cadres receive training in Vietnam, and Vietnamese advisers are assigned througout the LPDR bureaucracy. Patterns of change in Laos generally follow those of Vietnam, with a lag of some months.

THE LAO COMMUNIST LEADERSHIP

In 1960 the American journalist Edgar Snow was told by a high-ranking Communist Party of China (CPC) member that, for practical purposes, China was being run by 800 cadres who had survived from the party's earliest years and had moved to the top of the hierarchy.[1] In the spirit of this comment it could be said that the Lao Communist movement, from its origins in the late 1940s until the present, has been dominated by seven members of the party's politburo. In rank order they are: Kaysone Phomvihan, Nouhak Phoumsavan, Souphanouvong, Phoumi Vongvichit, Khamtai Siphandon, Phoun Sipaseut, and Sisomphon Lovansai. Each was a member of the Indochinese Communist Party (ICP) and was one of the original twenty-five ICP members who founded the Lao People's Party, now the Lao People's Revolutionary Party, on 22 March 1955.[2]

The remarkable record of continuity of these seven men is equalled by few regimes (if any) in the contemporary world. These leaders have also given evidence of impressive unity. Outside observers have scrutinised this leadership for factions, and some have postulated that it might be divided along lines of Marxist–Leninist ideologues versus pragmatists, or pro-Vietnamese versus nationalists (or pro-Chinese). But there has been no solid evidence that this leadership has been seriously divided on any critical issues. As noted earlier, the Lao leaders worked closely with the Vietnamese communists during the revolutionary struggle, and indeed their rise to power can be directly attributed to Vietnamese assistance.

After long periods of penury and sacrifice these leaders are now enjoying the fruits of victory in Vientiane. The politburo members live in the American-built housing development at KM-6, referred to as the 'golden ghetto' by Americans who lived there before 1975. The party general secretary, Kaysone Phomvihan, makes his headquarters in the former USAID compound. They preside over a system in which the posts of power and influence are disproportionately distributed to the families and friends of those who served the revolution. Access to the two high schools of Vientiane is easier for the children of party leaders and their associates than for ordinary folk. Scholarships to the Soviet Union and other socialist bloc countries are unevenly distributed to those with connections to the revolutionary leadership. Political linkages, loyal service, and family connections to party leaders are widely known to be stronger assets for educational opportunities, jobs and promotions than pure merit. Those with close connections to the old regime are at a distinct disadvantage. There are few internal constraints to keep the leaders responsible to the public interest. Laos has little mobilised public opinion. There is no independent judiciary – indeed there is almost no system of courts. The feeble press is controlled by the government. There are few organised groups through which interests can be transmitted and limits imposed upon the rulers.

Laos now has a mélange of traditional politics, characterised by patron-client relations, and the intra-institutional competition associated with communist systems.[3] Several power centres are said to have developed around key party personalities: it has been reported, for example, that Nouhak, second-ranked politburo member and presumed czar of economic affairs, is being challenged by Sali Vongkhamsao, head of the State Planning Commission, who was added to the Politburo in 1986, each distributing favours based, in part, on clan membership. It is not surprising that those in power are targets of opportunity for members of their extended family and friends. Kaysone's wife, Thongvin, president of the revolutionary youth organisation, is said to be eagerly sought after by those wishing to curry favour with her husband. Kaysone, in his report to the Fourth Party Congress, alluded to the growth of special privilege when he levelled criticism at party and government cadres who 'remain narrow-minded and selfish' and who are concerned only about 'protecting their interests'.[4]

The Individual Leaders

For most of their long revolutionary career the Lao communist leaders seemed shadowy figures, particularly to the Western world. There has been increased access to the Lao leaders in recent years, as a few Western powers, particularly Japan, Australia, Sweden, and France, have been offering aid to the LPDR.

Several Western ambassadors report that Kaysone, in his meetings with them, appears bright, energetic, and alert. He speaks excellent French, reflecting his study at a lycée and at the Faculty of Law in Hanoi during the French colonial period in the early 1940s. Kaysone does not harangue listeners in doctrinaire terms. He acknowledges the low level of development of his country and the shoddy work habits of his people, and he is frank in stating that Laos needs help from the more developed countries. Kaysone is recognised by most Western observers to be clearly in command. Although Kaysone may be pragmatic, open to the ideas of outsiders, and zealous for economic growth, he has not translated his commitment to development into achievement.

Kaysone provides little access to himself from the Lao population. He gives speeches at major events of state, government, and party, and presides at formal functions, but he does not mingle easily with the people, nor display the attributes of a popular politician. (Perhaps Kaysone and his advisers remain concerned about his security, since several attempts were made to assassinate him in 1976 and 1977.)

Nouhak, second in the party hierarchy, party chief and presumed czar of economic affairs, is even less accessible than Kaysone to the Western diplomatic community. It is difficult to get a description of his personality and operating style. By contrast, Phoumi Vongvichit, the Acting President (since Souphanouvong's stroke in 1986) and often characterised as the 'intellectual' of the top leadership, gives the appearance to his Western interlocutors of a grandfatherly school-teacher or Buddhist philosopher. Phoumi and Souphanouvong, both born in 1909, are the seniors in age in the politburo. Phoumi's age has taken its toll of his short-term memory, and he is now prone to some confusion and embarrassment when called upon to exercise it in public.

Souphanouvong, third in the party ranks, Chairman of the Supreme People's Assembly and President of the Republic, suffered a stroke in September 1986 en route to the eighth non-aligned conference in Harare, just before the LPRP Fourth Party Congress. He made an appearance in a wheelchair at the Congress but did not speak, raising the question as to whether his speech had been impaired. Souphanouvong has resigned as President (replaced by Acting President Phoumi Vongvichit), and Sisomphon Lovansai was moved up from his post of Vice Chairman of the SPA to be its Acting Chairman. I heard reports in Vientiane in December 1987 of an improvement in Souphanouvong's health. He had attended several receptions in a wheelchair. The right side of his face was said to be slightly paralysed but he was able to talk, if with difficulty. He was not yet considered strong enough to take up his formal duties.

Another veteran party leader, Foreign Minister Phoun Sipaseut, who was born in 1920, suffered a heart attack in 1979 and is carrying on a schedule of reduced activity. Phoun retains his post on the politburo as well as that of Foreign Minister, although his five Vice Ministers carry the bulk of the burden of his ministry.

General Khamthay Siphandone, military chief, and General Sisavat Keobounphan, former Minister of the Interior, provide little accessibility to Western observers, presumably because they deal in matters of security, not a subject for which Western observation is invited. Indeed incoming Western ambassadors, who normally make courtesy calls on each of the government ministries, are informed that the Ministry of the Interior is not to be visited.

Unlike the 1986 Sixth Congress of Vietnam, which selected a new General Secretary and dropped five members from its fourteen-member politburo, the Fourth Congress of the LPRP, which met in November 1986, reconfirmed Kaysone as the Party's General Secretary and re–elected his six veteran colleagues. But the Congress did expand the Politburo, adding four new full members and two alternates. Following the top seven members mentioned above the new members in order of ranking were:

8   General Sisavat Keobounphan, who had served as Minister for the Interior, Secretary of the Vientiane Party Committee, and Chief of the LPLA General Staff;
9   Sali Vogkhamsao, Chairman of the State Planning Commission;
10 Maichantan Sengmani, Member of the Secretariat of the Central Committee and Head of the Party – Government Central Control Commission;
11 Saman Vignaket, Member of the Secretariat of the Central Committee and Head of the Party Central Organisation Committee;

The two alternate members were:

12 Oudom Khattigna, who served as secretary of the Xieng Khouang provincial party committee and was thought to be of the Hmong ethnic minority;
13 Brigadier General Choumali Saignakon, Vice Minister of National Defence.

With these new members, the Congress added some younger men to the party's highest leadership and brought in an economic planner and at least two high-ranking military officers.

A few changes were made in the important nine-man party secretariat, which directs the daily business of the party. Dropped were three veteran members, (Nouhak, Phoun, and Sisomphon) who nevertheless retained other important functions and three younger men were added: Oudom Khattigna, Secretary of the Xieng Khouang Party Committee; Chounmali Sainakon, Vice Minister of National Defence (see above); and Somlak Chanthamat, who served in Central Propaganda and was a Training Committee Chief.

At the second echelon of power, just below the politburo, is the Central Committee of the party, which was increased from forty-nine to fifty-one members and from six to nine alternates. Four members had died since the 1982 congress and another ten were dropped, while eleven new full members and nine alternates were selected. Some of the older members were replaced by younger cadres, lowering the average age of the Central Committee in 1986 to 52, with the oldest 77 and the youngest 33. The number of women on the committee rose from three to five including Mrs Thongvin Phomvihan, General Secretary Kaysone's wife, who worked with the LPRP Revolutionary Youth Organisation and was first appointed to the Central Committee in 1982. Fifteen per cent of the newly constituted Central Committee had university or 'pre-university-level training' in the words of an official communiqué.[5]

Below the party's Central Committee, at the second echelon of party rank, is a new generation of leaders, likely soon to replace certain aged and incapacitated members of the politburo.[6] A handful of these younger leaders are said to be technically competent, some with training in the socialist countries. They are described as less doctrinaire than the top political leaders, and more pragmatic in their approach to development. The emerging leaders appear most prominent in assignments calling for economic expertise, reflecting the fact that the political posts have been monopolised by the veteran revolutionary leaders. Most of the second echelon leaders have travelled in many of the socialist countries, either as students or members of government delegations, and some have visited the West. They are aware of the higher level of development abroad, and they aspire to a higher standard of living for their backward country.

They may be more sensitive than their elders to the aspirations of the Lao population for a higher standard of living. They seem to understand that the easy contact with Thailand over the 1,000-kilometre border (notwithstanding the intermittent frontier problems and the closing of official entry ports by the Thai government) and especially the increasing impact of Thai television on Lao viewers reveal that material goods are available in much greater abundance just across the Mekong River. The letters and packages sent by 250,000 of their relatives resettled in affluent countries – the US, France, Canada, Australia, New Zealand – are a constant reminder to them of how low Laos is on the income scale.

Foreign observers differ as to the depth and impact on Laos of a second echelon of leadership that is pragmatic, open-minded, committed to development, and technically competent. Those optimistic about Lao development see a promising number of such cadres. The more pessimistic find such people to be rare, and generally with little impact, smothered by the older, more doctrinaire, isolated, revolutionary party veterans.

It is difficult for a foreigner, even a resident one, to pick out personalities who have promise of future prominence. A name frequently mentioned in this category is Khamsi, one of many of Souphanouvong's sons, who was recently appointed Vice Chairman of the State Planning Commission. Educated in the Soviet Union, Khamsai is said to be competent and self-confident. His chief, Sali Vongkhamsao, the Chairman of the State Planning Commission, who joined the Politburo in 1986 and thus is already in the higher ranks of power, is reputed to be pragmatic and seriously committed to development.

CONSTITUTIONAL DEVELOPMENT

The LPDR has been functioning without a constitution since its establishment in 1975. At the Third Party Congress in 1982 General Secretary Kaysone appeared to give priority to the task of writing a constitution, stating that 'in order to promote the effectiveness of the administration', the party should 'urgently undertake the major task' of 'preparing a socialist constitution at an early date.' Although party leaders alluded to progress in constitutional drafting during 1983 and 1984, it was not until 22 May 1984 that the Supreme People's Assembly (SPA) Standing Committee, led by Souphanouvong, formally appointed a fifteen-person constitutional drafting committee, to be directed by SPA Vice Chairman Sisomphon Lovansai, with two-subcommittees. In January 1985, addressing the SPA, Kaysone stated that the constitution must be drafted and translated into reality. The SPA responded with a resolution by its plenum on 26

January, stating that 'it is expected that the drafting will be completed within 1985', in time for the LPDR's tenth anniversary celebration, to be held in December. But the bureaucracy of Laos works even more slowly than most, and there was no announcement of a constitution at the tenth anniversary celebration, nor the following year at the Fourth Party Congress in November 1986, which had been subsequently targeted by Party spokesmen.

In December 1985 I interviewed Souvannalat Saignavong, Chairman of the Sub-committee responsible for studying, collecting and compiling the work of the Constitutional Drafting Committee. Souvannalat had studied in France and returned to join the Lao revolutionary movement in Sam Neua in 1974, rising to the post of Deputy Secretary General of the SPA. Souvannalat took pains to assure me that the absence of a constitution did not present a serious problem for the LDPR's political and legal development. He contended that an adequate legal basis had been established for the LPDR by the Congress of People's Representatives, which had met on 1 – 2 December 1975. This congress of 264 representatives, selected to represent each province and the Vientiane municipality, as well as Buddhist bonzes, youth, intellectuals, and the Patriotic Nationalist Front, had met secretly in Vientiane and dissolved the 600-year-old monarchy as well as the incumbent government. The congress issued nine resolutions of a 'constitutional nature', according to Souvannalat, creating the fundamental institutions of the President, the government, and the Supreme People's Assembly.[7]

Elaborating on the work of the drafting committee, Souvannalat noted that 'the LDPR constitution will be a political document which institutionalises the political line, the political options, and the specific policies of our party'. The most important documents guiding the work of the drafting committee are the basic party rules and the party resolutions. He added, 'the party for us is like a light which illuminates our path'. Within this context, he noted, the committee has been studying the LPDR's experience during the past 10 years, developing an electoral law for selecting a new National Assembly, which will be constituted to replace the present SPA. The electoral law, he said, will be based on universal suffrage, with a secret ballot and direct vote. He noted that a census upon which electoral districts could be based had already been completed. The new constitution will include certain fundamental laws. He mentioned, in particular, a law adopted and issued to local authorities in October 1978, which presumably governed the arrest and trial of persons suspected of specific criminal or political offences. Souvannalat said that the committee had already completed a comparative study of the constitutions of a variety of countries, especially socialist ones. It had also examined the special political, social and cultural characteristics of Laos, in order to shape a document that would be relevant to the country's needs. Souvannalat declined to estimate when the constitution would be ready for public presentation, and by mid-1988 it had still not appeared.

Even in the absence of a formal constitution, the LPDR's governmental and political organs have been evolving. The party, which dominates the political system, had grown by March 1982 to an announced 40,000 members.[8] As in communist systems elsewhere, the party assigns cadres to key positions throughout the principal institutions of the society, exerting its control through them. Unlike most other communist parties, no party members except for the top leaders are publicly acknowledged, so that some of the secrecy characterizing the revolutionary struggle is retained.

At the apex of state power stands the Supreme People's Assembly (SPA). The role of the SPA is largely honorific, with members convened semi-annually to listen to speeches of key party leaders. Members of the SPA include prominent members of various ethnic groups, regional political leaders, chairmen of mass organisations, several women activists, some 'patriotic neutralists', and a few personalities formally associated with the Royal Lao Government. As a body, the SPA is supposed to symbolise the variegated elements of Lao society unified behind its revolutionary leadership.

The Government of the LPDR, like its legally superior organ, the SPA, was proclaimed by the founding congress on 2 December 1975, and is guided by a Council of Ministers led by chairman and party chief Kaysone. The government was restructured by a basic law, dated 10 July 1982 (after the Third Party Congress), which formed three levels of government. At the top level, the Chairman of the Council of Ministers and five Vice Chairmen are charged with major policy-making and coordination of major sectors of national life. At a second level lie the ministries, which have technical functions. At a third level are about eighty deputy ministers, who include a sizeable proportion of technically trained personnel.

While these basic political institutions have been evolving in the absence of a constitution, the system gives power to party leaders and assigns little importance to legal safeguards for the rights of citizens. Amnesty International notes its concern about the 'continuing lack of legal safeguards for accused criminal and political offenders'. It states that 'in the absence of a Constitution and of formally promulgated and published penal and criminal procedure codes, citizens of the DPRL (LPDR) are effectively denied proper legal guarantees of their internationally-recognized human rights'.[9]

GOALS OF THE LEADERSHIP

The declared aims of the party leadership can be discerned in their speeches, party documents, and five-year plans. Party leaders have declared that they are pursuing the twin economic goals of 'socialist transformation with socialist reconstruction'. These are to be achieved through 'three revolutions': (1) a production-relations revolution, (2) a scientific and technical revolution, and (3) an ideological and cultural revolution. The production-relations revolution is meant to convert private economic enterprise into state-run and collective enterprise, and envisages the gradual establishment of agricultural cooperatives. The scientific and technical revolution aims to bring in a new technology and efficiency for the expansion of production. The ideological and cultural revolution is meant to expunge the decadence of the old system, raise people's consciousness to Marxism – Leninism, expand the level of education, and nurture the national culture, all leading to the emergence of a 'new socialist man'. In the pursuit of these revolutions there must be respect for the right of 'people's mastery', a notion similar to the 'mass line' in China, which defines people's rights and duties in controlling and improving their destiny. In brief, the Lao leaders are committed to developing Laos within a socialist context.

The Socialist Republic of Vietnam offers the LPDR a model, and Vietnam serves as its primary guide and leader. The Soviet Union and its East European junior partners are next in importance in providing guidance. Although the goals provide for the collectivisation of agriculture and the nationalisation of industry and trade, the reforms initiated in the Soviet Union under the labels of *perestroika*, which have appeared in modified form in Vietnam, have their counterparts in Laos. In sum, the LPDR has also been experimenting with economic liberalisation.

The Second Five Year Plan (1986–90) lays out rational objectives, and asserts that lessons have been drawn from the shortcomings of the First Five Year Plan (1981–85). Its goal is to sustain the attainment of basic food self-sufficiency, which the government claims to have achieved in 1985. A drought in 1987 produced a shortfall in rice production, a reminder that Laos is still dependent upon the vagaries of the weather. Further, the Plan has the following objectives:[10]

  (i)   diversification of agricultural production, emphasising export-able food products;
 (ii)   reform and strengthening of economic management, including public enterprise management, in order to increase investment efficiency;
(iii)   reconstruction and rehabilitation of major trunk routes giving access to sea ports, and of rural feeder roads;
 (iv)   increased savings and reduced wastage of development res-ources;
  (v)   reform of general education and training so that the training of professional cadres will be consistent with the human resource requirements during the plan period;
 (vi)   the implementation of small and medium-scale projects on the basis of appropriate economic analyses.

Stated in the clear, pragmatic language of the United Nations Development Program (UNDP) report, these goals seem reasonable. Yet there is a serious problem of financial resources available to pursue these developmental goals.

FINANCIAL RESOURCES FOR DEVELOPMENT

The LPDR does not have adequate domestic resources to finance its own development, since domestic savings in Laos are less than 3 per cent of the Gross Domestic Product. Laos must rely almost entirely upon external assistance for its development funds. Availability of money from foreign sources is not a problem for Laos – there appear to be ample funds.

Funding for development in Laos is available from three primary sources:

  1.   *bilateral assistance* from (a) Socialist bloc countries, in non-convertible currency, and (b) Western countries, in conver-tible currencies;

2. *multilateral assistance* from such agencies as the United National Development Program (UNDP), Food and Agriculture
   Organisation (FAO), United Nations High Commissioner for
   Refugees (UNHCR), UNICEF, World Health Organisation
   (WHO) and the Mekong Committee;
3. *non-governmental organisations*, including the Quakers, Mennonites, Save the Children Fund, and World Concern.

Among the bilateral donors, the largest amount of assistance
comes from the socialist countries, of which the largest contributor is
the Soviet Union and the second is probably Vietnam.[11] An article
published in the Soviet party newspaper, *Pravda*, under the signature
of Kaysone, summarised the contribution of the Soviet Union to
Laos:

> Over the past ten years LPDR has received from the Soviet Union
> materials, equipment, construction technology, petroleum pro-
> ducts, and consumer goods. The Soviet Union helped to construct
> Highway 9, major bridges across the (Nen Ngim) and (Kading)
> Rivers, an oil storage depot, workshops to repair motor transport
> and agriculture equipment, a hospital with modern equipment, a
> space communications station, and a radio station. Soviet special-
> ists are helping the LPDR to construct economic, cultural, and
> scientific–technical facilities, above all for tin concentrate produc-
> tion, for timber processing, for mineral prospecting, and for the
> communications and transport sector.[12]

Despite the poverty of their own economy, assistance by the
Vietnamese to Laos adds up to a significant sum. A Lao government
radio broadcast in October 1985 provided an estimate of the value of
Vietnamese aid to the LPDR during its first 10 years:

> The SRV has rendered enormous economic assistance to the
> LPDR–worth more than 1,334 million dong or an equivalent of
> $133.4 million – in the past ten years to help build more than 200
> projects in Laos, half of which were *gratis* aid. The mutual
> economic assistance and cooperation between the two countries
> that have encompassed all social, economic, education, public
> health, communications, agriculture, industry and trade services
> and have involved medium and small size construction projects –

such as the construction of several bridges along routes 7, 8 and 9, a brick factory, a (? stone-grinding) factory, and a gypsum mine – as well as the all-round relations and cooperation between the sister provinces, have effectively and significantly contributed to the Lao people's tasks of national defence and construction.[13]

The major Western donors, in order of importance in US dollars, are Japan (explained, in part, by the rise in the value of the yen), Sweden, Australia and, most recently, France.

In 1986 Japanese aid amounted to approximately $20 million. Construction of the Ngam Ngum Dam, which produces electricity for export to Thailand, Laos's major foreign currency producer, was largely financed by Japan. Japan has been exploring the construction of a second dam, aimed at generating additional electricity for export to Thailand as well as for limited domestic use. A Japanese diplomat in Vientiane explained to me that Japan follows a development assistance policy which selects only a few important projects, and carries them to full fruition. The Japanese believe that Lao development needs are best served by concentrating on a cluster of projects in the Vientiane region, and organising this region as the locomotive of development for the rest of the country. This development doctrine challenges the notion that resources should be distributed first to the more backward, remote regions.

Sweden is the second largest Western donor. Its aid, which was estimated at $12 million in 1986, provides assistance mostly in two sectors: (1) timber exploitation and processing; and (2) transport and communication, including road-building and heavy vehicle maintenance.

Australia, whose economic assistance totalled about $6 million in 1986, invests most of its funds in agricultural development, including irrigation and livestock management, and in heavy plant maintenance.

France joined the ranks of Western donors to Laos in 1987. A high-level French delegation visited Laos in November of that year and signed the first bilateral document with Laos since the revolutionary takeover in 1975. Implementation of French assistance was made contingent upon settlement of the outstanding Lao debt to France, which included approximately $5 to $6 million in private debt. A debt of some 70 million French francs (roughly $11 million) owed by Laos to the French government was cancelled. France was also an interlocutor for the European Economic Community, which in July 1987 appropriated 6 million ECUs for assistance to Laos. An important portion of French aid was for French language training and cultural development.

In summary, bilateral aid programs concentrated on projects in agriculture, transport, forestry, and mining. Agriculture development included livestock management and the expansion of irrigation projects. Road development retained high priority, with work continuing to complete Route 9, which would provide an outlet to the sea through Vietnam, and rehabilitation of Route 13, the single road running from north to south in Laos. Assistance in forestry was aimed at strengthening state forest enterprises. Most of the asssistance in the mining sector was provided by the socialist bloc countries.

Multilateral assistance in 1986 concentrated upon agriculture, hydropower, wood processing, communications, and integrated rural development.

Finally, non-governmental organizations, a comparatively minor source of external funding to Laos, offered support in small projects, especially in health care.[14]

Competition among Donors

Foreign donors to Laos compete to expand their programs and gain recognition for them. A rivalry is evident between socialist and Western blocs. (There appears to be cooperation among the donors within each bloc, although some competition is inevitable.) The Lao government derives benefit from this rivalry – there is an obvious advantage to the recipient as donors vie to increase their aid.

A variety of motives drive the donor nations to provide assistance to Laos. Each donor asserts that its primary purpose in giving aid to Laos is humanitarian. With a per capita income estimated at $135 in 1985, Laos, among the poorest nations in the world, certainly needs assistance, and there is no reason to challenge the humanitarian claims. However, certain political motives may have equal, if not greater, importance. For Vietnam, which wields the greatest influence of all donors in Laos, integrating Laos economically as well as politically into the Indochina bloc is of critical importance.[15] The creation of 'Indochinese solidarity' is high on Vietnam's list of priorities, and its economic assistance to Laos is part of that plan. As the leader of the socialist bloc, the Soviet Union has the interest of a big power in maintaining a direct presence in socialist countries aligned with it, and in helping to develop their economies.

Among the non-communist donors, Japan's aid to Laos is part of a pattern of increasing Japanese economic assistance to Southeast Asia. Japan seeks to achieve political influence commensurate with its remarkable economic growth. Swedish aid to Laos grew out of that country's massive popular sympathy for North Vietnam during the Vietnam War. Swedish aid to Hanoi had begun during the 1960s and, as an official of the Swedish aid mission explained to me in December 1987, Sweden's Ambassador to Thailand and Laos, Jean Christof Oberg, who had a real affection for Laos, was instrumental in persuading the Swedish government to extend its assistance to Laos.

The Australians see their aid program as a continuation of assistance to the Lao people which they have offered for some 30 years. An Australian diplomat pointed out to me in December 1987 that an important political motive is to show the Lao an approach to organising their society that is an alternative to the one on which they have been launched. As the former colonial power, the French have a sentimental attachment to Laos. They recognise what a French diplomat referred to as a French cultural 'capital' remaining in Laos, if greatly diminished, and following the inclinations of its forebears, the French government is making a modest effort to preserve in Laos a bit of *la civilisation française*.

In addition to these humanitarian and political purposes which motivate foreign assistance to Laos, there is the well-known bureaucratic impulse for national and international aid agencies to expand their turf. If Laos were able to absorb more foreign assistance, it seems likely that ample funds would be available. The principal restraint upon the flow of foreign aid funds is the limited absorptive capacity of Laos.

LIMITATIONS ON THE LAO ABSORPTIVE CAPACITY

Administrative and Managerial Constraints

The UNDP report notes that 'the low levels of *human and institutional capacities*, although improved in relation to past years, are inadequate enough to cause concern:[16]

(a) on the level of the conception of development plans, programs and projects, because of the lack of statistical informa-

tion, the scarcity of studies (on sectoral, regional and project levels) and an inadequate number of qualified managerial personnel;
(b) on the level of project implementation, because of the inadequate number of specialists and technicians, which hinders the proper and timely implementation of projects, often resulting in cost over-runs'.

Prime Minister Kaysone publicly acknowledges the low level of competence of the LPDR bureaucracy. In his report to the Fourth Party Congress, Kaysone noted that 'cadres' economic management skills are low and that assignments are sometimes made on the basis of personal connections rather than qualifications'. He chided those in authority who gave 'preference only to (their friends) or those from the same locality or race; paying attention to only their birth origin, habits and one particular sphere of education'. He emphasised that 'we must oppose bureaucracy, dogmatism, privatism, racial narrow-mindedness, regionalism and localism'.[17]

The Lao bureaucracy is composed of layers which reflect the country's historical evolution. Its foundation is set in traditional Lao royal customs and Buddhist practices. Next there is an overlay of French influence, the product of French colonial rule, which lasted from 1890 to 1954. This period saw the development of several generations of Lao bureaucrats, often subordinated to French-imported Vietnamese civil servants competent in the French language and imbued with French colonial administrative practices. There followed from 1954 to 1975 two decades of American influence. Although the American impact was far less pervasive than the French because of its brevity, the Americans offered training and educational opportunities, and employment in US agencies. After 1975, the ranks of those associated with the Americans were severely thinned, as were those who served under the French. A new layer of bureaucrats has been put in place since 1975 by the new revolutionary government. The external power with the most important impact on this layer is Vietnam, with the Soviet Union and its Eastern European allies coming next.

Many of the French-trained and US-influenced bureaucrats fled across the Mekong when the Communists seized power. Of those who stayed, many – perhaps 10,000 to 15,000 – were sent to 're-education' camps. However, a certain number continued to serve the new government, though it is usually difficult to understand why some who had served the former regime were committed to detention camps, while others with similar pasts retained their freedom. But sometimes the reasons are evident. One official was out of the country during the communist seizure of power, when many assignments to re-education camps were made. In another case the bureaucrat had a powerful patron in the party. Certain people were apparently spared because their technical skills were judged useful to the new regime. These few Western-trained bureaucrats constitute the bulk of those individuals who have the French or English language skills and the technical competence to deal effectively with foreign-aid donors.

In regard to those who are most able to deal with Westerners, one experienced official of an international organisation suggested that the Lao officials who are the most competent in French or English, and can get on most easily with Westerners, are often the least able to deliver on their commitments. It is not surprising, when one thinks about the current calculus of power, that the revolutionary 'cadres', who served with the Pathet Lao before 1975 and now dominate the bureaucracy, have little formal education and are unable to speak foreign languages. In most cases, too, they are not equipped with the technical or managerial skills necessary to run an economy, and many are suspicious of the outside world and of their colleagues from the former royal regime who were shaped by it. Members of the foreign-aid community from Western as well as socialist bloc countries report that only a few cadres in each ministry are capable of implementing management tasks adequately. These few are often not available, since there are so many demands on their services. They are frequently occupied with visiting foreign delegations, travelling to international meetings, or assigned to political training.

There seems to be unanimity among observers – within the Lao bureaucracy as well as the socialist bloc and Western diplomatic community – that morale in the Lao bureaucracy is very low. One major cause is the low pay. A middle to upper level bureaucrat earns from 7,000 to 10,000 kip monthly ($20 to $30), an insufficient sum to sustain a family. Some bureaucrats say that is not enough to justify their working. They simply do not show up for work, or they come at 9 am. and leave at 10 am. They must search for supplemental income through gardening, petty commerce, tutoring, and a variety of small business activity. A Vice Minister explained to me that all civil servants, including himself, are expected to plant gardens and raise chickens and pigs to supplement their income. Some civil servants devote time that they should be on official duty to this activity. In a system which is so low on morale, and lacks discipline, supervisors are reluctant to impose sanctions.

Few members of the Lao bureaucracy are willing to take an initiative. Initiative is seldom rewarded, and there may be dangers connected in moving too far out on a limb. Since there is no established system of justice, there is no clear definition as to what constitutes a crime against socialist morality, or against the party, or the state.[18] Officials have been intermittently arrested on suspicion of corruption or ideological deviation ('pro-Chinese' sentiment). There have been no formal trial procedures, no legal safeguards, and no organised system of appeal. These conditions dampen initiative and paralyse action. Under the present conditions rapid or forceful action by the bureaucracy cannot be expected.

There is a special bureaucratic bottleneck within the Ministry of the Interior, one of the most powerful and most closed agencies of government. This guardian of the country's internal security has to answer many bureaucratic questions and make numerous decisions (e.g. on refugee matters, visas, internal travel passes, and permissions of all sorts). The ministry seems impervious to access by outsiders. Ambassadors, who normally make courtesy calls on each ministry upon arrival in Laos, are advised explicitly *not* to include the Ministry of the Interior on their itinerary. Lao citizens seem fearful of this ministry. Foreign officials say that papers get lost in Interior, causing monumental bureaucratic delays, but outsiders cannot pry into the ministry to expedite a decision. Thus the Ministry of the Interior compounds the sluggishness of the Lao bureaucracy.

Foreign-aid donors frequently point out that, in view of the constraints imposed by the low-level administrative capacity described above, the Lao government can focus its attention upon only a few issues. For example, during 1985 the LPDR's primary concern was to prepare Vientiane for the government's tenth anniversary celebration. Its attention was riveted on painting and finishing the public buildings that would be on display, paving the necessary roads, installing the grandstands, the electricity, and other paraphernalia required for the ceremonies and distinguished visitors. The LPDR's limited resources and even more limited administrative attentiveness were almost totally devoted to these concerns, and little else was accomplished.

Within this context a Hungarian diplomat explained to me in December 1985 the problems that his relatively small aid mission confronted in Laos. He pointed out that these problems were characteristic of those facing other COMECON donors. Hungary had three principal development projects in Laos: (1) the modernisation of poultry-raising, (2) the expansion of Mahasoot Hospital to include a seventy-bed wing for children, and (3) the improvement of Routes 9 and 13, which run from Vientiane through Savannakhet and Pakse in the south. Poultry farming seemed to match Lao needs and Hungarian competence. Twenty years earlier the Hungarians had adapted an effective chicken broiler system after studying the process in the US. Lao delegations visited Hungary to inspect the Hungarian broiler farms, and requested assistance to develop them for Laos. An agreement to develop a chicken-broiler enterprise was reached in 1980 but by the end of 1985 only a few buildings had been constructed, and there was little prospect that production could begin.

Aiming to involve the LPDR in adding a pediatric wing to Mahasoot Hospital, the Hungarians set as a condition for their assistance – which would include fully equipping the new wards and training the personnel – that Lao government construct the building shell. When the building shell was 90 per cent completed, the Hungarians promised to bring in beds and surgical and operating equipment, and to train the necessary staff. A children's wing was badly needed – children were packed into overcrowded hospital wards. Five years after the agreement the Lao government had not yet started the construction. Lao officials claimed that they did not have funds to buy the cement for the construction of the shell, yet in 1985 alone, the Hungarian diplomat noted, they were pouring tons of cement into the roads, meeting halls, and other preparations for the tenth anniversary celebration. Finally, in late 1985, the Hungarians, with Lao government agreement, decided to abandon the paediatric project, giving equipment already delivered to other hospitals.

There was more substantial progress on the road-building. Vietnam wants to improve its road and communication links with Laos as part of its effort to reduce Lao dependence on Thailand and to promote the integration of Indochina. The SRV has encouraged the LPDR to give this activity the highest priority. But even on these projects the classic bottlenecks appeared. For example, the Hungarians bought cement in North Korea for the construction of a bridge. The cement was to be delivered to a Vietnamese port. Upon inquiry after a long delay, the Vietnamese declared that it was lost. The Hungarians assumed the Vietnamese had diverted the cement for their own use, but they could not accuse the Vietnamese of diversion. The Hungarians next ordered cement from Thailand. In the meantime, however, a follow-up inquiry produced delivery of the cement from Vietnam. A lab analysis revealed that it was not of suitable quality for bridge construction.

Summarising the problems of COMECON countries with development projects in Laos, the Hungarian diplomat noted that the Lao had no organised budget or foreign aid plan. They seem to live life from day-to-day and cannot plan ahead. They concentrate upon only a few projects to which they attach great importance. He estimated that the Lao had been able to use only about 50 per cent of the aid available to them during the first five-year plan (1981 – 5). The COMECON nations have concluded therefore that their projects should be small-scale, fewer in number, and concentrated in fewer fields.

These problems of the LPDR bureaucracy must be understood within the cultural context of Laos. As a peasant society at the lower end of the modernisation scale, Laos has adopted few of the work routines associated with modern administration. A UN official from a Western country told me that, despite the friendly cooperation he encounters from Lao administrators, 'each time we accomplish it is a new time. Each little step seems to be done for the first time. (The Lao administrators) don't seem to create patterns, precedents, or learn by experience'. He added parenthetically, 'It seems like losing your data on a computer – you must start again each time'. He speculated that the explanation for this behaviour lay in Lao cultural traits and inexperience. A diplomat from a socialist country, describing similar experiences, offered the *bo pinh yan*' syndrome 'never mind – don't worry about it') of Laos to explain the languid pace of administration.

Development planners hope that the level of Lao administrative competence will improve with the return of students. Laos sent abroad 11,000 students and trainees during the first decade of the LPDR, according to the Minister of Education (in an interview with me in December 1985), and 5,000 had returned by the end of 1985. Most had been sent to the socialist countries, which offer scholarships. The largest number study in the Soviet Union, the second largest in Vietnam, followed by East Germany, Czechoslovakia, Bulgaria, Poland, Hungary, Mongolia, and Cuba. A few have been studying in the capitalist countries under government scholarships provided by Australia, Japan, Sweden, and, more recently, France, and with support from international organisations such as UNESCO.

Serious problems which confront Lao students are inadequate language skills and poor basic education. Most students go abroad knowing little of the language of the country to which they are sent. The Minister of Education explained that students are assigned to a year of language training when they first arrive in their assigned country, and afterwards they are channelled into their substantive classes. He stated with (possibly feigned) confidence that their language problems are then minor.

Reports from knowledgeable observers give another picture. Lao students, they insist, have serious language deficiencies (compounded by problems of adjustment to the strange land, the absence of family, a colder climate, and new food). With inadequate preparation, they must devote much of their time to language study, and some never actually acquire enough competence to learn much subject matter. One French-educated bureaucrat expressed her frustration that most of her younger subordinates who had returned from study in Eastern Europe were incapable of writing even a coherent brief memo in Lao, or indeed in any language.

The Hungarian diplomat offered an illustrative case of the language problems of Lao students sent to his country. Approximately 300 Lao students were studying in Hungary (as of December 1985, the date of my discussion in Vientiane with him) and another 300 had already returned to Laos. Most were in health-related professions or agriculture, and they spent about 4 years in Hungary. Of the 300 students who had returned to Laos, a study by the Hungarian mission in Vientiane produced an estimate that three (sic), at most, were competent to translate a Hungarian newspaper into Lao, or to serve as interpreters for visiting Hungarian delegations. After one year back in Laos many lose entirely whatever Hungarian they may have learned. When student returnees visit the Hungarian Embassy, he noted, 'they try to speak to us in English or French'.

An added, and perhaps equally serious, problem for Lao students is their poor educational formation. Many have had only rudimentary instruction in maths and science. They have limited training in problem-solving and analysis, and few have developed adequate study habits and skills. Some have been selected through family connections rather than on merit. I heard reports, during interviews in Vientiane in December 1987, that the Soviet Embassy was so disturbed by the poor quality of the Lao students to whom it had been granting scholarships that the Embassy insisted it must be more directly engaged in the selection process.

Another issue in the training of future cadres is appropriateness of the instruction in the socialist countries to the conditions of Laos. Most socialist bloc countries do not have long experience or recognise expertise in tropical countries. Some observers point out that Lao trainees in the Soviet Union often work on large-scale projects which have limited relevance to little Laos.

Still another training problem concerns the assignment of the trainees once they return home. An official of a nation which gives substantial technical assistance to Laos told me that of 300 Lao who had been trained under the sponsorship of his mission in the use of irrigation equipment during the past several years, only two (sic) were working at tasks for which they were trained.

Optimists note that these problems are not unusual in underdeveloped countries and are being addressed in Laos. Official spokesmen say that some measures have been undertaken to improve foreign language teaching within Laos before the trainees set off for study abroad. A few Western nations – notably Japan, Australia, Sweden and France – have increased opportunities for study and training assignments. Plans are under way for the upgrading of education in Laos. A polytechnic training institution is projected, to be developed with the assistance of the UNDP. It is possible that the continued return of trainees from study abroad will create, at some point, a critical mass with enough skills as well as enhanced aspirations to raise the development curve of Laos substantially.

The Problem of Statistics

Another limitation on Lao absorptive capacity is the notorious unreliability of statistics. Not only is there a paucity of means to collect statistics but also their recent revolutionary victory may incline party leaders to exaggerate their achievements; it is often impossible to even guess the reality beneath the exaggeration. For example, LPDR pronouncements claim that illiteracy has been defeated. The Minister of Education estimated, in my interview with him in December 1985, that more than 98 per cent of the population were literate. When I noted, perhaps a bit puckishly, that Laos was doing better in literacy than New Zealand, he showed not the least trace of a smile but added with apparent confidence, 'Yes, we work hard at it'. Spurious figures pronounced by government leaders must be repeated by subordinates. The Deputy Director of the Social Science Research Council, a division of the Ministry of Education, cited these same literacy figures to me in an interview in December 1987. When I pointed out, in disbelief, that Laos does better than Japan and the United States in literacy, he did not budge from his assertion but added that perhaps the literacy is not very deep. Yet these claims are clearly absurd.

A study by a UN expert, published in July 1985, noted that in Luang Prabang province, 'despite the widespread provision of primary schools literacy appears to have declined in the surveyed villages during the last seven years. . . While the literacy campaign immediately following the revolution had good results, indicated by the literacy rates for the 15–24 year age group, the level of literacy among 7–14 year olds is somewhat lower'.[19] A UNICEF Report on children and women in Laos, published in 1987, notes that 'recent data show that both child and adult illiteracy is still substantial in the Laos PDR'.[20] This report notes that only five other countries in Asia have illiteracy rates as high as or higher than that of Laos: Afghanistan (80.8 per cent), Bangladesh (74.2 per cent), Papua New Guinea (67.9 per cent), India (65.9 per cent), and Iran (63.5 per cent).[21]

It is not surprising that literacy levels may have dropped, since so many teachers had fled to Thailand, and resources for school materials had declined with the economic tailspin following the accession of the new communist government.

Another example of statistical obfuscation can be found in the reporting on agriculture. A Vice Minister of Agriculture told me in December 1985, reading from an official report he had prepared, that Laos then had '3,184 cooperatives, containing 163,188 families, or 51.6 per cent of the rural population, cultivating 199,139 hectares of collective property, or 50.2 per cent of our riceland'. The Socioeconomic Report of the Fourth Party Congress one year later showed figures slightly higher: 'the number of agricultural cooperatives reached 3,420 by the end of 1985; they encompassed 53 per cent of all peasant families and 52 per cent of land cultivated with rice in the whole country'.[22] By the end of 1986 there were 3,976 cooperatives, with 74 per cent of all farm families, according to government announcements. Yet a socialist bloc agricultural adviser, deeply committed to the collectivisation effort and frustrated at the snail's pace progress in collectivisation, told me that these figures are largely formalistic 'paper figures', and do not reflect the reality that

Laos has almost no genuine agricultural cooperatives. Another UN expert made the same point to me in December 1987, noting that Lao authorities, with foreign assistance, had not yet been able to establish even a model cooperative which would set an example for others. At most, these figures may suggest that there has been some change in rural land ownership, but not a fundamental alteration in the pattern of agriculture production.

It is difficult to judge the effect of fictional figures upon development in Laos. One consequence is to increase the uncertainty quotient in economic planning. It is possible that government ministers may themselves come to believe, at least in some corner of their psyche, their own recitation of numbers showing progress in their jurisdiction, and even use these figures in their planning. These spurious data confound experts in international organisations who are responsible for helping the LPDR with economic development. Foreign experts are generally aware of the spurious quality of the statistics provided by their government hosts and they diplomatically enter the standard caveats about the soft quality of the statistics when they cite them. However, since these reports are submitted to the host government, they often find it impolitic to challenge the statistics provided for them. When the government-generated figures are then cited in reports by such respected international agencies as the World Bank or International Monetary Fund, they become legitimised and attain a new credibility, even among Lao and international civil servants who should recognise their spuriousness. Thus there is a chain of self-deception which cannot but have a deleterious effect on rational economic planning. Several foreign experts with whom I discussed this problem expressed cynical frustration, noting that the production of cloud-cuckoo land statistics reflects a lack of disciplined commitment to economic development. However, they recognise the political reality, certainly not confined to Laos, that ministers and bureaucrats may have a greater interest in showing progress in their field of responsibility than in reporting an unpleasant truth.

Popular Attitudes towards the Regime

Although it is difficult even for long-term residents, let alone short term visitors, to discern Lao public reaction to the regime, I conclude that the level of popular support for the LPDR is low. One measure of popular attitudes can be drawn from the number who flee. More than 350,000 of the approximately $3\frac{1}{2}$ million Lao have crossed the Mekong to Thailand, suggesting dissatisfaction among a significant segment of the population. Of course not all who flee are necessarily dissatisfied with the regime (nor are all who stay satisfied).

A thoughtful article in the *Asian Wall Street Journal*, written by a Lao government agronomist on the occasion of the tenth anniversary celebration, gives a rare Lao perspective on the question of popular attitudes toward the LPDR. For Lao over the age of 45, the author notes, the first 10 years of the LPDR brought little cause for cheer, since they witnessed the physical and economic decline of their country, the flight of friends and relatives, and food shortages and hardship. The young, especially those in school, he contends, are much more positive than their parents, and many identify with the goals of the government. Exposed to the official line in school, many young people are hopeful about the economic future and regard their parents' complaints as indicators of decadence produced by the previous 'corrupt capitalist system'. The youth have been heartened by the modification, beginning in 1980, of the heavy-handed measures at 'socialist transformation'. A further cause for optimism might be found in the achievement of self-sufficiency in rice production. Among the serious problems confronting the nation, however, are mismanagement, poor planning, and lack of trained personnel and funds. Most serious is the lack of motivation pervading the entire system, affecting workers, peasants, and civil servants. A variety of explanations has been offered for this low morale, which keeps production low. The government blames the devastating effects of the 30-year Indochina War and limited resources, and notes that socialist transformation is in an early stage. Government agronomists and technicians blame the pricing and distribution system for the low agricultural productivity. They say the government has priced agricultural produce too low and consumer goods too high to provide incentives for farmers to increase production. Moreover, the government provides little help to farmers in such things as fertiliser, insecticides, and machinery. When coerced to produce, the farmers work with little enthusiasm.[23]

While it is easy to blame inept, heavy-handed, socialist style bureaucratism for the low productivity, it is well to recall the cultural dimensions of Laos. The Lao are known for their light-hearted, easy-going manner, traditionally following subsistence farming rather than production for the market place. The Lao agronomist completes his analysis of Lao economic problems with the old story of the Lao peasant, sitting by his little pond under the shade of two coconut trees adjacent to his rice field, responding to the admonitions of a government extension worker to improve production. The peasant notes that he is already living in paradise – he has fish, coconuts, and rice – why would he want more?

One Western ambassador, unusually sensitive to Lao developmental problems, suggested that the Vietnamese and the Soviets are unlikely to succeed in making Laos a Marxist–Leninist style socialist state, even though they will continue to dominate their foreign policy. Nevertheless the SRV is showing the LPDR a Vietnamese version of the socialist path, and the Lao are stumbling forward upon it. The system, which derives so heavily from foreign sources, tends to reduce motivation, create discontent, and erode the legitimacy of the government.

POLITICS AND LAO DEVELOPMENT

In drawing some conclusions about the Lao development process, it may be useful to refer to my first two propositions concerning long-standing attributes of Lao political behaviour – (1) Laos is poor and (2) Laos is an ethnically plural society, dominated by a lowland Lao Buddhist elite – and the last two propositions describing more contemporary political phenomena – (3) Laos is a recently victorious communist revolutionary state, and (4) Laos is a weak state, dependent upon its more powerful senior partner, Vietnam. Regarding the first two propositions, there are signs of some, if slow, development in Laos, although, because of the poor statistics, concrete data on improvement is difficult to cite. I draw upon my informal observations during my visits in 1985 and 1987 to note some changes in appearance which reflect, I believe, modest economic progress.

During my visit to Vientiane in December 1985, just a few weeks after the gala tenth anniversary celebration, I was struck by how much brighter the city looked than on my previous visit just 5 years earlier. Public buildings were freshly painted, flower beds lined some of the main streets, many had been newly paved, and street lights had been mounted on several public squares. This spruced-up look contrasted sharply with the desultory city I had found in December 1980, a look which then reflected the urban collapse in Laos following the termination of American aid in 1975, the flight of almost 10 per cent of the population – including a large proportion of those with education and technical skills – the removal to re–education camps of some 10,000 to 15,000 people associated with the former regime, and the imposition of Marxist–Leninist measures aimed at collectivising agriculture, nationalising commerce, and bringing Laos into the socialist world.

Some economic and social progress had clearly been made in the subsequent 5 years.[24] The program of modest 'liberalisation' inaugurated in December 1979, following similar measures undertaken in Vietnam, eased the level of social control, slowed agricultural cooperativisation, reduced the burden of tax collection, and gave some encouragement to economic incentives. By the tenth year of the LPDR, the downward economic spiral that followed the communist consolidation of power appeared to have halted, and there were signs of economic stabilisation and, in some sectors, even improvement in life. The single most encouraging element in the economic picture was the fact that Laos appeared to have achieved self-sufficiency in rice production, if at a low level of consumption. A poor transportation system continues to be a problem, hampering the distribution of rice from areas which had a surplus to those that were short. In sum, while Laos may have a lower per capita income than Vietnam, its rural poverty is less visible and grinding, and life seems easier for the Lao than for the Vietnamese.

Although there has been a drastic change in the leadership of the Lao political system, many of the fundamental contours of Lao society have persisted. The Lao Loum continue to dominate the polity. However, as modernisation proceeds, there is little reason to believe that Laos will escape future demands from minorities for a greater share of political power, as has been the case in other plural societies.

As for the revolutionary fervour that has accompanied the recent victory of the Lao communist leadership, age will diminish it – indeed, it has already done so. There is evidence of a bit of *glasnost* in Laos, which has percolated in from Vietnam, in turn influenced by the Soviet Union.

The integration of Laos into Indochina, under Vietnamese guidance, has been proceeding with assurance. Vietnamese domination is likely to continue. There are, however, constraints upon the guidance which Vietnam can impose on neighbouring Laos. If pressure for conformity to Vietnamese-inspired Marxist–Leninist standards were to grow too heavy, there would remain the escape hatch to Thailand for many Lao. Further, there is a more natural affinity of the Lao toward the Thai than toward the Vietnamese. This Lao cultural orientation imposes additional restraints upon Vietnam's efforts to draw Laos more tightly into its orbit. If, or when, tensions reduce in Indochina (with a solution to the Cambodian problem), and Vietnam turns to its own great internal problems of economic development, Laos may have more room for manoeuvre with its development process, still, however, within the context of a communist Indochina.

A Postscript, May 1989

Important changes have taken place in Laos since the foregoing part of the chapter was prepared. Just as other nations in the communist world are undergoing fundamental transformation, Laos has been making dramatic changes in its domestic and foreign policies. This postscript, written one year after the preceding text, will provide a brief summary of some of the significant changes, focusing particularly on issues discussed in the chapter. I shall draw upon observations and interviews during a research visit to Laos in April 1989, when I again spoke with Lao government officials, members of the diplomatic community, and experts in international organisations.

Laos has recently launched a major effort at economic reform. The basic principles of this reform were set forth by Party Secretary Kaysone Phomvihan in an article published in *Pravda* (Moscow) on 2 December 1988, commemorating the thirteenth anniversary of the Lao People's Revolutionary Party:[25] Kaysone announced that while achieving socialism remains the ultimate goal of the Lao People's Revolutionary Party, Laos must pass through a stage of 'state capitalism' under the leadership of the party in order to expand the country's productive forces. Following the example of Gorbachev's *perestroika*, Kaysone declared that state enterprises are now being cut from central direction and will be financially autonomous, with the requirement that they must become self-sustaining. He reached back to Lenin's New Economic Policy to emphasise movement toward a market economy, and the desirability of stimulating private initiative. He pointed out that Laos is reaching to the outside world, not simply the socialist, but the capitalist countries as well, and particularly to neighbouring nations for trade, technology, capital, and expert advice. Affecting the largest segment of the Lao population is Kaysone's acknowledgement that the campaign to collectivise the agriculture of Laos was imprudent. Henceforth land will be allocated to families for private exploitation, for which they will pay only a tax.

The implementation of these reforms, as in other communist countries, has produced ferment and vitalised economic activity. There are visible changes in Vientiane, as well as in the provincial towns, especially those along the Mekong River. The markets are now brimming with produce, with more Thai and foreign goods. New private shops and stalls have opened. Small business enterprises have sprung up, including lumber-processing, furniture-making and textile production. In Vientiane there is a clutch of new restaurants, movie theatres with foreign video films, and even a few new nightclubs and discos. Taxis and three-wheeled motor scooters are now available for hire, and hotel rooms are becoming scarce. (I was not able to reserve a room in the Lan Xang Hotel which was half empty when I visited 16 months earlier. It is now filled with Thai businessmen and tourists, and a variety of official and private foreign visitors.) The Lao population appears to be encouraged by these new developments, with new hope that their meagre standard of living will rise. Peasants appear to be relieved that the campaign for collectivisation has subsided and that the government recognises private family farms as legitimate.

A limited number of political measures have been introduced to accompany the more dramatic economic reforms. Elections were held for people's councils at the district level in June 1988, for provincial councils in November, and for membership in the Supreme People's Assembly at the national level in March 1989. Elections had much in common with recent elections in the Soviet Union. Although the party was active in guiding the election, nominating 60 per cent of the candidates from the party membership, there were multiple candidates for most seats, balloting was secret, and the voting procedures were generally regarded as fair. Government spokesmen have noted that the newly elected Supreme People's Assembly will be charged with studying and approving the draft constitution, with the possibility that it may then be submitted to a national plebiscite.

The most dramatic development in foreign policy has been the improvement of relations with Thailand. In place of the tension and intermittent border violence which characterised relations between the two countries at the outset of 1988, there have been signs of growing cooperation. The Thai Prime Minister and the Thai Army

Chief of Staff each led delegations to visit Vientiane, and high-level Lao delegations reciprocated with visits to Thailand during the latter half of 1988 and 1989. A foreign observer noted that the Lao and Thai military chiefs of staff who, one year earlier, were ordering their soldiers to shoot at each other, were seen in Vientiane dancing the *lamvong* together. A joint Lao–Thai border commission has been formed to recommend measures to settle contentious territorial disagreements that have produced armed hostilities during the past several years. In December 1988 Thailand cut the list of banned exports to Laos from sixty-one to nineteen, and Lao trade with Thailand has been expanding. Thai businessmen, with official Lao encouragement, have proposed a variety of joint ventures in Laos. Thai entrepreneurs are particularly interested in the rich supply of logs still available in Lao forests, as well as in plentiful Lao mineral deposits. Thai tourists have been arriving in unprecedented numbers, often in large tour buses, to sightsee and visit with Lao relatives, and Thai Buddhist delegations have been meeting with each other on both sides of the Mekong River. Lao and Thai academics met in seminars at Thammasat and Khon Kaen Universities in Thailand in November 1988 to discuss Lao–Thai relations. Prime Minister Kaysone met Thai Prime Minister Chatchai in Nakon Phanon province on 17 February 1989 to announce that a 'friendship bridge' would be constructed across the Mekong River, with Australian assistance.[26] The Lao government, with the encouragement of international aid donors, has begun to send civil servants and students for training in Thailand, where similarities in language and culture facilitate adaptation for the Lao trainees.

Thailand, whose rapidly expanding economy far outperforms Vietnam's, is now regarded as a model for economic development by many members of the Lao government, quietly challenging the Vietnamese model that the Lao communist leadership has almost automatically followed since 1975. However, not all Lao officials are pleased with the rapid rapprochement with and emulation of Thailand. The second-ranking party leader, Nouhak Phoumsavan, was quoted as saying at a Politburo meeting in late 1988, 'Is this what we fought for? Are we becoming Thai?'[27] Some Lao are counseling caution about the new Thai embrace, pointing out that the Thais, who have overlogged their own timber and drained their minerals, may now be too eager to strip the Lao forests and cart away Lao ore.

The Vietnamese have not displayed concern about the Lao rapprochement with Thailand – indeed, they seem to endorse it.

Improvement of relations with Thailand and the West have been active goals of Vietnam as well. Symbolic of the Vietnamese, as well as Lao and Cambodian, interest in improving commercial relations with Thailand was the public seminar held in Bangkok hotel on 28 April 1989. Entitled 'Indochina: From War Zone to Trade Zone', and sponsored jointly by the *Asian Wall Street Journal* and *The Nation*, an English-language Thai newspaper, the seminar was attended by high-level officials of each Indochina country. More than 800 participants, 80 percent from abroad, each paid 3,900 Baht (approximately US $150) to attend the seminar, advertised as an exploration of 'trade and investment opportunities in Indochina'. Thai Prime Minister Chatchai, in his keynote address, urged ASEAN and Indochina to join in common economic development efforts. Vietnam's Deputy Prime Minister Nguyen Co Thach responded with a call for increased economic interchange between Indochina and ASEAN, endorsed the Thai Prime Minister's suggestions, and proposed that 'Thailand be the coordinator of our common efforts in future regional economic cooperation'.[28] In view of their own eagerness to improve relations with Thailand Vietnamese leaders must see their interests served by stronger ties between Laos and Thailand.

Concomitant with the improvement of Lao–Thai relations, there appears to be a decline in the active role of Vietnam in Lao affairs. Vietnam reduced its troop presence in Laos from an estimated 45,000 at the beginning of 1988 to 10,000 to 20,000 at the end of the year, according to Western diplomatic sources in Vientiane, and to zero, according to Lao spokesmen. Vice Minister of Foreign Affairs Souban Salitthilat noted, in a speech in Bangkok in December 1988, that Vietnamese troop protection is no longer necessary because of improved Lao relations with China to the north and Thailand to the south.[29]

Probably more important as a reason for the troop withdrawal was the Vietnamese desire to signal a goodwill gesture to China, against whom their troops were deployed in the northern tier of Laos. Foreign observers report that there has also been a reduction in the number of Vietnamese civilian and military advisers in Laos. Additionally there has been a diminution of Vietnamese activities to promote Indochinese integration through high-level leadership conferences. No Indochina summit meetings or Indochinese Foreign Ministers meetings – regular features of the earlier years of the three newly victorious communist countries – have been convened in the past several years. Deputy Foreign Minister Soubanh explained to me, in an interview in Vientiane in April 1989, that because of the forthcoming withdrawal of Vietnamese troops from Cambodia and the relaxation of tensions in the region, these meetings are not necessary. He dismissed the notion that Lao rapprochement with Thailand might be seen as a source of concern by Vietnam. The solidarity between Laos and Vietnam is so well developed, he maintained, that both countries can pursue independent relations with the outside world with full confidence in each other.

The Soviet Union has been supportive of the new Lao policies. A diplomat at the Soviet Embassy in Vientiane explained to me that the Lao Government's attempt to reform its economy is consistent with Soviet efforts at *perestroika*. Laos, like the Soviet Union, is eager for Western technology and increased trade with the capitalist world. The Soviets believe that the Lao accommodation with Thailand will serve the development efforts of Laos, and they do not appear to be disturbed by the prospect of a relative decline of Vietnamese influence – they may even be pleased by it as their own relative influence in the region increases.

Just as the outcome of *perestroika* in the Soviet Union is in doubt, so is the impact the reforms will have on the economic development of Laos. An economist with an international organisation in Vientiane with whom I discussed this question quoted Mao Tse-tung's response to a question about the impact of the French revolution: 'It's too soon to tell'.

In summary, the unusual policy changes described in this postcript are a product of both internal and external influences upon Laos. Changes in the communist world, especially the new orientation of the Soviet Union and Vietnam, or even the example of China, have stimulated change in Laos. The emergence of a new prime minister in Thailand, interested in converting Indochina from 'a battlefield to a market place', provided an opportunity for rapprochement with Thailand. Internally, 13 years after the establishment of their revolutionary government, the Lao leaders have come to recognise the inadequacies of their policies and the malaise of their population. With the conjuncture of these forces for change, they have seized the opportunity to launch new policies. It is noteworthy that, while change in the Soviet Union has been introduced by a new leader, Gorbachev, and Vietnamese change has been proposed by Nguyen Van Linh, also a recent arrival to power, the reforms in Laos are directed by the veteran Kaysone, who has been at the helm of the

Lao communist movement for almost four decades. It is normally more difficult for a longtime incumbent than for a new arrival to acknowledge the shortcomings of his own policies and set a new course.

To return once again to the four propositions set forth at the introduction of this chapter. The first two – Laos is poor, and Laos is a traditional ethnically plural society, dominated by a lowland Lao Buddhist elite – summarise long-term, structural attributes of Lao politics and remain useful in explaining Lao political behaviour. The third proposition – Laos is a recently victorious communist revolutionary state – is rapidly losing its explanatory utility as a guide to Lao politics. The Lao leadership no longer exhibit a zeal for creating a 'new socialist society and a new socialist man'. As in other communist nations, the content of Lao socialism is in flux. Revolutionary socialist ideology is giving way to pragmatic measures aimed at increasing productivity. Private ownership and initiative in agriculture are replacing collectivisation, and market-place economics, in NEP-like fashion, have been inserted into the system. The fourth proposition – Laos is a weak state, dependent upon its more powerful senior partner, Vietnam – also requires modification as a guide to Lao political behaviour. Clearly Laos has been moving into closer economic relations with Thailand in recent months, without Vietnamese objections. Closer economic ties with a more powerful neighbour are often accompanied by the neighbour's increased political influence. Since Laos and Thailand are so closely linked by geography, language and culture, if the present rapprochement solidifies, it is logical that Thai influence will increase and Vietnamese influence decrease.

For the present, as the final sentence of the previous section suggests might happen, the Lao leaders enjoy a growing measure of latitude from their Vietnamese allies.

With the Vietnamese commitment to withdraw all their troops from Cambodia by the end of September 1989, providing a reduction of tensions in Indochina, and their absorption in efforts to ameliorate their own lamentable economic situation, the Lao leaders have found room for independent manoeuvre in their development process and foreign policy. They still pay homage to their 'special relations' with Vietnam and Cambodia, but, for the present at least, these connections impose less restraint upon their independence.

Notes

1. Cited by Harold C. Hinton (1978) *An Introduction to Chinese Politics* (NY: Holt, Rinehart & Winston/Praeger), 2nd edition, p. 130, citing Edgar Snow (1961) *The Other Side of the River: Red China Today* (NY: Random House), Ch. 44.
2. While the names of the founding members of the Lao People's Party (later the Lao People's Revolutionary Party) have never been officially revealed, they appear to be the following: Kaysone Phomvihan, Khamtay Siphandone, Maisouk Saisompheng, Nouhak Phoumsavan, Phoumi Vongvichit, Phoun Sipaseut, Sisavat Keobounphan, Sisomphone Lovansai and Souphanouvong. For a list of the surviving members of the LPRP on the 1982 Central Committee, see MacAlister Brown and Joseph J. Zasloff (1986) *Apprentice Revolutionaries: The Communist Movement in Laos, 1930–1985* (Stanford: Hoover Institution Press), Appendix C 2. Founding members who were on the Central Committee in 1982 but not in 1986 (presumably death, illness or political decline had overtaken them) were: Ma Khaykamhithoun, Meun Somvichit, and Souk Vongsak (died 7 February 1983).
3. See Martin Stuart-Fox, 'Politics and Patronage in Laos', *Indochina Issues*, October 1986.
4. 'Political Report', *FBIS Supplement*, 6 January 1987.
5. A significantly larger proportion of the Vietnamese Communist Party's Central Committee, 43 per cent, have university or higher academic degrees, and 32 percent have graduated from senior high school. The new VCP Central Committee, which was reconstituted in the December 1986 Sixth Party Congress, is more than three times as large as its Lao counterpart, with 173 members, of whom 124 are full members and forty-nine alternates. Only ninety-two of them were re-elected. The average age of the new VCP Central Committee is 56, only slightly older than the LPRP Central Committee, with sixteen from age 40 to 59 (67%), fifty-six from age 60 upward (32%) and one below 40. Twenty members of the new VCP Central Committee were admitted to the party before 1945 (12 per cent), 142 between 1945 and 1965 (82 percent) and ten between 1965 and 1969 (6 percent). The data on the Central Committee of the Vietnamese Communist Party were taken from a broadcast by Hanoi NVA in English, 25 December 1986, in *FBIS*, 29 December 1986. The data for the LPRP were taken from a speech by politburo member Sisomphon Lovansai, broadcast by Vientiane Domestic Service in Lao, 15 November 1986, in *FBIS*, 17 November 1986.
6. Phoumi Vongvichit and Souphanovong were 79 in 1988; Phoun, at age 68, has been ill; Nouhak is 74; Khamthay, 64. Kaysone, born in 1920, appears to be vigorous and in good health.
7. For the text of these resolutions, see Joseph J. Zasloff, 'Lao People's Democratic Republic', in Albert P. Blaustein and Gisbert H. Flanz (eds) (Sept. 1985) *Constitutions of the Countries of the World* (Dobbs Ferry, NY: Oceana Publications, Inc.).
8. Statement by Minister of Information Sisana in 'Counting the Cadres', *Far Eastern Economic Review (FEER)*, 115, No. 13, 16 March 1982.
9. Amnesty International, 'Background Paper on the Democratic People's Republic of Laos (DPRL) Describing Current Amnesty International Concerns', AI 26/04/85, April 1985, p. 8.
10. The Plan is summarised in the United Nations Development Program (UNDP) Documentation prepared for the Country Review Meeting, Vientiane, June 1987.
11. The socialist countries do not publish the amounts of their aid; these estimates are derived from interviews with officials of international organisations during

December 1987. For figures on total assistance, see UNDP Report, December 1987.

12. *Pravda* (Moscow) in Russian; *FBIS*, 2 December 1985.

13. Mémoire on LPDR Ties to Socialist Countries, Part I, Vientiane Domestic Service in Lao, 23 October 1985; *FBIS*, 8 November 1985.

14. Above data from UNDP Documentation Prepared for the Country Review Meeting, Vientiane, June 1987, pp. 20–1.

15. See Part I, 'Vietnam and Indochina', especially Chapter 2, Joseph J. Zasloff, 'Vietnam and Laos: Master and Apprentice'; Chapter 3, Nayan Chanda, 'Vietnam and Cambodia: Domination and Security'; Chapter 4, MacAlister Brown, 'The Indochinese Federation Idea: Learning from History'; and Chapter 5, Hollis C. Hebbel, 'The Special Relationship in Indochina' in Joseph J. Zasloff (ed.) (1988) *Postwar Indochina: Old Enemies and New Allies* (Center for the Study of Foreign Affairs, Foreign Service Institute, US. Dept. of State, US. Government Printing Office).

16. UNDP Report Documentation Prepared for the Country Review Meeting, Vientiane, June 1987, p.5.

17. 'Political Report', *FBIS Supplement*, 6 January 1987, p.37.

18. See Martin Stuart-Fox (1986) *Laos, Politics, Economics and Society* (London: Frances Pinker), pp. 157–163, for discussion of the LPDR failure to establish an adequate system of justice.

19. *Women in Food Production*, TCP/Lao/4405, Report on the Findings of a Socioeconomic Survey in Two Provinces of the Lao PDR. Prepared by Magda Maroczy Ing. Agr., Vientiane, July 1985, 9.

20. *An Analysis of the Situation of Children and Women in the Lao People's Democratic Republic*, United Nations Children's Fund (UNICEF), 1987, p.53.

21. Quoted from Asian Cultural Centre for UNESCO (ACCU) *Guidebook*, 1985, pp. 88 and 89. The *Guidebook*, in a section on child illiteracy, states: 'Nationally, based on UNESCO findings, the number of illiterates in the Lao PDR is estimated to have increased by 3.6% between 1970-1980'.

   The UNICEF Report, in quoting the *Guidebook*'s data, notes: 'This suggests that in spite of the rapid expansion in education, population growth continues to outpace school enrollment and many young children are still unserved or under-served by educational programmes and facilities. The problem is especially serious in the provinces where ethnic minority populations predominate. This has been verified by examining primary school enrollment figures. Given that literacy is the window to learning and a tool for combatting ignorance, its eradication, especially among the young, is vital for the improvement of child welfare' (p. 53).

22. Radio Vientiane, 1 Jan., 2 Feb.; KPL, 17 Jan., 1987; FBIS, 8,21 Jan., 2 Feb., 1987.

23. Sombath Somphone, *Asian Wall Street Journal*, 9 December, 1985.

24. For a thoughtful assessment, see Martin Stuart-Fox, 'The First Ten Years of Communist Rule in Laos', *Asian Pacific Community*, Winter 1986, pp. 55–81.

25. *Pravda*, 2 December 1988; a mimeographed French-language version entitled, 'La Renovation et le Développement', was given to me by a Lao government official in Vientiane; an English-language version entitled, 'Renovation and Development', appears in *FBIS*, 19–22 December 1988.

26. *Bangkok Post*, 18 Feb., 1989.

27. Grant Evans, 'Laos Faces Daunting Future, Despite Reforms', *The Asian Wall Street Journal*, 14 Feb. 1989, Part I of a three-part series on recent changes in Laos. Parts II and III are in *AWSJ*, 15 Feb. 17–19, 1989.

28. For an account of the seminar, see *The Nation* (Bangkok), 29 April 1989.

29. *The Nation*, 5 Dec. 1989.

2 Communists in Coalition Government: Lessons from Laos
MacAlister Brown

The Cold War began with shocking demonstrations of the inability of non-communist parties to survive in coalition governments containing communist parties. This was the pattern in Poland, Bulgaria, Rumania, Hungary, and Czechoslovakia, although not in France or Finland. The lesson seemed almost self-evident, that the Comintern's national front tactic adopted against fascism in 1935, and used against the German and Japanese enemy in World War II, was a potent vehicle for boosting communist parties to the point of seizing full political power within a previously anti-communist state. Particularly striking to Americans was the takeover in Czechoslovakia.

The Czechoslovak coup of February 1948 has even been called the 'elegant' takeover, or the 'classic manoeuvre', but it remained a unique case until the takeover of Laos in 1975.[1] The Prague seizure of power was different from the others in that it did not depend upon military occupation nor follow a civil war. In an eight-part typology of communist takeovers historian Thomas T. Hammond distinguishes the Czechoslovak case as a unique occurrence: *a semi-legal takeover through considerable popular support combined with armed threats.*[2] The Communist coup d'état in Laos seems to match the Czechoslovak model.

The democratic tradition was strong in Czechoslovakia. Its wartime government-in-exile, headed by Eduard Beneš, survived World War II in the West, and American troops had shared in liberating the nation from Nazi occupation. Even though its postwar National Front government was headed by a communist, after his party won 38 per cent of the vote in the 1946 election, the Soviet Red Army returned home without installing a full communist regime. In 1947, however, as the USSR reacted to the US determination to defend West European democracy, the Czechoslovak communists stepped up their preparations for a showdown over their nation's choice of alignment. The government withdrew abruptly from the Marshall Plan planning conference, and within 6 months the stage was set for a bloodless coup d'état, using semi-legal methods.

The twelve anti-communist cabinet members forced a showdown by resigning over the misuse of the police, only to find their departure ultimately accepted by an infirm President Beneš. He had to face the intimidation of militant action committees springing up throughout the government and society, a Central Council of Labour under a communist chairman, armed workers' militia, mass demonstrations by workers, communist-controlled Ministries of the Interior and Information, a pro-Soviet Minister of Defence, and defecting oppor- tunists among the democratic parties. Casting its shadow over all this was the Soviet Red Army on the border, and a Soviet Deputy Foreign Minister visiting Prague to monitor the progress of events. The takeover was quick, semi-legal and unexpected. Since no milit- ary force was directly applied, it seemed to be the quintessential demonstration of the trap of coalition government arrangements with communist parties.

This 'fixed pattern'[3] starts with patriotic expressions of respect for the nation's cultural, economic, and political traditions, democratic principles and private property. With these reassuring postures a coalition government is established and the gates are opened to 'systematic infiltration into all spheres of national life and, particu- larly important, to an exclusive entrenchment in the command of the armed forces, the police and mass communication'. A National Front embracing all political parties is established, along with national committees with vast local authority and mass organisations. There is courtship of the intellectuals, division of the ranks of the social democrats, collaboration with opportunists, and the maintenance of illegal military organisations.

In 1988 the suggestion of forming coalition governments has arisen in nations where the United States has supplied anti-communist resistance forces during the past decade. Diplomatic movement toward negotiated ceasefires and political settlements in Nicaragua, Afghanistan, Angola and Kampuchea has raised the idea of coalition government as a conceivable option. Much manoeuvring remains to be done, and coalition may well be rejected, but the possibility of negotiated power-sharing is more real as the Reagan era draws to a close than at any time since 1975.

A curious reversal of positions now presents itself, however. Unlike the situation in postwar Czechoslovakia, where the communist party challenged the political tradition, the four American-supported anti-Marxist movements are challenging the existing order in their nations. In fighting from the periphery to acquire their power and legitimacy they resemble the Pathet Lao, which moved gradually into ever larger representation in the Council of Ministers in the nation's capital. Thus the coalition government experience in Laos can be examined both as traditional parties attempting to share power with revolutionary rivals (as in the post World War II models in Eastern Europe), and also as a guerrilla movement fighting from the periphery to increase its power via participation in the central government. The purpose of the author is not to chasten the contras, mujahedeen, UNITA nor Kampuchean fronts against creating coalitions with their rivals, nor to provide them instruction from the tactics used by the Pathet Lao. Rather the case of Laos will be examined to uncover its unique features, and thereby to test again the validity of a so-called classic model of exploiting coalition government based on the Prague experience.

SUCCESSIVE COALITIONS IN LAOS

The First Coalition: 1957–8

A striking feature of the experience in Laos is the fact that three successive coalitions were formed before the seizure of full power by the communists. The Lao communist movement originated as an offshoot of the Indochina Communist Party (ICP), founded in 1930 under Vietnamese leadership and Comintern supervision. Before World War II scarcely any indigenous Lao members were recruited into this clandestine, hazardous party. After World War II a bid for independence from France, led by young members of the elite political families of the Mekong River towns, foundered in the face of French military re-entry and collaboration by the royal dynasty in Luang Prabang. Most of the leadership of this independence movement, called the *Lao Issara*, retreated into exile in Thailand in 1946, but returned home 3 years later with a political amnesty. The more anti-colonial and ambitious elements, however, made common cause with the Vietnamese independence front, the Viet Minh, led by the

Indochina Communist Party. Prince Souphanouvong was the most prominent member of this faction, but lesser known figures who were partially tied to Vietnam by birth or marriage played decisive roles in shaping the movement. Even though the ICP officially disbanded in 1945, a small number of Lao revolutionaries (and thousands of Vietnamese) remained under its discipline. Eventually, in August 1950, the Lao kernel met in the mountains to found a new independence organisation which also purported to be a government of resistance. Its manifesto nonetheless demanded a coalition government, in clear acknowledgement that the movement lacked authentic national authority. Five years later a secret Lao Revolutionary Party was founded in the same border region, and in January 1956 an open patriotic front, the *Neo Lao Haksat (NLHS)*, was publicly established under the secret guidance of the clandestine party.

Before reaching this level of organisation, however, the independence movement engaged in guerrilla warfare, supported by Viet Minh units, to the point that it laid claim to territorial control of the northeast provinces of Laos. This enabled the movement, known in the West as the *Pathet Lao* (meaning Lao nation), to seek representation at the Geneva Conference of 1954 on Indochina.

This meeting produced ceasefire agreements between France and the communist-led Democratic Republic of Vietnam (DRV) and its cohorts in Laos and Cambodia. Even though the Pathet Lao (PL) was denied representation by the conference (in spite of demands by the North Vietnamese, China and Russia), the so-called 'Fighting Units of the Pathet Lao' were tangible enough to require provisions in the Agreement for their regroupment in the two northeast provinces 'pending a political settlement', and their integration into the national army. Out of these provisions grew the first claim by the PL to representation in the nation's Council of Ministers.

It took 3 years of sporadic negotiation between the half-brother princes Souphanouvong, the president of the NLHS, and Souvanna Phouma, the leading believer in national reconciliation, to settle the issue of reintegrating the two northeast provinces and the PL military units under royal Lao authority. With this finally settled in principle the PL was invited to take two cabinet portfolios in November 1957, even before supplementary elections were held. This poll in May 1958 shocked the Vientiane politicians, as the NLHS and a leftist party ally won thirteen out of twenty-one available seats in the National Assembly. In a sharp swing to the right, the other parties then excluded the PL from the cabinet, and the new prime minister declared his government no longer bound by the neutrality requirements of the 1954 Geneva Agreement on Laos. Thus the first coalition lasted less than a year, with the popular Souphanouvong and the educated Phoumi Vongvichit briefly heading the Ministries of Reconstruction and Planning, and Religion.

The Second Coalition: 1962–3

The road to the second coalition started from the low point of July 1959, when the Royal Lao Government put sixteen NLHS leaders in prison in Vientiane. This action followed the refusal of two Pathet Lao battalions to complete their integration into the Royal Lao Army (with the loss of some officer ranks) in May 1959. The right-wing government had thereupon arrested Souphanouvong and three of his top NLHS cohorts. Two months later twelve other NLHS personalities were also charged with treason and joined the four in military prison.

The new militancy of both parties had coincided with the secret decision by the Vietnamese communist leadership to resume 'armed struggle' in South Vietnam. This change of strategy (decided by the Vietnamese Communists' Central Committee in January 1959) was implied in the party's statements in mid-May. The escape of one PL battalion from incorporation into the Royal Army in May 1959 was consistent with this strategy, and as the Lao Revolutionary Party's General Secretary, Kaysone Phomvihan, later said, it announced 'to all the population the new style of combat of our party'.[4] The resumption of guerrilla warfare in South Vietnam would rely upon securing north–south infiltration routes through mountainous eastern Laos, maintained by North Vietnamese forces.

The jailing of sixteen NLHS leaders in July 1959 put the secret party in a difficult position, but militant cadres continued their recruitment and administration in the eastern provinces. Ten months later, the sixteen won over their guards and made their escape back to PL headquarters in northeast Sam Neua province. Then a totally unexpected coup d'état by Captain Kong Le in August 1960 put political power into the hands of Souvanna Phouma and the followers of a 'neutralist' persuasion, who were anxious to end civil war and exclude outside interference. The neutralists were not allowed to prevail, however, once General Phoumi Nosavan, with the help of southern political families, the CIA, and Thailand organised a quasi-legal counter government in Savannaket. His subsequent takeover of Vientiane in December 1960 forced Souvanna and Kong Le and their followers to seek refuge on the Plain of Jars, in concert with leaders of the NLHS. A Russian airlift out of Hanoi provided them with arms and sustenance, and North Vietnamese military personnel provided aggressive stiffening for the PL military units. With a nasty confrontation now brewing between American and Soviet military support operations, the Great Powers backed off, and sought another agreement in Geneva which would neutralise Laos and remove it from the bipolar chessboard.

Between May 1961 and 1962 three Lao princes (Souvanna Phouma, Souphanouvong, and the rightist southerner Boun Oum) haggled and manoeuvred over the composition of a new coalition government. The basic formula in both the North Vietnamese and Souphanouvong's proposals was (a) parity of cabinet positions for the Pathet Lao and the rightists, and (b) neutralists identified with Souvanna Phouma holding more seats than any other party. The Great Powers agreed that Souvanna should be the prime minister; but only after the incompetence of the rightist military had displayed itself at the siege of Nam Tha could Prince Boun Oum be prevailed upon to strike a bargain. On 12 June 1962 a new government of national union was announced, with Souvanna as Prime Minister and Minister of Defence. General Phoumi Nosavan and Souphanouvong were Deputy Prime Ministers (each with a veto over cabinet decisions), and respectively responsible for Finance, and for Economy and Planning. The Pathet Lao was also given charge of the Ministry of Information and two state secretaryships, while Phoumi's side held four portfolios, Souvanna's cohort received seven and rightists from Vientiane received four. Integration of the Royal Lao Army and the Pathet Lao plus Kong Le's neutralist forces was not spelled out in the agreement, a crucial omission. The fourteen-nation Geneva Conference put its stamp upon the settlement with a 'Declaration on the Neutrality of Laos', and the United States pulled back its show of force in Thailand and hoped for minimal violations of the neutralisation agreement by North Vietnam.

This was not to be. North Vietnamese military forces never withdrew from southern Laos, where the Ho Chi Minh Trail developed into a crucial asset in their struggle for South Vietnam. The so-called 'tacit understanding' engineered at Geneva by Ambassador Averell Harriman precluded a North Vietnamese campaign to occupy the royal and administrative capitals of Laos, but in return the United States would not send ground forces into Laos to close the corridor to

South Vietnam.[5] The Kong Le forces at the Plain of Jars soon found themselves polarised between allegiance to Souvanna Phouma, who could supply them, with the help of an American airlift, and the Pathet Lao, which sought to prevent such relief operations. The struggle led to an ominous exchange of assassinations by the rival factions of the neutralist forces, and shortly thereafter, in April 1963, the two top PL ministers withdrew themselves from the insecurity of Vientiane.

The anti-Kong elements in the neutralist group were consolidated by the NLHS into a quasi-independent leftist front called the Patriotic Neutralists, and Kong Le gradually drifted into obscurity. The Government of National Union continued to be served by two state secretaries from the Pathet Lao, and the departed PL ministers were not replaced for more than a year. The NLHS declared itself ready to discuss the possibility of its two ministers returning to the cabinet, but government military actions against PL positions repeatedly set back the idea. By June 1964 the possibility of tripartite goverment seemed unrealistic. Although the NLHS denounced Souvanna Phouma as prime minister at various times, not until 1966 did they unequivocally denounce the Vientiane government as illegal, while maintaining their own liberated zone apart.

Thus the first two coalitions had foundered on the shoals of Royal Lao Government reaction to NLHS self-assertion. In the first coalition the election shock of 1958 and dispute over integration of the PL forces in 1959 persuaded the anti-communist parties to stop including the Pathet Lao in the cabinet. Nonetheless NLHS personalities had gained public exposure for several months as legitimate party politicians and office-holders. Their arrest without trial, and the subsequent conversion of their prison guards, generated an air of martyrdrom and prowess about them. In the second coalition cooperation also ended abruptly in April 1963, but it served again to demonstrate the capacity of a few PL leaders to serve intelligently in the government.

The Third Coalition: 1974–5

The coalition device was not tried again until after the ceasefire between the Democratic Republic of Vietnam and their adversaries in January 1973. By this time the NLHS (still secretly led by the Lao

People's Revolutionary Party), with military and administrative
control over four-fifths of the national territory and one-third of the
population, negotiated for parity in cabinet positions with the Vientiane parties. The subsequent ceasefire agreement provided for this
in a Provisional Government of National Union (PGNU), and also
required unanimity of the two sides in its decisions. This coalition was
to govern pending general elections, but the Pathet Lao zone of
control was to be administered separately from the PGNU zone along
the Mekong River. The National Assembly was effectively nullified
until new elections might be conducted under the guidance of a new
body, the National Political Consultative Council (NPCC), which was
negotiated into the ceasefire agreement by the NLHS.

The elections never took place, as the civil war in Vietnam
unexpectedly raced to a conclusion in the spring of 1975. With the
capture of Saigon on 30 April, 2 weeks after the Khmer Rouge had
overrun Phnom Penh, Indochina contained but one remaining
obstacle to the Communist military tide. The PGNU in Vientiane
readjusted itself in a revolutionary direction, by the departure (after
denunciations and demonstrations) of its most right-wing elements,
the merging of Royal Army units and Lao People's Army units, the
dispatch of thousands of police and military officers to 're-education'
camps, and the denunciation and purging by people's committees of
the anti-revolutionary elements in the civil service. With Thailand as
a temporary haven across the Mekong River, thousands abandoned
their occupations and nation to a socialist new order. In August,
Vientiane was officially 'liberated' without resistance, and on 1–2
December 1975 a Congress of People's Representatives secretly met
to dissolve the PGNU and NPCC, accept the resignation of the king
and proclaim the Lao People's Democratic Republic (LPDR), under
the now publicly heralded Lao People's Revolutionary Party.

Such was the bare scenario of successive coalition governments
through which a secret revolutionary party positioned itself to seize
full power in a quasi-legal, semi-popular way. The outcome was a
vast departure from the intentions of the non-communist players in
the political games of 1957, 1962, and 1973, yet the hazards were
known. Does the success of the Lao communist party reinforce the
conventional thinking that coalition governments inevitably fall into
the hands of the most disciplined and purposeful element? Is there an
almost categorical rule revealed in the fate of the Lao anti-communist
politicians?

RECENT HISTORICAL COMMENTARIES ON LAOS

Hardly a handful of scholars have traced the full course of the revolutionary struggle in Laos, and the coalition government phenomenon has not engaged their full attention. Arthur Dommen's book[6] breaks off in 1970, before the third coalition, and stresses the 'miserable ... failure' of the international peace-keeping commission set up by the first Geneva Conference, as well as the bowing out of the Soviet Union as an influence for the neutralisation of Laos, and the failure to find a political settlement in South Vietnam. In later writing, after the 1975 finale, he mentions the PL's use of coalition government to expand its mass base of support, and the ineffectiveness of the rightist politicians in coping with the vote-getting ability and propaganda of the NLHS. He sees Souvanna Phouma in the spring of 1975 as a realist swimming with the tide.[7]

Another American study, by Charles A. Stevenson, also finishes before the third coalition. His perspective fixes on the American role in Laos, which he criticises for its ideological approach (obsessive anti-communism), lack of control from Washington, and selfdestructive use of secrecy. He asserts that more sensitivity by the Americans toward ethnic and generational cleavages, and *greater* willingness to accept PL participation in government, might have prevented the civil war that was raging as he completed his book.[8]

An Australian, Grant Evans, has essentially reinforced Stevenson's critique of US thwarting of the neutralist politicians, particularly Souvanna Phouma, the dogged middleman. In a book review[9] he asserts that social conditions would have favoured Souvanna's approach, and coalition government would have drawn the communists into the mainstream of political life, had Souvanna not been undermined by Cold War Warriors. Indeed he cites the American intervention itself as providing social conditions that favoured the PL's reformist programme.

Another observer from Down Under, Martin Stuart-Fox, has pointed out how unexpected and premature was the demise of the PGNU, as the Lao People's Revolutionary Party took its chance to assume full power. An 'historic opportunity' presented itself, with the rapid collapse of the anti-communist regimes in Saigon and Phnom Penh, and though the party's planning was still very fresh, it felt impelled to act.[10] As a result, 'a small number of revolutionary cadres faced the problem of how to exert control over a much larger and better educated urban population which had come to expect an artificially high standard of living', based almost entirely on foreign aid.[11] Whether the PGNU would have had a moderating effect on its communist half, if it had lasted longer, is a question not addressed by Stuart-Fox. Evans avoids this line of thinking, however, by suggesting that the PL programme for Laos should not be regarded *ipso facto* as bad for the nation.

Public testimony of the key Lao personalities in the coalition experiments is scarce to non-existent. Only a few interviews have touched upon the question, and PL personalities seem to be making no provision for individual historical records. Souvanna Phouma, in an interview with Brown and Zasloff in December 1980, made clear his criticisms of the Vientiane politicians who fled in 1975.[12] In his opinion they should have stayed and sought understanding with their Lao brethren across the ideological divide. His own retirement from office in December 1975, however, and his final years in Vientiane as an adviser to the government, were passed more comfortably than ranking members of the opposition might have hoped for. It would be enormously instructive to know what his private thinking may have been during the turbulent years of manoevre between the revolutionary left, the reactionary right, dominating neighbours and intrusive Great Powers. One US ambassador believed that the PGNU could have survived considerably longer had it not been for events elsewhere in Indochina.[13]

Brown and Zasloff's full history of the Lao communist movement up to 1985 reaches a general conclusion that the final breakdown of the coalition government in 1975 reflected geopolitical realities, which were exploited by a disciplined and doctrinally oriented party.[14] The historic opportunity arrived surprisingly early because of the collapse in morale of anti-communist military forces in Cambodia and Vietnam after the retirement of the United States from direct engagement in the armed struggle. The ceasefire agreed to at Paris in 1973, and expected by Washington to provide a 'decent interval' before a local resolution of the struggle for South Vietnam, proved to be a fatal juncture for the opponents of communist rule throughout Indochina. Two years later, with Richard Nixon no longer in office to honour his pledge of American air support, and the Congress no longer willing to match South Vietnam's requirements in arms, the balance of forces in the region tilted abruptly in favour of the North Vietnamese Army. The loyal apprentice revolutionaries in Laos reaped an easy, bloodless victory.

The preceding special emphases by historical interpreters do not in themselves contradict the thesis that coalition government with communist parties is inherently unstable and leads inevitably to anti-democratic outcomes. The ways in which the Lao experiment failed may be but local variations of a larger pattern that predictably promotes communist domination. The 'classic model' provided by Czechoslovakia in 1948 was not replayed in every respect in Laos, but can we conclude that the Lao revolution of 1975 essentially demonstrated the model's applicability? And can one argue that any American-backed anti-communist resistance forces would be well advised never to enter the game of coalition government?

THE SPECIAL FEATURES OF THE LAO COALITIONS

The peculiarly Lao features of this case should be underscored before deciding whether Laos reinforces the Czechoslovak model. A striking feature of the Lao coalition government experience is that the coalitions grew out of successive attempts, encouraged and supported by outside powers, to negotiate both a military ceasefire and agreements on domestic political cooperation and neutralisation. In the third attempt the warring Lao parties alone signed a formal ceasefire on 21 February 1973, and a detailed protocol on 14 September 1973 providing for an interim government of equal parts for 'the Vientiane Government side and the side of the patriotic forces'.[15] On each of these occasions the distribution of cabinet seats was a matter of considerable negotiation before the NLHS was formally accepted into the government, and Souvanna Phouma was the prime minister on each occasion. The two, then four, then twelve cabinet positions held by the NLHS were decided upon after periods of negotiation lasting as long as 3 years and no shorter than 6 months,[16] with Souvanna as the key player. During the first episode the American ambassador, Graham Parsons, struggled, as he testified to Congress, 'for sixteen months to *prevent* the formation of a coalition government'. During the second episode, however, Special Ambassador Averell Harriman struggled for a year against elements of the State Department, Defense, and the CIA to get the three princes to *agree* on a coalition.[17] He resorted to withholding US aid and eventually capitalised on the military failure of Phoumi Nosavan's forces at the battle for Nam Tha.

The third coalition grew out of the 21 February ceasefire agreement, necessitated by the American withdrawal from Vietnam. The PL entered serious discussions on a ceasefire in October 1972 with a demand for one-third NLHS portfolios, one-third for the 'Vientiane side'.[18] This was changed by negotiation to equal parts for the Vientiane and the 'patriotic side'. Agreement on specific ministries in the PGNU required 7 months of talks, and the PL did not gain either the Ministry of Interior or defence; but the principle of unanimity of the two sides was an important check on self-serving actions by either side.

The most effective move by the PL was Souphanouvong's surprise assumption of the presidency of the National Political Consultative Council (NPCC)[19] in April 1974. He quickly moulded it into a powerful propaganda instrument for reformist thinking. Both his powerful personality operating in the royal city of Luang Prabang, and his manipulation of non-partisan seating and the unanimity rule, catapulted the NPCC to the vanguard of political thinking in the period of the putative national reconciliation. Souphanouvong's eighteen-point 'program for achieving peace, independence, neutrality, democracy, unification, and prosperity of the Kingdom of Laos', which won the NPCC's endorsement, was propagated by the members 'consulting' the nation, as authorised by the protocol of 1973. This took place before the PGNU gave its official endorsement (with slight amendments). The NPCC's provisional regulations on democratic freedoms, adopted as part of the preparation for general elections, were also inspiring in tone but quite at odds with the 'secret non-legal activities of the Party', which were inspired by the secret Second Resolution of the Central Committee of the LPRP, also fashioned in 1974. The latter document laid the ground for the Central Committee's call on 5 May 1975 for a national insurrection.[20]

Whether two contrasting factions within the party were developing alternate lines of action remains an intriguing line of speculation. It is now realised that only two of the top ranking leaders of the secret party participated in the PGNU or NPCC – Souphanouvong and Phoumi Vongvichit (the Foreign Minister and Vice Prime Minister). Five other members of the Party's Politburo (apparently formed in 1972), and all but two of its Central Committee members,[21] stayed home in the safety and the discipline of the PL zone. Even at that, as Kaysone later avowed:

Vis-à-vis the cadres and Party militants who participated in the coalition organization, it was necessary to continually watch their political behavior and remind them of the position and task of a militant revolutionary, to fight against their tendency to break away from the masses and avoid all contact with them, to combat the illusion of a confidence in 'the spirit of national concord' on the part of the enemy, which would weaken the fighting spirit of the masses.[22]

After the decisive events of May 1975 both Phoumi Vongvichit and Souk Vongsak left Vientiane for medical leave abroad, before resuming service in the revolutionary government.

A critical part of the 'juridical' or legal struggle[23] by the party during this period was the status of the National Assembly elected in 1972. In the negotiation of the ceasefire, which started in Vientiane on 17 October 1972, the NLHS insisted upon a new provisional political council to replace the existing National Assembly. The issue was not clearly confronted by the Royal Lao Government nego-tiators, and was more or less settled by indirection. The existing National Assembly was not mentioned in the ceasefire agreement or its protocol, whereas the National Political Consultative Council was spelled out in both, and its presidency was reserved for a member from the patriotic forces side. Notwithstanding, leaders of the Vientiane side attempted to have the National Assembly reopen on Constitution Day, 11 May 1974, only to be voted down by the 'patriotic side' in the fledgling PGNU. Souphanouvong's neatly crafted political manifesto would face no legislative challenge until the 'general elections to set up the National Assembly, and a definite National Union Government'[24] were held. In October 1975 the revamped PGNU announced that national elections would be held in April 1976, but the declaration of the Lao People's Democratic Republic intervened and Souphanouvong dissolved the NPCC in favour of a party-appointed Supreme People's Council.

Another special feature of the Lao experience, which Dommen deplored in 1971, was the failure of international control machinery, provided for in both Geneva agreements and reactivated by the 1973 ceasefire, to guarantee the neutralisation of Laos and the observance of restrictions on outside forces and arms entering the country. The tripartite commissions (Canada, India, Poland) were hobbled with respect to any decisions or recommendations by the requirement of unanimity and the expected partiality of two of the members, by ambiguity about whether the commission could interpret the agree-ment, the lack of sanctions, the distraction or indifference of the sponsoring powers once the Geneva conferences adjourned, the lack of fixed access to areas within the PL zone, and the readiness of the Vientiane side to dispense with the commission when expedient.[25] The idea of such a balanced international control mechanism may have been reassuring to the outside powers seeking a ceasefire in a civil war that fed on outside support, but the neutral commission could contribute no more to a stable solution than the intervening powers were willing to allow. The North Vietnamese strategy of supporting its 'resistance war' in the South via mountainous eastern Laos dictated a calculated disregard for restrictions recorded in Geneva; and their violations helped to rationalise the breaches by the American side.

COMPARING LAOS AND CZECHOSLOVAKIA

Similarity

In reflecting on the Czechoslovak model of power seizure the relative infirmity of ageing President Eduard Benes invites comparison with Souvanna Phouma, who suffered a severe heart attack and convalescence abroad after 3 months at the helm of the PGNU. Both men have been blamed by the losing parties for not fighting. Souvanna has even been accused by some former colleagues of conspiring to bring his half-brother to office as chief of state. The wear and tear of bitter cabinet debate over the eighteen-point programme and relations with Vietnam in July 1974 laid Souvanna low for 4 months. In his absence the Vientiane side attempted to organise itself as a cohesive bloc to counter the disciplined NLHS team of fifty-odd ministers and lesser officials living and working together in Vientiane. Although Vice Prime Minister Phoumi Vongvichit was designated by Souvanna to run the prime minister's office during his convalescence, the Vientiane side's counterpart, Leum Insisiengmay, held a veto over any actions. So, little was undertaken until Souvanna Phouma's return to duty in November 1974. At that time he dismayed many conservative stalwarts by suggesting during a reception at his home that those not satisfied with the peace arrangements should leave the country.[26]

The period of his absence had been punctuated by successive strikes for better pay and administration in numerous governmental institutions, ranging from US embassy guards and staff of a Philippine-run hospital to junior police officers, postal workers, students and teachers in various schools, and soldiers in a northern town. At first students stepped forward to mediate such disputes, but by early 1975 demonstrations in the streets in two southern towns led Souvanna to arrest eight leaders (students, teachers, and civil servants) and ban future demonstrations nation-wide. A bloc of Twenty-one Organisations for Peace was organising nonetheless, and it led demonstrations against the right-wing ministers on May Day and 9 May. Two weeks earlier the prime minister had ordered General Vang Pao not to fight at the critical road junction between Vientiane and Luang Prabang. Perhaps a healthy Souvanna Phouma would somehow have shut down on strikers in a wide variety of places, or have countered civil insurrection in May by unleashing the former secret army leader, General Vang Pao, and his light aircraft against Pathet Lao positions, and have thereby avoided the flight of the rightist leaders.

A similar query can be made regarding President Benes' decision to give in to communist demands. In both cases the kingpin was caught up in events beyond his control and chose not to resort to force. Benes faced not only action committees, armed militia, militant trade unions, mass demonstrations and communist-run police, but potentially the Soviet Red Army.[27] He chose in 1948, as in 1938, not to fight against unequal odds. Souvanna Phouma faced a year-long epidemic of strikes and growing demonstrations by consolidated protest organisations, linking Lao People's Army forces in a 'liberated' zone of the country, an unwillingness of the US Congress to maintain military aid in Indochina and the proximity of overwhelming North Vietnamese military power. The health or convictions of these agonised constitutional figures probably mattered less than the balance of forces – which they could realistically read – and their distaste for violent conflict.

The question yet remains whether actions that could have been taken earlier might have avoided the no-win situation confronting Benes and Souvanna. A valid critique of the Czechoslovak anti-communist parties is that they failed to unite, and did not persuade the social democrats to join forces with them, that they lacked a unifying idea, did not create a paramilitary force of their own, and grossly miscalculated the possibilities in submitting their resignations.[28] The Vientiane side in the third coalition also lacked unified organisation and a credible leader, partly due to Souvanna's illness and his preference to act as intermediary. They were ready to resort to armed force against the Lao People's Army (LPA), as some of the skirmishes in March and April 1945 demonstrate, but the morale of their troops was uncertain, and they had no assurance of support by the United States or Thailand, without which they would be no match for North Vietnam and the LPA. Their fate had been decided on the battlefields of Vietnam and in the political halls of Washington.

Souvanna Phouma continued the façade of provisional national union until the proclamation of the LPD, and lived half a decade in retirement in Vientiane. Benes left the presidential palace in despair after accepting a communist-dominated cabinet and resigned without approving a revised constitution. He died within 6 months.

Contrast

A striking difference between the communist coup in Laos and the one in Czechoslovakia was the clandestine nature of the party itself. Although some tracts and statements published by the NLHS spoke of the importance of the 'Lao revolutionary Party'[29] in leading 'the Lao revolution', there was no clear public acknowledgement of the Lao Revolutionary Party, founded in 1955, as the controlling element behind the patriotic front, until after the insurrections of May–June 1975.[30] As the veteran Phoumi Vongvichit put it a year after the final seizure of power: 'The Lao People's Revolutionary Party now functions openly, although in the past it hid in the background to provide leadership to the Lao Patriotic Front; now it is taking direct charge of the leadership'.[31]

Even after being overwhelmed by the LPRP in 1975, some Lao politicians in exile lacked a clear impression of the secret, disciplined party they had contended against.[32] Langer and Zasloff had identified the party through careful research in 1970,[33] but the Lao nation's perspective on the struggle for its political orientation was little affected by such documentation. The informed public continued to think in terms of rival personalities, families, neighbouring nations, and availability of aid. The Front was known to have revolutionary ideas, while also professing support for the monarchy and democratic liberties, but the fact that it descended directly from the Indochina Communist Party was scarcely known. Such knowledge may have been superfluous for inspiring opposition to the NLHS, but the low public awareness of the genesis of the Front was a product of careful deception throughout a decade by the clandestine party.[34] In Czechoslovakia no such pretence was conceivable or necessary. The Communist Party sought the maximum value from association with wartime resistance efforts, liberation by the Soviet

Red Army, and postwar land redistribution and economic reforms. In Laos the calls for revolution were dressed in nationalist garb and insulated from the negative reverberations of Marxism–Leninism. It seems unlikely that any future coalition governments will be formed in the midst of such ignorance of the communist origins, inspiration and discipline of a so-called national front.

One of the reasons the party's role could remain so little known was the base area maintained by the Pathet Lao, with the help of North Vietnamese forces. This also differs sharply from the Prague model. The virtual partition of the nation was never fully undone after Geneva 1954, and it shifted through the years of civil war. The PL denied access to its zone of control to all but a handful of journalists sympathetic to the revolutionary cause, even after the formation of the third coalition government. PL headquarters in northeast Sam Neua province provided refuge for leaders from the hazards of political arrest, exposure or assassination in the Royal government areas. As we have seen, after 1959 most hard core leaders of the secret party did not expose themselves to politics in the Mekong River towns, for they were relatively close to military posts and CIA facilities in Thailand, which provided a secure base for anti-communist forces. The 1973 ceasefire agreement' [took] into consideration' the 'present realities of Laos where there are two zones separately controlled by the two sides', and pending General Assembly elections allowed each side to 'keep the areas under their temporary control'. Meanwhile the establishment of normal relations between the zones 'with a view to unifying the country at an early date'[35] was to be stepped up.

Surely the existence of a separate territorial base, and a separate armed force which was not under the authority of the Ministry of Defence, gave the PL a peculiar advantage during the coalition governments. Under the PGNU it could hold up government action in Vientiane by means of the unanimity provision, and in the other four-fifths of the nation it could work its will without supervision. At the same time it was able to proselytise throughout the PGNU zone for the eighteen-point programme pending general elections. The arrangement was grossly asymmetrical between the 'patriotic forces' and the 'Vientiane side', yet the latter group had reason to believe that the PL lacked the skilled cadres to aspire to full control of national affairs, especially the economy. Even if its strategy of coalition was merely a delaying tactic pending the development of such administrative capacity, some Lao nationalists could hope that the process of union government would soften and tame their revolutionary rivals and produce a gradual reconciliation based on social reform.

COULD THE PGNU HAVE SURVIVED?

Given the actual historical record and commentaries offered by the LPRP, however self-serving, a PL strategy of consolidation and participation in a PGNU for several years does not seem far-fetched. Party resolutions to guide the final phase of the 'people's national democratic revolution', had been adopted[36] but the party did not have sufficient educated bureaucrats to manage even the fledgling Lao economy, as it demonstrated in the years after 1975. The timing of the revolution was clearly accelerated, to its advantage and disadvantage, by the external events in Vietnam and Cambodia. As Kaysone later said: 'Our preparations were not complete, the cadres who had to take practical charge of the action were notably limited in number'.[37]

Had this acceleration not occurred, would reconciliation and convergence have begun to take place? Seemingly some self-modification might have occurred on both sides, but the party's record in the 're-education' of its erstwhile adversaries after May 1975 underscores how jagged were the ideological differences between the hard core of the rival parties. Here the deep significance of the Pathet Lao's exclusive zone of control again comes into focus. The so-called 'cave mentality' of the veteran party leaders who hid from Royal military forces after 1959 and American bombers between 1964 and 1973 probably hardened and narrowed into irreversible orthodoxy, tied to the heroic outlook of their Vietnamese mentors. After such trial by fire their capacity to consider any outcome but final victory was virtually eliminated. Compromise, except as a tactic, had been purged from their mentality by a prolonged civil war, years of deception, the relentless example of the North Vietnamese, and the Leninist doctrine of their most dedicated revolutionary leaders.

In his speeches after the seizure of power the party's general secretary has made it very clear that the periods of coalition government were tactical devices, in keeping with the dicta of Lenin:

The period of coalition was one of legal and semi-legal struggle in coordination with the clandestine and illegal activities of the Party. It was a period of mobilization and political education, extensive and as rapid as possible, of numerous people in the zone under enemy control. In each period of coalition our Party has known how to profit from the legal and semi-legal conditions; to rely on basic revolutionary organizations, to use the channel of progressive organizations of the intermediate levels, especially the youth, and students, to enlist tens of thousands of persons under their marching orders.[38]

The general conclusion drawn by Kaysone after appropriate quotations from Lenin is: 'coalition, which has been of extreme importance to our revolution is none the less but a tactic, in the given conditions, for reaching the strategic objectives'.[39]

In addition to this theoretical reaffirmation, it should not be overlooked that the NLHS's proposed programme of action during the PGNU period, while partly fraudulent – for example, with respect to venerating the monarchy and honouring democratic elections – contained items of genuine interest to the people of the Vientiane zone, who were susceptible to the promise of reform. The ability of the LPRP to trigger the formation of local revolutionary administrations in 1975 to 'seize power from the ultra-rightist reactionaries' was rooted in its relentless critique of the privilege and corruption visible in the traditional social structure. There was a real target for its propaganda, seen again in the overgrown infrastructure which Western aid supported. Thus it was not simply the fact of letting the revolutionary party into a coalition government that wrote its death warrant, but also the conditions, both internal and external, which the communists could exploit from the nation's capital cities, that were critical to the outcome.

Conclusions

Coalition with communists has been incisively analysed by Gerhart Niemeyer to expose a number of 'dangerous illusions'.[40] Principal among these are the belief in 'common interest', or limited goals on the part of communists, and false hopes regarding 'controlling' communists or experiencing peace and harmony as the result of joining in coalition. Not every resort to coalition government with communists has degenerated in their favour, as France and Finland can remind us, but Niemeyer's warnings lean in the direction of probability, and they can surely be applied to Laos. In addition the Laos experience highlights other conclusions of general significance.

The Intrusion of Power

1 Coalition governments in a revolutionary context are inherently unstable, and unlikely to last in nations racked by bitter civil conflict. They are an expedient, sometimes preferable to continuing civil warfare, but they should not be expected to resolve the national conflict. They may temporarily reduce the use of revolutionary violence, but they will not eliminate the theoretical commitment to its use.

2 Coalitions that are quite unbalanced in the distribution of seats, and/or in external support for the parties, may easily break down, as the stronger side resorts to force or coercion.

3 The morale of parties in contention in a coalition government is deeply affected by the international balance of forces in the region, and the key national leaders may give way to this fact rather than usher the coalition into a terminal trial of arms.

4 Communist parties may be better designed to increase their power through a coalition arrangement because of their doctrine, discipline, unity, planning and intransigence. Leninist doctrine specifically refers to coalitions as tactical expedients on the road to full power. Non-Leninist parties in a coalition should not expect to survive unless they generate greater public appeal, loyalty and readiness to struggle (with help from the outside, if possible) than their adversaries.

Special Advantages

5 Any party to a coalition that camouflages itself by clandestine modes of operation is by definition hostile to the coalition enterprise.

6 A party which retains an exclusive territorial base while participating in a so-called national coalition enjoys a distinct advantage and discounts the value of the political compromise.

The Limits of Negotiation

7 International control mechanisms, even when balanced or neutralised, cannot impose solutions on determined adversaries, especially if they are backed by outside powers. Great Power

declarations of neutrality and guarantees of independence are not reliable.

8   The policy issues that divide the parties in a national coalition remain alive and potentially crucial with respect to winning popular support, even after a compromise on distribution of cabinet seats.

9   Coalition agreements between parties in control of armed forces cannot expect the merger or cooperation of previously hostile military commands and units to be achieved without great care and deliberation. In Laos the first two coalitions split apart in 1959 and 1963 over issues of allocating ranks and weapons among the rival military organisations. These issues had not been clearly settled in the ceasefire agreements, but were left to future negotiation between the local parties. This deferral may be the only feasible negotiation option, but it leaves exposed a critical area of infection that can bring down the coalition enterprise.

Notes

1.   Paul Tirgrid, 'The Prague Coup of 1948: The Elegant Takeover', in Thomas T. Hammond (ed.) *The Anatomy of Communist Takeovers* (New Haven: Yale University Press), pp. 240-1. Ivo Duchacek, 'Czechoslovakia: The Classic Maneuver', in Jeanne Kirkpatrick (ed.) (1963) *The Strategy of Deception: A Study in World-wide Communist Tactics* (New York: Farrer Straus & Co.), Ch.3.
2.   T.T. Hammond, *op. cit.*, p. 639. A general review of the coalition government phenomenon is provided in Gerhart Niemeyer (n.d.) *Communists in Coalition Governments* (Orlando: Council Against Communist Aggression).
3.   Joseph Korbel (1959) *The Communist Subversion of Czechoslovakia, 1938–48: The Failure of Co-existence* (Princeton University Press), p. 290.
4.   As quoted in MacAlister Brown and Joseph J. Zasloff (1986) *Apprentice Revolutionaries: The Communist Movement in Laos, 1930–1985* (Stanford: Hoover Institution Press), p. 67.
5.   Norman B. Hannah (1987) *The Key to Failure: Laos and the Vietnam War* (New York: Madison Books) is particularly incisive on the strategic significance of the Geneva agreements of 1962. A brief chronology of this period can be found in Charles A. Stevenson (1972) *The End of Nowhere: American Policy Toward Laos Since 1954* (Boston: Beacon Press).
6.   Arthur Dommen (1971) *Conflict in Laos: The Politics of Neutralization* (New York: Praeger), rev. ed.
7.   Arthur Dommen, 'Communist Strategy in Laos', *Problems of Communism*, Sept. 1975, p. 65.
8.   Charles A. Stevenson (1972) *op. cit.*, p. 268.
9.   Grant Evans, 'Apprentice Communists', *Far Eastern Economic Review*, 5 June 1986, pp. 54-5.
10.   Martin Stuart-Fox, 'Reflections on the Lao Revolution', *Contemporary Southeast Asia*, 3, no. 1, 1981.

62 Communists in Coalition Government

11. M. Stuart-Fox, 'The First Ten Years of Communist Rule in Laos', *Pacific Commentary*, Winter 1986, p. 56.
12. M. Brown and J.J. Zasloff, *op. cit.*, p. 154.
13. Interview with Ambassador Charles Whitehouse, Bangkok, 24 March 1977.
14. MacAlister Brown and Joseph J. Zasloff, *op. cit.*, pp. 133-4. See also MacAlister Brown, 'The Communist Seizure of Power', Ch. 2 in Martin Stuart-Fox (ed.) (1982) *Contemporary Laos* (St Lucia, Queensland: University of Queensland Press).
15. 'Documents', *Journal of Contemporary Asia*, 1973, pp. 244–53.
16. Between August 1954 and November 1957 the first coalition was discussed by Souphanouvong, Souvanna Phouma and Katay Dan Sasorith; between October 1960 and 11 June 1962 Souvanna and Souphanouvong conferred; and between February and September 1973 the third coalition was negotiated.
17. Charles A. Stevenson, *op. cit.*, pp. 168–73.
18. M. Brown and J.J. Zasloff,'The Pathet Lao Moves Toward Reconciliation', *Pacific Community*, 6, no. 3, April 1975.
19. Souphanouvong did not announce his choice of office until after his popularly acclaimed return to Vientiane on 3 April 1974 to inaugurate the provisional government.
20. M. Brown and J.J. Zasloff, *Apprentice Revolutionaries, op. cit.*, pp. 114–18.
21. Party Central Committee member Souk Vongsak served as Minister of Information, Propaganda and Tourism; and Sanan Soutichak was a member of the NPCC and perceived as a stern figure.
22. As quoted in M. Brown and J.J. Zasloff, *Apprentice Revolutionaries, op. cit.*, p. 115.
23. Kaysone Phomvihan uses this phrase in recounting the phases of the revolution. *La Revolution lao* (Moscow: Editions du Progrès, 1980), pp. 36–41.
24. 'Agreement on Restoring Peace and Achieving National Concord in Laos', art. 8, in *Journal of Contemporary Asia, op. cit.*, pp. 251–2.
25. Robert F. Randall, *Geneva 1954: The Settlement of the Indochinese War* (Princeton: Princeton University Press, 1969), pp. 560–6; and Charles A. Stevenson, *op. cit.*, p. 190.
26. M. Brown and J.J. Zasloff, *Apprentice Revolutionaries, op. cit.*, p. 318.
27. Dana Adams Schmidt (1952) *Anatomy of a Satellite* (Boston: Little Brown), p. 120.
28. *Ibid.*, p. 139.
29. For example, Phoumi Vongvichit (1969) *Laos and the Victorious Struggle of the Lao People Against U.S. Neo-Colonialism* (Neo Lao Haksat Publications), pp. 178, 194, 209, etc.
30. The first clear reference noted by the author was in September 1975, via *Foreign Broadcast Information Services (FBIS)*, APA, Laos. Dennis Duncanson first identified the Party's new name (the addition of 'People's') in *The World Today*, Sept. 1975.
31. Radio Vientiane, *FBIS*, Laos, 18 Jan. 1977.
32. See M. Brown, 'The Communist Seizure of Power in Laos', in M. Stuart-Fox, *Contemporary Laos, op. cit.*, p. 36, footnote 18.
33. Paul Langer and Joseph J. Zasloff (1970) *North Vietnam and the Pathet Lao* (Cambridge: Harvard University Press).
34. Only in October 1975 did Kaysone Phomvihan, identified as Vice Chairman of the Central Committee of the NLHS (rather than as General Secretary of the LPRP)), forthrightly reveal the NLHS's political genealogy. Cf. *FBIS*, APA, Laos, 4 Nov. 1975.
35. Article 10, 'Agreement on Restoring Peace and Achieving National Concord in Laos', 21 Feb. 1973.

36. Kaysone Phomvihan, *La Revolution lao, op. cit.*, p. 129.
37. *Ibid.*, p. 129.
38. *Ibid.*, p. 116.
39. *Ibid.*, p. 119.
40. Gerhart Niemeyer, *op. cit.*, pp. 94-8.

Part II
Economics

Map 1 Lao People's Democratic Republic

3 The Economy of Laos: an Overview
United Nations Development Program

INTRODUCTION

With a population of 4 million, and a large land area of 236,000 square kilometres, rich in agricultural, forestry, mineral and power resources, Lao PDR offers good prospects and opportunities for accelerated development. The country is confronted with formidable obstacles to exploiting these opportunities: lack of infrastructure, lack of manpower skills and lack of domestic and foreign savings. The government has adopted new policy and programme directions, incorporated in the New Economic Management System, which are designed to remove some of these constraints. Deregulation of pricing and markets has created new incentives for state enterprises (which have also been delegated greater autonomy) and for the private sector, whose contribution to development is now more fully appreciated.

Since the Second Round Table Meeting held in 1986, the government and the donor community have broadened their contacts, and there is a better understanding of the development potential of Lao PDR. New investment opportunities have been identified through the preparation of master plans, sectoral studies and elaboration of project ideas. The UNDP-financed Southern Area Development Master Plan identified over sixty projects. Many others have been identified within the framework of the Mekong Basin Development programme. Other multilateral and bilateral donors are engaged in identification of projects and are undertaking feasibility studies. In 1987 the Government convened a local Round Table Meeting in Vientiane, with UNDP support, to strengthen coordination among aid donors. The positive results of this meeting have facilitated preparations for the third RTM, which comes at a time of growing economic and political stability in this Asian sub-region.

CURRENT ECONOMIC SITUATION[1]

GDP per capita for 1987 is estimated at US$177, calculated at the early 1988 exchange rate for official transactions in convertible currencies (US$ = KN 95). About 60 per cent of GDP is accounted for by agriculture, while industry is a mere 7 per cent. The rate of growth of the population is estimated at 2.9 per cent. Life expectancy at birth is 50 years, highlighting the importance of primary health care in future development strategies. A striking feature of the economy has been the volatility of its growth performance. Real GDP growth rates since 1983 have been as follows:

1983	1984	1985	1986	1987
		(percentages)		
3.1	6	7.9	7	−3

The government sector occupies centre stage in the Laotian economy. The private sector is largely limited to subsistence farming and, at present, occupies only a minor role in other sectors; 92 per cent of industry, and 30 per cent of exports are handled by the state sector. In transport the state sector controls 70 per cent and the co-operative sector 22 per cent. Efficiency and productivity in the 400 state enterprises are therefore crucial to economic performance. Since 1986 these state enterprises have been delegated increased responsibility and greater autonomy in their management.

Government expenditures are large relative to GDP – estimated at between 40–50 per cent. Government revenues, though in surplus over current expenditures, cover only 25 per cent of the capital budget. Capital expenditures must therefore largely be met from external donor resources.

Inflation has been persistent in recent years. The rate of inflation averaged 55 per cent annually between 1981 and 1985, rising to more than 100 per cent in the latter year. In 1986 the effective rate declined to 35 per cent and in 1987 dropped to 5.5 per cent. However, according to the most recent IMF estimate, the rate of inflation increased to 30 per cent in 1988. Lao PDR is not a fully monetised economy yet and has many features of a barter economy, including payments in kind. The process of monetisation is, however, under way. The monetary authorities have eliminated the multiple exchange rate system, and the local currency has been devalued by about 300 per cent against the US dollar to enable a convergence of all these official rates with market rates. The table 3.1 illustrates the broad features of the balance of payments.

Table 3.1   Laos: balance of payments, 1983–7 (US$m)

	1983	1984	1985	1986	1987 Est.
1. Exports	40.8	43.8	53.6	55.0	50.9
Conv. area	27.8	30.0	34.6	39.4	32.0
Nonconv. area	13.0	13.8	19.0	15.6	18.9
2 Imports	−149.4	−161.9	−193.2	−185.7	−216.8
Conv. area	−76.3	−59.3	−77.6	−78.4	−83.0
Nonconv. area	−73.1	−102.6	−115.6	−107.3	−133.8
3 Trade balance	−108.6	−118.1	−139.5	−130.7	−165.9
Conv. area	−48.5	−29.3	−42.9	−39.09	−51.0
	−60.1	−88.8	−96.6	−91.7	−114.9
4 Services (net)	−12.5	−9.8	−7.2	6.6	3.2
Conv. area (net)	−9.8	−4.8	−2.0	10.2	8.2
Nonconv. (net)	−2.7	−5.0	−5.2	−3.6	−5.0
5 Private transfers (conv. area)	0.3	2.8	3.5	3.7	4.0
6 Official transfers	25.1	42.1	49.6	30.5	29.5
Conv. area	25.1	27.7	45.4	26.0	25.0
Nonconv. area	—	15.4	4.2	4.5	4.5
7 Current account	−95.7	−82.9	−93.7	−89.9	−129.2
Conv. area	−32.9	−4.5	3.9		
Nonconv. area	−62.8	−78.4	−97.6		
8 Capital account	76.5	86.0	101.9	106.7	134.1
Conv. area	13.7	7.6	4.3	15.9	18.7
Long-term loans	8.2	2.0	1.0	12.3	15.2
Drawings	(9.5)	(10.1)	(12.1)	(20.8)	(22.0)
Amortisation	(−1.3)	(−8.1)	(−11.1)	(−8.5)	(−6.8)
Private import/ financing	4.8	5.6	3.3	3.6	3.5
Other	0.7	—	—	—	—
Nonconv. area	62.8	78.4	97.6	90.8	115.4
Long-term loans	35.2	28.3	46.7	33.1	56.5
Drawings	(35.8)	(30.2)	(50.0)	(34.9)	(58.3)
Amortisation	(−0.6)	(−1.9)	(−3.3)	(−1.8)	(−1.8)
Bilateral clearing arrangements	27.6	50.1	50.8	57.7	58.9

Source: IMF.

The trade balance has been in continuing deficit. Imports have exceeded exports by almost four to one; about half of total imports are financed under aid programmes. In the 5 years 1983–7 exports have yielded about US$52 million annually, while imports have averaged US$181 million. Around two-thirds of the exports have gone to convertible currency area countries and one-third to the non-convertible area. Sixty per cent of imports have come from the non-convertible area and only 40 per cent from the convertible area. This means that 70 per cent of the trade gap was with non-convertible countries. Exports are confined to a few items – logs and wood products, coffee, tin and gypsum, and, in addition, hydro-electric power to Thailand.

The long-standing trade imbalance has led to a heavy accumulation of external debt. In 1987 the external debt outstanding was estimated at US$ 884 million, of which US$ 689 million was owed to non-convertible countries, and US$ 195 million to convertible area countries. In 1987, however, the external debt service ratio (i.e. the payment of principal and interest as a percentage of exports of goods and services) was about 13 per cent, which is not unduly excessive. Amortisation payments to the non-convertible area have been small, due to the highly concessional terms offered and debt relief measures.

Rice dominates the agricultural economy of Lao PDR; 80–85 per cent of the cultivated land is devoted to growing paddy. Crops, other than rice, include maize, coffee, tobacco, sugar cane and root crops. The only significant export-earner among these is coffee. Though non-rice crops play a minor role in agricultural production, a marked trend towards increased production of non-rice crops can be seen. During the 1980s the total area under non-rice crops increased by about 12 per cent, with a corresponding decline in paddy area. Livestock production accounts for 30 per cent of total agricultural output. Between 1982 and 1987 the livestock sub-sector increased its output by 34 per cent, whereas crop production increased only by 20 per cent. During the 1980s the number of cattle and poultry has nearly doubled.

Fifty per cent of Lao PDR is covered by forests. FAO estimates that 6 per cent, or 80 million cubic metres, of timber are currently of commercial value. This works out to a sustainable felling rate of 2 million cubic metres per year, which is ten times the current rate of harvesting. Logs are a major export-earner and the potential exists for greatly increased export earnings from forestry.

Lao PDR is well endowed with hydropower resources. Currently installed capacity is 153 MW, of which 80 per cent is exported to Thailand and 20 per cent is consumed domestically. Hydropower generation could be increased significantly with additional investments. Mining, industry and tourism are sectors which make a relatively marginal contribution to GDP, though opportunities for further development are being explored in the context of the government's development strategy.

Social improvements, especially in education and health, are critical to the country's progress. A marked improvement in school enrolment is noticeable since 1975. Eighty-three per cent of primary age schoolchildren attend school, though this declines to 13 per cent at the secondary school level. In 1987, 8 per cent of the government development expenditure, or 4 per cent of the total budget, was on education. In the health sector Lao PDR has experienced high levels of morbidity, through malaria, water-borne diseases and malnutrition. The infant mortality rate (151/1,000) is one of the highest in the world. Increased investments in the health sector are an important prerequisite for the country's economic development.

MAJOR CONSTRAINTS TO ECONOMIC DEVELOPMENT

Four key, interrelated constraints to the economic and social development of Lao PDR can be identified. The first concerns obstacles of a structural nature to be overcome in the agricultural and forestry sectors. The second relates to the narrow, relatively weak export base. The third concerns the poor condition of the country's transport infrastructure and the limited access it provides to domestic and external markets. The fourth constraint is the lack of skilled manpower in key development sectors. As these constraints to development are all interrelated, each affecting progress in the others, they will have to be addressed on an integrated basis.

Appropriate and effective investment programmes must be developed to overcome these broadly identified constraints. Programmes and projects have to be formulated within the framework of sectoral strategies, to ensure coordination and exploit fully the intra- and inter-sectoral linkages. Careful planning at a sectoral level enables the most effective use of scarce capital and manpower resources. A logical prerequisite is therefore the elaboration of detailed sectoral strategies, and technical assistance can make an important contribution in this context.

Agriculture and Forestry

Agriculture, which employs over 80 per cent of the labour force, is largely based on subsistence farming systems. Improved agricultural practices have failed to penetrate the countryside. Of the over 2 million hectares suitable for agricultural crops, less than 800,000 hectares are currently utilised. It is estimated that another 1 million hectares could be economically used for livestock production. The scope for increasing agricultural productivity on existing land is also considerable. To achieve this requires a greater degree of crop diversification and intensification by farmers to take account of the comparative advantages of soils, weather and internal and external market opportunities.

Recent price, marketing and transport policy reforms have had a favourable impact on agricultural production levels, especially for non-rice agricultural commodities, and hence on crop diversification. Major investments in increased irrigation, flood control and distribution of improved seed varieties will be essential, as will strengthening of storage and distribution systems, agro-research, seed multiplication programmes and extension services and increased use of appropriate chemical fertilisers. A related problem is the extensive practice of slash-and-burn cultivation, which destroys an estimated 100,000 hectares of virgin forest cover each year. The government has attempted to discourage this method of cultivation by giving priority to the introduction of crop substitution programmes.

Livestock production has made important gains during the 1980s, with cattle and poultry production nearly doubling since 1981. However, endemic diseases and poor animal nutrition constrain the further growth of the livestock industry, requiring urgent vaccination and drenching programmes. Investment in marketing outlets and facilities are also urgently required.

Lao PDR has very extensive forestry development potential that has not been effectively exploited. As has been pointed out, it is estimated that sustainable forest exploitation levels are about ten times current annual harvest yields. The development of the country's forest industry potential will require control and eventual elimination of the destructive slash-and-burn cultivation practised extensively in upland areas. It also calls for the expansion and upgrading of primary and secondary wood-processing facilities and related transport infrastructure, reforestation of felled areas and related technology transfer, including introduction of effective forest resource management and harvesting skills.

Exploitation of the country's considerable agricultural and forestry sector potential is critical for the expansion of Lao PDR's export sector and national development. More generally, three basic actions appear to be reqired:

1 continued economic policy reforms in the agriculture and forestry sectors to encourage more intensive, efficient production and processing practices;
2 continued improvement of rural transport and communications infrastructure;
3 continued priority to training in improved production and harvesting practices.

The government has included in its project proposals for donor funding, major crop diversification and livestock development schemes, several irrigation development studies, an agricultural planning study in the southern provinces and a forestry management survey. These proposals should help to cope with the constraints to the development of the agricultural and forestry sectors and help give them an export orientation.

The Export Sector

It is a matter of high priority that the country increases its foreign exchange earnings. The broadening and deepening of its export base is its essential prerequisite. The government has recently adopted various measures to promote the expansion of the country's export base. This has included monetary measures, one being a major devaluation of the local currency, providing a more than threefold increase in the return to the exporters. In addition the government has given priority to the development of hydropower, the expanded processing of logs and the increased production of coffee for export markets in Thailand and elsewhere.

The government has given priority to the development of the country's abundant hydropower potential for export. About 80 per cent of the present installed capacity of the country's major Nam

Ngum power station, serving Vientiane, is exported to Thailand. Apart from the Xeset Hydroelectric project in Champassak Province, whose first phase will be completed in 1991, the government is giving priority to another hydro project – the Nam Theum II – which has major potential for the export of power to Thailand. The export of power offers the possibilities of greatly expanded foreign exchange earnings for the country, though power supply is affected by occasional droughts. The economics of such investments will also depend very much on energy prices in world markets.

Aid and trade are closely linked to each other in the development of the export sector. External assistance can and should help expand the capacity for export trade. Trade can also be further facilitated through expanded private investment – both local and foreign – in the production, processing and marketing of local resources.

Transport Infrastructure

Because of its landlocked situation, Lao PDR is confronted by difficult, high-cost transport routes to external markets. Export marketing is further complicated by the poorly developed local road network and local transport infrastructure, which has prevented development of even domestic markets. During the wet season domestic transport systems break down extensively, leaving large areas of the country inaccessible by land transport. In many instances roads, bridges and other transport infrastructure have deteriorated as a result of inadequate maintenance and operating budget provisions. Until recently the movement of products to external markets was also restricted by domestic and foreign regulations.

The Lao PDR has given high priority to the development of major road arteries and to the upgrading of local transport infrastructure. National plans have allocated up to 20 per cent of total investment in road rehabilitation and construction projects. Lack of equipment and funds has prevented road construction schemes from meeting projected completion dates. This has lessened the impact of the 1987 economic reforms to liberalise the internal trade regime and expand the role of the private sector in transport and marketing. Moreover, improving road links with Vietnam's road network and port facilities would offer prospects for improving access to export markets.

While river transport accounts for only about 15 per cent of Lao PDR's freight traffic, it is important in the handling of forestry and coffee exports to Thailand and for general transport in areas not served by the road system. For these reasons a major river transport development project is being considered.

Manpower Development

Lao PDR's current economic reforms have already had a positive impact upon agricultural production levels and have generated increased income and foreign exchange earnings. However, the country's development objectives can only be attained if manpower resources are trained or retrained to function effectively in a deregulated economic system.

The development of trained manpower in Lao PDR is severely constrained by the very low levels of educational achievement – quantitatively and qualitatively – at the primary, secondary and post-secondary levels. The quality of instruction is severely compromised by the lack of qualified staff, teaching materials and equipment. While, to some extent, Lao PDR's trained manpower needs have been met by extensive training programmes abroad, this has not proved altogether satisfactory, underlining the need for the urgent upgrading of the capacity and curriculum of the local education system, especially in vocational and technical training. There are a number of project proposals intended to help expand and upgrade the formal education and vocational and technical training institutions within the country to help meet projected future requirements.

DEVELOPMENT STRATEGIES

Following the proclamation of the Lao People's Democratic Republic in 1975, measures were introduced to establish a socialist system of production and to encourage agricultural cooperatives. Lao PDR then adopted a highly centralised form of planning. During the first decade of the Republic, the primary goal was food self-sufficiency. The goal of food self-sufficiency was largely realised and rice production doubled between 1975 and 1985. Urban expansion was curtailed and the foreign exchange earnings sector was mainly confined to forestry, mining and hydro-electric power. In education the number of students attending school doubled, and literacy increased by 10 percentage points to 40 per cent of the total population. Progress was also made in building up the country's physical and social infrastructure.

The five-year plan for 1986–90 endorses basic economic objectives similar to those of the first half of the 1980s:

(a) to ensure food self-sufficiency and food security;
(b) to reduce the area subject to slash-and-burn cultivation and to conserve forestry resources;
(c) to expand the agro-forestry industrial processing sector;
(d) to improve the balance of payments by reducing non-food imports and increasing exports, particularly to convertible currency countries;
(e) to improve the transport and telecommunication system;
(f) To strengthen managerial capabilities and to overcome the constraints of lack of qualified manpower.

The annual growth target for the economy was set at 10 per cent. Thirty per cent of investment expenditures were allocated to industry, 26 per cent to transport and 18 per cent to agriculture. Now into its fourth year, the achievement of plan targets has suffered considerable setbacks, due mainly to the inability to raise required levels of domestic savings and investment capital; shortages of foreign exchange for essential supplies, fuel and spare parts; and severe drought conditions in the country affecting crops and hydro-electric power generation.

Since 1986 the government has focused its attention on implementing its New Economic Management System (NEMS) to introduce new vigour into national economic performance. The NEMS is an integral part of the government's development strategy, as it emerged from the recognition that controlled planning should give way to a more flexible system of indicative planning and decentralised economic management. The NEMS constitutes an attempt on the part of government to introduce economic reforms bringing about greater efficiency and profitability in economic enterprises and thereby helping to achieve the objectives of the five year plan. The main features of the system are described below.

Market Pricing

Until early 1988 there were two distinct systems in Lao PDR – a public sector market and a private sector market. Goods and services needed for the public sector were acquired by the government at officially designated procurement prices. These prices bore no relation to prevailing market conditions. To illustrate, in 1982 the government purchased paddy from farmers at less than one-fifth of the market price. Public sector employees were paid mainly by coupons cashable at state stores. The dual price system was also used to purchase goods to be sold under bilateral trade agreements. The government, under the NEMS, has deregulated prices, which are now allowed to be established by market demand and supply conditions.

In eliminating the gap between official procurement prices and market prices, the government has created important incentives to agricultural producers to expand production of cash crops for local and external markets, eliminated subsidies to state enterprises, and helped to ensure that scarce investment resources are used efficiently and channelled into uses of highest returns.

Exchange Rate Policy

The official exchange value of the local currency, kip, was fixed much lower than the market rate of exchange. In December 1986 the official exchange rate was only one-tenth of the market rate. Exports were therefore discouraged, and undervaluing the true cost of imports led to serious economic distortions. In September 1987 the kip was devalued almost 300 per cent relative to the US dollar, finding a new equilibrium determined by market forces. The introduction of a market exchange rate and the unification of multiple official exchange rates signalled a major policy adjustment away from support to a subsistence economy to the development of an export-oriented cash economy.

Business Accounting for State Enterprises

State enterprises are now obliged to operate on a commercial basis – paying market prices for capital and factor inputs, introducing business accounting and management practices, developing their own market development strategies, and retaining profits for reinvestment and other operational requirements. In this respect the NEMS has stripped away subsidies to the state sector. Not all state enterprises have successfully transformed themselves into efficient business units, as the NEMS had envisaged, and external advice and assistance to such enterprises will be helpful.

Decentralisation in Decision-Making

Autonomy for state enterprises is one aspect of decentralisation. A larger role for the private sector on an equal footing with the public sector in competition for scarce resources is another. Under the Foreign Investment Code local entrepreneurs are allowed to form joint ventures with foreign investors. The structure of government has itself been reorganised to reflect greater decentralisation of decision-making power and responsibility to the provincial and district governments. Since 1987, for example, provincial governments have assumed full responsibility for the administration of health and education services.

Banking Reforms

In March 1988 a radical restructuring of banking services was initiated. The responsibilities of the State Bank, which was the sole financial intermediary in Lao PDR, has been confined to the monetary functions expected of a central bank. Management of foreign exchange, and commercial and development banking functions, have been reassigned to other autonomous banking institutions. These institutions will mobilise savings and extend credit on a commercial basis. Foreign banks have been offered facilities in the country. Private and public sector enterprises will be extended credit privileges on an equal basis.

Monetisation of the Economy

The NEMS encourages the movement away from barter and payments in kind to a cash economy. Taxes and wages are to be paid in cash. The real resource cost of goods and services will become more evident with the switch to cash exchange. Trade is likely to increase as a consequence.

Trade Liberalisation

Greater flexibility has been introduced into trading operations, both foreign and local, with increased responsibility for initiatives being given to enterprise management. The export of goods necessary to fulfil bilateral trade agreements is still a monopoly of central government. However, foreign firms may now establish offices in Lao PDR, and Lao PDR enterprises may send representatives abroad to establish trade contacts. Import of goods can now be undertaken directly by mixed public/private enterprises.

Tax Reforms

Under the reforms private and public enterprises are now taxed equally. The tax on paddy production is a land tax scaled to expected yields per acre, and is intended to encourage stationary rather than shifting slash-and-burn forms of rice cultivation. Export taxes are scaled to the degree of processing. The tax system is being reassessed with bilateral technical assistance.

The Foreign Investment Code

The Code has been formulated to encourage opportunities for economic, scientific and technological cooperation with foreign countries. Foreign organisations and individuals are authorised to invest in agriculture, forestry, transport and tourism. Investments may take the form of contract business, joint venture or 100 per cent foreign-owned enterprise. Tax concessions and repatriation of profits are provided for.

THE ROLE OF EXTERNAL RESOURCES

Resource Availability and Needs

Aid disbursements for the period 1983–7 were equivalent to $443 million, the annual average being $90 million. Annual aid receipts were as shown in Table 3.2.

Table 3.2   External aid disbursements, 1983–7 (US$m)

	1983	1984	1985	1986	1987
Aid in kind	16.6	8.2	10.3	6.0	11.0
Convertible zone	14.1	1.5	6.1	4.0	5.2
Non-convertible zone	2.5	6.7	4.2	2.0	5.8
Project aid	40.7	56.3	78.0	67.1	67.2
Convertible zone	10.1	22.4	33.2	33.3	20.9
Non-convertible zone	30.6	33.9	44.8	33.8	46.3
Technical assistance	13.1	17.9	23.4	13.1	14.3
Convertible zone	10.4	12.9	18.2	9.5	10.3
Non-convertible zone	2.7	5.0	5.2	3.6	4.0
TOTALS	70.4	82.4	111.7	86.2	92.5

This table does not reflect the highly concessional arrangements made by non-convertible zone countries to manage the deficit in bilateral clearing arrangements. See Table 3.1 for magnitude of bilateral clearing arrangement deficits.

There has been a decline in external assistance disbursements since the peak year of 1985 and the decline is even more significant in real terms. The reduced level of disbursements is mostly from the convertible currency zone, especially for project aid (mainly equipment imports) and technical assistance. This decline is directly counter to Lao PDR's increasing requirements for external assistance, as demonstrated by its widening resource gap (the difference between domestic savings and investment requirements), and needs to be reversed. As convertible donor commitments, as distinct from disbursements, have continued to increase during this period, a reversal of convertible currency zone disbursement trends will require urgent measures to expand Lao PDR's aid absorptive capacity. This issue is discussed further below.

The non-convertible zone has disbursed a little over 50 per cent of total aid, and the convertible zone has provided the rest. The major donor of the former group is the USSR, the other contributors being Bulgaria, Cuba, Czechoslovakia, the German Democratic Republic, Hungary, Mongolia, Yugoslavia and Vietnam. From the convertible area the key donors have been Japan, Sweden, Australia and the Netherlands. The World Bank and the Asian Development Bank have committed significant funds, and the UNDP has been an important source of funds for technical assistance.

In preparing the current five-year plan (1986–90), the government has made a realistic assessment of resource availability and has planned its investments accordingly. For the five-year period the government projected an inflow of foreign resources of about $93 million annually, or $465 million, of which $220 million was expected from the non-convertible area and $245 million from the convertible area.

Project Finance

The government has submitted twenty-seven projects with a total external funding requirement of US$497 million. Of this amount, US$489 million is for various capital assistance proposals, and US$7.9 million for high priority technical and preinvestment assistance.

One infrastructure project, for the construction of the Nam Theum II Dam for hydropower generation purposes, accounts for $400 million. This project is central to the government's strategy to boost power production to meet growing local requirements, and also to expand power exports to Thailand to generate increased foreign exchange earnings. The balance of the project proposals are all of high priority and are intended to expand and diversify local agricultural production, including exports; increase harvesting of commercial grade timber for local and foreign markets on a properly supervised and sustainable basis; promote integrated rural development for populations in several particularly disadvantaged, remote areas of the country; upgrade basic road and river transport to facilitate internal commercial expansion; strengthen primary and secondary education, teacher training and curriculum reform; and renovate provincial hospitals and strengthen the training of medical personnel at all levels.

These project proposals are all of high priority in relation to the government's current national development strategy, and will help to lay a solid foundation for the successful implementation of the country's major economic reforms. Accordingly, they are strongly recommended for positive consideration by the donor community.

Aid-absorptive Capacity and Improved Management

It will be critically important to strengthen Lao PDR's aid-absorptive capacity in order to improve foreign assistance disbursement performance, and more generally to enhance the impact and usefulness of capital and technical assistance provided to the country. This will require attention by both the government and the donor community to additional measures to expedite project formulation, appraisal and approval, as well as to more streamlined implementation and monitoring procedures. The government identifies the following specific measures to help increase the efficiency and timeliness with which external assistance is utilised:

1 strengthen project design, taking note of key obstacles to successful implementation (especially local transport/communications, skilled manpower and capital shortages);
2 increased stress on technical assistance required in support of capital investment programmes and to strengthen local development administration capability;
3 include provision in capital assistance for funds-in-trust and other arrangements to help meet operating and maintenance expenses for a number of years after project completion;
4 longer-term donor commitment to Lao PDR on a multi-year country programme basis, rather than on a project-by-project basis, if possible, allowing for greater flexibility to plan projects according to local capacity to utilise funds effectively;
5 for projects financed on a concessionary loan basis, eased conditions of repayment where rates of return on investment are low or below those anticipated;

6 owing to Lao PDR's large external debt and heavy repayment burden, assistance on grant terms to the greatest extent possible.

The government has expressed its desire to improve aid coordination, and one of its proposals is to organise data which are essential to understanding the spatial and sectoral impact of externally assisted projects. The primary objective of the Development Cooperation Report (DCR), published by UNDP, is precisely the same, and more comprehensive information from all donor agencies should enable the DCR to play its intended role of facilitating local aid coordination. Apart from organising the information base, the central agencies of government require further donor cooperation in coordinating project and programme aid and in monitoring and assessing the impact of external assistance. Such assessments should identify problems encountered, and ways to minimise these problems, through more integrated and consolidated design of projects and programmes. Discussions and decisions should be followed up at the country level through introduction of formal and informal institutional mechanisms for aid coordination.

Note

1 Any variations from statistics contained in Lao government documentation are due to the availability of more recent statistics from the IMF.

4 Planning Problems in Peripheral Socialism: The Case of Laos

Grant Evans*

Globally, communist states are in the throes of radical economic reforms (notable exceptions being North Korea and Albania), and Laos too has been caught up in the process. The Lao People's Revolutionary Party (LPRP) began to change direction in late 1979, but its most fundamental policy reorientation came after 1985. These dramatic shifts inside world communism have led to considerable confusion about the nature of socialism itself, and questions long buried in the socialist tradition have re-emerged to be hotly debated. What looks like a crisis in world socialism from one angle is from another viewpoint a rediscovery of the diversity of socialist thought.

There are, however, some basic premises adhered to within this debate, and they are that socialism inevitably means a strongly managed economy or planning, and a major role for public as against private ownership of productive resources. Planning is of course an attempt to influence or control the key economic variables in an economy – investment, consumption, savings, exports and imports, etc. The *command* economy, as developed in the Soviet Union during Stalin's rule, tries to directly regulate all these variables according to a centrally formulated plan.[1] The market and private production are marginalised within such an economy. Largely an accident of Soviet political history, the proliferation of this model was ensured by the predominance of the USSR in the world communist

*I would like to acknowledge the assistance of two friends who took the time to read and comment on an earlier draft of this chapter: Kelvin Rowley, who broadly agrees with its assumptions; and Bob Moreland, who does not.

84

movement until the 1960s. It is the model the LPDR first set out to emulate after taking power in December 1975.

Other approaches to economic development were advocated in the USSR, not least by Lenin himself in the New Economic Policy, adopted by the Soviet regime between roughly 1921 and 1925.[2] It downplayed direct state intervention in the economy and gave the market a vital role in the transition to socialism. These views were developed further, especially by Bukharin, and also by Trotsky. In 1922 the latter, for example, advocated ideas which ran counter to total centralised planning, and indeed could have been lifted from recent LPRP programmatic statements: 'In the course of the transitional epoch each enterprise and each set of enterprises must to a greater or lesser degree orient itself independently in the market and test itself through the market. It is necessary for each state-owned factory with its technical director to be subject not only to control from the top – by state organs – but also from below, through the market, which will remain the regulator of the state economy for a long time to come'.[3] These were not the views inherited by the LPRP.[4]

Bukharin articulated a radically different policy on the peasantry to what was finally adopted under Stalin. A fully collectivised agriculture was for him a distant prospect, and its growth would depend on properly equipped and run collective farms being able to prove their superiority in competition with private farmers. 'Collective economics is not the main highway, not the high road, not the chief path by which the peasantry will come to socialism', he wrote.[5] He challenged a pillar of Marxist orthodoxy up to that time which asserted that peasant *production* relations had to be transformed before any progress could be made towards socialism. Bukharin asserted that progress could be achieved through 'the process of circulation', through the formation of marketing and credit cooperatives.[6] He argued, as Lenin had, that socialist possession of state power was the key to their success, and in conjunction with their control of industry and the banks the peasants, 'independent of their will; must 'grow into socialism'.[7] The ability of the state to control what was called the 'commanding heights' of the economy would ensure the success of socialism.

Complementing Bukharin's strategy were the policies promoted by a leading Russian economist, Shanin, who advised greater investment in agriculture in order to lift marketable surpluses, especially for exports through which industrial goods, especially capital goods, could be imported.[8] Far from a strategy which insisted on the attainment of self-reliance in the shortest possible time, Shanin envisaged long-term dependence on the developed West.

These were heretical ideas during the tyranny of Stalinism, and they were only rediscovered, and in some cases reinvented, by Polish, Hungarian and some Soviet economists in the late 1950s and early 1960s (leaving aside socialist economists in the West). Bukharin has only recently been rehabilitated in the USSR, and Trotsky and others are waiting in the wings. Therefore when the Lao began looking for new economic policies in 1979, they began, as good orthodox communists, with Lenin's NEP articles. Subsequently, however, the LPRP has become more acquainted with alternative approaches to socialist planning through debates in Eastern Europe, and from Soviet advocates of reform.

Many authors, including several in this volume, argue that Lao economic thinking bears a strong Vietnamese imprint. I dissent from this view because I believe it can be demonstrated that there is nothing which distinguishes Vietnamese economic thinking from orthodox Stalinist communism. Both the Vietnamese and the Lao inherited this body of economic thought. Only in recent years have they learned of alternative approaches to economic planning and socialist development, and I would argue that the Lao have taken on these ideas much more rapidly than the more hidebound party and state apparatus in Hanoi. There is no question that for a long time the Lao communists have been the 'apprentices' (to use Brown and Zasloff's apposite description)[9] of the Vietnamese, and for obvious reasons. But had they been the 'apprentice' of the Soviets or the Chinese, I am certain they would have been instructed in the same Stalinist mode of thought. Even had the LPRP been no one's apprentice, it is unlikely to have produced a new approach to socialist development. The Vietnamese have clearly played an important role in the implementation of specific Lao policies, however; as I have argued elsewhere, their influence has been mediated by various conjunctural political and economic factors.[10]

THE ECONOMIC ISSUES

Poor countries facing the 'steep ascent' of economic development must solve the problem of capital accumulation if they are to create economic growth. The fundamental question for state elites therefore is what is the best way to promote accumulation?

Development economics as a sub-discipline is premised on the positive role that state planning and state enterprises can play in developing economies. This approach grew out of the post World War II phase of decolonisation when nationalist elites took power in countries with only small or non-existent bourgeois classes possessing entrepreneurial skills and capital to invest. In this context the state was seen as the one institution capable of promoting national economic development. Thus many developing countries created substantial state-owned corporations. These accounted for as much as 70 per cent of gross fixed investment in, for example, Algeria (1978–81), or 23 per cent each in Brazil (1980) and South Korea (1978–80).[11] It was the era of state capitalism in the Third World.[12] Indeed until the 1980s the World Bank preferred to channel loans and aid through public enterprises, and multinational corporations preferred to do business with state enterprises.[13]

The late 1970s to early 1980s saw a dramatic reversal of this approach, as opinion worldwide swung against state ownership of economic resources. This mood coincided with the maturation of two long-term trends: an acceleration of global economic integration, which challenged previous strategies of economic nationalism and 'self-sufficiency' (partly a product of post-colonial nationalism); and, secondly, the intervening period had seen the growth of a bourgeois class which came to oppose the state's appropriation of a large share of national investment to their detriment.[14] This has led to a redefinition of the role of the state and to a decline of state capitalism in parts of the developing world. It can be argued that communist states too have come under similar pressures, although their response has been more problematic.

While there are obvious historical reasons for the role of the state in economic development, there are also more general theoretical arguments put forward to justify active state intervention in economic affairs. A key premise of state planning is that it is able to achieve the best possible use of scarce resources for economic development, and is better placed than an individual private enterprise to recognise the externalities of a particular investment or economic activity, that is, the costs and benefits to others which a single privately owned firm is not bound to take account of. For example, it will invest in infrastructure to promote the long-term economic integration of a country regardless of short-term profitability, or invest in education, or legislate to protect natural resources against indiscriminate exploitation for immediate profit. In other words, the state not only has broader horizons, its plans have longer time frames. Thus, it is argued, by recognising externalities benefits can be maximised for the society as a whole. This is in contrast to an argument which claims that individually rational decisions by entrepreneurs acting in an unfettered market add up to or are homologous with benefit to society as a whole.

The 1980s have produced an avalanche of simplistic commentary in the West on the virtues of the 'free' market versus the dead hand of the state. For example, one representative of this 'New Right' orthodoxy argues that the 'vast array of government controls on economic activity is the key to understanding low living standards and slow growth in poor countries'.[15] Less government will equal more growth. In this world view state action is identified as 'socialist' and the market as 'capitalist'. This, however, poses the debate in 'mythic terms', writes Robert B. Reich:

> The idea of a free market somehow separate from law is a fantasy. The market was not created by divine will. It is a human artifact... What is mine? What is yours? What is ours? And how do we define and deal with actions that threaten these borders – theft, force, fraud, extortion or carelessness? What should we trade, and what should we not? (Drugs? Sex? Votes? Babies?) How should we enforce these decisions and what penalties apply to transgressions? As a culture accumulates answers to these questions, it creates its version of the market.[16]

Reich sees the state operating in a capitalist context, and consequently the role of government is to design the right market rules and not dictate the right market results. The basic issues, however, also apply in a socialist context, although the lines are drawn differently because different social forces are at work and these dictate alternative political priorities.

Socialists have approached the problem of accumulation from two basic directions. The first, and to date dominant, model has been the 'command economy', which attempts to harness internal economic surpluses by directly controlling all investment and consumption in the economy. As an economic system it tends to be autarchic and encourages plans which tend to reproduce identical rather than complementary economic structures between states. As a model it is most feasible in large countries with varied resources. The second approach, which has only begun to be experimented with recently, opts for more indirect methods of controlling investment and consumption, and therefore gives considerable scope to the market. It is also more open to the world market and less concerned with national 'self-sufficiency'. We will return to this approach in greater detail after we have looked at the LPDR's attempt to implement the first model, followed by its gradual adoption of the second.

For both strategies, however, harnessing an investable surplus is the fundamental task of economic development. Naturally investment can only take place if there is a surplus over and above what is required for current consumption and replacement of the wear and tear on instruments of production. Paul Baran's discussion of capital accumulation makes a useful distinction between an *actual* economic surplus and a *potential* surplus. He defines them in the following way:

1 *Actual* ecomomic surplus, i.e. the difference between society's *actual* current output and its *actual* current consumption. It is thus identical with current savings...
2 *Potential* economic surplus, i.e. the difference between the output that *could* be produced in a given natural and technological environment with the help of *actually* employed productive resources and what might be regarded as essential consumption.[17]

The latter concept is central to his thought in that it involves a critique of the status quo by not accepting that, for example, the market has already allocated all resources efficiently. In other words mobilization of the potential surplus for investment may call for a more or less drastic reorganisation of production and distribution, which is the task of socialism. Baran isolated three broad sources of potential surplus: excess consumption by elites; unproductive workers (e.g. state officials or the armed forces); and irrationalities and waste in prevailing economic organisation.

Socialists stake a large part of their claim to economic and political legitimacy on their ability to harness the unrealised *potential* surplus of the previous regime and thereafter produce an ever-expanding investable actual surplus – or dynamic economic growth.

ACCUMULATION IN LAOS[18]

What sources of actual surplus were available to the new socialist state in its first year, 1976? The answer is simple. Almost none. Over 80 per cent of Laos' $3\frac{1}{2}$ million people worked in agriculture as either slash-and-burn hilltribe subsistence cultivators who produce no surplus, or as largely subsistence-oriented peasants. The economy of the previous regime had been dependent on massive injections of foreign aid dollars (mainly from the United States) which provided little incentive for productive investment, and led to the creation of a bloated services sector accounting for 57 per cent of GDP (compared with 21 per cent in 1986). The government depended for 80 per cent of its budgetary expenditure on bilateral and multilateral aid. As this aid was withdrawn over 1975–6, the Lao communists found themselves in charge of a bankrupt state and an increasingly bankrupt economy. The urban service-oriented economy ground to a halt along with the few manufacturing firms producing for it. Capital took flight, as did the owners of some companies, and often not before they had either dismantled or sabotaged machinery. Thousands of internal refugees displaced by the civil war remained dependent on imported food, and their resettlement added further costs. Production declined and therefore the actual surpluses available to the new government diminished to virtually nil.

The collapse of dollar inflows and of production led to severe shortages and thence to rapid inflation. This was aggravated by a rapid growth in the money supply as the government extended credit to newly established state enterprises for investment, and to pay salaries. At the end of June 1976 the old Royal kip was replaced with the Liberation kip, whose official rate was KL200=US$1. On the parallel market it was initially KL400=US$1, then plummeted to KL1000=US$1 by the end of July. The government attempted to cope with panic buying and selling by a crack-down on 'speculators' and merchants, causing a further decline in commerce, and therefore of circulation of anything that was produced.

Per capita income, estimated at US$80–90, was extremely low even compared with the poor northeast of Thailand. A World Bank mission remarked that 'the *average* per capita national income in Laos (let alone private consumption) is lower than the poverty line. Thus, the incidence of poverty in Laos must be extremely high even if the incomes are evenly distributed'.[19] The grim reality was that the population had little money to buy what was produced, let alone to invest.

Over 1976 Western aid inflows were steadily replaced by aid from the USSR and other Eastern bloc countries, and from Vietnam, and hence the state was kept functioning. One index of the paucity of actual surpluses in the economy is the fact that by 1977 sources of revenue for the new government mirrored those of the previous regime in that foreign aid accounted for 81 per cent of it.[20] These inflows also financed the serious imbalance in foreign trade.

Thus Laos in the years immediately following the communist takeover had no actual surplus available for accumulation. As a World Bank report stated: 'in 1977 Laos had no national savings, and...the country was fully dependent on the outside world to finance its development needs'.[21]

What about the potential surplus? Prospects here were little better.

Firstly, there was no surplus available from an old landed elite, for such an elite was not significant in Laos, and the former urban elite's conspicuous consumption had been financed by foreign dollars. So, little was available in savings on elite consumption.

There were also few immediate savings to be made by eliminating unproductive demands on the surplus. The former administrative elite, police and army were sent off for 're-education' through 'productive' labour. But they were quickly replaced by a new bureaucracy whose desire to extend state control over the society in fact led to a growth in the bureaucratic apparatus. Similarly the army was not demobilised because of continuing security fears, and in fact attempts were made to expand it. In this context (leaving to one side foreign policy and political issues) the presence of Vietnamese soldiers in Laos to help with security alleviated pressure to expand the army, and therefore unproductive expenditures, further.

The main source of potential surplus, therefore, was in underutilised or inefficiently utilised productive resources. The distribution of these resources is shown in Table 4.1.

When considering the category of industry in Table 4.1, we need to realise that within manufacturing about 75 per cent of the value added was in activities such as rice-milling, rural production of charcoal, distilling local rice whisky, and handicraft and cottage industry, all of which hardly qualify as manufacturing in the usual sense.[22] In 1977 capacity utilisation in industry was estimated at 30 per cent, and as low as 10–15 per cent in some activities. The reasons were shortages, especially of imported raw materials and spare parts, and of trained staff at all levels, besides the disruptions stemming from changes in ownership and management. Thus resources, especially foreign exchange, had to be allocated to this sector if

Table 4.1   Structure of GDP, 1977–84 (%)

	1977	1982	1984	1985	1986	1987
Agriculture	59.0	62.0	62.5	63.5*	63.6*	62.2*
Forestry and industry	6.0	6.5	5.6	7.6	7.4	7.5
Construction	9.3	3.3	4.2	3.8	3.3	3.7
Transport and communications		1.5	1.4	1.2	1.2	1.4
Commerce	(7.9)	9.1	8.8	7.9	7.7	8.3
Government and other services	17.8	17.6	17.5	16.0	15.8	17.0
	100	100	100	100	100	100

Source: World Bank Report, June 1986. p.40 for years 1977–84. For years 1985–7 Draft Document for the 3rd Round Table Meeting on the LPDR for March 1989.
*Agriculture and forestry.

potential productive capacity was to be realised. Rice-mills were also functioning below capacity, owing to lack of spare parts or sabotage. Some of these parts could be supplied by local machine tool shops, but these too were short of raw materials and spare parts, and required foreign exchange to acquire them.

Export income was therefore crucial to generating funds for investment in productive activity in Laos. However, commodity exports had declined. There had been a serious drop in forestry exports from around $12–14 million in 1974 to $1.5 million in 1977, owing to lack of equipment and imported fuel, the weak management of wood-processing industries, and poor price incentives. Mining also went into decline, with production and exports falling from around 1,500 tons of concentrate in the early 1970s to 600 tons in 1977. Considerable potential also existed in coffee exports. Before the escalation of the civil war some 6,000 ha had been planted to coffee, two-thirds of which was abandoned as a result of fighting. But considerable rehabilitation, plus shifts to better varieties and marketing practices, would be required before this potential could be exploited. Only in 1978 did new electricity-generating capacity come on stream from Nam Ngum dam north of Vientiane, and about 90 per cent of the electricity generated was sold to Thailand.

Tables 4.2 and 4.3 list commodity exports and the balance of payments respectively in the late 1970s.

Table 4.2   Commodity exports, 1976–80 (US$m)

	1976	1977	1978	1979	1980
Wood	0.7	0.9	2.7	8.5	6.1
Tin	1.3	0.9	0.8	0.2	0.5
Coffee	2.2	3.1	1.0	4.1	1.1
Forestry products	0.6	0.4	0.2	0.2	0.2
Electricity	1.6	1.8	1.9	6.1	5.3
Total exports	6.5	8.0	8.1	19.4	13.5

Source: *LPDR Report on the Economic and Social Situation: Development Strategy and Assistance Requirement*, prepared for Round Table of the Least Developed Countries of Asia and the Pacific, Geneva, May 1983. p.88.

Table 4.3   Balance of payments, 1975–79 (US$m)

	Average 1972–4	1975	1976	1977	1978
Trade (net)	−51.0	−50.0	−41.5	−55.0	−64.0
Exports	6.0	3.0	6.5	9.0	11.0
Imports	57.0	53.0	48.0	64.0	75.0
Services (net)	−15.0	−8.0	−15.5	−20.0	−20.0
Receipts	24.0	8.0	4.5	3.5	6.5
Expenditures	39.0	16.0	20.0	23.5	26.5
Current balance	−66.0	−58.0	−57.0	−75.0	−84.0
Capital and transfers	83.0	52.0	52.0	70.0	82.0
Overall balance	15.0	−7.0	−1.0	−4.8	1.3

Source: World Bank (1979) *Socialist Transformation in the LPDR: An Economic Report*, Vol. 1., p.47.

Of course the other major source of surplus was agriculture, in which approximately 80 per cent of the population laboured. The country as a whole was not self-sufficient in food, but this was because of refugee movements before 1975 and the expansion of an urban population dependent on dollar imports to finance food requirements. The peasants themselves were largely self-sufficient, even though their rice productivity was, and remains, among the lowest in Asia. Lao agriculture was at the mercy of the weather, as it always had been, but bad years were fatalistically accepted along with the good. Up until 1975 the peasantry had largely remained beyond the reaches of the state and of commerce. The state had been able to sustain itself through foreign aid and taxation of trade and commerce, and had little reason seriously to attempt to tax the peasants. The communist government, however, saw agricultural taxation as a vital source of revenue, and therefore introduced it in September 1976. Predictably it was not welcomed by the peasants, causing Phoumi Vongvichit, Vice Premier and Minister of Education, Sport and Religion, to respond in December 1976:

> Some people have rejected the collection of agricultural taxes. They want the government to pay these taxes and the people not to pay for anything. However, they say the country must be built. If we followed that idea, then the country would have to be dependent on foreign countries and could only ask them for money to carry out construction work. However, it is not easy to get other countries to give us as much as we want... After we have found other sources of income then the agricultural tax may be reduced or abolished.[23]

Poor harvests, evasion and problems of administering the tax, however, limited proceeds from it to less than 1 per cent of GNP (about 4 per cent of total paddy production in 1977), rather than the hoped for 5 per cent. Yet there was considerable room for lifting productivity in Lao agriculture through irrigation, new rice varieties and some mechanisation, and attempts were begun in this direction in 1976–7 as people were mobilised to construct irrigation channels. However, the resources available for agriculture were minimal, so that the impact of these attempts at improvement on production were marginal; and the continued vulnerability of Lao agriculture to the elements was dramatised by severe drought in 1977 and serious flooding in 1978. International food relief was required, especially for city dwellers.

At the end of 1977 the situation looked grim for the Lao leaders. The economy was generating no actual surplus, and the potential surplus was proving extremely difficult to mobilise. A hostile Thai government had faced them throughout 1977, had severely restricted imports and given unofficial encouragement and support to insurgents inside Laos, especially the remnants of the former Vang Pao forces. Furthermore, disagreements between its Vietnamese ally and Kampuchea and China had begun. It was against this backdrop of growing insecurity, economically and politically, that the three-year development plan in early 1978, and the collectivisation campaign soon after, were formulated.

Taxation had shown itself unable to mobilise sufficient surplus and had caused dissatisfaction among peasants, both because it was new and was poorly administered. Another option open to the state, namely garnering of surpluses produced in agriculture through manipulating the internal terms of trade, depended on having something from industry to trade with peasants, or imported goods to trade. However, there were insufficient quantities to stimulate rapid growth in production, hence any surpluses produced by peasants were likely to be consumed by them. Therefore both these avenues for mobilising the agricultural surplus, which, in the words of Baran, 'constitutes the indispensable condition for any developmental endeavour',[24] were inadequate.

So between 1975 and 1977 the economy contracted, and GNP at the end of 1977 stood 10 per cent lower in real terms than in 1974. Instead of developing, the economy went backwards, and this in turn undermined the government's endeavours to establish its legitimacy.

THE LOGIC OF CENTRALISATION

The centralising logic of the new state, and the new government's ideological emphasis on 'self-reliance', pushed economic policy in an autarchic direction, and placed strong emphasis on the importance of raising surpluses internally rather than, for example, through foreign trade or investment. This led inevitably towards collectivisation. Through collectivisation any surpluses in peasant production are able to be 'siphoned off' through the new structure's ability to regulate consumption and output. Baran states the classic case for this move:

> ...if there were no other powerful reasons for the desirability of collectivisation of agriculture, the vital need for the mobilisation of the economic surplus generated in agriculture would in itself render collectivisation finally indispensable. By transferring the disposal of agricultural output from individual peasants to government-supervised collective farm managements, collectivisa-

tion destroys the basis for the peasants' resistance to the 'siphoning off' of the economic surplus.. the share of agricultural output consumed on the farm can be fixed by direct allotment to collective farm members, while farm consumption of nonagricultural commodities can be regulated...[25]

Moreover this new institutional form could be used to mobilise labour for capital construction, such as irrigation, and be a channel through which agricultural improvements could be directed. What Baran and governments who have attempted this strategy overlooked, however, was the degree to which this would provoke both active and passive resistance from the peasants, and destroy the incentives to produce within agriculture.

However, even according to Baran, collectivisation may not be imperative in the short run. Peasants, he says, may 'sit it out' for a while if the country has an industrial nucleus able to generate a sufficient economic surplus, or if aid from abroad releases the state from having to extract a surplus internally. It may 'save the beneficiary country the necessity of hasty collectivisation of the small peasant'.[26] This, however, is dependent on a government's assessment of the desired pace of development, and that more often than not is a political question. Rapid change seemed urgent in Laos in early 1978, despite the fact that it was receiving considerable foreign aid, and collectivisation promised it. Furthermore, during this politically volatile period, collectivisation not only promised greater control over consumption and production, but greater political control over the population as well.

A Three Year Development Plan was announced in March 1978, with the aim of expanding and strengthening the socialist sector of the economy. Collectivisation was integral to the plan. The plan's fundamental aim was to achieve food self-sufficiency by 1980, which was to be done both through the extension of the cultivable surface area, irrigation construction, and agricultural intensification. Increased funds were allocated to industry and manufacturing to provide inputs into agriculture, and for the processing of timber. Reflecting the government's economic and political–strategic concerns, stress was also placed on the construction of an all-weather road through Vietnam to the sea. Considerable funds were therefore allocated to this project, and to transport and communications within the country.

Clearly an important part of the government's thinking at the time was to finance at least part of this investment through controlling personal consumption. Rationing had been in effect for state officials from the beginning, and salaries consisted largely of commodity sales to public officials at subsidised prices. The government had attempted to control prices through establishing a monopoly over internal financial transactions and over foreign trade, and by placing limitations on internal private trade and attempting to expand state trade. Low official prices for rice were also meant to keep costs down. Shortages meant high prices for commodities in the parallel market, although the state obviously hoped that its officials would not need to resort to that market for essential items. On this premise the Plan froze salaries at 1977 levels. Thus a policy framework was established for beginning state-centred socialist development in Laos. However, within a year it came unstuck, primarily because the state sector could not fulfil its prescribed role. The drive for collectivisation was suspended in mid-1979, and a radical rethinking of economic policy began later the same year.

The problems the communist government encountered in Laos were inevitable, given the poverty of the country. Any government would have difficulty in promoting economic 'take-off' in Laos. However, the solutions adopted by the Lao leaders contributed to a decline in economic activity and therefore a decline in the potential surplus realizable. The basic mistake, as General Secretary Kaysone Phomvihan admitted in late 1979, was that they had adopted an over-centralised model of socialism.

In its attempt to establish a centralised system, the government had either completely taken over industrial or commercial enterprises, or established joint state–private companies, and when allowing private enterprises to continue their operations, had required them 'to operate in much the same way as state enterprises, submitting each year a budget and production plan to the Ministry of Commerce and Industry for approval'.[27] The state enterprises were not unlike government departments, in that managers followed directions from above and had little control over production decisions, or the flow of funds to and from their enterprises. They simply attempted to fulfil specified physical targets, and it was a matter of relative indifference whether their enterprise ran at a profit or a loss, as these categories were simply absorbed in the state budget. Private companies, on the other hand, were expected to absorb losses even if the cause of them was a failure of the state to provide planned-for inputs, such as imports of spare parts or raw materials, on time. For many the risks and costs of staying in business became too high.

A centralised system demands coordination of several and ultimately all sectors of the economy, and places a premium on efficient management and flows of information. Neither of these preconditions was present in Laos. Competent management is a function of literacy, education and experience. However, not only were people with sufficient education in short supply in Laos, but much of the little managerial experience had joined the exodus from the country after the communist victory. Information flows, which become increasingly complex as one moves from agriculture to industry, are dependent on general literacy, bureaucratic efficiency, and the communications system, all of which were extremely rudimentary in Laos. Centralisation was undoubtedly partly a result of these same scarcities, in that only a very small number of people were sufficiently competent to make the decisions demanded by the system. Information therefore flowed towards the pinnacle of the bureaucracy, where it became ensnared in bottlenecks. The structure therefore had a self-reinforcing (self-defeating) logic.

An example of problems of coordination and information flows can be seen in the forestry area, where the upstream work of logging was handled by the Ministry of Agriculture and downstream wood-processing was handled by the Ministry of Industry. The non-arrival of logs at particular mills would be a result of the information travelling upwards becoming jammed and therefore not being transmitted to those responsible for delivery. This was one contributing factor to idle capacity in the mills. On the other hand the logs might arrive but the mill was idle because the order for a new saw blade, or whatever, had still not reached the enterprise responsible for importing and distributing spare parts.

Furthermore there were no economic sanctions for non-delivery. There was no point, for example, in one part of the state suing another part of the state for non-fulfilment of its task because the state itself absorbed all losses. Therefore there were few incentives to fulfil production targets efficiently, except perhaps promotion within the bureaucracy for the manager. There were definitely no incentives for innovation; bureaucracies reward the obeying of orders.

The consequences of this were low or declining production, which meant of course fewer goods available for trade and therefore stagnant commerce. State commercial enterprises were favoured with supplies of scarce goods, but they too suffered from the same problems of administration and coordination as other state enterprises. Therefore the distribution of what was available was inefficient. In addition restrictions on private trade limited the extent to which it could plug the gaps left by the state sector; and the scarcity of low-price goods against which to exchange their rice meant there was little incentive for peasants to produce or exchange any surpluses, while prices for manufactured goods in the small parallel market were too great for the ordinary farmer.

Collectivisation had aimed at both raising productivity and ensuring cheap supplies of rice to the the non-agricultural sectors. However, it simply caused widespread disruption of production and disaffection, and burdened the weak administration with yet one more task to oversee.[28] Short of extremely authoritarian measures to ensure rice deliveries, such as those adopted in Pol Pot's Cambodia, the programme had to be suspended.

Thus the strategy formulated in the Three Year Plan was undone. It had been premised on the state's ability to maintain basic consumer goods supplies to all sectors, and on raising the productivity of the export sector in order to generate investable surpluses. It had been unable to do either.

THE ROAD TO MARKET SOCIALISM

At the end of 1979 a reversal of previous policy was begun, and by 1987 it had been substantially completed, with the most important shifts occurring over 1985–6. The immediate cause of the change was a growing realisation in 1979 that the state's food self-sufficiency target for the country would not be reached in 1980. Resolution VII of the LPRP Central Committee, passed in December 1979, sanctioned an increased role for private enterprise and lifted some restrictions on market transactions. The private sector thereon was to fill gaps left by state enterprises either because of the latter's inefficiency or because of incapacity.

Kaysone appealed to Lenin's NEP texts to give the changes a mantle of orthodoxy and legitimacy. Consider the following statement from Lenin's 'The Tax in Kind' (1921) where he pondered

which policies should be adopted, given the inability of state industries to supply goods for exchange with peasants:

> What is to be done? One way is to try to prohibit entirely, to put
> the lid on private, non-state exchange ...But such a policy would be
> foolish and suicidal for the party that tried to apply it. It would be
> foolish because it is economically impossible. It would be suicidal
> because the party that tried to apply it would meet with inevitable
> disaster.[29]

Kaysone adopted identical formulations in his speeches on the new
policies. However, it took the government several years to evolve a
new model of accumulation, one which broke with previous autarchic
assumptions that squeezed consumption.

The model they have been moving toward is similar to that
outlined by E.V.K. Fitzgerald, one of the more innovative contemporary theorists on the problems of what he terms 'peripheral
socialism'. He has seriously questioned the surplus-generating potential of a strategy which depends on 'squeezing' consumption, and has
shifted the focus of socialist economic theorising from a closed-
economy model to one which places issues of foreign exchange and
trade at its centre. Small, peripheral socialist economies are, he
argues, inescapably dependent on the international economy because
of their need to import producer goods, and their inability in the
medium and perhaps long term to provide import-substitutes. This,
he says, is the true meaning of their 'dependency'. In this context
therefore the export sector must become a surrogate producers'
goods sector.[30]

Combined with a situation where basic consumption goods are
produced by independent peasants, the macroeconomic framework
confronted by planners is one where the socialist sector 'can only
obtain capital goods and wage goods by trading with two sectors
outside their own direct control'.[31] The branch providing non-basic
consumer goods – televisions, fashion clothes, household appliances,
etc. – central to any strategy of incentives is therefore the most
plannable area of the economy, with services naturally being more
decentralised than manufacturing. This therefore is where socialist
planning should direct its energy. Fitzgerald writes:

> Central aspects of economic strategy must therefore be the mana-
> gement of commercial relationships with the world economy

(covering price stability and credits, as well as the external terms of trade as such) and with the small-producer sector (covering community welfare and infrastructure support as well as the internal terms of trade), rather than planning of production in the state sector itself. Avoidance of 'accumulation bias' will involve less emphasis on the large export projects beloved of planners and more on popular consumption...[32]

By 'accumulation bias' he means the tendency of state socialism to subordinate popular consumption to high rates of investment and accumulation in the modern sector. This is caused by unconstrained enterprise budgets ('soft budgets') and the absence of bankruptcy provisions, resulting in the 'crowding out' of non-state investment, especially in the small-scale consumer goods sector, including peasants and other small producers. This has the seemingly paradoxical result of the national accumulation rate falling as state investment rises because labour surpluses in the non-state sector remain unmobilised. This raises the opportunity cost of state investment, or wastes part of it, as a result of squeezing consumption.[33] An 'accumulation bias' of sorts had been occurring in Laos, and the new policies have sought to overcome this.

By and large, up until 1985, Laos was still failing to produce a significant investable surplus. In 1984 government revenue for the first time exceeded government expenditure, but the agricultural surplus which had been generated was essentially consumed and the country remained dependent on external sources to finance development expenditure. Thus of 1985's high rate of investment, 25 per cent of GDP, Laos contributed only 2.9 per cent. Furthermore the returns from this high rate of investment were low.[34] For example, investment directed towards some relatively large-scale irrigation projects had been underutilised because of inadequate price incentives, and in some cases canals had fallen into disrepair, thus degrading the investment. These examples of 'accumulation bias' were not going to be tolerated by Laos' international donors and creditors indefinitely.

One of the most important early changes initiated by the government was increased flexibility on pricing and market exchange with the agricultural sector. Thus in 1980 the prices of most crops and export products were raised between 300 and 500 per cent; retail prices of commodities marketed by the state went up by 200 to 300 per cent and approached parallel market prices, while wage increases of 200 per cent partially compensated state employees. Increased consumer goods were imported by the state for sale to farmers in return for state procurement at negotiated prices. One immediate result of these increased incentives was a 16.5 per cent increase in rice production. Government purchases of rice rose six times, and tax income tripled, the latter being a partial consequence of a tax reform in mid-1980 which lowered average tax rates and was simpler to administer. Production in 1981 rose to 1.15 million tons of paddy, which was a 52 per cent increase over 1977, and brought the country close to self-sufficiency. Table 4.4 shows rice production in the early 1980s.

Table 4.4　Production, supply and government procurement of rice, 1980–4

	1980	1981	1982	1983	1984
Total rice supply ('000 tons)					
Paddy	1053	1155	1093	1001	1321
Rice equivalent	612	673	636	583	775
Rice imports	46	0	5	0	20
Per capita rice supply	207	206	192	170	226
Official rice procurement ('000 tons)					
Purchases	4	29	31	32	39
Agric. tax	10	20	26	23	22
% Net production	2.3	7.3	9.0	9.4	7.9

Source: World Bank Report, June 1986, p.154.

The improved procurement prices for paddy, however, were achieved at the expense of the manufacturing and industrial sector, where the state was able to hold down prices. One consequence was a decline in manufacturing output over 1981–4. In fact over this period the share of industry, transport and trade in the GDP fell, suggesting that the economy had become increasingly subsistence-oriented. However, this was partly a statistical mirage, in that it reflected the increase in agricultural productivity over the period from an average of 1.4 tons/ha to 2.1 tons/ha of paddy. Nevertheless it indicates little or no improvement in the 'modern' sectors of the economy, and therefore meagre success in the aim of modernisation and economic development. In 1985, with the beginning of new policies, the official prices for manufactured goods were readjusted once again, worsening the terms of trade between paddy and the industrial sector. These swings back and forth in administered prices helped push to the forefront the need for a more responsive pricing system.

Having begun to take steps away from the command model in late 1979, the LPRP was drawn inexorably toward a greater use of the market, and therefore of prices, which could provide more accurate information on supply and demand within the economy.[35] New institutions for accumulation had to be established in what later came to be called the New Economic Mechanism. A process of gradual decentralisation of the economy was begun, and firms, previously little more than government departments, became semi-autonomous enterprises, with their own internal accounting systems, dealing with other enterprises and the state as external agents rather than internal ones. This policy was introduced gradually, no doubt because of disquiet in the party, and necessary prudence, which demanded that controlled experiments be made in order to isolate potential problems and attempt solutions before promoting the system more widely. In mid-1981 Resolution 11 of the Political Bureau instructed enterprises to meet a dozen compulsory plan targets, determined by the supervising authorities. Beyond these the enterprises were given a degree of operating autonomy and allowed to retain 10 per cent of their profits for reinvestment. In 1983 certain enterprises were granted even more autonomy through being allowed to keep 40 per cent of their profits and a proportion of any overseas earnings generated, and to engage in some direct sales on the open market. In 1985 these measures were further extended until in 1988 the majority of the 380 state-owned enterprises in the country had become basically autonomous. By late 1988 around fifty enterprises had still not been cut adrift but, according to Dr Sompavanh Inthavong, Vice Minister of Trade, Commerce and External Relations, if they cannot become self-sustaining then they must be allowed to 'disappear'.[36]

Consequently they became responsible not only for their own profits but their own losses as well. In other words, 'soft budgets' were abandoned. However, they did not become private enterprises. They remained fundamentally state-owned, although shares have been offered to employees (the proportion of employee shares allowable is unclear). Managers and workers receive wages and salaries and do not have the right, independently of the state, to sell the firm or buy another, although they do have rights to dispose of assets they no longer require for their operations. They are obliged to pay the state taxes and have to negotiate with the state concerning investment plans, and therefore the amount of surplus which can be retained within the firm for accumulation.

By mid-1987 the government had also logically moved to a pricing system which reflected the new structure, by abolishing almost all administered prices and the multi-tiered foreign exchange rate, lifting all barriers to internal trade, and giving enterprises direct access to international markets. The process of change was further consolidated during the fifth session of the Council of Ministers in March 1988, which passed several key decrees on the economy – on taxation, finance and banking, state pricing, goods circulation, and an outline of state policy on the private sector. One result was a reorganisation of the state's planning apparatus, given its withdrawal from direct economic management. Thus the State Planning Committee headed by Sali Vongkhamsao was abolished and Sali took over the Ministry for Planning and Finance, while other key figures in the old SPC joined the Ministry of Trade, Commerce and External Relations, headed by Phao Bounnaphon. The task of these ministries is macroeconomic planning, not microeconomic decision-making.

Sali Vongkhamsao's ministry is responsible for indicative planning and the formation of general investment priorities for the whole economy. Thus it not only oversees the general investment decisions of state enterprises but is required to monitor the investment programmes of the provinces and districts. To do this, however, it will need to learn techniques of macroeconomic monetary and taxation adjustments in order to bend the economy in the direction desired by the state. The March 1988 meeting also established a framework for reforming the state banking system, leaving the central bank to manage money supply, while a separate system will operate on a commercial basis in which state enterprises are not granted preferential interest rates but have to approach the banks on the same basis as private businesses. A major problem facing this reform, however, is the shortage of personnel in the banking sector capable of carrying out project and creditworthiness analysis. The latter will be crucial, for in this system the banks will have to adopt a more active planning role in the economy (more or less as management consultants) in their relations with firms if their loans are to conform with priorities set by the Ministry for Planning and Finance. Table 4.5 lists exchange rates.

Table 4.5 Exchange rates, 1981–7 (Kip per $US)

	Official	Commercial	Import Valuation	Pvt Remittance	Import Export	Parallel Market
1981 December	10	30		—		56
1982 December	10	35		—		105
1983 December	10	35		108		140
1984 December	10	35		108		250
1985 December	10	35	95	108		380
1986 June	10	35	95	270	300	440
1987 February	10	35	95	270	300	390
1987 September	350	350	350	350	350	350–370
1988 May	350	350	350	350	350	345
1988 November	460	460	460	460	460	460

The aim of the LPRP is to transform Laos from a minimal surplus natural economy into a 'socialist commodity economy'. Kaysone and his comrades have recognised that the exchange of goods on a wide scale is a prerequisite of economic development, for exchange at least registers that some surpluses are being produced in the economy, rather than none at all. But what is most intriguing about the latest shift is the attempt to create socialist entrepreneurs. As I said at the beginning of this chapter, it has been the role of the state in underdeveloped countries to perform the role of a 'collective bour-geois'. In Laos the state is delegating this role to its various autonomous enterprises, while the state continues to act as ring-master. Thus in February 1988 Kaysone exhorted his cadres 'to become communist traders in accordance with Lenin's teachings which say: the Party, the communists and the proletarian state must act as major traders and must study civilised trading practices from Western capitalists. Only by doing this shall we be able to make a small agricultural country advance towards socialism'.[37]

Leaving aside the agricultural sector for a moment, the Lao government does not envisage a dramatic shift in production relations within industry and commerce towards private enterprise. If the policies were somehow a reversion to capitalism, it certainly was not reflected in the sectoral distribution of production in 1987 – though it could be suggested that it is too soon to tell (see Table 4.6).

Table 4.6   Sectoral distribution of production (%)

	Private	State	Cooperative
Agriculture	77	0.5	22.5
Industry	8	92	—
Transport	9*	78	13
External Trade	21	79	n.a.

*Most of this 9 per cent claim to be in cooperatives.

The plan is one in which state enterprises occupy the 'commanding heights' of the economy (to steal a formulation from Bukharin), or 'key links' in Lao statements, i.e. those areas with most potential for accumulation and with most influence over the long-term direction of the economy. State-capitalist enterprises (i.e. mixed private and state capital) occupy the next rung, cooperatives the next, and private 'capitalist' trading the next, along with petty commodity producers. Kaysone formulates the structure in the following way:

> The first and foremost role of the state economic sectors is to engage in internal and foreign trade, banking and finance... Through this network, the role of trade as primary link will be enhanced, thereby transforming the state into a wholesaler, as pointed out by Lenin. After that effective management and control of the whole of society can be exercised by the state. Under state control and supervision through the state economic sectors, other economic sectors will be merged, intermingled and reshuffled in the various forms of transitional economies.[38]

The general preference appears to be that capitalists who wish to engage directly in production should attempt to do this in conjunction with the state. According to a *Sieng Pasason* editorial, the state will 'allow private individuals to rent production means in the form of natural resources such as unexploited land, forest and mineral deposits'.[39] In other words, the state will act as a collective landlord. A similar situation will arise with the entry of foreign capital to develop minerals, for example.

Most of the larger state-owned enterprises (95 per cent) are located within Vientiane prefecture and employ somewhere from 5,000 to 8,000 workers, 2,500 of whom are engaged in electricity generation and tin and gypsum mining. In medium and light industry there are around 173 enterprises nationally. (These include weaving cooperatives, metal handicraft, brick and ceramic products, bamboo rattan handicraft, wood handicraft, salt making, clothes making cooperatives and food and beverages and processing of farm products.) Half of these enterprises are located in Vientiane (93), 13 per cent in Savannakhet (24), and from 4 per cent downward in other centres. Over 50 per cent are under state and provincial control, employ about 4,000 workers and range across the whole spectrum of economic activities; 5 per cent are cooperatives whose activities are concentrated in weaving; and 45 per cent are private enterprises which are almost totally concentrated in processing food and beverages. Beyond this there is simply a diffuse 'informal sector' based on intermittent household activity. Therefore the 'industrial' structure is *very* rudimentary, and is unlikely to attract a great deal of private investment. One of the main areas for private economic opportunity is trade, involving small owner–operators and small capitalist trucking and trading firms. Here, however, the state has continued to put in considerable effort to expand its operations because of the importance placed on trade as a 'key link' by the new policies. There has been a rapid expansion of state and state-orientated trading and marketing networks. From 1981 to 1987 the number of state shops throughout the country more than trebled to 745, and the number of collective and cooperative shops grew five times to 1977. This network is the basis for Kaysone's aim of 'transforming the state into a wholesaler', and therefore vertically integrating cooperative and private commerce.

A similar strategy has evolved in agriculture. Here the state trading networks have been encouraged to negotiate contracts with farmers or cooperatives for the procurement of rice or other output, while supplying commodities farmers want. This is to be done in competition with private traders. Thus through taxation of the peasants and through the hoped-for profitability of trade with the peasants, and subsequent transfers to the government through taxes on state trading enterprises and taxes on trading cooperatives and private traders, the state hopes to mobilise the agricultural surplus for the purposes of accumulation.

Agriculture remains the most widespread private economic activity in the Lao economy, and the Lao communists continue to carry inherited suspicions concerning the long-term tendencies of private production in agriculture, namely that it will inevitably develop into capitalist agriculture if unchecked. As I have argued elsewhere, the sociological foundations for this belief are weak;[40] nevertheless Kaysone thought it important to circumscribe landownership rights in his February 1988 speech: 'Under our new system, the entire land is the common property of the entire society with the state as the representative'.[41] Land is not to be a source for the consolidation of capitalist property rights. This partly explains the state's previous emphasis on forming producers' cooperatives, a policy which has been modified to one where it is considered more appropriate for the peasants to be drawn into marketing cooperatives, and through trade and contractual relationships become part of the 'transitional' economy. Thus a government statement in late August 1988 underlined the regulating role it envisaged for the contract system: 'It should be clearly understoood that this contractual mechanism is not a path which will lead farmers back to the independent production system. ...Due to the implementation of this contractual mechanism and the double service system [supplying commodities and credit], a close relationship between state and farmers will be firmly established.'[42]

A crucial source of LPRP anxiety, however, comes from its recognition that the situation in Laos is truly a transitional one. As Kaysone told his cadres at the 1986 Party Congress: 'It would be incorrect to say that our country is not at all a socialist society, and it would also be wrong to say that our society is a socialist one'.[43] The dilemma for the developmental state is that it is presiding over the formation of a new social structure and in this role it is largely autonomous from specific classes, yet it wishes to establish its legitimacy through claiming to represent the interests of a worker and peasant majority. But the former class, as we have seen, hardly exists, while the latter's long-term spontaneous trajectory is seen to be capitalism. It is in this context that cooperatives become a 'most important strategic task' in the transition period, because 'with the transformation of the relations of production through the process of agricultural cooperativisation there emerges in the rural areas of our country a *new class*, namely the collective peasantry'.[44] With the formation of classes and social groups characteristic of industrial socialism decades into the future in Laos, the 'collective peasantry' is to form the social base of the regime.

Like Lenin in his final NEP reflections, however, the LPRP's expectations for cooperatives have been tempered by experience, and the party is prepared to countenance 'various types of cooperation at different levels [as] transitional forms to socialism'.[45] This is not only a more economically rational approach to cooperative formation, but its flexibility also has the advantage of consecrating all forms of cooperation, including traditional peasant cooperation, as somehow transitional to socialism. The peasantry's normal everyday actions are thereby brought within the orbit of state-sanctioned action rather than peasants feeling that what they are doing is in some way illegitimate in the state's eyes. Undoubtedly this pragmatism also explains why official cooperative numbers have risen steadily since 1983.[46]

As in other communist countries which have attempted radical reforms, one can expect some opposition from within the bureaucracy, not necessarily because of any particular ideological predilection but because the former power and privileges of some members, party cadres in particular, are challenged by the reforms. Many cadres achieved positions of influence within the economic system by virtue of their role in the revolutionary movement, regardless of their expertise.[47] The new decentralised system places much greater emphasis on expertise, and Kaysone has called for the formation of a new contingent of cadres. In choosing them he instructed, 'We must not pay too much attention to their class origin, biography, behaviour or lifestyle',[48] which contrasts with the importance placed on revolutionary credentials and class background in the years immediately after 1975. The shift in emphasis has unquestionably caused considerable friction in the implementation of the new system, as old cadres refuse to cooperate with, or actively hinder, the implementation of the new economic mechanism. The following example was given by Sali Vongkhamsao in a report on the new economic mechanism in early March 1988:

> ...in certain enterprises, mass organisation directors and party secretaries are at odds all the time and the higher echelons of the enterprise can do nothing to settle it. The masses' rights to ownership, the principles of democratic centralisation, and the chief ruling system in many enterprises have been seriously violated, as a result of which mass movements have come to a standstill, internal solidarity has been disrupted, and various negative phenomena have grown widely.[49]

Some ministries – Interior, National Defence, Health were singled out – continue their 'interference' in the 'internal affairs of enterprises', and in some cases refuse to allow enterprises any accounting autonomy.

The reforms have caused a major squeeze on state revenues. Before 1988 a crucial source of state revenue was direct transfers from state enterprises into the budget. Now enterprises are financially autonomous and revenue can only be raised from them through taxation. There is naturally a temptation by the state to maintain its income through higher taxes, but this runs the risk of stifling incentives to increase production and profitability. Thus the state has had to rationalise its own operations, in two forms: the gradual phasing out of subsidies to state employees, and cutting public service employment or pruning 'unproductive labour'.

Before 1988 Lao state employees received approximately 90 per cent of their salaries in kind, a system of payment which functioned as a form of state-controlled consumption. They have been forced to use coupons (what public servants caustically refer to as their 'monthly book money') which can only be redeemed in designated state shops for a limited number of goods (when available) whose low prices were fixed by the government. It has been estimated that implicit consumption subsidies of this kind absorbed 29 per cent of budgetary revenues in 1987.

Following the introduction of the 'one-price' policy in mid-1987, aimed at eliminating most administered prices, consumer prices in state shops also began to rise – accelerating more rapidly in some more financially lucrative ministries and state enterprises than in others, so that prices were no longer uniform in state shops. By the end of 1988 many of the prices in state shops and in the open market had evened out. A spot check in Vientiane in December 1988 revealed that a kilo of rice sold for 105 kip per kilo in a state shop and for 110 kip in the open market; beef was even at 700 kip per kilo; while pork was cheaper in the market at 400 kip per kilo compared with 530 kip in the state shop. But as public servants who were still using coupons sourly remarked, whatever the prices, one could not depend on state shops having supplies.

The government recognised that wages have to rise with prices and has moved to fully monetise wages. However, it has tried to introduce these changes slowly so as to avoid triggering an inflationary spiral. Inflation in fact fell in Laos from 115 per cent in 1985 to 6 per cent in 1987, one of the success stories of the economic reforms. Despite price rises and the growing demand for money in the economy, it remained at manageable levels throughout 1988. Further inflation in the future, however, seems unavoidable, and could cause considerable dissatisfaction among public servants, whose wages will probably be the first to suffer from any price hikes.

One other avenue for limiting the burden of wage rises on the budget has been to cut the number of public servants, and some ministries are said to have shed up to 50 per cent of their staff. But cuts in this direction are necessarily limited unless the state wishes to run down its already depleted health and educational services, which is unlikely. In reality these areas must continue to receive subsidies if the state wants to improve the nation's health or wants children in remote areas to buy school textbooks. Other transfers from the wealthier provinces of Vientiane, Savannakhet, Saravane and Champassak will be necessary to maintain an administrative apparatus in such poorer provinces as Houa Phan or Attopeua.

Other problems have arisen out of the very nature of decentralisation. Certain areas have rushed to cash in on the opportunities
offered by the new policies and attempted to monopolize all local
resources. 'For example, the administrations of many provinces have
not allowed enterprises of other provinces or the centre to carry out
natural resource exploitation activities in their provinces'.[50] This
contradicts government policy on free internal trade and commerce.

A further unintended consequence of devolving financial responsibility to state enterprises, and to provinces and districts, was their
attempts to make quick profits, or compensate for their drop in
budgetary funds, through indiscriminate logging. Thus wood exports
from Laos rose from US$7.2 million in 1986 to US$32.8 million in
1987. The Sixth Resolution passed in June 1988 rails against such
practices, but it is unclear how the central government can stop them.
There was talk of a forestry master plan and a decree banning all log
exports from the beginning of 1989 which would only allow the export
of processed wood. However, this is likely to be thwarted by the
insufficient capacity of local sawmills to process the logs, and by
pressures on Laos to maintain its foreign exchange earnings, which
would inevitably fall if such policy was enforced. Thus the government may have to evolve some enforceable form of tax on log exports
as an alternative. However, the newly autonomous companies have
already shown that they are as wily as managers in the capitalist West
when it comes to tax. According to Dr Inthavong, some companies in
the southern provinces of Saravane and Champassak exported a
greater volume of logs in 1987 than in 1986 and yet they paid less tax
to the government because they made less profits – they had redistri-
buted them through higher salaries![51] To finance itself under the new
economic mechanism therefore, the government will also need to
develop a more sophisticated taxation system and better auditing
skills.

The new commercialisation of relationships between enterprises
has also caused 'credit hoarding' – strangely reminiscent of a peren-
nial distortion in command economies, where insecurity of supply
and the use of physical units for accounting cause the hoarding of
physical inputs. Thus a major debt problem emerged between
enterprises:

An example of this is that in 1987, the Lao electrical company had
a total debt of 1.58bn kips, the water supply company had 174.9m

kips, the material and supply company had 225m kips, the trade company of Champassak province had 1.2bn kips, and the Lao fuel oil company had 718 m kips debt. Many enterprises, not being allowed [not being able?] to withdraw their money, have had to delay the payment of wages to workers...[52]

This appears to reflect the precarious financial state of many enterprises in the new competitive context, and many would seem to be teetering on the brink of bankruptcy. Thus it was reported that twenty-two out of seventy-one enterprises in Vientiane which had switched to the new accounting system experienced significant falls in production and revenue in 1987 compared with 1986. A similar situation was reported from other localities in the country.[53]

No doubt many of these difficulties are teething problems, and it remains to be seen whether the government will really allow state industries to go to the wall. Current policy, as enunciated by Sali Vongkhamsao, for example, suggests that failures should be 'privatised': 'state enterprises must have a high level of efficiency. This means that enterprises which are dramatically inefficient and are not so important must switch to the form of state–private partnership or any other appropriate and more effective form'.[54] This policy can be contrasted favourably with attempts to 'privatise' the public sector in capitalist countries, where only the most profitable state enterprises are able to be sold, leaving the public sector to prop up its least profitable sectors. Another crucial problem is that the new economic mechanism requires a stable, enforceable framework of commercial law. The legal structure in Laos is skeletal, and there have been scattered reports of legal problems arising out of failures to fulfil contracts. According to one report, the gravel grinding factory under the Construction Ministry was being sued by No. 5 construction company.[55] Until such a body of law is developed, use of 'contacts' instead of contracts will prevail, and the Lao economy will continue to be permeated by corruption.[56]

Despite problems in certain areas, the new policies have led to a growth in production, and greater use of the market has led to a more effective use of investment capital. The economy nevertheless remains dominated by a rudimentary agriculture, which is still vulnerable to the vagaries of the weather. Drought over both 1987 and 1988 seriously reduced rice production, cut heavily into agricultural surpluses and raised costs throughout the economy. Although major efforts are being made to improve irrigation facilities, especially on a local scale, agriculture and therefore most of the economy remain at the mercy of the elements.

FOREIGN TRADE AND INVESTMENT

As a 'peripheral socialist' economy Laos has been dependent on foreign trade to provide producers' goods and on foreign finance for investment, because of low domestic savings. It was the country's rapidly growing debt service ratio from 13.5 per cent in 1982 to 22.4 per cent in 1985 which formed the backdrop to the radical reforms of economic management begun in 1985. Although the debt service ratio had returned to its previous level by 1987, conjunctural factors conspired to ensure that the reforms saw no improvement in domestic savings. In fact they fell to −3.9 per cent of GDP in 1987, one of the lowest rates in the world. A key cause of this was a dramatic 54 per cent fall in the dollar value of electricity sales to Thailand, following a renegotiated contract between Vientiane and Bangkok in 1986. The fall in electricity sales to Thailand highlighted the narrowness of Laos' export base and the economy's vulnerability. Only a quadrupling of log exports to the convertible area and a sixfold increase to the non-convertible area averted a balance of trade crisis in 1987, although it led to indiscriminate felling of forests throughout the country.

The narrowness of Laos' export base is typical of peripheral economies, and underlines the importance of economic diversification for the country. A rapid spurt in the export of logs in 1987 and into 1988 was able to avert a foreign exchange crisis, yet unless logging is closely regulated, it may cause serious deforestation and ultimately destroy Laos' forestry potential. As noted earlier, the government is aware of this problem and banned log exports from the beginning of 1989 in favour of processed timber with a high value-added content. However, an incapacity to process the timber, combined with the demand for foreign exchange, is likely to undermine decrees of this nature.

Perhaps a countervailing factor, however, is that rapid forest destruction caused an unexpected drop in electricity production. In the last quarter of 1988 the Nam Ngum hydroelectric station north of Vientiane had to reduce its production of electric power from 716.65 to 566.07 million kW/h because the reservoir had fallen to its lowest level in 16 years. This was a result of heavy tree felling in the area over the previous 2 to 3 years. Thus evolving a system for rationally exploiting Laos' forest resources is a key to future economic growth.

Further export diversification could also be achieved through boosting coffee production. However, its potential as an export earner for Laos is yet to be realised, because of the insulation of coffee prices from international prices, and the payment of low state prices to coffee producers in the Bolovens Plateau in southern Laos. Farmers have lacked incentive to produce more coffee or to grade it carefully for marketing. Yet according to the World Bank, coffee has the potential to double its production over 5 to 7 years, resulting in it becoming the country's main export earner (about US$30 million by 1995 compared with US$9.5 million in 1987).[57] An extension of the 'one-price' policy to this sector is inevitable.

Coffee was one of a package of 'strategic goods' earmarked by the government when it initiated a series of reforms in mid-1987. (Coffee, tobacco, cardamom, benzoin, lac, logs, sawed timber of various types, rattan, cattle, wild animals, minerals and other 'special goods' – 'Decree on Strategic Goods exports', *SWB*, 29 July 1987.) The central Import-Export Company uses the provincial trading companies and other designated companies to collect these 'strategic goods' through contracts. Income from these transactions is then divided according to a stipulated formula. Strategic goods collected over and above the contract signed can be sold directly by the provincial trading companies, or other companies with rights to import and export. The proceeds are divided between the company and the provincial budget according to another fixed formula.[58] The assertion of a state monopoly over strategic goods, along with the granting of rights to deal directly with foreign companies to Laos firms and government agencies, reportedly ended the role of approximately 200 Thai 'middlemen' in Vientiane.[59] This is one way the socialist state hopes to control crucial foreign exchange earnings.

There is little in the composition of Lao trade which suggests that its chronic trade imbalance could be redressed by cutting back on imports. The increased inflow of consumer items, restricted in the past, provides vital economic incentives for ordinary workers and farmers, and there is a large and growing demand for imports of capital equipment in the new economic environment in Laos. Given the high demand for foreign exchange, a major problem for Lao planners in the immediate future will be how to distribute, or rationally allocate, it within the economy, given the state's continued control over foreign exchange earnings by the socialist sector. This central control will no doubt lead to institutional conflicts within Laos, but it is a vital channel through which the state can try to ensure that its planning priorities are followed.

Recognising its inability to mobilise sufficient foreign exchange for investment (leaving aside the issue of expertise) led the LPDR to formulate a foreign investment code in mid-1988. Not surprisingly Thai capital moved swiftly to take up the opportunity, and in September 1988 a Thai company signed the first major contract under the new code for a Lao-Thai joint venture manufacturing garments. Of the US$10 million required for construction of the factory, 85 per cent was Thai, although the Lao partner, Dan Xang Cooperative, retained an option to increase its share to 40 per cent at a later stage. By late 1988 it had become a standard joke in Vientiane that if you were a Thai businessman, then no door in the capital was closed to you. Out of a list of eighteen applications for joint ventures and other investments held by the Ministry of Commerce, Trade and External Relations in late November, nine (or half) were by Thai business-men. They ranged from plans to construct a perfume factory through to furniture construction and mining. One Thai businessman who was setting up an office in Vientiane told me that because of the shortage of foreign exchange, he had a barter arrangement whereby he would provide local authorities with whatever they wanted – goods or roads – in return for wood. This increased business cooperation was also reflected in the trade figures, which showed that in the first half of 1988 the volume of trade between Laos and Thailand was 82 per cent higher than in the first half of 1987. By the year's end Thailand had decided to further reduce its list of items of supposed 'strategic significance' from sixty-one down to twenty-nine. These goods requi-re a special government permit to be exported to Laos, and in 1985 consisted of 273 items.

Other joint ventures between Laos and capitalist and socialist companies were in the pipeline in late 1988: for example, joint production of furniture with an Hungarian company: and Hunt Oil Co., the large US firm, had also applied to establish a business in Vientiane. Various Lao who are now citizens of foreign countries have also enquired about investing, and one from America in particular is investigating investment in tourist development. In late December a small Australian company was still negotiating for mineral rights over an area just north of the capital, in return for a generous profit-sharing arrangement with the Vientiane municipality. Generally profits from foreign ventures will be exempt from tax for a period of 2 to 4 years. Even after that, according to the Vice Minister of Trade, Commerce and External Relations, Sompavanh Inthavong, they may be granted further 'tax privileges' if they are still not turning a profit.[60]

The failure of the previous more autarchic strategy to solve Laos' acute surplus shortage undoubtedly explains the attractions of foreign investment. And as Joan Robinson once remarked, the one thing worse than being exploited is not being exploited at all. The Lao (like their Vietnamese allies) are obviously hoping for investment which will at least provide some income for the state, construct industrial infrastructure, provide industrial training, pay wages, and generally increase economic activity. They would obviously like to garner all the proceeds from any endeavour, say mineral exploitation, but the choice is one of having some or none at all, in the short run at least.[61] Moreover large multinational firms are one of the major institutions within capitalism committed to long-range planning, and therefore, perhaps most compatible with the aims of socialist planning.

As can be seen from Table 4.7, a large percentage of Lao trade is conducted with the 'non-convertible area' – the socialist bloc. This trade runs parallel to the world capitalist market, in that prices for

Table 4.7 Official exports, 1981–7 ($USm)

	1981	*1982*	*1983*	*1984*	*1985*	*1986*	*1987*
Convertible area	16.9	27.8	27.8	30.1	34.8	39.4	35.1
Coffee	—	—	1.6	0.6	0.7	2.1	0.9
Electricity	10.8	23.9	24.0	25.2	27.4	29.8	18.7
Logs, wood prods	5.1	3.5	1.7	3.7	5.6	5.8	19.5
Other	1.0	0.4	0.6	0.5	1.1	2.0	1.0
Non-convertible area	6.2	12.2	13.0	15.0	19.0	15.6	29.2
Coffee	3.1	8.1	6.9	8.1	8.2	7.1	8.5
Logs, wood prods.	—	0.5	1.3	1.3	5.6	2.3	18.3
Tin and gypsum	1.6	2.6	3.7	4.0	2.5	2.2	n.a.
Other	1.5	1.0	1.1	1.6	2.7	1.2	3.1
TOTAL EXPORTS	23.1	40.0	40.8	45.1	53.6	55.0	64.3

Source: LPDR authorities.

Planning Problems in Peripheral Socialism

Table 4.8 Balance of payments, 1981–7 ($USm)

	1981	1982	1983	1984	1985	1986	1987
Exports	23.1	40.0	40.8	43.8	53.6	55.0	64.2
Imports	109.5	132.2	149.4	161.9	193.2	185.7	216.2
Trade balance	−86.4	−92.2	−108.6	−118.1	−139.5	−130.7	−152.0
Services and Transfers	17.2	23.9	12.9	35.1	45.8	40.8	37.7
Current acount	−69.2	−68.3	−95.7	−82.4	−93.7	−89.9	−114.3
Capital account	51.4	60.2	76.5	86.0	101.9	106.7	115.0
					18.7		
Overall Balance	−4.6	−4.3	11.9	−6.0		9.1	11.1

Source: World Bank Report: June 1986; September 1988.

exports and imports are determined by averaging dollar prices on the world market. At the same time, however, they are fixed by long-term agreements,[62] which often resemble barter trade because of their divergence from world market prices over time. The production of Lao tin and gypsum, plus most of the coffee produced, is tied up in such trade arrangements with the countries of the Council for Mutual Economic Aid (CMEA or COMECON), and the USSR in particular. The costs and/or benefits of such a system of trade to the Lao economy remain to be analysed; and it is doubtful that it will proceed much further in its present form in the face of radical economic reforms throughout the CMEA area. The Lao have already felt the winds of *perestroika* in Soviet insistence on stricter Lao accounting of their assistance. Laos apparently had been in default of its commodity payments to the USSR since 1984. This probably explains the steep 25 per cent drop in Soviet imports in Laos in 1986.

Table 4.8 covers the balance of payments, 1981–7, and the value of LPDR – Soviet trade is shown in Table 4.9.

In fact part of the motivation behind the decree on strategic goods in mid-1987 was prompted by a need to direct more exports to the socialist bloc. The preamble to the decree said it was required 'so that an adequate supply of strategic goods can be maintained and delivered to meet orders from foreign countries in accordance with prior agreements signed with them, such as with socialist countries...'[63] Subsequently exports to socialist countries in 1987 were

Table 4.9 Value of LPDR–Soviet trade, 1980–7 (Rb m)

	1980	1981	1982	1983	1984	1985	1986	1987
Turnover of which:	37.3	37.1	66.2	77.8	67.1	87.9	67.3	71.0
Imports	37.0	36.2	64.2	75.5	65.0	85.6	62.2	62.0
Exports	0.3	0.9	2.0	2.3	2.1	2.3	5.1	9.0

Source: LPDR Ministry of Trade, Commerce and External Relations.

reported to have increased 10 per cent compared with 1986,[64] and exports to the USSR almost doubled. Laos' large external debt is mostly owed to the socialist bloc (70 per cent in 1985) and in 1988 it owed the USSR 500 million roubles, which is expected to grow to 700 million by 1990. But most of this, fortunately for Vientiane, has been obtained on extremely favourable terms.[65]

Plans for future relations between Laos and the USSR are more in line with the new economic policies in both countries. Thus instead of the USSR providing direct government to government aid in the future, direct contacts between enterprises are to be encouraged, along with mutual enterprises in which each country will hold a 50 per cent share. If the Lao are unable to raise their share of the capital, then the USSR will provide commercial credit on a basis slightly more favourable than the prevailing world credit market. A joint Lao–USSR enterprise has been established to supply spare parts for the thousands of Soviet vehicles in the country; and a Soviet–Thai joint trading venture (ASPAC), which has been operating in Bangkok since 1986, plans to engage in processing Lao wood. Thus while the Soviets will remain a major aid donor to Laos for the foreseeable future, they hope that the proportion of direct government assistance will progressively decline.[66]

Managing external relations in a small weak economy presents formidable problems, and Laos' recent plunge into the market will bring with it a whole range of unanticipated ones, as Yugoslavia's decentralised socialism discovered to its cost. Concluding her detailed study of Yugoslavian trade experience, Diane Flaherty cautioned that small developing countries must use careful and systematic macroeconomic planning to evolve 'a trade policy that protects the domestic economy from the most extreme vagaries of the world market. The market, domestic or international, cannot provide the primary institutional framework within which such a country can at the same time ensure domestic stability and growth and keep a payments deficit within manageable limits'.[67]

INTERNATIONAL PLANNING?

Kaysone, not surprisingly, has turned his thoughts to the complexities of the contemporary international division of labour. The world economy, he observed in early 1988, 'has become a single universal entity. That is, each individual country cannot be separate and cannot develop alone in a self-sufficient manner'.[68] This may have been possible for a while in larger socialist economies with wider resource bases, but is impossible for smaller ones. Vertical integration on a global level is, he suggests, to some degree inescapable, and includes cooperation not only with capitalist multinationals but also joint ventures between, for example, Soviet and Lao firms.[69] In recognising the need for some international specialisation, however, the LPRP is obviously also trying to work out a basis on which this could take place without freezing Laos into its existing pattern of development – which is a criticism levelled at orthodox theories of free trade and comparative advantage.[70]

The main attempt at planning international socialist trade and specialisation has been among the states belonging to the CMEA, of which Laos is not a member. Since the mid-1950s members have attempted to avoid needless duplication of industries and products. However, many obstacles have been encountered because of command style planning, currency non-convertibility, and a predominance of bilateral trading arrangements. The fundamentally national basis of command planning militated against the extension of integration within COMECON, contrary to theories of planned socialist cooperation. A Hungarian economist wrote in the early 1970s: 'commodity trade between the CMEA countries is organised on a bilateral basis... The advantages of a united socialist world market cannot assert themselves. The system of bilateral relations puts a brake on the efficiency of foreign trade. And the principle of identical commodity patterns simply contradicts the requirements of efficiency'.[71] Some socialist multinationals have been formed but they too tend to only have bilateral relations.[72] In other words, in a world of independent nation states, a break from command planning is a prerequisite for international specialisation and cooperation, among socialist economies, and full currency convertibility, as adopted in Laos, is fundamental to its success.[73]

Baran and some other socialist economists have written optimistically about cooperation among socialist countries,[74] but they seriously underestimate the strength of national interests in relations between socialist states. For example, in the admittedly hypernationalist context of the command system prevalent in COMECON both Rumania and Bulgaria once argued that because they are developing societies, new industrial activities in the organization should be located in their countries,[75] and CMEA literature does boast that its 'specialisation and trade [is] not "vertical", between producers of raw materials and manufactures, typical of capitalist trade, but "horizontal", i.e. involving all stages of production without the division of the countries into "developed" and "underdeveloped"'.[76] But there has been at times considerable suspicion of exploitation between COMECON members, firstly because of the practice of socialist imperialism by Stalinist Russia in Eastern and Central Europe and in China after 1945. The Soviet Union used its dominant political position to orient trade to its benefit and to establish pseudo-joint enterprises. These companies were dissolved after the death of Stalin in 1953, and since then evidence suggests that the terms of trade have favoured the USSR's partners in COMECON.[77] Suspicion of double dealing is also found in the pricing system, which, as we remarked above, makes it very hard to establish realistic comparisons between domestic and foreign prices. Thus in the serial bilateral trading arrangement between COMECON countries the price of the same commodity can vary up to 100 per cent. Once again this underlines the importance of a rational pricing system. Eastern Europe is only now moving toward full currency convertibility.

There are attractions and problems entailed in any regional system of cooperation for Laos, such as an 'Association of Indochinese Nations'. The Lao market is too small to support any range of modern industries, and the formation of a regional economic grouping is sensible if economies of scale are to be achieved. Such a grouping could, for example, cooperate in locating a particular factory or industrial process in one country, but selling in all three. One major problem would be establishing an institutional form for such supra-national planning.

But the mere suggestion of such a grouping is anathema to leftist writers on Laos, who are influenced by dependency theory, which sets a premium on economic 'self-reliance'. Hans Luther, for example, claims that there is a Vietnamese 'masterplan' for Indochina in which Vietnam would be the industrial centre, Heng

Samrin's Kampuchea the rice bowl, and Laos the supplier of raw materials and hydro-electric power:

> Most probably the 'terms of trade' between the three unequal partners will be determined, as in the Soviet dominated COME-CON organisation, according to political seniority and military power and not by the urgent needs of the peasants... Hence [Laos] will lose out the most in long terms through this kind of coopera-tion. Thus, the political liberation from American and French influences has so far not resulted in national self-determination, but has rather been reproduced in a new more *structural* form of economic dependency.[78]

Leaving aside the fact that Luther produces no evidence for such a 'masterplan', we can agree that problems of national self-interest and regional disparities are important considerations and can present serious problems.

It should be recognised that regional disparities can occur in the context of free trade, and are most evident within national borders. But free trade does not operate at the global level, because nation states are able to pursue national interests, through protectionism, for example. The ability of nation states to bargain with one another or with multinational corporations in an attempt to maximise national interests and therefore direct resources toward themselves is wilfully either underestimated or denied by dependency theorists.[79] Consis-tent with these latter assumptions, Luther denies that the Lao state has control over its economic destiny and assumes it has no bargain-ing power, but he provides no evidence for this. In fact state policies in the Third World would seem to suffer from the opposite problem, that is overcompensating for the dangers of regional disparities in their attempts to create identical structures in each national eco-nomy. This tendency, i.e. the assertion of national sovereignty, has been the main factor obstructing attempts at coordinating industrial planning in either capitalist or socialist regional groupings.[80]

Disparities of power obviously exist between states, and for this reason it is generally considered preferable that regional groupings be made up of states of relatively equal size and at equal stages of development. Vietnam would unquestionably be the dominant member in any formalised Indochinese regional grouping, and this would contain dangers for Laos and Cambodia of Vietnam pursuing its national interests at their expense. No doubt this would be a potential source of tension between Laos and Vietnam, and Cambodia and Vietnam, should any such grouping come into existence. (We should note that Vietnam, as a member of COMECON, is likely to have similar problems with its more powerful partners.)

While there have been attempts to coordinate economic relations between the three Indochinese nations, there are recent signs that this is being downplayed. The director of the Institute of International Relations in Hanoi is reported to have said in August 1988 that such coordination will be restricted to trade in the immediate future, and will eventually be superseded when the three states are permitted to join ASEAN.[81] A similar perspective was offered by Sompavanh Inthavong, who saw a need for Laos to benefit from the 'spill over' of prosperity from its ASEAN neighbours.[82] When I asked Kaysone if the Indochinese states had any plans to build an economic organization like ASEAN, he responded:

Up to now we have not built one and no one has proposed such an organisation. Each country remains independent and in control of itself and cooperation will continue as always.

During the period when the French Administration was here we joined forces to protect our countries. During the past ten years we have helped each other and engaged in economic exchanges between the three countries. We cooperate with each other in order to become richer than before. That is how it is with the 'new way of thinking', and that also goes for the world at large. No one can stand alone. You rely on me and I rely on you. We cooperate in order to improve the economy and to keep peace in the region. And from the three countries we will expand our contacts. For example, Laos has become involved with Thailand. And in the future if Indonesia or Malaysia want to get involved then that's fine. According to the 'new way of thinking' that is how things are going in the world and in the region.[83]

The options available to a small state like Laos are few. The futility of 'self-reliant' autarchic development (the dependency theorists' option) has been tried already, leaving the alternative of participation in a world economy in which Laos is a bit player. A regional grouping could at least offer Vientiane some collective bargaining power in the broader world economy and allow it to achieve some rational economies of scale. But it remains to be seen whether this will be done through a Third World socialist regional grouping or through ASEAN.

The latter has so far had much greater success as a political grouping than as an economic grouping, which was ASEAN's original purpose. After 20 years it has made little progress in forming a common market or in planning the channelling of aid and techno- logy.[84] Yet although its members compete against one another more often than they coordinate, ASEAN has had some success in lobbying on behalf of its members against, for example, Japanese rubber restrictions, changes in New Zealand's generalised system of preferences, and European Community edible oils policies. This is, perhaps, all ASEAN could do for Vientiane if it was a member, but going on ASEAN's record the organisation would appear to offer few possibilities for regional planning which would allow Laos' fledgling industries to achieve economies of scale and modernise. Whether a socialist regional organisation could offer more remains an open question.

CONCLUSION

The Lao communist government learned in a relatively short space of time that its capacity to plan national economic activity was limited both by its inability completely to control production and consump- tion internally, and by its dependence on a sphere totally beyond its control, the world market. It has therefore adopted a system of planning which relies less on direct state intervention and more on state control of macroeconomic levers in order to achieve its priori- ties. That is, state regulation of foreign exchange, credit, taxation, and a commitment to developing a body of commercial law, as well as laws on conservation. The new system also demands the exercise of much greater economic skill and initiative on the part of state financial institutions and enterprises than before. It is uncertain whether the state apparatus or state enterprises are up to the task.

This chapter has emphasised that the Lao economy is heavily reliant on outside sources to finance its development, and on foreign trade. The government's plans are therefore vulnerable to shifts in the world economy and the vagaries of world politics, which must seem as unpredictable as the weather that dogs Lao agriculture. Perhaps the preceding chapter has underplayed the degree to which Lao perceptions of external political hostility, from Thailand in particular and from the United States, reinforced preferences for an autarchic model of development. In the late 1980s this political conjuncture has passed, as barriers to political dialogue and trade are crashing in Southeast Asia, creating an environment which is favourable to an outward looking socialism.

The Lao government has been moving to limit the impact of external fluctuations by diversifying its exports and its sources of aid and investment.[85] But how income derived from external sources is distributed and invested within the new structure will be one of the major planning problems faced by the Lao state in the future. These problems will occasionally become acute as export income fluctuates – as it must inevitably, given Laos' export structure – and conflicts will arise over national investment priorities.

How these conflicts are resolved will partly depend on the evolution of the social structure, in particular the evolution of what Kaysone and the LPDR refer to as 'State Capitalism'. That is, the role of state–private ventures in the Lao economy. Sali Vongkhamsao has made it clear that 'enterprises which are regarded as the main arteries of the economy and are of significance in various aspects to the foundation of the national economy must be directly controlled by the state.'[86] Nevertheless that leaves a large swathe of the economy in the hands of state-capitalist ventures and capitalist companies. The significance of this is twofold: the Lao elite is very small and there is increasing evidence of a growing overlap between a re-emergent old business elite and the new party elite,[87] therefore family-based alliances could become decisive in conflicts which will arise over the distribution of foreign exchange, for example, and the setting of national investment priorities. Such conflict in itself is not necessarily a problem, but the way it may come to be resolved is. There is a real danger of the Lao social and political structure developing into a one-party oligarchy typical of Third World state-capitalism, whose elites are more concerned with lining their own pockets than with economic development, let alone socialist development.[88] Kaysone and his comrades obviously hope to avert such a possibility through maintaining a high-minded vanguard party capable of leading Laos through the 'necessary' state-capitalist stage. However, they appear to seriously underestimate the importance of simple sociological processes such as marriage and family alliances in the Lao social structure.

An obvious solution to nepotism is greater political pluralism and the encouragement of a critical press able to pursue corruption and question national policies. Unfortunately little consideration has been given to this in Laos, although it is undoubtedly vital to the new model of socialism the LPRP is pursuing. Furthermore it remains unclear to what degree the LPRP realises that planning of any sort demands a free flow of information and maximum feedback if the most rational decisions are to be made. This is one of the fundamental issues of *glasnost* in the communist world. Yet states presiding over social transitions in both the capitalist and socialist Third World are all cursed with an authoritarian reflex which will probably hamper the efforts of rational planners for the foreseeable future.

As we have seen, Laos is a poor country with as yet little surplus to allocate for accumulation, and with few of the skills required by a modern economy. Whichever route it took into the modern world, capitalist or socialist, neither would have offered easy options or simple solutions. Market socialism is not a utopia, and it will bring with it its own unique and perplexing problems, but it offers Laos a greater chance for success than the now discredited Stalinist model of planning.

Notes

1. The main features of this system have been summarised by W. Brus as:' (1) one-level decision-making. All other elements of the centralized model follow therefrom, namely (2) strictly hierarchical structure of the plans, plans of lower levels formally subordinated sectors of the corresponding plans on the higher level, and predominance of the vertical links between central level and enterprises; horizontal links between enterprises themselves are of a purely technical, implementary character; (3) communications from the top to the bottom are transmitted in the form of direct *orders* which determine what has to be done and how (obligatory target planning); communications from the bottom to the top can be called "reports"; they supply material for the central decisions; (4) necessarily connected with this system of organization is the predominance of economic calculation and allocation of resources in physical terms; monetary forms do appear but their role is passive.' Wlodzimierz Brus (1973) *The Economics and Politics of Socialism* (London: Routledge and Kegan Paul), p.8.
2. See Alec Nove (1976) *An Economic History of the USSR* (London: Pelican Books), Chapters 4 and 5. Also Moshe Lewin (1975) *Political Undercurrents in Soviet Economic Debates* (London: Pluto Press), Chapter 4.
3 Cited in Alec Nove (1986) *Socialism, Economics and Development* (London: George Allen and Unwin), p.89.
4. I queried Kaysone Phomvihane, the Lao Prime Minister, on this matter during an interview in December 1988. He said he knew very little of Bukharin and others because these matters were simply not discussed in the world communist movement for a very long time.

5. Cited in Stephen F. Cohen (1979) *Bukharin and the Bolshevik Revolution* (London: Oxford University Press), p.195.
6. *Ibid.*, p.196.
7. *Ibid.*, p.197.
8. See Michael Ellman (1979) *Socialist Planning* (London: Cambridge University Press), p.124.
9. MacAlister Brown and Joseph J. Zasloff, *Apprentice Revolutionaries: The Communist Movement in Laos, 1930–1985* (Stanford: Hoover Institution Press), 1985.
10. Grant Evans (1988) *Agrarian Change in Communist Laos* (Singapore: ISEAS).
11. Nigel Harris (1987) *The End of the Third World: Newly Industrializing Countries and the Decline of an Ideology* (London: Pelican), p.163.
12. Mieczyslaw Szostak, 'Le Secteur Public dans les Pays du Tiers Monde: Sa Formation, son Expansion', *Revue Tiers Monde*, t.XXIV, No.93, 1983.
13. Yacob Haile-Mariam and Berhanu Mengistu, 'Public enterprises and the privatization thesis in the Third World'. *Third World Quarterly*, October 1988,p.1569.
14. Nigel Harris, 'New Bourgeoisies?', *Journal of Development Studies*, Vol. 24, No.2, 1988.
15. Edwin S. Mills (1986) *The Burden of Government* (Stanford: Hoover Institution Press), p.122.
16. Robert B. Reich, 'Of Markets and Myths', *Commentary*, February 1987.
17. Paul A. Baran (1969) *The Longer View* (New York: Monthly Review Press). 'Economic Progress and Economic Surplus', p.273.
18. For previous discussions of the Lao economy see: Nayan Chanda, 'Economic Changes in Laos, 1975–1980', in Martin Stuart-Fox (ed. 1982) *Contemporary Laos* (St Lucia, Queensland: University of Queensland Press); MacAlister Brown and Joseph J. Zasloff (1986) *Apprentice Revolutionaries* (Stanford: Hoover Institution Press), Chapter 12; and Martin Stuart-Fox (1986) *Laos: Politics, Economics and Society* (London: Frances Pinter) Chapter 4.
19. World Bank (1979) *Socialist Transformation in the Lao People's Democratic Republic: An Economic Report*, Vol 1, Main Report, p.8.
20. W. Worner, 'Money, Prices and Policies in Laos: 1969–1980', *Proceedings of the International Conference on Thai Studies*, The Australian National University, Canberra 3–6 July, 1987. Vol. 3, Part Two, compiled by Ann Buller, p.489.
21. World Bank, *Socialist Transformation*, *op.cit.*, p.9.
22. *Ibid.*, p.6.
23. *BBC Summary of World Broadcasts: Far East*, 8 January 1977. Hereafter *SWB*.
24. Paul A. Baran (1962) *The Political Economy of Growth* (New York: Monthly Review Press) 2nd ed., p.266.
25. *Ibid.*, p.268.
26. *Ibid.*, p.290.
27. World Bank, *Socialist Transformation*, *op.cit.*, p.36.
28. Myrdal observed that in the Indian context state-sponsored cooperatives increased the burden of administration and made it more complex for no apparent gain. Gunnar Myrdal (1968) *Asian Drama: An Inquiry into the Poverty of Nations* (New York: Pantheon), Vol. II, p.915.
29. V.I. Lenin (1967) 'The Tax in Kind', *Selected Works* (Moscow: Progress Publishers) Vol.3, p.596.
30. E.V.K. Fitzgerald, 'The Problem of Balance in the Peripheral Socialist Economy: A Conceptual Note', *World Development*, Vol. 13, No.1, 1985. Baran *The Larger View*, pp.284–5, makes a similar point about the role of the export sector, though he clearly sees it playing this role for a short period.
31. *Ibid.*, p.7.

32. *Ibid.*, p.11.
33. See E.V.K. Fitzgerald, 'State Accumulation and Market Equilibria: An Application of Kalecki-Kornai Analysis to Planned Economies in the Third World', *Journal of Development Studies*, Vol. 24, No. 4, 1988.
34. World Bank, *LPDR Country Economic Memorandum*, June 1986. pp. 12–14.
35. On prices as information and the complexities of price information see Janos Kornai (1971) *Anti-equilibrium* (Amsterdam: North-Holland Publishing Company), pp. 67–9.
36. Interview with the author, 15 December 1988.
37. *SWB*, 25 February 1988.
38. *Ibid.*
39. *SWB*, 12 March 1988.
40. Grant Evans, 'The Accursed Problem: Communists and Peasants', *Peasant Studies*, Vol. 15, No.2, Winter 1988.
41. *SWB*, 25 February 1988.
42. *SWB*, 3 September 1988.
43. Kaysone Phomvihan, *Political Report* to the Fourth Party Congress of the LPRP, Vientiane 1986. Mimeograph.
44. *Ibid.*
45. *Ibid.*
46. For details see Grant Evans, *Agrarian Change in Communist Laos, op. cit.*
47. Such problems are not exclusive to communist systems in the Third World, as Myrdal writes: 'political difficulties have been much increased by the dearth of highly educated, rationalist individuals with long experience of participation in colonial government and administration or with professional competence, and by the excessive numbers of leaders with training chiefly as plotters, schemers, agitators, and fighters'. Myrdal, *op. cit.*, p.731.
48. *SWB*, 25 February 1988.
49. *SWB*, 13 April 1988.
50. *Ibid.*
51. Interview with the author, 15 December 1988.
52. *SWB*, 12 March 1988.
53. *SWB*, 13 April 1988.
54. *Ibid.*
55. *Ibid.*
56. For a discussion of some of these problems, see Martin Stuart-Fox, 'Politics and Patronage in Laos', *Indochina Issues*, 70, October 1986. By underlining the importance of commercial law for market socialism I do not, at the same time, wish to subscribe to the complacency of liberal modernisation theory, which envisages a decline in corruption with development. Corruption scandals surrounding the Pentagon (June/July 1988), or widespread corruption in the Australian police, should soon dispel such naive beliefs. For a discussion of the degree to which 'corruption' is endemic in certain social systems, see Larissa Adler Lomnitz, 'Informal Exchange Networks in Formal Systems: A Theoretical Model', *American Anthropologist*, 90, 1988.
57. World Bank, 'Lao People's Democratic Republic Country Economic Memorandum', 21 September 1988.
58. For details, *SWB*, 29 July 1987.
59. Economist Intelligence Unit, *Indochina: Vietnam, Laos, Cambodia, Country Report*, No. 4, 11 December 1987, p.18.
60. Interview with the author, 15 December 1988.
61. Criticising leftist dependency arguments against foreign investment, Bill Warren writes: '...private foreign investment in the LDCs is economically beneficial irrespective of government control. This should come as no surprise to Marx-

ists – Lenin attempted to attract foreign investment in the early years of the Soviet republic,.. and it is an elementary principle of Marxism that under capitalism exploitation presupposes the advance of the productive forces. To the extent that political independence is real, private foreign investment must normally be regarded not as a cause of dependence but rather as a means of fortification and diversification of the economies of the host countries. It thereby reduces "dependence", in the long run', Bill Warren (1980) *Imperialism: Pioneer of Capitalism* (London: Verso), p.176.

62. See Jozef M. van Brabant, 'The Relationship Between World and Socialist Trade Prices – Some Empirical Evidence', *Journal of Comparative Economics*, Vol.9, 1985.
63. *SWB*, 29 July 1987.
64. EIU, *Indochina: Country Report*, No.1, 1988. p.20.
65. A US Department of Commerce estimate, however, claims that repayments of these loans to the USSR could consume over half of Laos' export earnings beyond 1990. *Bangkok Post*, 22 June 1988.
66. These comments are based on discussions with Soviet officials in Vientiane over November and December 1988.
67. Diane Flaherty, 'Economic Reform and Foreign Trade in Yugoslavia', *Cambridge Journal of Economics*, Vol.6, 1986. p.142.
68. *SWB*, 25 February 1988.
69. See also *SWB*, 18 November 1987.
70. See Michael P. Todaro, *Economics for a Developing World* (London: Longman) 2nd ed., Chapters 19 and 20.
71. Csikos-Nagy, cited in Alec Nove (1977) *The Soviet Economic System* (London: George Allen and Unwin), p.280.
72. Ellman, *op.cit.*, p.242.
73. Predictably Rumania, once the country in Eastern Europe most committed to Stalinist command style planning, refused to join its CMEA neighbours in a plan to create an integrated market. *Age* (Melbourne), 8 July 1988.
74. Baran (1968), *op.cit.*, pp.291–5.
75. Nove (1977), *op.cit.*, p.281.
76. J. Wilczynski, *The Economics of Socialism* (London: George Allen and Unwin), p.198.
77. Ellman, *op.cit.*, p.230.
78. Hans U. Luther (Jan. 1983) *Socialism in a Subsistence Economy: The Laotian Way* (Bangkok: Chulalongkorn University Social Science Research Institute), p.29.
79. See Warren, *op.cit.*, Chapter 7.
80. Todaro, *op.cit.*, pp.332–6.
81. Michael Haas, in the Letters columns of the *Far Eastern Economic Review*, 5 January 1989. Also the 'Intelligence' column, *FEER*, 29 September 1988.
82. Interview with the author, 15 December 1988.
83. Interview with the author, 16 December 1988.
84. 'ASEAN', *Asia 1988 Yearbook*, December 1987, Hong Kong. Also Amado Castro, 'ASEAN Economic Cooperation', in Alison Broinowski (ed. 1982) *Understanding ASEAN* (London: Macmillan Press). For problems elsewhere in the capitalist third world see the special report 'Latin American Integration', *South*, March 1988.
85. For a discussion of the importance of diversification, see Barbara Stallings, 'External Finance and the Transition to Socialism in Small Peripheral Societies', in Richard R. Fagen et al. (eds)(1986) *Transition and Development* (New York: Monthly Review Press).
86. *SWB*, 13 April 1988.

87. Maritn Stuart-Fox (1986) *op.cit.* was the first person to draw attention to the significance of this.
88. See Myrdal, *op.cit.,* Part Four, "A Third World of Planning"; Alec Nove, 'State Capitalism and the Third World', *Development and Change,* Vol.8, 1977.

Part III
Society

Map 2 Laos and its neighbours

5 After the Revolution: Ethnic Minorities and the New Lao State

Wendy Batson

In April 1901 French Commissioner Remy wired from remote Saravan Province in southern Laos for assistance, saying 'It is a general uprising, all the villages on the Plateau are deserted, the rebels have formed seven groups, stronger than 1,000 men each'.[1] Thus began a rebellion of the southern hill tribes which lasted for 35 years and cost the French considerably in terms of money and men.

Nor was the south the only segment of Laos which suffered such uprisings. In 1919 the Hmong of northern Xieng Khouang responded to a call to revolt from one Batchay, a rebel from Vietnam who had fled to Laos, in hopes of establishing an independent Hmong kingdom with its capital at Dien Bien Phu. Local Hmong supported him by attacking all the Lao, Tai and French installations in the province. When local garrisons failed to quell the uprising, regular troops from Saigon and Hanoi were sent in. These troops 'launched a systematic pacification program – moving villages, burning crops, and incarcerating the Meo population – with such success that by March of 1921 Batchay had lost most of his support'.[2]

Such hill tribe uprisings were not solely the consequences of a sometimes harsh French colonial administration during the nineteenth and early twentieth century. Various accounts from the Lao Royal Court going back many hundreds of years attest to the king's own problems with the minorities in his realm.

Often as not, the revolts which occurred with considerable regularity throughout the early decades of the twentieth century pitted highlanders not just against the French but against their Vietnamese and Lao administrative agents as well.[3] Many of the tribes of Laos clearly felt no more loyalty towards the lowland Lao population than they did to the recently arrived Europeans. Who then were these fiercely independent peoples who populate much of the mountainous regions of Laos?

THE MAIN GROUPS[4]

The single largest ethnic group in Laos is composed of the Lao of the Tai linguistic family, who make up about half the country's population. These are the people who gave Laos its name. Migrating from southern China, the Lao-Tai settled along the lowlands of the Mekong Valley before the thirteenth century. Swept up in the great cultural migration of ideas from India, the Lao became Theravada Buddhists, and village life today still centres around the Buddhist temples. Ethnic Lao peasants prefer to grow wet rice in the valleys of the Mekong and its major tributaries. They dominate the provinces of Vientiane, Luang Prabang, Khammuane, Savannakhet and Champassak.

Other Tai groups live in Laos as well, notably the Lu of Luang Prabang and areas north, the Tai Neua of Houa Phan, and the Tai Dam and Tai Deng of Phong Saly and Houa Phan. These Tai peoples, who settled in an arc reaching down from southern Yunnan through Laos and Vietnam, and who present a minority in all those areas, represent the largest ethnic group without a nation state in Southeast Asia, a fact not lost on either the current Vietnamese or Lao leaders.

These thirteenth-century Tai arrivals displaced the original inhabitants – Mon-Khmer peoples most often referred to as Kha, or slave, by the lowland Lao until recently. This group includes the Kasseng, Loven, So and Bru, all inhabitants of southern Laos, and the Lamet and Khmu from the north. The largest single grouping of Mon-Khmer comprises the Khmu, now concentrated in parts of Luang Prabang, Houa Phan, and Oudomsy provinces.

Much of upland southern Laos, particularly the Bolovens Plateau in Champassak and the seldom visited mountains running between Laos and Vietnam, are also heavily populated by Mon-Khmer peoples from a wide variety of ethnic backgrounds. An 8 April 1981 article in *Vientiane Mai* listed thirty-three Mon-Khmer tribes, 'among others'.

Finally there are the Meo, or Hmong, as they prefer to be called, and the Yao. Originating from somewhere near Kweichow, China, these latter two groups came to Laos only a century and a half ago and settled on lands above 3,000 feet. They, like the Mon-Khmer tribes, practice swidden agriculture, growing upland rice and maize as well as opium as a cash crop. Family and clan have traditionally been the only important groupings among the Yao and Hmong. Like the

Mon-Khmer, they are animists and their shamans play important roles in village life and in clan decision-making.

Other smaller Tibeto-Burman-speaking groups from Yunnan, like the Yi, Akha and Lahu, now live in Laos near the Burmese and Chinese borders.

THE POLITICS OF TERMINOLOGY

I have lost count of the number of times I have blithely stated that the Lao People's Democratic Republic is made up of sixty-eight different ethnic groups speaking mutually unintelligible languages. Somewhere along the way it occurred to me to wonder where I got that figure. The central government authorities of the Lao PDR have yet to publish an official list, but provincial officials are more willing to take the plunge – the governor of Phong Saly, while briefing my husband in 1984, included a list of all sixteen nationalities inhabiting the area in order of numerical superiority. Lowland Lao were at the bottom of the list.

Martin Stuart-Fox, while researching his most recently published book, was told by researchers in the ethnographic section of the Ministry of Culture that the list did not include urban-dwelling ethnic Chinese, Vietnamese, Thai or Indians resident in Laos, even if they possessed Lao citizenship. Such a conversation does assume that a list exists but has not been made public. Numerous reasons for such reluctance can easily be guessed at. Stuart-Fox says that agreement has evidently not been reached on a definitive basis of classification: whether the primary criterion should be cultural or linguistic.[5]

The count may simply be wrong. Census-taking has not been a regular feature of Lao life. Ethnographic work done before 1975 was certainly not complete and it is not likely that the financially constrained Lao authorities are going to commit limited resources to achieving ethnographic precision any time soon.

The war too may well have made some of what was known about tribal settlement patterns no longer accurate. The heaviest bombing – according to public records the Lao hold the dubious distinction of being the most heavily bombed people in the world's history on a per capita basis – occurred in the tribal areas.[6] Large-scale migrations resulted, and the exodus continued for other reasons through much of the late 1970s.

The desire to play down ethnic differences and create a Lao state less dominated by its very variety gave rise to the practice of classifying all Lao under one of three groupings: Lao Loum, or lowland Lao; Lao Theung, or mid-level Lao; and Lao Soung, high mountain Lao. Lao Loum refers to the Tai-speaking peoples who dominate the plains, Lao Theung covers the Mon-Khmer groups living on the mountain slopes, and Lao Soung the mountain-top dwellers such as the Yao and the Hmong.

This terminology was first introduced into Laos by Toulia Lyfoung, one of the Hmong chieftains allied with the Royal Lao Government. It proved far more popular with the Pathet Lao, however, and its usage continues in Laos today. Often when travelling with various government representatives to outlying areas, our inevitable questions as to what these people were called were almost always answered by Lao Loum, Theung or Soung. Our occasional insistence on further clarification was met with a baffled shrug of the shoulders.

A final interesting note: the Lao PDR government decided not to include questions about ethnicity on the country's first official census form. The original drafts did ask, but latter versions omitted the question. I was in Attopeu Province in the remote, difficult to reach southeastern corner of the country during the time when the census information collected there was being tabulated. I asked provincial representatives for an ethnic breakdown of Attopeu, and received the most overtly political answer I'd yet got in the Lao PDR: 'We are all Lao here'. When I asked if the census had provided new information on this question, I was told Vientiane did not want ethnic questions asked.

BEFORE 1975

A journalist writing in 1964 described Laos as 'less a nation state than a conglomeration of tribes and languages... less a unified society than a multiplicity of feudal societies. The family clan is all important'.[7] The politically and economically dominant lowland Lao were never particularly interested in the tribal minorities (unless they were in revolt) and thus tended to ignore their presence. The only known census taken in Laos before the recent 1985 effort was done in the fifteenth century by the monarch in Luang Prabang whose records noted that all Lao were counted except the kha. (Kha, which translates as slave, is also used primarily by lowland Lao in a derogatory manner to refer to a number of the more primitive ethnic tribes.)

Geography and climate have contributed to a pervasive sense of isolation among and between the various occupants of Laos. It is a land of limited plains, and over half the country is covered with razor-edged, steep and heavily forested mountains. Such terrain has made it possible for the numerous ethnic minorities to maintain their strong cultural and linguistic identities intact. Living in narrow valleys which are often cut off from the remainder of the country during the long wet season discouraged the development among the mountain tribes of any sense of national identity.

If any of Laos's many and varied hill tribes did aspire to nation-building, it was not a Lao nation of which they dreamed. At a minimum, hopes of freeing themselves from the nominal rule of Luang Prabang or Vientiane motivated them; at times more ambitious dreams of creating a Tai Dam or a Hmong nation drove them. In the main, however, the ethnic minorities kept to themselves, ignored by lowland Lao and Westerners alike.

The Lao Theung groups resented the lowland Lao as the people who had forced them into the mountain slopes in the first place. The Hmong, late arrivals, immediately challenged the Lao Theung for both territory and economic control of certain northern areas such as Xieng Khouang. The lowland Lao looked down on both groups as savages, barbarians, people who were to be distrusted.

The Tai Dam related to their principalities or muong, each ruled over by a prince. The mountain Tai principalities were originally organised into a loose federation called the Sip Song Chau Tai (the Twelve Tai Principalities) – territory which is now mostly within the northwestern region of Vietnam. In 1984 when I visited Muong Et, an area of Houa Phan province lying along the Vietnamese border, many of the Tai Dam villagers spoke Vietnamese as their second language, not Lao; and the Lao spoken was heavily influenced by Vietnamese pronunciation and vocabulary.

Although the French abolished slavery, their presence did little else to benefit minorities. French taxes were levied individually and were often higher than the traditional tribute of gold dust paid communally by the villages to their Lao overlords.[8] The Lao Theung particularly resented demands for corvée labour, as they did not have the means to redeem their share through payments.

Apart from constructing 5,000 kilometres of road with corvée labour, France did little to stimulate the economic development or improve social welfare.[9] What was done primarily benefited the lowland Lao and the Vietnamese settlers, not the ethnic minorities in the hinterlands. Thus the Lao Theung in particular correctly perceived themselves to be paying more and still getting nothing in return.

BIRTH OF THE PATHET LAO

As the French colonial period drew to a close following World War II, several events which have had critical implications for the role of minorities in the new Lao state took place. The small independence movement led by members of the Lao elite was defeated in battle at Thakhek by French colonial troops in 1946. The remnants of this army split into two groups. The larger, led by Prince Phetsareth, fled to Bangkok, where it withered away when no outside support was forthcoming. French amnesty and the grant of partial self-rule to the Lao Kingdom in 1949 completed the disintegration.[10]

A smaller group, however, led by Prince Souphanouvong, would not concede defeat and searched for alternatives. Unwilling to flee Laos and unable, owing to French control, to remain in the Mekong valley areas, this group retreated to where the French were both unable and uninterested in going, the territory on either side of the Annamite Mountains which form the Lao–Vietnamese border. Sam Neua (later renamed Houa Phan) and Phong Saly provinces became home for the leaders of this group, who maintained close fraternal relationships with the North Vietnamese government.

As they moved into the mountains, the Lao communists openly courted those very people who had traditionally been shunned by elite lowland Lao. The first eighteen-man Central Committee of the Neo Lao Issara, founded in 1950, included Sithon Kommadan (son of the Lao Theung leader of the nineteenth-century revolt mentioned earlier) and Faydang (chief of the Hmong families united in opposition to both royal rule and those Hmong clans allied with the French).

The earliest documents of this new movement stress the importance of uniting the various nationalities and of improving the living conditions of the tribes. Although lowland Lao dominated the Lao party hierarchy, the army, including the officers, increasingly reflected a balanced cross-section of the country's population. During the 30-year struggle to take Laos, the Pathet Lao invented its own symbols of nationhood – a flag, an anthem, national days, a currency – for people 'whose previous psychological field was often restricted to their village or tasseng'.[11]

The Pathet Lao (PL), once established in the northeastern provinces of Sam Neua and Phong Saly, set out to create a model society on which to base the socialist reconstruction of the country once it had won. Meanwhile they were prepared to participate in the coalition government of Prince Souvanna Phouma established following the second Laos Conference and the regime it prescribed in 1962. Part of this drive included the recruitment of ethnic minorities into positions of responsibility in roles other than that of soldier. The communist leadership did this in a variety of ways.

Beginning in the mid-1960s, the PL organised schools for ethnic minorities in the territory it controlled. These fledgling institutions served several functions. Orphaned children from the area's hill tribes were sent to these places if no relatives could be found to take them in. More important, in a political sense, bright children were selected to be educated at these schools, often the first in their village to receive such attention. Under the watchful eye of local communist cadre, young Hmong, for example, learned to read and write Lao while also imbibing the basic tenets of socialism as taught by Lao Marxists. Many students from such schools can be found scattered through rural Laos administering the district governments.

I met one such man in 1984 while travelling by jeep through four of the six districts of Houa Phan province. Introduced to me as the secretary of the district and an influential member of the Party in Houa Phan, the man was dressed simply in Hmong costume.[12] From a peasant village located about a 7-day walk from district headquarters (80 km), the secretary had never been to any place larger than his Hmong village until 1966, when he was chosen by area PL cadre and his village elders to study teaching at the first ethnic minorities school in Houa Phan province. It was at this school that he first learned Lao.

He is now the most highly educated man in the district. After completing his studies at the ethnic minorities school, he was chosen once again because of his abilities as an organiser to spend the years 1972 through 1974 in Hanoi at the prestigious Nguyen Ai Quoc School for Political Study. Clearly respected everywhere we went, he dominated, in a quiet but intense way, most of the discussions.

The leaders of the Pathet Lao often displayed considerable tact in ways both large and small when dealing with their hill tribe brethren.

The Pathet Lao officer training school in Sam Neua Province was named the Kommadan School after the greatest of all the southern hill tribe leaders who revolted against the French.[13] Pejorative terms for ethnic minorities like Kha and Meo, in general use throughout Laos, were studiously avoided by the Pathet Lao and their followers.

In 1984 during a trip to northern Houa Phan I was treated to an evening of film clips. We sat on a hillside for hours watching Vietnamese war movies (no subtitles) while shivering from the cold. The highlight of the evening, however, was a remarkably sophisticated colour film made by the Chinese for the Neo Lao Hak Sat some time in the early 1960s. The film featured dancers representing each of the ethnic groups of Laos – dancing at first only with their own kind, each group slowly intertwines with the others until all are dancing together under an enormous Pathet Lao flag, now the flag of the Lao PDR.

During my stay in Laos I occasionally travelled with a lowland Lao cadre from the Ministry of Irrigation. I used to wonder why the older staff of the ministry treated him with a mixture of fear and respect, for he was both younger than many of them and lower in administrative rank. He was born in 1949, as was I. Discovering this shared birth year during long lazy evening conversations when travelling together led us to compare lives, so to speak, and to share perspectives on a long war understood from opposite sides of the world which had deeply affected us both.

My friend was from a village in Saravane Province, and that geographic fact explained much about his current position in the Lao regime. Partly in consequence of the success of the Pathet Lao campaign in the early years, the eastern half of all the southern provinces, including Saravane, became liberated areas early in the Lao Civil War. This fact and the presence of the Ho Chi Minh trail in the eastern border areas of the southern provinces had important consequences for Pathet Lao recruitment. Repeated clashes between Royal Lao government soldiers and local communist supporters on the borders of the territory controlled by the PL caused havoc among the lives of peasants living in the contested areas. By the time my friend reached adolescence Royal Lao government soldiers had burned his village several times, robbed the people of what little they had, and, as he put it, committed other crimes against them. By the age of 14 he was in touch with Pathet Lao cadres, first in Saravane and later in the city of Savannakhet, where he was sent to high school.

The French gave automatic scholarships to the top three students to graduate from the country's grade schools. As high schools existed only in Vientiane and the larger province capitals, the recipients of these awards, often the brightest and most ambitious children of peasants living in the back-woods, were sent to the cities in early adolescence to enter high schools, which were, by the mid 1960s, hotbeds of Pathet Lao activity.

At 21 my companion decided, without consulting his parents, to walk to Sam Neua and join the revolution. Traversing the country during a period of increasingly heavy aerial bombardment, he took seven months on the journey. During that time, as well as his stay in Sam Neua, he got to know, and sometimes depend on for his life, the ethnic minorities living in the territory between Savannakhet and Sam Neua.

Adversity and fear led him, and other bright lowland Lao like him, to get to know his Khmu and Hmong brethren. Such relationships are new in Lao history. Still a lowlander by preference (to this day he loathes walking and avoids it whenever possible, a fact which meant we spent an inordinate amount of time waiting for jeeps to take us two blocks), he nonetheless does not question the right of ethnic minorities to become part of the Lao polity.

While the Pathet Lao was recruiting among the hill tribes, the Royal Lao government continued in the main to ignore them. Although the Armée Clandestine of Hmong leader Vang Pao became among the best-known fighters in Laos, its recruitment and support was done by American Special Forces, not by the government in Vientiane.

Journalist Arthur Dommen wrote a highly critical book in 1964 trying to account for the failure of the United States to achieve its goal in Laos, which he felt to be the creation of a state secure in its independence and livelihood. He believed that the Royal Lao government's failure to pay any attention to the hill tribes was one of the more critical mistakes of the war. He wrote

The Royal Government's authority did not extend at all into the territories of the mountain tribes, because of their almost total lack of previous political organization and the age-old animosities between them and the lowlanders... when the [Royal Government] army appeared in the upland villages, even outside the Pathet-Lao controlled provinces of Sam Neua and Phong Saly, it was feared as an army of foreigners rather than welcomed.[14]

COME THE REVOLUTION

The country taken over by the Pathet Lao in 1975 was, and remains, one of the least developed and poorest in the world. It is a country with few roads, and a weak infrastructure which dwindles to the nonexistent in the hinterlands.

The problems of illiteracy, poor health, and poverty which beset all Lao plague the ethnic minorities more severely. Infant mortality, high by Southeast Asian standards (the Lao PDR's infant mortality rate is 150 per cent higher than that of Vietnam, for example),[15] is far higher in the upland areas than in the lowlands, and higher in the rural areas than in the cities. A recent survey carried out in one of the districts of Bokeo, an upland province with large concentrations of ethnic minorities, found that nearly three out of ten babies died before reaching their first birthday.[16]

Although rice self-sufficiency was once again achieved nationally in 1984, rice is not adequate everywhere. Uneven production, poor land, poor transportation, and climatic vagaries have left people in the rugged, highland areas without enough rice or with very marginal surpluses.[17] A recent UNICEF study found food shortages among certain ethnic minority communities in the mountains of Sekong, Phongsaly, Luang Prabang, and Bokeo.

Although malnutrition is considered negligible by experts, one recent survey found a significant number of undersized among young children in three very remote villages. UNICEF and WHO staff assume, probably correctly, that whatever severe malnutrition exists in Laos will be found in the highly isolated rural locales mostly inhabited by ethnic minorities.[18] Most upland minority groups depend on slash-and-burn cultivation, which demands more work with less return per hectare than conventional methods, thus exacerbating their food problems.

Illiteracy is a serious problem in Laos, and once again there is substantial regional variation. In the more developed provinces, such as Vientiane Municipality and Savannakhet, literacy is now 80 per cent or more.[19] In provinces where ethnic minorities predominate, however, illiteracy is high, especially among women, children, and the elderly.

Finally what transportation, communication, social services, and agricultural infrastructure existed in Laos in 1975 were concentrated almost entirely in the Mekong Valley towns. Where service networks of some sort (such as the village temples of northern Luang Prabang) had existed in the remote, mountainous areas of the country, they had rarely survived the intensive bombing campaigns of the 1960s and early 1970s. In short Laos was poor and underdeveloped and the Lao Theung and Lao Soung were comparatively much worse off than their lowland countrymen. Ethnic minority Pathet Lao cadres who entered Vientiane in 1975 brought with them certain expectations as to the benefits their support would bring but little in the way of training which would prepare them to administer a state.

The party leadership meanwhile hoped to expand its base of support to include lowland Lao previously beyond its organising reach. The city of Vientiane was also full of students who had participated in the anti-USAID demonstrations in May 1975 and who, although not actually party members, could be counted on for support. Many of these students and others like them, all lowland Lao, would soon be in direct competition with their more poorly educated but politically more committed Lao Theung and Lao Soung countrymen for jobs within the newly evolving ministries, as well as for positions within the higher level education system.

Thousands of vacancies opened up within the varied ministries and committees that make up the national government. Between May 1975 and December 1987, more than 375,000 people, representing 10 per cent of the country's population, left the Lao People's Democratic Republic. Of that total, refugee camp registration figures show that 205,251 were lowland Lao (a figure including Chinese and Vietnamese) and 121,424 were ethnic minorities, most of them Hmong. The United Nations High Commissioner for Refugees estimates that at least another 50,000 have been absorbed into Thai society, bypassing officialdom entirely.[20]

Those who had left included most of the former Lao elite and a substantial proportion of the educated middle classes. Laos lost most of its middle level managers, accountants, mechanics, doctors, and teachers.

The lowland Lao outflow doubled in 1976, held steady in 1977 and doubled again in 1978. In contrast, over the same period hill tribe departures dropped dramatically. In 1979 Hmong exodus once again increased dramatically as a result of the final crushing by Lao and Vietnamese troops of the residual Hmong resistance around the Phu Bhia mountain in the border region between Vientiane and Xieng Khouang Provinces. Since 1981 refugee outflow has slowed among all groups of Lao probably because political and economic liberalisation coincided with tighter Thai and Western controls over who would be accepted for resettlement abroad.

The gaps created within the governing structures of the country were filled by lowland Lao and hill Tai from Houa Phan and Xieng Khouang provinces and from villages in Vientiane province. In the cities of Luang Prabang, Pakse, Champassak and Thakkek, a number of Lao Theung appeared to replace the fleeing lowlanders.[21] Thus a visitor to any of the major cities, including the nation's capital in the years following 1975, would have found many members of ethnic minorities running departments, schools, vet centres and so forth. This was not so, however, at the ministerial and central committee level.

MINORITY PARTICIPATION IN NATIONAL INSTITUTIONS

Minority participation in the governing institutions which had grown up during years of struggle was impressive. The Central Committee of the Front had significant Lao Theung, Lao Soung and hill Tai representation.[22] Sixty percent of the party members before 1975 were drawn from minority groups and at all times minority recruits made up the bulk of the Pathet Lao armed forces.

In the first few years after 1975 the minorities were somewhat better represented in the Supreme People's Assembly than before 1975. The four vice-presidents were Sithon Kommadan, a Lao Theung; Faydang Lobliayao, a Lao Soung; Sisomphone Lovansy, a hill Tai; and Khamsouk Keola, a lowland Lao.

Representation in the Supreme People's Assembly proved the exception rather than the rule. Since taking control of the country, the Central Committee of the Lao People's Revolutionary Party and the government of the Lao People's Democratic Republic have remained overwhelmingly ethnic Lao. The Third Party Congress in April 1982, in expanding the Central Committee, increased minority representation somewhat: eleven of the fifty-four members and alternates were from ethnic minorities.

The dynamics of reorganisation during 1982 and 1983, however, reduced minority representation within the national government. Increasing evidence of administrative inefficiency in the ministries coincided with the return of large numbers of lowland Lao educated in the Soviet Union and Eastern Europe. Many politically trusted cadres were removed from jobs awarded them in the heady days following victory in 1975 to be replaced by technicians with the skills necessary to build dams and allocate scarce resources.

Beginning in 1980, mid-level administrators from the former regime began to be released from re-education camps in the north and assigned to work within the Vientiane ministries. Those returning home were among the last of the well-educated bureaucrats left in Laos, and the government could not afford not to use their services. Many of the cadres with whom we worked in the ministries of Education and Agriculture, and within the Social Welfare Committee from 1981 on, had been released from the camps during the previous year. The availability of both students returning from overseas and political prisoners from the camps made it possible for the Party to replace the politically trusted but administratively incompetent with better-educated people. By the early 1980s the government felt confident enough in itself to do just that.

PROVINCIAL AND DISTRICT REPRESENTATION

While the government at the national level remains an ethnic Lao stronghold, at the provincial and district levels, minority representation is far more impressive both in the party and in the government. In the northern provinces, including Luang Prabang and Houa Phan, as well as in the southern provinces of Saravane, Sekong and Attopeu, ethnic minorities hold at least one if not both of the two most powerful positions available in provincial politics: Secretary of the Party and Chairman of the People's Administrative Committee. (The chairman is often referred to as governor of the province.) The governor is usually deputy secretary of the party, while the secretary is deputy governor, thereby ensuring that minority representation is significant in both party and government affairs at the provincial level. Members of minorities are even better represented at the department head level in the provincial ministries.

The district offices of both the party and the administration are usually entirely in the hands of minorities in the minority areas. It is this level of government which is most directly concerned with the day to day lives of villagers. During my husband's 1985 visit to Nong Het, a Hmong stronghold on the Xieng Khouang border with Vietnam, negotiations for a variety of local aid projects were handled entirely by local Hmong government officials.

Provincial and district authorities can be an independent group, willing to experiment, to cut through red tape and ignore the bureaucratic niceties when it comes to getting something they really want done. Foreign aid agency staff often prefer to work at this level because of this relative freedom to make decisions and because intra-ministry cooperation is far more evident at the provincial than at the national level.

More than once during negotiations to thrash out the details of some aid project we would turn to our Vientiane Ministry travelling companions for guidance when local people changed the plan in some significant manner, only to find that the provincial leaders held ultimate decision-making power. District authorities also can rework plans to their own satisfaction even when their wants differ from the stated objectives of the provincial staff.

One example: Lao Lu villagers in northern Luang Prabang decided to rebuild destroyed temples with the portable sawmill we provided rather than construct housing for government cadres, as requested by the province. We returned to Luang Prabang convinced that this reworking of the plan would be denied. The governor, however, agreed that they needed the temples more than they needed houses.

Nor does local independence stop at reallocation of aid funds. My husband once spent days travelling for the first time to the capital of Phong Saly province in the far north. Finally arriving, he was told to wait on the boat until his guide had located the proper authorities to welcome him. After 3 long hours the Vientiane government people accompanying him finally returned, properly chagrined, to tell him that the provincial authorities had decided they didn't like the location of the new capital, so that three months earlier they had all moved back to the traditional one at Phong Saly Neua, another day's trip up the Ou River.

NEW APPROACHES

It is at the district level that new approaches to national problems are being worked out. Some of the more intriguing examples are evolving in Houa Phan Province in what are called 'workers' villages'. I visited one such village in the district of Muong Houa Muong in early 1984.

Muong Houa Muong is the poorest, most war-damaged district of Houa Phan province, and has the highest percentage of ethnic minorities. The district is completely lacking in electricity. It has one old truck used by the district staff, one small rice mill which runs on diesel fuel, and a small projector with a built-in generator used to show movies. The above represents all the machinery in the district.

Most of the 416 families living in Muong Houa Muong are Lao Soung and Lao Theung. Approximately 30 per cent of the population became refugees during the war. Having lost their traditional villages during the bombing, they are now grouped in new villages along the area's major river or along the province's only road. These displaced persons are the district committee's responsibility.

When I visited the district, most of its populace depended on forest clearing to open up land for the cultivation of their rice. The most critical problem was lack of paddy fields and the water systems with which to irrigate them.

The national government has declared hardwood trees a national resource of considerable value on the world market and so has mandated an end to slash-and-burn cultivation. So not only does the Muong Houa Muong district committee want to assist war refugees to resettle, it hopes to get them to take on new ways of rice farming as well. If they can't produce many new hectares of paddy land, the people now along the road and river will wander off into other provinces, other districts or simply higher up into the mountains in search of more fertile slopes to burn.

The problems facing this district and the solutions under considera-tion by local leaders present an example of the evolving relations between ethnic minorities and the lowlander majority. The provincial government has assigned a group of workers to live in the district and figure out ways to solve the area's problems. Organised as a working unit in 1972, the group's members moved to the current location in 1976. (Before 1972, everyone lived higher up in the mountains either to avoid the war or to fight in it as soldiers.)

This 'workers' village' is now the district capital of Muong Houa Muong and houses the 346 workers and their families assigned by the provincial government to assist the peasants of the area. The government group is an ethnically mixed lot, although lowland Lao predominate. Describing themselves as 'not in the productive sector', because they don't grow rice, their task is to assist the people of this district to make plans, raise animals, construct needed buildings, transport goods, educate themselves and, most important, to introduce irrigation schemes to enable inhabitants to grow more wet (paddy) rice and, consequently, less upland rice. Not all the workers live at headquarters; some are placed in villages around the district.

The workers see their assignment as temporary. They were there just to see what they could do to help provide paddy land to an area sorely in need of it.

The district leadership running the worker's village is representative of the kind of relationships forged by the long years of civil war and the resulting coming together of young, relatively well-educated lowland Lao and ethnic minority youth from the mountains. The secretary of the District was Hmong, the president was Khmu, and the deputy was lowland Lao. The Hmong secretary clearly dominated.

The workers' village is a new concept which evolved during the war and which breaks with tradition in several ways. Each Lao ethnic group almost always lives with its own kind; thus the mixed Lao Loum, Lao Theung, and Lao Soung workers' village would have been unheard of before the war. Mixed leadership is new, too, and a Hmong in charge of a committee which includes a Khmu as well as a lowland Lao is evidence of the new roles slowly evolving for the country's ethnic minorities.[23]

UPWARD MOBILITY

What about upward mobility in government circles? It is happening, but slowly. Although no numbers are available, ethnic minority students are being sent to provincial schools: to the national training centres in Vientiane to study medicine, agricultural techniques, and teaching; and even overseas. My personal experience in Laos suggests that their numbers are small. However, as more educated minority youth enter the job market, representation within the ministries will increase at the critically important deputy minister and departmental head level. How fast that happens depends in part on the decisions made about allocation of national resources.

ALLOCATION OF NATIONAL RESOURCES

The pledge to 'pay attention to education, develop primary and secondary education systems [and] to help all people, especially mountain people, to learn to read and write'[24] runs through all the Pathet Lao statements from the 1950 Program of the Neo Lao Issara through contemporary *Pasason*[25] editorials. So do promises to improve health conditions, transport networks, and the economy of the minorities. The government has tried to distribute social services more equally throughout the country, thereby living up to one of the many promises made during years of civil war.

Education

Following the intensive national literacy campaigns of 1976, the Ministry of Education put considerable effort into creating a primary and secondary school system. Although problems, of which lack of funds and trained staff loom largest, have been numerous and continuous, a rudimentary school system does now exist. Many minority villages in Laos have a small, open-walled, thatch-roofed school with an earthen floor, one blackboard and rows of crude desks. At least a third of all minority children now complete 3 years of elementary schooling.

Progress beyond the first three grades is still very unlikely for most, however, and the obstacles facing educators are legion. Since a multi-lingual system is too expensive (and the PL is committed to Lao as the national language anyway), all instruction is in Lao, a language few minority children speak. But the government also recognises that many minority children from the remote rural areas are in a sense educationally handicapped and in need of special assistance to catch up with their brethren in the valley areas. So it has organised ethnic minority schools which serve as special institutions for minority children.

The curriculum is identical to that of similar schools in the lowland areas but the pace is slower and the emphasis is on learning to read and write Lao. It is primarily from these schools that bright minority children are chosen to attend the nearest high school and, if they continue to progress, to study in one of the Vientiane academies or overseas.

There are also now fifteen ethnic minority teacher training colleges turning out teachers who will be sent back to their villages to set up primary schools. I cannot overemphasise the rudimentary nature of all of this. Teacher candidates at the minority teacher schools, for example, will complete grades 1–5 so that they in turn can teach grades 1–3.

My notes from a 1985 visit to an ethnic minority training school in Houa Phan begin with the sentence, 'Life is still very hard here'. As I left, the head teacher asked me if we could help him get cement, roofing, wood, and nails to build wooden classrooms, a kitchen, an eating place and dormitories. 'And then', he added, 'perhaps you could send notebooks, pencils, a volleyball, mosquito nets, sweaters, and blankets.' On the other hand, when I visited Attopeu, a remote southern province with a large Lao Theung population in 1985, provincial and district authorities were elated that the province had, for the first time in its history, a high school with 167 students as well as an ethnic minority orphanage.

Health

Progress is also being made, though at a snail's pace, in health. Using its own limited resources as well as foreign assistance, the government has built hospitals in all the provinces and some of the larger district centres. Vietnamese sister provinces have made provincial and district hospital construction something of a speciality. The very method of twinning Lao and Vietnamese provinces, however, is emblematic of the problems facing minorities in both countries.

A health cadre in Attopeu once tried to explain to me why the lovely new 100-bed hospital building in the provincial capital was but an empty shell. 'Sister provinces are chosen for their proximity so ours is just over the mountain [Annamite Chain] but they're all minorities over there [Vietnam], too, and they don't have any money either', I was told.

Health workers are venturing into the villages, setting up clinics, training sanitation and public workers and trying to collect data on how many children really die in infancy. Even a well-trained health worker, primed to teach much-needed lessons about infant nutrition and clean water, lacks credibility in the eyes of his/her potential audience because he/she carries few or no 'foreign medicines'.

Hope springs eternal, however. My husband was once entangled in string while trying to enter a Lao Theung village in northern Luang Prabang. Questioned as to the purpose, the village headman explained that there was sickness in the area and so the village was tied off with string and powerful incantations to keep the disease bearing bad spirits out. 'That will keep us going', he said, 'until you', meaning Western aid agencies, 'or the government, bring us some medicines.'

State Stores

To meet the plea for more consumer goods, the government has set up a network of very popular state stores which stock a variety of goods at low, government-subsidised prices. Resembling general stores on the American frontier, the state stores stock Thai and Russian cloth, rubber flip flops, Vietnamese sewing machines, Russian bicycles, and, in the former liberated territories, cooking utensils manufactured from the metal taken from downed American planes. To a lowlander from Vientiane, used to the American 'glory days' or just the morning and evening markets as they are now, these places appear pathetic. To minorities who have had no access to consumer goods except for an occasional small trader, the state stores are the equivalent of the local shopping centre.

Complaints about them usually concern lack of stock, especially during the rainy season, when the rudimentary transportation network tends to fall apart. The minorities also complain about the prices, because, even at subsidised rates, the more coveted items, such as bikes and sewing machines, are beyond the means of most minority families.

ALLOCATION OF DEVELOPMENT MONEY

The monies available for development are not going to improve living conditions for the country's minorities in any significant fashion in the near future. This is not because of poor intentions, but because in an economy like Laos the needs are very great everywhere, and competition for resources between ministries and areas is likewise great.

Education and health were allocated 3.7 per cent and 5.2 per cent of the monies available for development projects between 1981 and 1985, while transport, agriculture and industry consumed a whopping 62 per cent of the national budget during that period.[26] Much of that 62 per cent was spent on upgrading existing road networks and extending the total hectarage of irrigated wet rice production. Such projects by their very nature do not immediately affect minorities, who, for the most part, do not live near Laos's major roads or paddy fields.

There are exceptions in that the roads now connecting Pakse with capitals in Sekong and Attopeu, as well as the road into Sam Neua from Xieng Khouang province, are clearly spurring development in minority areas. A few years ago it took 2 or 3 days to drive across the Bolovens Plateau into Attopeu, a drive I did in $6\frac{1}{2}$ hours in mid-1985 on the new road.

Such roads do lead to new enterprises. While in Samakhisai, the capital of Attopeu, I was intrigued to see people beginning to congregate in front of a rundown little storefront. I pulled up a chair and sat down too to await developments. About an hour later an ancient Russian Zis truck, looking like something out of a World War II movie, came bumping down the road. Within minutes of its stopping in front of us young men from the store had it unloaded. It was full of ice packed in straw, and the clever proprietor quickly set up a brisk business in iced coffee which lasted about 2 hours until the ice ran out. Basically, though, the major routes now being upgraded or constructed to the provincial capitals will become useful in developing the hinterlands only when feeder roads are built. I suspect those will be a long time coming.

RESETTLEMENT PROJECTS

The government over the years has shown a continuing interest in resettling ethnic minorities from the mountains in lower-lying territory. The rationale given for the approach shows a combination of social work instincts, security concerns, and economic considerations. According to a report by a leading UNDP consultant to one such undertaking, the objectives of integrated rural development projects to assist minorities are as follows:

1 geographically and economically integrate those remote areas into the country;
2 progressively attract and integrate the minority populations into the development process of the country;
3 set up the preliminary conditions for rational exploitation of existing but as yet almost untouched potential resources.[27]

Members of the Nationalities Committee have, over the years, approached various foreign donor agencies with plans to resettle hill tribes on lower-lying lands in the provinces of Vientiane, Xieng

Khouang, Sekong, Savannakhet and Champassak. Donors have
tended to be wary of such projects for obvious political reasons.

Nonetheless, as Quaker staff in Laos in 1983, we agreed to provide
the funds for a dam in the vicinity of Pha Hoi in northern Vientiane
province. The project was to complement a larger UN effort. The
plan represented the best and the worst of lowland Lao instincts
towards the hill tribes, especially the Hmong. The proposed recipients, a group of Hmong who gave Long Chen, Vang Pao's CIA
base, as their 'home village', were unwilling to live at the project site
itself. They built a small village about 7 kilometres away, where they
went about the business of daily life, paying minimal attention to the
efforts of the government to restructure their lives. They let it be
known, however, that they would indeed resettle if and when the new
site was completely finished.

Meanwhile, a group of lowland Lao and a UNDP/FAO consultant
laboured away on their behalf against what turned out to be
overwhelming odds. Communication between the two groups was
minimal and all the project staff, with the exception of two Hmong
trainees, were lowland Lao. Nonetheless, it must be noted that the
untrusting Hmong were genuinely interested in, although suspicious
of, resettlement, while the Government, by 1983, was committed to
persuade by example, not coercion.

Since our experience with such projects the United Nations Development Project has underwritten several very ambitious plans to
assist Hmong living in the vicinity of Muong Hom in Vientiane
Project and Lao Theung in the remote province of Sekong. Both
project administrators and outside consultants concerned with the
projects feel that the Lao government has improved in its ability to
plan and administer such projects. They also report that the minorities involved are enthusiastic participants and much more helpful in
both planning and execution than the Hmong in the Pha Hoi project
mentioned earlier.

RACISM AND CULTURAL BIAS

Lao communist leaders realised early on that traditional lowland Lao
attitudes of contempt toward the minorities must be overcome if
there was to be a Lao nation state. Their attempts at achieving a less
racist attitude have been considerable. Derogatory labels like Kha
and Meo are discouraged and are rarely if ever used by government

cadres. Children's primers in use in the schools emphasise the multi-ethnic nature of the Lao state. State holidays and celebrations always include women dressed in the various costumes of the hill tribes. Provincial dance troops learn dances from the various tribes as well as the lamvong, the dance of the lowland Lao. Newspaper and magazine articles emphasise the importance of the minorities' contribution to the socialist victory in 1975.

A reader wrote to the editors of *Siang Pasason (Voice of the People)* in November 1976 to ask the following: 'I would like to know where racism still exists under the new system ...I would like *Siang Pasason*, in giving its view, to state clearly which nationality, the Lao Loum, Lao Theung, or Lao Soung, is really greater'. The editors chose to quote from the political report of the party and government of the Lao People's Democratic Republic which was read during the Congress of People's Representatives from throughout the country on the occasion of the formation of the People's Democratic Republic on 2 December 1976:

> Lao people of all nationalities constitute the larger family of the Lao national family. They are bound by solidarity and mutual love, assistance and progress, and work to play a part in building the nation and preserving unity on a foundation of equality with emphasis on striving to preserve a united country, the new social order, and the happiness of all nationalities.

The editors go on to explain that this shows that there 'will be a complete intermingling of people from the leading organizations at the highest level down to branch party and government offices; there will be representatives of all nationalities and tribes, especially the Lao Soung and Lao Theung'.[28]

The party lets it be known that ambitious lowland Lao had best display a proper attitude of respect toward minority peers. One lowland Lao medical student, for example, told me that Mahosot, the main hospital in Vientiane, was so dirty because the Hmong and Khmu students had no standards of cleanliness. I asked my informant if such behaviour was criticised by the other students. Shocked, my friend said any such comments would be frowned upon and could adversely affect a student's future.

Yet in 1984 on a visit to Houa Phan Province, my husband walked all day before finally arriving in the Tai Dam village where he was told he would spend the night. Although the sun was now going down, my husband asked that the aid discussions begin immediately. That was impossible, he was informed; the village to receive the dam in question was 6 kilometres back down the trail. When asked why the party hadn't stopped there, his guides looked surprised at his stupidity, pointing out that that village was Khmu and so he wouldn't want to spend the night there.

Even official publications occasionally reflect minority concerns that the promises of the state are far from fulfilled. A *'Vientiane Mai'* column of 5 April 1985, called 'Conversations with the Editor', carried a letter asking if the Lao Theung language would ever be broadcast on the national radio and if the magazine could tell him if there are any Lao Theung on the Party Central Executive Committee, the Politburo or on the Central Committee. The editors wrote back 'Dear Comrade Bounchan Sopaseut ...we talked with the comrades in national radio broadcasting, and we found that they would like to broadcast in many Lao ethnic languages. However, the present situation is not ready for doing so, and they can broadcast only in the [H]mong language. .. It is good to listen to the central dialect so that all Lao will get to know the central dialect well'. The answer went on to regret that the editors could not answer his second question but suggested that the reader 'review the names in detail and then you will know the ethnicity of each individual'.[29] In actuality it is often difficult to guess which nationality any individual is from names alone, given the confusing tendency of some ethnic minorities to take lowland Lao names. The editors' answer is indicative of the ignorance about hill tribes' role in national government often found among lowland Lao.

There is also a strong cultural bias running through even the most enlightened party pronouncements. Although, for example, some Buddhist practices came under criticism during the first 5 years following 1975, the heavier critical analysis was always reserved for hill tribe superstitions, which were seen as far more inhibiting to modern progress than was Buddhism.

Kaysone himself, in a speech given in 1981, emphasised that the people must strive to overcome traditional attitudes of condescension and superiority. He went on to suggest, however, that the state create 'economic, political, cultural and social models in nationality areas so that they can be imitated by our fraternal ethnic minority people in building the villages and in enabling the mountainous areas to gradually catch up with the plains areas, thereby creating conditions for achieving true equality among our fraternal nationalities'.[30] The same speech went on to say that '...we must introduce culture...to free our nationality brothers from backward customs and traditions and supernatural beliefs so they can build a new, modern life'.

Much of the harsher rhetoric directed towards tribal traditions has been mitigated since 1980. The emphasis today is more on change through example rather than change through coercion and exhortation. Nonetheless hill tribe leaders are sometimes suspicious, with reason, that the catching up they are supposed to do includes more than just achieving parity with lowland Lao areas in terms of schools, clinics and other material improvements.

CONCLUSION

If Laos is to become a nation state, with all that that entails in terms of national identity and allegiance, the tribal minorities must be included. National security and economic development hang in the balance.

The Second Five-Year Development Plan (1986–90) calls for the exploitation of mining resources (iron in Xieng Khouang, gold in northern Luang Prabang, copper south of Pakse), of coffee on the Bolovens Plateau and fruit trees in the mountainous regions with colder climates, and, of course, all those hardwood trees, including valuable teak, growing on the slopes of Laos' mountains.[31] Such development planning is predicated on the government's commanding a strong sense of loyalty from the minorities living in the areas containing these riches. The hill tribes must feel enough of a stake in their future as Lao to welcome the extraction of wealth from 'their' territory.

Progress has been made. The new Lao government has committed itself, publicly and often, to the notion that the Lao PDR is a multi-ethnic state. Encouraging too are the signs that Lao leaders are willing to re-evaluate and change course when initial efforts don't work. The liberalisations, both economic and political, of 1980 are a case in point. So too is the decision to tone down government rhetoric regarding tribal customs and to switch from attempted coercion to persuasion over issues of methods of cultivation and resettlement. Finally the party has proven itself willing to rein in over–zealous officials when the result of their efforts is massive disaffection among the people.

The creation of a nation state must inevitably, however, raise issues of government control versus tribal independence. Census-taking, conscription, the collecting of taxes – all are potential sources of conflict, of struggle between submitting to some sort of national consensus versus denying the government the right to undertake such actions at all.

The tribal minorities of Laos are unique by dint of their traditions, yet the very nature of progress wars against tradition. The minorities must consider it worth the cost of loss of traditional identity and freedoms to achieve economic, political and social welfare parity with the plains. It is much too soon for any of the participants (or observers) to know whether the sacrifices entailed will be worth the gains.

Notes

1. Alfred W. McCoy, 'French Colonialism in Laos, 1893–1945', in Nina S. Adams and Alfred W. McCoy (eds) *Laos: War and Revolution* (New York: Harper and Row), p. 88.
2. *Ibid.*, p. 92.
3. MacAlister Brown and Joseph J. Zasloff (1986) *Apprentice Revolutionaries: The Communist Movement in Laos, 1930–1985* (Stanford: Hoover Institution Press), p. 11.
4. Basic information on minorities taken from Guy Morechand, 'The Many Languages and Cultures of Laos', in Nina S. Adams and Alfred W. McCoy (eds), *op. cit.*, p. 31.
5. Martin Stuart-Fox (1986) *Laos: Politics, Economics and Society* (London and Boulde: Frances Pinter and Lynne Rienner), p. 44.
6. For more information on the air war in Laos, see Raphael Littauer and Norman Uphoff (eds) (1972) *The Air War in Indochina* (Boston: Beacon Press), rev. ed.
7. Arthur J. Dommen (1971) *Conflict in Laos: The Politics of Neutralization* (New York: Praeger), second edition, p. 17.
8. Stuart-Fox, *op. cit.*, p. 15.
9. *Ibid.*, p. 16.
10. Brown and Zasloff, *op. cit.*, p. 270.
11. *Ibid.*, p. 270.
12. Anecdotal material taken from Trip Reports and Field Notes prepared between 1981 and 1985 by Wendy Batson and Robert Eaton.
13. Arnold R. Isaacs, Gordon Hardy, MacAlister Brown, and the editors of Boston Publishing Company (1987) *Pawns of War: Cambodia and Laos* (Boston: Boston Publishing Company), p. 80.
14. Dommen, *op. cit*, p. 383.
15. *An Analysis of the Situation of Children and Women in the Lao People's Democratic Republic* (Vientiane, Lao PDR: UNICEF, 1987), p. 17.
16. *Ibid.*, p. 19.
17. *Ibid.*, p. 36.
18. *Ibid.*, p. 33.
19. *Ibid.*, p. 54.
20. Refugee numbers from United Nations High Commissioner for Refugees.
21. Stuart-Fox, *op. cit.*, pp. 53 and 54.

22. *Ibid.*, p. 130.
23. *Trip Report to Xieng Khouang and Houa Phan,* Jan–Feb. 1985, pp. 62–70.
24. 'Principal Points of the First Program of the Neo Lao Issara, 1950', in Brown and Zasloff, *op. cit.*, p. 290.
25. *Pasason* is the official newspaper of the Lao People's Revolutionary Party.
26. UNICEF report on women and children, p. 24.
27. From UNDP consultant Michel Guttleman's report 'Area Based Integrated Rural Development Projects', given at the Round Table Meeting, Vientiane, Lao PDR, June 1987, p. 3.
28. JPRS, translation of letter to *Siang Pasason*, 2 November 1976, p. 3.
29. JPRS, 28 May 1985, translation of a letter from *'Vientiane Mai'*, 5 April 1985, p. 2.
30. *FBIS*, 13 February 1981.
31. Information on development plans from second Five-Year Plan taken from 'Report on the Economic and Social Situation Development Strategy and Assistance Needs', (Geneva: Prepared for the Asia-Pacific Round Table Meeting Concerning the Implementation of the Substantial New Programme of Action for the Least Developed Countries, April 1986). Round Table reports are usually available from the United Nations Development Program (UNDP).

6 Social Developmen the Lao People's Democratic Republ Problems and Prospects

Ng Shui Meng

BACKGROUND

The Lao People's Revolutionary Party (LPRP) came to full power in Laos in 1975 after more than 30 years of struggle. From its earliest inception it had promulgated a strong social agenda to mobilise popular support. Promising to improve the living conditions and social well-being of the people, its social agenda was constructed largely around the following points:[1]

1   the eradication of illiteracy and advancement of education and national culture;
2   expansion of health care for all;
3   promotion of equality of the sexes;
4   protection of the interests of all national minorities;
5   respect for all religions.

Throughout the period of revolutionary struggle and even during the Indochina war (perhaps more so during that period) the Pathet Lao leaders were mindful of their promises and made efforts towards meeting some of these goals. Hence, despite the harsh conditions of the war years and lack of financial and material resources, the party helped build a rudimentary social infrastructure in its base areas in Sam Neua and Xieng Khouang. Basic literacy and elementary education and health services were made available, especially for cadres and members of their families. In certain places education and health workers also reached the village level.[2] At the same time, through intensive social mobilisation via the party's mass organisaons, women's rights and rights of national minorities were pro-moted. And despite some uneasiness and occasional confrontations with religious leaders, the practice of religion, especially Buddhism (the religion of the great majority of the Lao), was largely tolerated as long as it was not seen to subvert the revolution.

In 1975, with the end of the Indochina war and the establishment of the Lao People's Democratic Republic (Lao PDR), the Pathet Lao finally gained complete control of a unified Lao state. As the legitimate government of a fully unified Lao state, the Pathet Lao is thus obligated to put its revolutionary agenda, including its promises on social development, into practice on a national basis. Understand-ably such an endeavour is far from easy, especially given Laos' underdeveloped economy and historical, political, and social background.

This paper attempts to discuss development in three of the five areas mentioned above, namely education, health and sexual equality for women, in the Lao PDR since 1975. It will focus on the progress made in the last 12 years, the problems encountered and the prospects for change.

IDEOLOGICAL CONTEXT OF SOCIAL DEVELOPMENT

Before proceeding to discuss social development in Laos in the recent period, let us look at Laos' social policies within the state's ideolo-gical context. According to the party's theoreticians, Laos' develop-ment depends upon successfully carrying out the 'three revolutions', the attainment of which is considered necessary to enable Laos to progress towards socialism, 'bypassing the stage of capitalism'. This theory of the three revolutions, first expounded by the Party Secret-ary General, Kaysone Phomvihan at the Fourth Plenum of the Central Committee of the LPRP in December 1976, was essentially modelled on the Vietnamese theory of the 'three revolutionary currents'. According to this theory, Laos' transition to socialism is said to demand concurrently (1) a revolution of the relations of production, (2) a scientific and technological revolution, and (3) an ideological and cultural revolution – with the scientific and technolo-gical revolution as the keystone.[3]

What all this means briefly is that for Laos to progress towards socialism, there must first be a restructuring of the economy through socialisation of the means of production, that is, economic production should fall largely within the control of the state or the collective. Such a revolution of the relations of production is, according to the party, a prerequisite for transforming the economy from its current backward state to a modern industrialised one. However, the process of economic transformation itself is envisaged to hinge critically upon the acquisition of new industrial technology and scientific knowledge; hence the importance of the scientific and technological revolution. Last but not least, just as the economic relations and structures needed to be transformed, so too did social relations. Such social transformation is to be brought about through a comprehensive ideological and cultural revolution. Through the latter the party believes there will come about the evolution of the 'new socialist man' – a new type of man 'who engages in labor with a spirit of collective mastery, who profoundly loves the country and socialism and who has a clear spirit of internationalism'.[4]

The task of carrying out the 'three revolutions' was early recognised by the party as much more easily said than done, given the underdeveloped nature of the Lao economy and the critical shortage of trained manpower in the country. While the state is able to institutionalise certain changes pertaining to patterns of ownership and means of production in the economy, it cannot so easily decree a scientific and ideological revolution or the evolution of the new socialist man. For the latter two the key is seen to lie with social development, especially in the areas of education and general politicisation. Given this, assessment of social development in Laos will have to take into account how successfully the goals of the three revolutions are being met.

Educational Development

Educational development in Laos was largely neglected throughout the French colonial period and was but slightly improved after the 1960s under the Royal Lao Government (RLG). Access to education was a privilege available mainly to the rich and influential urban elite. In 1975, when the LPRP government took power, it was estimated that less than 2 per cent of the $3\frac{1}{2}$ million population had completed 12 years of education and less than 20 per cent had finished 6 years of elementary schooling.[5]

The dismal state of education meant that illiteracy was widespread, and it was especially high among females and ethnic minorities. Hence it was not surprising that, more than any other area of social development, the LPDR government's policy of eradication of illiteracy and extension of education was the one most enthusiastically embraced by the people.[6]

Goals and Achievements in Education

Development goals in Laos are set forth in the country's development plans. The country is currently into its third national development plan (called the Second Five-Year Plan).[7] These plans laid down the specific sectoral goals to be fulfilled within the plan period. In the case of education the government had set for itself the ambitious goal of complete eradication of illiteracy and the attainment of 100 per cent primary school enrolment by 1985. In addition it was planned that the number of students in the secondary and higher education levels were to increase in the following proportions between 1981 and 1985: 20 per cent for lower secondary, 51 per cent for upper secondary, and 25 per cent for higher education.[8]

Literacy
In 1975 the government estimated that 65 per cent of the population between 15 and 45 were illiterate.[9] Immediately after assumption of power, the government launched a literacy campaign in which students, teachers and workers mobilised to conduct literacy classes throughout the country. The immediate result was that people who could neither read nor write were exposed to basic reading and writing skills for the first time in their lives. Through such campaigns and the efforts of education expansion, the government claimed that 85 per cent of the population between 15 and 45 had learned to read and write by the end of 1980.[10] By the end of 1984 illiteracy was officially said to be successfully eradicated.[11]

While government efforts in literacy advancement were commendable, official proclamations of complete eradication of illiteracy must be interpreted with care. It cannot be denied that a substantial number of people were exposed to some form of literacy classes during the nationwide literacy campaigns, but it cannot be concluded that all these people have therefore achieved functional literacy in the true sense of the word. In fact it may be assumed that many, especially those in the remote rural areas, remained illiterate despite the brief literacy campaigns. Moreover, even among those who did acquire rudimentary literacy, many are believed to have lapsed back into illiteracy.

The reasons are clear. These early literacy campaigns were seldom comprehensive enough or of ample duration to have an enduring effect on the majority of the illiterate population, with the exception perhaps of limited localities where the local party leadership was unusually dynamic. Experience in other countries shows that for literacy campaigns to be effective there must be sustained, systematic follow-up programmes in adult or complementary education to help the neo-literate retain functional literacy. In the case of Laos such programmes, while available, are not widespread enough to have major impact.[12] Furthermore, outside major towns, reading materials remain even today in very short supply, so that there is little for people to read. Hence, despite government efforts and claims, illiteracy remains problematic in Laos. A 1984–5 UNESCO survey of fifteen provinces in fact revealed that illiteracy among the 15–45 age groups is still estimated to be 56 per cent.[13]

More recently there has been renewed effort to establish literacy centres, especially for women in ethnic minority areas, but such attempts have had limited success, owing to lack of funds, suitable teachers and teaching materials as well as poor community response.

However, despite the fact that government claims of illiteracy eradication are over-exaggerated and the problem of illiteracy in Laos remains, the trend of illiteracy decline, especially among the younger age groups, is nonetheless clear. As education expands, literacy levels in Laos are expected to rise, but probably not as rapidly as the government hopes.

Education

Literacy improvement in Laos is closely linked to access to education. Statistically speaking, in the past 12 years, the Lao PDR can be said to have made impressive gains in the sphere of general education expansion. Between 1976 and 1985 the total number of students receiving general education increased from 346,300 to 584,600 (68.8 per cent), with primary school enrolment increasing by 56.2 per cent, lower secondary enrolment by 160.0 per cent and upper secondary enrolment by nearly 700 per cent. Given the large backlog of children awaiting access to schools, the most rapid rate of increase of student enrolment took place between 1975 and 1980. After 1980 student intake at all levels of education levelled off. Between 1981 and 1985 primary enrolment increased by 3.4 per cent, lower secondary enrolment by 8.2 per cent and upper secondary enrolment by 34.5 per cent.

With rapid expansion of student intake, the number of schools and teachers too increased markedly. Between 1975 and 1985, schools increased from 4,527 to 8,033 (77.0 per cent) and teachers from 13,057 to 23,885 (82.9 per cent).[14] In terms of enrolment ratios, primary enrolment reached 85.4 per cent in 1983–4 compared to 67.5 per cent in 1974–5, and secondary enrolment increased from 4.2 per cent to 16.8 per cent for the same period.[15]

However, if assessed according to the targets the government has set for itself, they are still short of the plan. All school enrolment ratios in 1985 show that they have not reached the targets set by 1985. Nonetheless it should be pointed out that from a regional perspective the primary school enrolment ratio in Laos today is comparable to that of most Asian countries. But while primary enrolment ratios have reached a satisfactory level, secondary level enrolment ratios are still low for the region.

Achievement in the sphere of higher level professional and technical education, which is perhaps ultimately more critical in determining the rate of scientific and technological advancement, has been more patchy. In-country higher level and university education is now provided only at a few institutions, namely the School of Medicine, the School of Civil Engineering, the Teacher Training Institute at Dong Dok, the School of Agriculture and Forestry and the National Polytechnic Institute.[16] In addition there are other lower and mid-level technical and vocation schools operated by the Ministry of Education and ten other sectoral ministries at the central and provincial levels. These provide training in basic electrical and mechanical engineering, architecture, agriculture, nursing and teacher training.

In all, according to official statistics, the number of students enrolled in university and higher level education totalled 5,209 in 1984–5 (455 in 1975 – 6), and those in vocational and technical schools (inclusive of first level and secondary technical schools) numbered 17,389 for the same period (2,537 in 1975–6).[17] Also, since 1980, an additional 1,000–1,500 students have been sent abroad each year, mainly to the Soviet Union and Vietnam, for university and higher level technical education.[18] Although the number of students enrolled in university and higher level education has increased, higher education enrolment is still miniscule. University and higher level education enrolment, including those studying abroad, represented only about 1.2 per cent of the population aged 20–29 (assuming 1,500 students studying abroad) in 1985.[19]

Quantity Versus Quality

What is of greater concern in education development in Laos is not that education expansion has fallen short of the plan. Objectively speaking, the rate of expansion of education in the Lao PDR in the last 12 years is a very credible achievement for a least developed country. In fact the criticism is that education expansion has taken place too rapidly and is achieved at the cost of education quality, which has plummeted at every level since 1975. The government in its headlong drive to expand education services nation-wide has set for itself goals which are perhaps not feasible or even practical in the Lao situation.

Many of the problems are linked to resource constraints, of which financial and manpower limitations are the most serious. The World Bank 1986 Report estimated that for the period 1981–5 the development expenditure for education was only 3.7 per cent.[20] This is a very low figure compared to some other sectors, such as agriculture (16.9 per cent) or transport (28.6 per cent), and in view of the needs of the education sector. Given such budgetary constraints, aside from others, the Ministry of Education simply did not have the funds or the manpower to maintain an adequate administrative and supply infrastructure needed to support such an extended network of schools and learning institutions.

The result is that schools (often little more than thatch and bamboo structures) are ill-equipped and teachers are inadequately trained[21] and poorly paid. Without an adequate salary, many teachers are compelled to turn to farming or other forms of employment in order to support themselves and their families.[22] This has given rise to low teacher motivation and high absenteeism. Furthermore, because of serious shortages of all kinds of didactic materials, students (and sometimes teachers) are often not supplied with basic textbooks and any other kind of reading materials.[23] Such a state of affairs prevails through all levels and at all educational institutions (with the minor exception of a few well-established schools in Vientiane) and is the major factor for the very high school drop-out and repeater rates.[24] It also accounts for the low standards of the graduates.

The low educational standards of students and the poor material support have a detrimental effect on those pursuing higher-level professional or technical education in-country or abroad. In-country higher-level education is even more seriously plagued with material and manpower shortages than general level education. As a result of the massive flight of educated people abroad following the change of government in 1975,[25] many of the higher-level institutions are staffed either by inadequately trained teachers or by foreign teachers from the Socialist bloc countries. The language problems, among others, encountered by students under such circumstances can only be imagined. Students attend lectures given by any number of foreign teachers in their respective tongues, which are then translated into Lao, usually by less than proficient translators. It is not surprising that many students flounder through the courses and eventually graduate with less than desirable skills or competence.

Students studying abroad do not fare much better. Until recently the selection of students sent abroad depended less on academic achievement than 'class' background and 'revolutionary spirit'. Through this process even poorly qualified students are selected. Complaints are often heard from donor institutions about the low quality of the Lao students they get. Many returning students candidly admit that they could not follow the courses because they had an inadequate academic base. Medical students, for instance, reported, not without some bitterness, that they went through their entire practical medical training courses without being allowed to handle certain medical equipment and patients because of inadequate background or skills. While such practices may not be general, there is reason to suspect that they are fairly widespread. To rectify this situation, if only in part, it was rumoured that the selection of students going abroad for the 1987–8 academic year was, for the first time, decided not by the relevant Lao authorities but by those of the countries offering the scholarships.

The poor quality and inadequacy of the education system is not unrecognised. Official party documents repeatedly bemoan this situation and urge improvement. Kaysone Phomvihan in his political address at the Fourth Party Congress (13–15 November 1986), for example, frankly stated that after 10 years, 'No adequate funds were allocated to the building of the material–technical infrastructure for education and culture. Education was not quite practical in content. The training of teachers was not good enough'.[26]

In view of the current failings of the education system the Lao government might have to reassess its entire education programme in terms of its objectives, projected output and available resources. Given that education is such a vital prerequisite to development, the national budget for education may have to be markedly increased, even if this means diverting resources from other sectors. Under the current five-year plan the allocated budget for education has been increased to 8 per cent,[27] but in view of the needs, development analysts still consider the figure too low. Also at this stage of the country's educational development it may be more realistic to forgo some less critical (but expensive and prestigious) areas of higher-level educational development and concentrate resources to improve general level education. As some development experts in the World Bank noted, the best route to overcome the chronic shortages of technical and professional manpower in Laos today is first by 'providing the workers with good general education [for it] offers the best foundation for filling current jobs and for retraining as circumstances arise'.[28] Otherwise the problems which plague the present education system and poor education standards will perpetuate themselves into the future and negate whatever statistical achievements appear on paper.

One positive step taken by the party during the Fourth Party Congress which could change the education system for the better is the proposed extensive reform of the general and vocational education system. This reform, according to Kaysone, is to be carried out 'with a view to raising the quality and effectiveness to ensure they reflect the demand for all-round education'.[29]

Education and the Transmission of Political and Social Values

Education in socialist Laos today is more than the transmission of academic skills or knowledge; it is to be the vehicle to form the 'new socialist man or woman of the future'. The new education system, by virtue of its implementation on a broad social basis, has a positive equalising effect on the population. Education in Laos today also emphasises physical and social labour. Student work teams led by teachers are sent out during weekends and holidays to clean up public places, dig public ponds, or harvest rice in cooperatives. This work has helped eliminate much of the elitism associated with education in the past.

Another aspect of the present educational system is that student assessment is based as much on academic performance as on 'correct' social attitudes and political attitudes. Correct social attitudes mean that students should demonstrate a spirit of mutual assistance and cooperation instead of competitiveness, which is regarded as selfish and individualistic. The merit and demerit of such an educational perspective is perhaps open to debate from a philosophical and a pedagogical point of view. In general educators would agree that the promotion of mutual cooperation is socially desirable, but it is questionable to what extent the discouragement of student competitiveness may be considered positive. A certain degree of competition is probably necessary if students are to excel, develop creativity, and achieve academic and professional excellence. Without such creativity and excellence, one may argue, there can be little real scientific and technological advancement.

Political attitudes are inculcated through political education, which now forms a major part of the students' curriculum both in and out of school. Besides formal and informal politics taught through the school subjects, students have regularly to attend political study sessions. It is through this process that the regime hopes to transmit 'desirable' political and social values to the youth who are the nation's future new socialist women and men. Again, without debating the desirability of such mass politicisation tactics, the government can be said to have been largely successful in this respect. Although some degree of cynicism among them exists, young people seldom question the social and political values of the state. On balance the Lao education system can be said to be more successful in meeting social and political objectives than the purely pragmatic educational ones. In view of the critical development needs of the country, the failure of the latter is a definite cause for concern.

Perhaps the best prospect for improvement in the education sector lies in the current attempt at educational reform, which is intended to be very extensive. It is to include wide revision of the school curriculum at all levels, rewriting and printing of textbooks, as well as setting of minimal standards for school buildings, classrooms and teaching equipment. The financial constraints, among others, for such an ambitious programme will be considerable. The government is nonetheless hopeful that it can obtain the bulk of the funds from national, international and non-governmental agencies.

HEALTH SERVICES

Development of health services, like education, received but scant attention under either the French or the RLG. Health services were available in major centres such as Vientiane, Savannakhet and Luang Prabang, but the rest of the country had little in terms of modern health care. People depended mainly upon traditional cures dispensed by village monks or medicine men. When the LPRP took power, the Lao PDR was listed as a country with one of the lowest life expectancies and the highest mortality in this part of the world.[30] With lack of clean water, proper sanitation and medicines, adults and children were exposed to all kinds of endemic, transmissible, respiratory and gastrointestinal diseases, such as malaria, diarrhoeal diseases, typhoid, cholera and tuberculosis. Such childhood diseases as diptheria, tetanus, polio, measles and whooping cough were rampant and took their toll, especially among infants and children under 5.

Goals and Achievements in Health

Upon assuming power the government attempted to extend health care on a nation-wide basis. According to the 1980–5 Plan, the government's goals in health were to develop a network of health stations and dispensaries from the centre down to the village; increase the ratio of medical facilities and personnel to population; improve maternal and child health and reduce infant and child mortality through immunisation and improved sanitation; and to provide potable water to 25 per cent of the rural population and 70 per cent of the urban population by 1985.[31]

As in education, the past 10 years have witnessed a substantial effort on the part of the government to build a health infrastructure through an ambitious programme of rapid construction of health facilities and training of health personnel. From time to time health campaigns such as the 'three cleanliness campaign' (clean food, clean water, and clean environment) were conducted to promote public health consciousness. Between 1978 and 1981 the government, with the assistance of such international health agencies as WHO and UNICEF and other private organisations, also incorporated a number of basic preventive services into its health care system, including:

1 an expanded programme for immunisation (EPI);
2 control of diarrhoeal diseases (CDD);
3 malaria control;
4 mother and child health services (MCH);
5 water and sanitation;
6 iodine deficiency control (IDD);
7 acute respiratory infections control (ARI).

By 1986 there was theoretically, a country-wide health network comprising four central hospitals, sixteen provincial and 111 district hospitals, 741 sub-district (commune) dispensaries, and 6,000 village health posts.[32] These facilities were manned by a total of 550 doctors, 2,200 assistant (auxiliary) doctors, 6,750 nurses and an unknown number of auxiliary nurses and health workers[33] supposedly capable of providing rudimentary primary health care for Laos' 3.6 million inhabitants.[34] At the same time the Water Institute of the Ministry of Health attempted to expand its programme to provide clean drinking water to many remote villages.

Slow Progress in Health

However, as in education, expansion of health facilities and services was done on such a broad basis and resources spread so thin that the ultimate impact of the government's health programme was largely ineffective. In its preoccupation to show concrete results, the Ministry of Health was more concerned with construction of health facilities all over the country than in providing proper health delivery systems. Many of these health facilities, especially in the more remote outer provinces, are crudely built and ill-equipped structures with little of the basic medicines and supplies needed for the medical staff to practise their trade. Hence, as in the case of teachers, the low level training, the poor working conditions and the low economic incentives have severely demoralised the medical workers.

The situation is not much better in the larger hospitals. Even in the Central Hospital (Mahosot Hospital) in Vientiane, syringes and bandages frequently run out. Most medicines are unavailable or if available have deteriorated.[35] Patients often have to obtain these from the private pharmacies. Services and sanitary conditions are also poor.

As a result, mortality rates in Laos have not been significantly reduced. Crude death rates are still about 17 per 1,000 population and infant mortality rates are 118 per 1,000 live births. Life expectancy has only gone up to about 50 years. These figures continue to mark Laos as a country with the highest mortality and shortest life expectancy in the region.

More discouraging is that the health services make little impact on most diseases. Malaria continues to be the country's greatest killer followed by diarrhoea, tuberculosis and pneumonia. Young children not surprisingly, are the most susceptible victims of these diseases

According to data drawn from limited sample surveys, four out of every ten children below the age of 10 have had malaria. In some villages the figure was as high as seven out of ten. The average diarrhoea episode rate per year among children 0–4 is reported to be 3.4, which partially explains why Lao children often appear stunted and weak.[36] At the same time the government's water and sanitation programme continues to fall way behind schedule, thereby denying many rural villages the benefit of clean drinking water and proper sanitation.

The lack of progress in the health sector led Kaysone to admit at the Fourth Party Congress: 'Health services are very poor, especially in the rural and remote areas. Infant mortality rate is high. A number of dangerous diseases especially malaria, have not been limited or eradicated'.[37]

Limitations of Health Programmes

Experience in other Third World countries shows that many diseases are preventable or controllable at fairly low costs. In the case of Laos, preventive health programmes are theoretically in place, but they were haphazardly conceived and poorly implemented. The expanded programme for immunisation (EPI), drawn up by the Lao government in collaboration with WHO and UNICEF in 1979, was one such example. The Ministry of Health had set very ambitious targets on paper, but the programme failed to make any impact on childhood diseases.[38] A mid-term evaluation of the EPI programme by a WHO expert showed that by 1984 only an estimated 2–3 per cent of children of 12–23 months nation–wide were fully immunised against all six childhood diseases: 10–12 per cent were vaccinated against tuberculosis, 2–4 per cent against diphtheria, pertussis (whooping cough) and tetanus, and 4 per cent against measles. And only 6–10 per cent of women are vaccinated against tetanus.[39]

The EPI programme's poor performance (also true of most other health programmes, such as malaria control, control of diarrhoeal diseases, mother and child health) was again due to budgetary, infrastructural and social constraints. On balance, budgetary constraint was perhaps of lesser importance than the latter two, because substantial programme inputs were provided (in the form of vaccines, cold chain equipment, and personnel training) by international aid agencies. More serious were problems linked to inept programme management, coordination and implementation by the ministry's officials and health workers. In addition the programme was hindered by the very inadequate and difficult transport conditions, which render outreach activities problematic, as well as by social inertia and ignorance on the part of the public regarding the causes of diseases and their prevention.

Apart from the need to improve the Ministry of Health's management and technical capacity associated with the implementation and delivery of health services, the government needs to place greater emphasis on primary health care and health education, which are by far the more effective and cheaper routes to health improvement. Unfortunately primary health care, both as a concept and in practice, is at an embryonic stage; and health education to raise public health consciousness, standards of personal hygiene and environmental sanitation is only very sporadically carried out.

As mentioned earlier, the Ministry of Health's priority, despite expressed goals, is in building provincial and district hospitals and producing doctors quite regardless of its actual resource capacity to support or train them. Such a strategy, apart from the disadvantage of reaching only a small number of people, is also of questionable utility. These provincial and district hospitals generally function at such a low level (lack of supplies and equipment) that their impact on health improvement is limited. More detrimental is that this cost has slowed the primary health movement.

Prospect for the Future

Despite the poor progress in the health sector, the most hopeful aspect is that a rudimentary health care framework is now established where none existed before. But for this framework to become functional and effective, the government must show more political will to ensure that the existing health programmes and health delivery systems operate satisfactorily. Recently the government has taken steps to restructure the reward system for doctors and nurses, including extra payment for night duty and other types of specialised services, in the Vientiane hospitals, with the result that health personnel in these hospitals have become more motivated. Services in these hospitals have become slightly more efficient and patient care has improved. To have impact, these reforms will have to be extended beyond the urban centres to provinces and districts, where they are most needed.

However, in the context of Laos' limited resources, the best health strategy, in the final analysis, is still improved health education and primary health care. For the health system to become sustainable and not to drain the national and local economy, the concept that people can and should be empowered to assume greater responsibility for their own and their community's basic health should be encouraged. People should be weaned away from the concept that health care is synonymous with going to hospitals and ingesting pills, and taught to look at health care in totality, including life-style, environment, nutrition and sanitation. This approach is the most rational way to move away from the Western concept of expensive institution-based health care, which is ultimately built upon dependence on expensive external inputs (expensive medicines, sophisticated medical facilities and equipment and foreign expertise).

There are indications that slowly some shift in this direction is being taken, although it is still relatively confined to the more developed centres. In Vientiane and the major towns people are slowly becoming more aware of the importance of basic hygiene and sanitation, and simple methods for disease prevention.

WOMEN IN LAOS

Social Situation

The position of women in pre-revolution or post-revolution Laos has rarely been the topic of academic enquiry. A serious study on women in Laos is certainly called for. In this chapter the issue can only be given superficial treatment, based more on personal observation than on firm data, because the latter are largely lacking.

What little one knows of the status of women in pre-1975 Lao society is that Lao women,[40] as in the tradition of most Southeast Asian societies, enjoyed a slightly higher status than women in South or East Asia. There was no overt discrimination against females, no evidence of female infanticide or predominant son preference. Lao women also often had similar inheritance rights as men, largely because of the prevalence of matrilocal residence among lowland rural Lao, whereby a newly married couple resided with the girl's family. This practice ensured some protection of the bride's interest vis-à-vis the husband. Land was therefore commonly (but not always) passed down through the females.

Despite this cultural advantage enjoyed by Lao women, there were other social practices which negated this apparent benefit and continue to perpetuate inequality between the sexes. Sex role differentiation is very clear-cut in Lao society, and women are trained from early childhood to accept a subordinate position in relation to men both in and outside the home. Female docility is viewed as a virtue and assertiveness is definitely discouraged. In the past girls seldom had the benefit of education, as the village 'wat' schools were only open to boys. In fact girls were essentially socialised to assume roles of submissive wives and doting mothers and very little else. While women were expected to shoulder almost the entire household and child care burden and work in the fields as well, female labour was seldom credited much social or economic value.

Women in Post-Revolution Laos

The LPRP quite early in its struggle promised to 'realise equality between men and women in all fields, political, economic, culture and social' and 'to do away with all acts of contempt or oppression toward women'.[41] This commitment to women's liberation was viewed by the leaders as not only ideologically consistent with Marxist–Leninism, but was also a politically powerful rallying point to gain women's support for national liberation. During the war years the Pathet Lao did make some effort towards widening women's political and social roles by encouraging them to participate in the revolution. Through this process a small number of women managed to rise within the system to hold fairly important positions within the party.

After the war government policy continued to encourage women to participate actively in the tasks of national reconstruction and the building of socialism. Hence the past decade has seen some advances made in the position of women. Women's progress can be seen particularly in the economic sphere, where female labour participation rates have markedly increased. This change reflects the government's policy to incorporate women into productive labour, which is seen as essential for national construction.

According to the statistics provided by the Union of Lao Women, women in 1982 made up almost half the active work force among the 15–44 age groups (21.6 per cent of the 43.9 per cent share of the economically active work force). Female labour in agriculture is especially high, comprising more than 60 per cent of the agricultural work force. In the industrial sector women's participation rate is lower. Among factory workers women constitute only about 20 per cent.[42] In the civil service women are fairly well represented particularly (but not unexpectedly) in the educational and medical services. While women are very conspicuous in the civil service, they are under-represented at the directorial/managerial and upper levels of all ministries.

Another area of definite improvement is in the sphere of education. At present there is roughly a 40:60 ratio in primary school enrolment between girls and boys (43 per cent girls and 57 per cent boys), but the disparity gets greater the higher the level, indicating that girls are still more likely to drop out after a few years of education.[43]

However, women's greater access to education and employment have only marginally improved their social and political status. In these areas the gains made by women are anything but impressive. Government institutionalisation of sexual equality in the socio-cultural and political spheres has in actuality gone little beyond ideological rhetoric and minor institutional concessions.

Institutional and Cultural Barriers to Women's Equality

In theory the government upholds the equality of women in society, but this is hardly reflected at all levels ranging from the party down. The Politburo is solidly a male domain. Of the sixty-strong Party Central Committee, only five are women (up from four only since the Fourth Party Congress in 1986). All these five women have strong revolutionary backgrounds and most are also linked, usually by marriage, to powerful males within the party. Few women independent of such patronage could ever rise up within the party system. Among rank and file party members women also constitute a small minority.

With the exception of Mme. Khampheng Boupha, who holds the position of president of the Union of Lao Women, no other woman has reached ministerial rank.[44] Even directors of ministerial departments are seldom women, although quite a few women do become vice-directors. In general, however, women concentrate in lower ranks of the political and administrative hierarchy. In the provinces women in leadership positions are even more rare.

One reason why so few women make it into the party ranks, let alone leadership ranks, is because they are overly burdened by domestic concerns. To qualify for nomination to party membership, a person must show herself/himself to be an exemplary worker and enthusiastic participant in activities encouraged by the state or other mass-based organisations. This means that, as a worker, the person must always be punctual at work, never be absent from work, and ever-ready to put in extra hours when needed. S/he must also volunteer to join all kinds of state/party-based activities and be willing to play a lead role in these activities.

Faced with such selection criteria, not many women can qualify for nomination for party membership, since domestic demands on the women's time are so great. Few women can claim that they are always punctual at work or are eager to work overtime, since they have to feed and wash the young, rush to the market and prepare the family meals with little or no assistance from their spouse. They are also more likely than men to miss work, since they are the ones who are expected to tend to the sick at home or take them to the doctors or hospitals. Similarly they are also less likely to participate actively in state/party-organised activities. Hence it is not surprising that there are few women in the party and fewer still make it to the top.

This is of course not such an uncommon situation in most other Asian societies, but its perpetuation nonetheless hardly augurs well for the empowerment of women. Furthermore, while in most other societies there are special interest groups and women's organisations to agitate for the improvement of women's position, that task in Laos is solely the responsibility of the Union of Lao Women. However, like other national mass-based organisations, the Union's primary task is to promote the political goal of the party to mobilise women in building socialism. The promotion of women's interests, sadly, has to take a secondary position. This is reflected in the Union's slogan calling upon all Lao women to uphold and practise the 'three goods and two responsibilities'. The 'three goods' call upon a woman to be a *good* citizen, a *good* wife and a *good* mother and the 'two responsibilities' refer to women's responsibility to safeguard and build the nation and to liberate oneself.

The political reason for such an agenda is clear. Stressing women's traditional domestic roles as wives and mothers ensures for the party a certain degree of social harmony and stability conducive to the development of the new 'socialist family'. On the other hand, the emphasis on women's nation-building responsibility is to ensure that women's productive labour is channelled to national development. The other aspects of women's needs are not adequately addressed.

That such an agenda may be contradictory to the goals of women's liberation seems not to be recognised by women leaders themselves. Or perhaps even if it is recognised, it is tacitly deemed expedient not to be challenged. In the same vein women leaders, when confronted, hardly see it as within their right to agitate for greater political representation for women. Instead they often mouth the male leaders' excuses that Lao women generally lack the education to assume such roles, or that by tradition women shy away from taking decisions and assuming leadership positions.

Even in the area of female reproduction, the Women's Union has refrained from opposing the party's policy of encouraging unlimited fertility and condemnation of contraception,[45] even though one of the leading causes of high infant and maternal mortality is the unending cycle of pregnancy and birth among village women. Only a few privately express concern on how uncontrolled fertility is detrimental to women's health, but none dare openly push for any policy changes.

A slight shift in this policy did come about recently, but ironically at the initiative of male leaders. Apparently after being shown the results of a recent fertility and mortality survey, certain high ranking male Party leaders became concerned about the implications of the current high population growth rate on future development. As a result, some form of birth spacing is now viewed as acceptable. It was after this that some women leaders began to support the concept of birth spacing to protect the health of mothers and infants. However, the idea of promoting contraception for the purpose of family planning or as a woman's fundamental right over her reproduction is still considered taboo.

To some extent the low status of women cannot be entirely blamed on inadequate government action. The problem can be said to lie as much in the cultural context of Lao society. The socio-psychological hold on both women and men that women are somehow innately inferior is very deeply entrenched. Quite clearly, even Party cadres, male or female, supposedly steeped in socialist ideology, have but a superficial understanding of the concept of what constitutes sexual equality and women's liberation. This may explain why there has been so little change in women's social position in spite of more than a decade of socialist rule and an increasing female economic role. Today's women, like women in the past, still almost never challenge the opinions or decisions of men either publicly or privately; and just like before, many highly intelligent working women still prefer to quietly withdraw from sight in face of male company. Even if they are present, most prefer to listen meekly. Such behaviour is, however, highly correlated with age. In general it may be said that the younger the woman, the more submissive and respectful she is expected to be.

In the rural areas such manifestation of female subordination are even more apparent. Foreign-aid workers often comment that in the provinces they seldom see women in any official capacity present at meetings. Even on the rare occasions when they are present, they seldom participate actively in the discussions.

However, this is not to imply that there are no prospects for change. Women today have greater access to education than ever before, and as women become educated, and as their world view extends beyond the narrow confines of home and village, their self-image and expectations will change.

This process is in fact just discernible. For example, some young urban women are beginning to complain privately about their subordinate position in relation to men. Quite a few openly laugh at the slogan of 'three goods and two responsibilities', asking why should women only and not men be urged to abide by such a manifesto. A number of independent-minded women have also voiced their unhappiness at the Women's Union during its internal meetings, in the hope that such criticisms will encourage the Union to promote women's real interests more actively. But, nonetheless, such criticisms are still couched in very subtle terms, and there is no indication whatsoever that these women are ready yet to assert their rights actively. However, one noticeable change, perhaps as a result of internal criticism or self-criticism of the kind mentioned above, is that the Women's Union (or one or two leading cadres within the Union) is now taking greater interest in developing village level women-related projects in cooperation with aid agencies.

These projects, by no means radical, are usually in the form of training programmes related to mother–child health, nutrition and child care, as well as in income-generating or labour-saving projects for village women. While much more can be done, especially in terms of skill development for rural women, this is a positive step forward for the Women's Union. As women become more conscious of their rights, it may be expected that they will make greater demands on the party and state to live up to their revolutionary promise to help women realise sexual equality in all spheres of life.

Another potential area of change for women, especially in the urban and sub-urban areas, has ironically been brought about by the very difficult economic situation in Laos today itself. Out of sheer economic necessity many women, including wives of government officials, have abandoned government jobs to resort to informal sector economic activities to supplement the family income. Such activities include small-scale market retailing, setting up of small food stands by the roadside, production or traditional handicrafts such as weaving and basketry, or even working as domestic help in the homes of foreigners. While these informal sector activities give the women very little social status in comparison even with a lowly post within the civil service, they are the sources of economic survival for many urban and suburban families. Some women are beginning to be aware of their economic edge over their husbands, and are utilising it subtly to improve their standing within the family. With the current trend towards economic liberalisation it will not be surprising that many more women can further capitalise on their knowledge of market conditions and marketing networks to strengthen their economic status further. Such developments are expected to have some positive impact on gender relations.

CONCLUSION

The last 12 years have witnessed some major transformations in Lao society and the economy. In the area of social sector development some significant achievements have been made, although these have often fallen short of the government's own planned targets.

The inability to meet social development targets seems to stem from over-ambitiousness and lack of realistic planning on the part of the government. This problem is further compounded by the shortage of trained planning personnel within government and the unavailability of reliable data and basic statistics. In the absence of basic information guiding policy formulation, government and party functionaries often arbitrarily draw up plans (generally preferring to err on the high side) which may have no relation with available financial, material and human resources. Of course there are also other limiting factors which have to be taken into account. The country's difficult physical terrain, pitifully inadequate transportation system, and complex historical, socio-cultural and ethnic background are but a few among others which hamper development.

Perhaps the most optimistic perspective for future development in the social sectors of education and health is that Laos today is in possession of a basic education and health framework where none existed before. To render these services effective the government will have to overcome the administrative and management weaknesses and failures which are already identified.

As regards women, the problems are more complex. Improvement of women's status will depend less upon availability of resources or better management capacity, than from the party's commitment to and understanding of the concept of sexual equality. This could come about only with major attitudinal change with respect to male and female roles and expectations. However, considering the conservatism of Lao society, women's liberation is not likely to emerge in the near future.

Notes

1. The social policies of the LPRP are contained in political agenda of the LPRP as published in the official documents of the party and its Front Organisation, the Neo Lao Hak Sat (earlier known as the Neo Lao Issara). For an easy reference to some basic documents of the LPRP, see MacAlister Brown and Joseph J. Zasloff (1986)*Apprentice Revolutionaries: The Communist Movement in Laos, 1930–1985* (Stanford: Hoover Institution Press), Appendix A (1–6), pp. 288–314.
2. Old revolutionaries in Laos today still recall their first exposure to education in the 'cave schools'. Similarly people in the northern provinces still talk about how the 'Aynon' (literally 'older and younger brothers', the name given to the Pathet Lao cadres by the people) taught them basic hygiene concepts and set up village health posts.
3. For an official discussion of the 'three revolutions', see Kaysone Phomvihan (1981) *Revolution in Laos* (Moscow: Progress Publishers), English translation, pp. 182–94. See also Amphay Dore, 'The Three Revolutions in Laos', in Martin Stuart-Fox (ed.) (1982) *Contemporary Laos: Studies in Politics and society of the Lao People's Democratic Republic* (St Lucia: Queensland: University of Queensland Press), p. 103.
4. Kaysone Phomvihan's speech to the joint session of the Supreme People's Assembly and the Council of Minister, Vientiane Radio, 17–20 March 1977 (*FBIS* Supplement, 11 April 1977, p. 27). Quoted by Martin Stuart-Fox, 'Agricultural Cooperativization in Laos', *Asia Quarterly*, 1980, 4, p. 279.
5. Jacqui Chagnon & Roger Rumpf, 'Education: The Prerequisite to Change in Laos', in Martin Stuart-Fox (ed.), *Contemporary Laos, op.cit.* pp. 167 and 169.
6. *Ibid.*, p. 163.
7. Laos' first national development plan was the Interim Three-Year Plan (1978–80). This was followed by the First Five-Year Plan (1981–5). The current plan, the third development plan, is hence the Second Five-Year Plan (1986–90).
8. The Lao education system comprises preschool, general education, university, vocational/technical and adult education. General education consists of a 5-year primary cycle and two 3-year secondary cycles, divided into lower and upper secondary levels. Higher education includes university and vocational technical education. The planned targets are included in Nouhak Phoumsavan's speech at the Third Party Congress (26–30 April 1982), 'The Report on the Orientation and

Tasks of the First Five Year Plan for Economic and Social Development', quoted in *Lao PDR Report on the Economic and Social Situation, Development Strategy and Assistance Requirements* (Report prepared for the Second Round Table of the Least Developed Countries of Asia and the Pacific, Geneva, 1986, Vol. 1, English Version), Vientiane, p.7.

9. *Khao San Pathet Lao* (Daily News Bulletin, English Verison), 3 July 1984. It is not clear how this estimate was derived. Given the state of educational development in Laos under the French and during the period of the Indochina war, observers generally doubt that illiteracy in 1975 for the nation as a whole could have been as low as 65 per cent. Many believe that the figure was an underestimate or that it had referred only to the more developed provinces along the Mekong rather than to the entire country.

10. *Lao PDR Report on the Economic and Social Situation, op.cit.* p. 53.

11. Martin Stuart-Fox (1986) *Laos: Politics, Economics and Society*, Marxist Regime Series (London: Frances Pinter), p. 148. This claim was reiterated by Kaysone Phomvihan during the Fourth Party Congress in his speech 'Political Report of the Central Committee of the Lao People's Revolutionary Party Presented at its Fourth Party Congress', 13–15 November 1986 (English version, mimeo.), p. 27.

12. Some educators claim that 4 years of education are required to maintain one's literacy through adulthood. See Randall Ireson, 'Laos: Building a Nation Under Socialism', *Indochina Issues 79*, Indochina Project, Washington DC, February 1988, p. 2.

13. UNESCO, 'Diagnostic du Sistem Educatif de la RDP Lao 1984/85', UNESCO Project Lao/82/010, Vientiane, 1985, p. 48.

14. All education figures are from the official source, *10 Years of Socio-Economic Development in the Lao People's Democratic Republic*, State Statistical Centre of the State Planning Committee, Vientiane, 1985, pp. 158–62.

15. *Esquisse d'une cooperation internationale pour le developpement de l'education et des ressources humaines*, UNESCO, Paris, 1985, pp. 3,4 and 7. The enrolment ratios given are gross enrolment ratios (GER), which refer to the number of *all* enrolled children in the given level of education. For GER the numerator would include over- or under-aged children. In Laos, given the recent expansion of education and large backlog of over-aged children, the tendency is for the GER to be high.

16. Martin Stuart-Fox, *Laos: Politics, Economics and Society, op. cit.*, p. 146.

17. *10 years of Socio-Economic Development in the Lao People's Democratic Republic, op.cit.*, pp. 170–4.

18. *Ibid*, p. 172.

19. According to the 1985 Census, the total population aged 20–29 numbered 559,475. *10 Years of Socio-Economic Development, op.cit.*

20. World Bank (1986) *The Lao People's Democratic Republic: A Country Economic Memorandum* (New York), p. 8.

21. The educational level of many teachers is very low. In 1984 it was estimated that 40 per cent of the primary school teachers were officially considered to lack the minimum qualification, that is, they had attained less than 5 years of primary education plus 1–3 years of teacher training. Some of these teachers had as little as only 3 years of primary education plus 1–3 years of teacher training. To rectify this situation, the Ministry of Education is attempting to move towards a system whereby a primary school teacher must have at least attained a lower secondary education (5 years primary + 3 years lower secondary education) followed by 1 year teacher training. (UNICEF, *An Analysis of the Situation of Children and Women in the Lao People's Democratic Republic*, Vientiane, May 1987, p. 63.)

22. Teachers in Vientiane are paid 5,000–7,000 kip a month, equivalent to about US$15–20. In the rural areas the salaries are lower, as the local community is expected to provide some assistance for the upkeep of the teachers. Unless the

teachers also come from the same community, the community is often reluctant to support them. Hence teachers who are placed outside their home communities often suffer the greatest hardships. The same goes for most other public employees. The problem of low salaries is not limited to teachers alone but is applicable to all government employees. Almost every civil servant has to have some other source of income or food to make ends meet.

23. Foreign-aid workers who have the opportunity to visit the learning institutions in Laos are often saddened by the bare state of the classrooms and the inadequate sanitation of most schools. Students usually without any books strain to copy the lessons for the day laboriously written by the teacher on the blackboard. The lesson usually ends with the students repeating after the teacher what they have just noted down. Many often wonder how much learning students can absorb in such an environment and through such a process.

24. It has been estimated that only 18 per cent of primary school students finish the 5-year course. Data on secondary completion rates are not available. (World Bank, *The Lao People's Democratic Republic, op. cit.,)* p. 57.

25. It is variously estimated that Laos has lost up to 90 per cent of its already minuscule educated population as refugees.

26. Kaysone Phomvihan, 'Political Report of the Central Committee by the Lao People's Revolutionary Party'. Speech presented at the Fourth Party Congress, 13–15 November 1986 (English version, mimeo.), p. 13.

27. Nouhak Phoumsavan, 'Guidelines and Tasks of the Second Five Year Plan (1986–1990) for Economic and Social Development in the Lao People's Democratic Republic'. Speech presented to the Fourth Party Congress, 13–15 November 1986 (English version, mimeo.), p. 10.

28. World Bank *The Lao People's Democratic Republic, op.cit.,* p. 60.

29. Kaysone Phomvihan, 'Political Report...', 1986, *op.cit.,* p. 58.

30. Reliable birth and death statistics are difficult to obtain in Laos. According to various estimates, Laos during the 1970s had a life expectancy of a little more than 45 years, a crude death rate of about 25 and an infant mortality rate of 145–50. UNICEF, *Statistics on Children in UNICEF Assisted Countries,* 1986. Some other sources estimate infant mortality rates to be even higher, above 250 per thousand. Martin Stuart-Fox, *Laos: Politics, Economics and Society, op.cit.,* p. 149.

31. *Lao PDR Report on the Economic and Social Situation, op.cit.,* p. 42.

32. Laos is administratively divided into seventeen provinces (including Vientiane Municipality, where all the central hospitals are located), 112 districts, 950 sub-districts, and 11,424 villages. The village is the smallest socioeconomic unit, usually comprising some 250–300 people.

33. *10 Years of Socio-Economic Development, op.cit.,* p. 183.

34. The ratio of medical personnel to population is still low for the region, but it has improved significantly from a decade ago. In 1976 there were 0.31 doctors and 1.28 auxiliary doctors respectively to 10,000 population. By 1985 the ratio had increased to 1.52 and 5.77 per 10,000 population respectively. *10 Years of Socio-Economic Development, op.cit.,* p. 185.

35. The most disturbing part is that large quantities of medical supplies are often available in the warehouses, where they often remain undistributed and left to deteriorate. Poor stocktaking and inventory procedures, bad warehouse management, as well as the troublesome bureaucratic procedures for access to government supplies are some of the causes of this sad state of affairs.

36. UNICEF, *An Analysis of the Situation of Children and Women in the Lao People's Democratic Republic,* Vientiane, May 1987, pp. 19–20.

37. Kaysone Phomvihan, 'Political Report...', 1986, *op.cit.,* p. 27.

38. The 1979 targets were subsequently revised downward and a new 1982–6 programme for EPI was formulated. Under the 1982–6 programme, the targets

set were to immunize:
- 50 per cent of children less than 1 year of age against all six childhood diseases (diphtheria, pertussis, tetanus, poliomyelitis, tuberculosis, and measles).
- 80 per cent of children 6–8 against tuberculosis.
- 50 per cent of women aged 15–45 against tetanus.
- 50 per cent of pregnant women against tetanus.
(UNICEF, *An Analysis, op.cit.*, p. 25.)

39. UNICEF, *Ibid.,* p. 24.
40. The term 'Lao women' used in this context refers mainly to lowland Lao (Lao Lum) women and does not pretend to generalise to apply to women in all of Laos. This point is very important, as Laos is a multi-ethnic society where social practices among the different ethnic groups can vary quite substantially.
41. 'Twelve Point Programme Adopted by the Third National Congress of the Neo Lao Hak Sat in November 1968'. See Brown and Zasloff, *op.cit.,* Appendix A, p. 292.
42. UNICEF, *An Analysis, op.cit.,* p. 71.
43. *10 Years of Socio-Economic Development, op.cit.,* p. 178.
44. Mdm Khampheng Boupha whose husband Khamphay Boupha is the First Vice-Minister of Foreign Affairs, was in fact not re-elected to the Party Central Committee during the last Party Congress for reasons of health.
45. In view of Laos' small population in relation to land and its critical manpower shortages, the government has consistently pursued a pronatalist policy, whereby the import of contraceptives for family planning purposes is discouraged.

Part IV
External Relations

7 Foreign Policy of the Lao People's Democratic Republic
Martin Stuart-Fox

It is virtually impossible when discussing the foreign policy of the Lao People's Democratic Republic (LPDR) to differentiate between initiatives adopted in pursuit of specifically Lao national interests and those beneficial to the interests of the Socialist Republic of Vietnam (SRV), as *primus inter pares* among the three Indochinese states. Or to put it another way, no clear analytical distinction exists between initiatives taken despite the constraints imposed by Indochinese (predominantly Vietnamese) interests and those taken in furtherance of these interests. This is because, despite the weakening of some ties cemented by the 'special relationship' between Laos and Vietnam, Lao foreign policy continues to be formulated to take account of both Lao and wider Indochinese (particularly Vietnamese) interests.

Nevertheless it is possible to argue – and this is the thrust of this chapter – that the evolution of Lao foreign policy in the late 1980s has, for reasons to do primarily with the climate of international relations in Southeast Asia, been in the direction of an increasingly even–handed 'non-aligned' position with respect to various power polarities: the USSR–China, the USSR–USA, and Thailand–Vietnam. As separate chapters are devoted to the LPDR's relations with Thailand and with the United States, emphasis will be placed on other developments – on the 'special relationship' with Vietnam, and its evolution from a bilateral Vietnam–Laos axis to a trilateral relationship including the People's Republic of Kampuchea (PRK); on relations with the Soviet Union and the People's Republic of China (PRC); and on changes brought about by international pressures towards solution of the 'Kampuchean problem'.

THE IDEOLOGICAL AND HISTORICAL FRAMEWORK

Any discussion of the formulation of Lao foreign policy must begin with the essential ideological framework, for important underlying ideological assumptions continue to influence the framing of Lao foreign policy. Paramount among these is belief in and commitment to proletarian internationalism and solidarity between communist states. The leaders of the Lao People's Revolutionary Party (LPRP) are well aware that without continuous political, military and economic support from the Vietnamese communist movement during the course of the 'Thirty Year Struggle' from 1945 to 1975, the Lao revolution would not have come to fruition. The ongoing revolutionary transformation of the Lao economy and society is still dependent on continuing international communist support. In order to ensure such support, Lao policymakers recognise that the LPDR must play its part. Solidarity is shown through endorsement of every initiative taken by the Soviet Union, and through proclaimed adherence to whatever common policy is agreed upon by the three Indochinese states. The revolutionary alliance of the three states is taken to be an historical 'law of development'.[1]

A second ideological assumption concerns the global context in which the struggle between communism and capitalism is fought out. Revolutionary currents may be more or less strong, but the ultimate victory of socialism is assured. Foreign policy formulation therefore revolves around the matter of tactics. The goal is to strengthen the revolution to the point where Laos can serve as the 'advance post' for the extension of socialism in Southeast Asia. In order to build socialism in Laos, revolutionary changes are necessary in the economic base (the means of production), in science and technology, and in the thinking of the multi-ethnic Lao people. All means to effect these 'three revolutions' must be seized.[2]

The progress of the 'three revolutions' in Laos since the LPRP seized power has, however, been disappointing. Attempts to socialise the means of production through the nationalisation of the country's limited industrial base and cooperativisation of agriculture led only to popular resentment and economic stagnation. Thousands of educated Lao fled to Thailand, thus depriving the country of badly needed technical expertise. The revolution in science and technology suffered from declining educational standards and reduced capacity to absorb technology transfer. Under such circumstances no amount of propaganda could create new socialist Lao men and women.

By 1980 a tactical change to more pragmatic economic policies had become a necessity. The economic changes ushered in by the party's Seventh Resolution should have had important implications for the formulation of Lao foreign policy. In fact new considerations intervened to limit Lao options – viz. the demands of the Lao–Vietnamese 'special relationship' and the problem of Kampuchea. It has taken almost a decade of intense international pressure, leading to isolation and economic collapse, to convince the Vietnamese to withdraw their forces from Kampuchea. By the mid-1980s, however, new opportunities were becoming available for pursuit of a more pragmatic Lao foreign policy. These found expression in the resolution of the Fourth Party Congress in November 1986 endorsing 'economic restructuring' at home, and 'the broadening of multiform economic cooperation with foreign countries' abroad.[3] Even so, policy formulation has continued to be rationalised in terms of strategies to be used in the building of socialism. Thus the 'ideological imperative' remains.[4]

THE LAO–VIETNAMESE 'SPECIAL RELATIONSHIP'

Despite Vietnamese attempts to discover deep historical roots for the 'special relationship' that is now said to exist between Laos and Vietnam,[5] the present relationship was primarily forged during the 'Thirty Year Struggle' over the period from the close of World War II to the victory of communist revolutions in both countries in 1975. During this period the respective revolutionary elites developed close ties, based on common ideology and shared revolutionary experience. The communist parties of both states proclaim a common origin in the Indochinese Communist Party (ICP) founded by Ho Chi Minh. These historic ties have been cemented by personal relationships forged over the years between the leaders of both communist movements, and in the case of a number of senior Lao cadres by education in Vietnam or marriage to Vietnamese. Kaysone Phomvihan, long-serving Secretary-General of the LPRP, is himself half Vietnamese.[6]

Immediately following proclamation of the LPDR in December 1975 the close relationship that had grown up during the years of revolutionary struggle was given substance in a series of political, economic and military agreements. The legal basis for the special relationship rests, however, on the 25-year Treaty of Friendship and

Cooperation between the LPDR and the SRV, signed in July 1977.[7] The treaty comprises six brief articles, but includes three attached protocols dealing with defence cooperation, frontier delineation, and economic assistance, the actual contents of which have never been revealed. Article 1 states in broad terms the purpose and ideological basis of the agreement, while article 6 commits both sides to regular exchanges on the development of their relationship. Articles 2 to 5 inclusive define specific provisions.

Article 2 provides for defence cooperation between the two states in the form of reinforcement of their joint defensive capacity in the face of 'all schemes and acts of sabotage by imperialism and foreign reactionary forces'. This article is taken by both Laos and Vietnam to justify both the presence of Vietnamese military units in Laos and the extensive assistance provided by Vietnam to the Lao People's Army (LPA) in the form of training, advice and equipment. Vietnamese forces were mostly withdrawn from Laos in 1975 and 1976, only to return early in 1977 to assist in destroying Hmong rebel bases in northern Laos and in countering anti-government insurgents operating from Thailand. Other Vietnamese units were based in northern Laos or were assigned to work on construction projects in the mountainous east of the country.[8]

Article 3 of the Treaty provides the basis for both economic cooperation and the provision of economic and technical assistance to Laos by Vietnam. In addition it provides for exchanges in the areas of culture, propaganda and education, all of which significantly reinforce commitment to the 'special relationship'. Cooperation and assistance in one form or another extend to every economic ministry and state commission, and entail the regular exchange of both high-level political and lower-level technical delegations. These have resulted in dozens of bilateral agreements covering everything from agriculture to tourism. Over the decade 1975 to 1985 Vietnamese aid to Laos, not including the cost of maintaining several hundred advisers and technical experts, amounted to US$133.4 million to finance some 200 separate projects.[9]

Article 4 of the Treaty refers to delineation of the Lao–Vietnamese frontier, but only in broad terms, by proclaiming a determination to turn the border into one 'of lasting friendship and fraternity'. Specifics were relegated to the relevant still secret protocol. Subsequent negotiations and delineation of the actual frontier conducted by a joint border commission lasted over 7 years. An agreement, finally signed in February 1986, reportedly includes a number of minor 'rectifications' of the previous French-imposed frontier, but its contents remain unpublished.[10]

Article 5 of the Treaty commits each side to respect the foreign policy of the other. Effectively this requires Laos to coordinate its foreign policy with that of Vietnam, and ensures that both countries will present a common front towards any third power. Bilateral consultations were subsequently replaced by regular twice-yearly tripartite meetings of the foreign ministers of Laos, Vietnam and the People's Republic of Kampuchea (PRK), beginning in January 1980. Since the thirteenth such meeting in January 1986, the foreign policies of the three states have been less formally, but just as effectively, coordinated by means of frequent contacts between respective ministries and special meetings of the three foreign ministers when necessary.[11]

The formal legal basis provided by the Treaty of Friendship and Cooperation defines only the framework for the Lao–Vietnamese 'special relationship'. Its articulation has been assiduously developed on a series of interlocking institutional levels. Notably these include party-to-party, government-to-government, military-to-military, and mass-organisation-to-mass-organisation interaction at the central, regional or provincial, and even district or local levels. Typically interaction is through mutual exchange of delegations, by education of Lao cadres and technicians in Vietnam, or by sending Vietnamese advisers to work in Laos.[12]

Party-to-party relations constitute the most important channel by means of which Lao and Vietnamese policies are coordinated and Vietnamese influence is exerted in Laos. Frequent contacts are maintained at the highest level, and are coordinated on the Lao side by the Central Committee Secretariat. But informal discussions between Lao leaders and senior Vietnamese political cadres, whether in Vientiane or Hanoi, are probably more important in arriving at common policy decisions. Such decisions are facilitated by common ideologically informed perceptions of both internal political and economic conditions, and external developments in the international balance of forces.

At lower levels of the LPRP the value of the Lao–Vietnamese 'special relationship' is promulgated as an article of belief. In fact, as Kaysone himself has clearly spelled out, commitment to strengthen the relationship further is a primary criterion for advancement within the party.[13] Senior LPRP cadres have almost without exception pursued advanced theoretical studies in Marxism–Leninism at the

Nguyen Ai Quoc school in Hanoi. In addition Vietnamese instructors have been instrumental in developing courses at the Party and State School for Political Theory in Vientiane, which is attended by all middle and upper level cadres.

Exchanges between party delegations frequently take place on a series of levels. Delegations to respective party congresses always include a number of the most senior party members, led by their respective secretary-generals. Exchanges also take place between specialist organizations of each party, such as the Organization, Propaganda, or Control Committees of the respective Central Committees. Exchanges are often of a technical nature, concerned with the internal functioning of each party, and provide the Vietnamese with an intimate knowledge of the Lao party. Other exchanges take place at the municipality (between Hanoi and Vientiane) or provincial level between party delegations of sister provinces. Contacts are thus both intensive and extensive, and are crucial for the development of common perceptions and policies.

Government-to-government interaction also takes place on a series of levels,though contacts at the state-to-state, ministry-to-ministry, and provincial-administration-to-provincial-administration levels. Because of the considerable overlap in Laos between senior personnel in government and in the party,[14] state-to-state relations and party-to-party relations tend to be conducted by the same people. The most significant interaction deals with the coordination of economic planning through synchronisation and inter-dependency of each country's successive five-year plans. It is on the ministry-to-ministry level that most of the economic assistance and technical exchange takes place. Under agreements at this level Vietnamese civilian advisers have been, and in many cases still are, attached to all ministries with the single exception of Foreign Affairs. Vietnam has provided assistance to the LPRP in agriculture and forestry, irrigation and cooperatives, mining and infrastructure, through conducting basic surveys and planning future exploitation. Vietnamese assistance has been particularly important in building roads, bridges and a fuel pipeline from Vinh to Vientiane.

Industrial assistance has concentrated on agricultural inputs such as farm machinery, fertilisers, insecticides and animal food, and on the processing of agricultural and forestry products. Other projects include the manufacture of cement and other construction materials, and engineering workshops servicing the Ministries of Posts and

Communications, Transportation, and Equipment and Technical Supply.

Agreements have also been concluded between the respective Ministries of Public Health, Social Affairs, Education, and Culture, and between state committees dealing with information and nationalities. Assistance in these areas relates particularly to the third of the 'three revolutions' – that aimed at creating new socialist Lao men and women. Vietnamese advisers have helped shape new educational curricula, including, notably, political education, and in some cases school texts are virtual translations of those used in Vietnam. Information and propaganda are also areas where important Vietnamese influence is exercised, and a careful Vietnamese watch is kept on content to ensure the 'correct' sentiments of Lao–Vietnamese friendship are encouraged.

At the level of provincial administration contacts are facilitated by the device of twinning sister provinces in Laos and Vietnam. The aid provided may not be significant, but exchanges, whether of trade or aid, do permit greatly increased personal contacts between provincial officials – something which can result in negative as well as positive responses.

Military-to-military interaction between the respective armies of the two states developed a strong basis of shared experience during the 'Thirty Year Struggle', and there is grateful recognition in Laos of the sacrifices made by Vietnamese military personnel in assisting the Lao revolution. This close cooperation continued into the post-1975 period with the reorganisation of the Lao People's Army, carried out under Vietnamese guidance and supervision in 1976. The following year Vietnamese troops returned to Laos in force to assist in establishing and maintaining internal security. Logistics, communications, and particularly construction units have provided considerable assistance in building up the Lao economic infrastructure. Most construction, including construction of military facilities, airfields, and barracks for Vietnamese forces, has been concentrated in the north and and east of Laos, and on the Plain of Jars.[15]

Actual numbers of Vietnamese troops in Laos have fluctuated according to circumstances. By the end of 1980 they had reached more than 50,000, as Vietnam committed forces to northern Laos along the Chinese border in order to deter any possible second Chinese 'lesson' against Vietnam via northeastern Laos. The bulk of these northern forces are believed to have been withdrawn to

Vietnam in the second half of 1987 and early 1988, as a concession to China, and in order to facilitate improved Lao–Chinese relations. Some construction and security units also appear to have been withdrawn, though, unlike the withdrawal of Vietnamese troops from Kampuchea, withdrawal of troops from Laos has been unannounced and without fanfare. By mid-1988 only between 15,000 and 25,000 Vietnamese troops were believed to still be in Laos.[16]

Progressive withdrawal of Vietnamese regular army units from Laos is not, however, likely to reduce Vietnamese influence within the LPA, since this is exercised by other, more important channels. Despite the provision of some heavier equipment by the Soviet Union, the LPA is largely dependent on the Vietnamese for military advice, for specialised logistic and communications support, and for advanced training. Vietnamese advisers and liaison officers are attached to the headquarters staff of most LPA units at battalion level and above. More significantly, Vietnamese officers assist in the political instruction of Lao military personnel, and influence the appointment and promotion of Lao officers. As in the case of the Lao People's Revolutionary Party, advancement in the LPA depends in large part on having a politically dependable commitment to Lao–Vietnamese solidarity.

Finally mention must be made of interaction between the mass organisations of the two countries. Exchanges of delegations between the Lao Front for National Construction and the Vietnamese Fatherland Front regularly occur at both the central and provincial levels. Exchanges between trade union organizations, women's associations, and the youth movements in both countries provide additional avenues of contact and influence. So too do the friendship associations of both countries, the respective peace committees, and delegations representing Buddhist organisations. These bring the intensity and frequency of official contacts between the two countries to a high level, indicative of the degree and extent of the 'special relationship'.

Effects of the 'Special Relationship' on Lao Foreign Policy

Formalisation of the 'special relationship' between Laos and Vietnam marked a turning pointing for Lao foreign relations, though the full implications of the Treaty did not become evident until 2 years after it was signed, with the Vietnamese invasion of Kampuchea. Before 1979 Laos pursued a foreign policy that sought to retain a degree of balance in the country's international relations. Even while favouring

Vietnam and the Soviet Union, the LPDR maintained cordial relations with China. Alone of the three countries of Indochina, Laos also retained its diplomatic ties with the United States. Even relations with Thailand, long strained over a series of border incidents and closures, markedly improved with the exchange of visits between Kaysone and the then Thai prime minister General Kriangsak Chamanand early in 1979. Joint communiqués pledged each side to terminate support for anti-government guerrillas operating against the other's country, and to create of the Mekong a river of peace.

The Vietnamese invasion of Kampuchea and consequent polarisation of international relations in Southeast Asia between opposing blocks had severe repercussions for Lao foreign policy. Before this the constraints imposed by the 'special relationship' were more than compensated for by the benefits to be derived from having a powerful guarantor for Lao unity and national integrity. The former *de facto* division of the country into antagonistic zones of influence – with the Chinese in the north, the Vietnamese in the east, and the Americans and Thais controlling the population centres along the Mekong river – was replaced by a regime in Vientiane able for the first time to administer the country as a whole, and thus to set about the task of building a single multi-ethnic Lao nation with a genuine sense of Lao national identity.[17] The 'special relationship' did not preclude the development of friendly relations with neighbouring states – China and Thailand – necessary to the construction of a socialist economy after years of war. Nor did it prevent acceptance of economic assistance from non-communist states. Laos seemed to possess, potentially at least, all the requirements for an effective and beneficial foreign policy.

The first casualty of the Vietnamese invasion of Kampuchea as far as Laos was concerned was that it destroyed what until then had been a carefully crafted relationship with China. Chinese aid during the first years of the LPDR was directed to projects in the north of the country, and the Lao maintained a studied balance between China on the one hand and Vietnam and the Soviet Union on the other. Not until mid-1978, as relations between Vietnam and Pol Pot's Democratic Kampuchea deteriorated towards war, were Lao leaders reluctantly forced to choose between Vietnam and China. Even so Laos, while quick to recognise the new regime in Phnom Penh, was slow to condemn China's incursion into Vietnam. By early March 1979, however, the die was cast. The LPDR denounced China in the same terms as did Vietnam. As the war of words and accusations between Vientiane and Beijing increased in intensity, the PRC was requested to withdraw all its construction workers and advisers and to reduce its embassy staff to twelve, the same number permitted the United States. Ambassadors were withdrawn but diplomatic representation remained at the level of *chargé d'affaires*.[18]

By 1980, as a direct result of the 'special relationship' with Vietnam, Lao foreign relations had entered a new and potentially damaging phase. The former policy of maintaining friendly relations with neighbouring states was in tatters. Relations with Thailand deteriorated sharply once Kriangsak was overthrown and replaced by Premn Tinsulamond. Relations with China were even more strained, with Vientiane accusing Beijing of training Lao anti-government guerrillas in Southern China and fomenting discord among Lao ethnic minorities.[19] Most alarming from the Lao point of view was Chinese–Thai collusion in supporting Khmer resistance forces against the Vietnamese-backed People's Republic of Kampuchea (PRK), a collusion which the Lao quickly detected in the relations of both states with the LPDR – in particular in their support for Lao resistance groups.

While Lao relations with China and Thailand were reaching their nadir, relations between the three states of Indochina were systematically consolidated under the direction of Vietnam. Less than 6 weeks after invading Vietnamese forces marched into Phnom Penh, the SRV signed a 25-year Treaty of Friendship and Cooperation with the newly installed PRK regime. This established the formal basis for a 'special relationship' between Vietnam and the PRK similar to that between Vietnam and Laos, the precise outcome the Khmer Rouge had been so desperate to avoid![20] Two months later Laos and Kampuchea signed an Agreement on Economic, Cultural, Scientific and Technical Cooperation to complete the bilateral agreements on which Indochinese solidarity was to be constructed.[21]

The institutional fleshing out of what has been called the 'Indochinese solidarity bloc' consisted of progressively extending the forms of bilateral exchange conducted under the Lao–Vietnamese 'special relationship' to include PRK representatives. Six-monthly tripartite meetings between the foreign ministers of the three states were inaugurated. Cooperation between respective planning commissions was extended to cover everything from transportation and communications to agriculture and public health. Political coordination, economic integration, and social contact were all encouraged, with corresponding limitations on independent policy initiatives. By the second half of the 1980s, however, developments in the international environment encouraged Lao policymakers to move back, cautiously at first but with growing confidence, towards what effectively amounts to a more 'traditional neutral' foreign policy. In large part this development has been due to the change of leadership in the Soviet Union.

RELATIONS WITH THE SOVIET UNION

During the Brezhnev era the Soviet Union, while gradually increasing bilateral contacts with the LPDR, was for the most part content to accept the Lao–Vietnamese 'special relationship' as defining the primary orientation of Lao foreign policy. In the post-Brezhnev period from 1982 to 1985, bilateral Soviet–Lao relations were progressively strengthened, a trend that has accelerated under Mikhail Gorbachev, to the point where Soviet influence in Vientiane was by 1988 perhaps more significant than that of Hanoi.[22]

There are a number of reasons for this development. Despite the ubiquitous nature of the Lao–Vietnamese 'special relationship', the actual value of Vietnamese economic and military assistance to Laos has never compared with that provided by the Soviet Union. Vietnamese economic aid during the first decade in power of the regime amounted to an average of just over US$13 million annually.[23] Figures for total Soviet aid over the same period have not been released, but it is generally accepted that the Soviet Union provides at least 50 per cent of the average annual US$80 to 100 million worth of foreign economic aid to Laos – an amount over 10 years of at least US$450 million, or more than three times the value provided by Vietnam. Add to this the bulk of up to US$100 million annually[24] in military aid – including the cost of running the Lao army and such major items as artillery, tanks and aircraft – and it is not surprising that Moscow has taken an increasing interest in how its significant level of assistance is utilised.

Soviet experts are permanently attached to the State Planning Committee, now the State Committee for Planning and Finance,[25] while special delegations of the Soviet Planning Committee (Gosplan) regularly arrive to put the finishing touches to the succession of Lao five-year plans. The Lao–USSR Intergovernmental Commission on Economic and Scientific-Technical Cooperation meets regularly in alternate capitals. The ninth meeting in January

1988 drew up agreements for Lao–Soviet joint enterprises in timber-processing and plywood production,[26] thus indicating that trade between the two countries is likely further to increase.

A similar pattern is evident in the military sphere. Soviet aid has included MIG-21 jet fighters, Antonov 24 and 26 transport planes, and Mi-8 helicopters for the Air Force. Aircraft are maintained by Soviet technicians, and Soviet experts train Lao pilots, both military and civilian. Soviet technicians also play a part in the air traffic control, communications and logistics. But while Soviet influence has always been dominant in the Lao Air Force, the army was virtually a Vietnamese preserve. Much military equipment, even when Soviet made, came from Vietnam. More recently, however, Soviet interest in the Lao army seems to have been growing. Exchanges of military delegations were reinforced in February 1988 by the visit of the chief of the Soviet Army and Navy Political Directorate at the head of a delegation for talks with officers in the LPA General Political Department.[27]

Soviet influence is also increasing in other ways. A Lao delegation from the Supreme People's Assembly visited Moscow in March 1988 for discussions on the new Lao constitution. A new agreement under which the USSR will increase its training of Lao cadres has been signed. Already more Lao students study in the Soviet Union than in Vietnam. Soviet teachers are employed to teach not only the Russian language at the Dong Dok Teachers Training College, but also mathematics, science and engineering subjects at the new Vientiane Polytechnic. Together these influences amount to an effective, multifaceted bilateral Lao–Soviet relationship which serves to counter-balance that between Vientiane and Hanoi – a development the Lao have not been reluctant to encourage.

The higher Soviet profile in both Laos and Kampuchea appears to be part of a deliberate move on the part of the Soviets to increase their standing throughout Southeast Asia. In both Kampuchea and Laos they have been assisted by the drastic collapse of the Vietnamese economy, and Vietnam's consequent reduced capacity to aid her two Indochinese neighbours. But the Soviets have also benefited from their participation in international efforts to resolve the problems of Kampuchea.[28] Moscow has made no secret of the fact that considerable pressure has been placed on Hanoi to withdraw Vietnamese forces, influence that has portrayed by Soviet leaders and diplomats alike as contributing to bring about peace in Southeast Asia.[29]

A further reason for the higher Soviet profile therefore is to enable the USSR to take advantage of the decline in Vietnamese presence and influence that is likely to occur with the withdrawal of Vietnamese forces from both Kampuchea and Laos. No commitment has been made by Hanoi to withdraw all Vietnamese troops from Laos by 1990, as in the case for Kampuchea; but force reductions have occurred, and it seems very possible that combined Chinese and Soviet pressure will lead to a complete withdrawal from Laos as well. The Soviet Union stands to be the principal beneficiary. So it is perhaps more significant for the future shape of Southeast Asian relations than might at first appear that a recent meeting of deputy ministers of transportation from the three Indochinese countries called to draw up plans to provide Laos with access to the sea via Kampuchea was attended by a Soviet deputy minister.[30] The future direction of both Soviet–Lao and Soviet–Kampuchean relations clearly warrants careful watching.

RELATIONS WITH THE PEOPLE'S REPUBLIC OF CHINA

As noted above, Lao–Chinese relations suffered most directly as a result of the Vietnamese invasion of Kampuchea. Diplomatic relations were reduced to the level of *chargé d'affaires*, the Chinese aid programme to northern Laos was terminated, and trade across the Lao–Chinese border was reduced to a trickle of contraband. Hostile armies faced each other, a number of armed incidents occurred, and the airwaves were full of shrill denunciation and propaganda. Vientiane accused Beijing of training a full division of insurgents,[31] with all that implied in terms of Chinese support for a possible invasion aimed at overthrowing the LPRP government, and replacing it by a regime loyal to the PRC – just as Vietnam had done in Kampuchea.

By 1983, however, what I have termed 'a curious disparity' was evident between Lao words and actions with respect to China.[32] Chinese criticism of the LPRP had become muted, border incidents and infiltration of agents reduced, and trade allowed to resume. In return, Lao denunciation of China focused not primarily, as before, on alleged Chinese hostility towards Laos, but on Chinese–Thai collusion to undermine the People's Republic of Kampuchea and on Chinese provocations along the Chinese–Vietnamese frontier. Surprisingly warm greetings were exchanged. Friendly contacts between respective armies even occurred. Vientiane was saying one thing – denouncing China for its policy towards Kampuchea, and thus towards the revolutions of 'the three Indochinese countries' – while doing another – rebuilding relations at the local level of cross-border contacts.

Towards the end of 1986 this policy began to bear fruit. Under the urging of the Soviet Union and with the reluctant agreement of Vietnam, Laos welcomed the first high-level Chinese diplomatic delegation to visit the LPDR for almost a decade. During the 5-day goodwill visit amicable discussions were held on the state of bilateral relations, and the possibility of resuming full diplomatic relations.[33] Almost a year later a Lao delegation, led by First Deputy Foreign Minister Kamphay Boupha, returned the visit. The Chinese reportedly gave verbal assurances that they would not encourage or supply armed resistance movements in Laos, and the Lao agreed to exchange ambassadors.[34] This occurred 6 months later, with the further prospect of a new trade agreement to come. Lao officials gave improved relations with China as the principal reason for withdrawal of some 25,000 Vietnamese troops from Laos by May 1988.[35]

Some suspicion yet remains in Vientiane as to Chinese motives for improving relations with the LPDR while maintaining both support for the Khmer Rouge and an intransigent attitude towards Vietnam. The very different treatment accorded the Lao is seen, at least by the Vietnamese, as an insidious attempt to undermine Indochinese solidarity. It may, however, reflect a more realistic acceptance by Beijing of the constraints which clearly operate on Lao freedom of action where foreign policy is concerned. More significantly it may signal a readiness by China to accept a considerable degree of Vietnamese and Soviet influence in the LPDR – and by extension also in Kampuchea.

CHANGING DIRECTIONS: THE IMPACT OF KAMPUCHEA

Paradoxically it has been the stalemate that has developed over Kampuchea that has been instrumental in creating conditions for the new initiatives that have marked Lao foreign policy in the mid-1980s. As early as the First Summit Conference of the three Indochinese states in February 1983 the withdrawal of Vietnamese forces from Kampuchea was foreshadowed – tacit recognition of their presence as constituting the principal obstruction to negotiations for a political settlement. Over the next few years proposals and counter-proposals were traded between Vietnam on one side and ASEAN and China on the other. In terms of conflict resolution, however, these constituted only a preliminary stage of pre-negotiation manoeuvring.[36]

By 1987 a number of new factors had entered into the Kampuchean equation. Prominent among these was Vietnam's increasing eagerness to resolve the Kampuchean recognition issue in the United Nations, and so open the way for Western aid to and investment in the SRV. In August 1985 Vietnam announced that its troops would be withdrawn from Kampuchea by 1990 – a move which was greeted with widespread scepticism. A second associated factor was the increasingly parlous state of the Vietnamese economy, allied to growing Soviet reluctance to continue virtually as Hanoi's sole provider of foreign aid. A third factor was the change in Soviet attitudes ushered in by Secretary-General Mikhail Gorbachev's Vladivostok speech of July 1986. Soviet interest in the Kampuchean problem, and pressure on Vietnam to negotiate a political settlement, increased markedly as a result both of the agreement to withdraw all Soviet forces from Afghanistan, and of the urgency with which the Soviet Union was determined to improve relations with both China and the ASEAN states. Other factors included some slight softening of Chinese attitudes, and some small readiness on the part of the United States to modify its hostility towards Vietnam.

The momentum towards holding serious negotiations to resolve the Kampuchean problem was maintained through 1987 and into 1988 by the willingness of the PRK government to embark upon negotiations with resistance factions aimed at national reconciliation, by Prince Sihanouk's three meetings with PRK Prime Minister Hun Sen in France, by Indonesia's determination to advance a Kampuchean settlement, and by continuing Soviet pressure in the face of the continuing collapse of the Vietnamese economy.[37] Throughout 1987 and 1988 the search for a breakthrough in the Kampuchean stalemate entailed a flurry of diplomatic activity, and figured as a topic of discussion from the capitals of Southeast Asia to the Moscow summit between Reagan and Gorbachev. It was in the context of this diplomatic activity that Lao foreign policy was shaped in new directions which furthered both Lao national interests and Vietnamese (and indeed, Soviet) goals.

Improvements in relations between the LPDR and China, as outlined above, are clearly beneficial to Laos – in the form of improved security, increased trade bringing consumer goods into remote northern regions, and the prospect of resumption of Chinese aid – and provided Vietnam with an additional indirect avenue of contact and influence in Beijing. It is evident that in the future not only must the SRV mend its relations with China, but the successor government to the PRK in Kampuchea will also have to establish friendly relations with the PRC. Given the continuing Lao–Vietnamese 'special relationship', the improvement of Lao–Chinese relations effectively prepares the way for improvements in Vietnamese–Chinese relations, which tacitly accept preponderant Vietnamese influence in Vientiane. In this way Laos' desire to further its own national interests by improving relations with China can be interpreted in both Vientiane and Hanoi as being in the interests of all three Indochinese states.

A similar rationale applies in the case of Lao–US and Lao–Thai relations. Laos alone of the three Indochinese states has at all times retained diplomatic links with the United States, though at the reduced level of *chargé d'affaires*. At first, in the period 1982 to 1984, moves on the part of the Lao Ministry of Foreign Affairs to improve relations with the United States encountered some opposition from Hanoi. Nevertheless Laos led the way on the MIA issue by cooperating with US investigators in the excavation of an aircraft crash site in Southern Laos in February 1985, and in despatching a delegation to visit the US Central Identification Laboratory in Hawaii. Laos has subsequently been removed from the Congress-approved list of enemy states, and the way is thus open for resumption of both aid and ambassadorial level representation. Again these improvements have been in both Lao national interests and concurrently in the interests of Vietnam in its campaign both to regularise relations with the US, and to encourage US support for a political settlement in Kampuchea.

The progress of Lao–Thai relations has been less smooth than that of Lao–Chinese or Lao–US relations. Lao–Thai relations have a dynamic of their own which tends to escape the rational formulation of policy in terms of joint Lao and Indochinese interests. Since 1975 a series of border shooting incidents have led to unilateral closure of the frontier by the Thai, much to the vexation of Vientiane. Suspicion and distrust runs deep on both sides, for each has seen the other as colluding with foreign powers to undermine its national security. In the eyes of the Lao Thailand has colluded with China to support both Lao and Kampuchean anti-government resistance forces in a deliberate attempt to undermine and eventually overthrow both regimes.

In the eyes of the Thai Laos is but a puppet of Vietnam and has collaborated with Hanoi to pose a military threat to Thai security.[38]

Only one Thai leader, former Prime Minister Kriangsak Chamanand, has been able to overcome this mutual distrust and suspicion. It was Kriangsak who signed with Kaysone the two communiqués of 1979; it was Kriangsak who led a delegation to Laos in August 1983 after relations had reached a new low following yet another shooting incident in which Vientiane's Lane Xang Hotel was damaged by Thai heavy weapons fire; and it was Kriangsak who undertook the shuttle diplomacy which brought about a ceasefire in the border fighting of early 1988.

Two serious outbreaks of fighting between Thai and Lao forces occurred in the 1980s – the first in mid-1984 over possession of three border villages in Laos' Sayaboury province and the second towards the end of 1987 over another small area further to the south. Both provoked angry media criticism and inconclusive diplomatic exchanges. But despite the fighting, both sides have quietly encouraged a steady build-up in mutual cross-border trade. In fact the second outbreak of fighting appears to have been both sparked off and terminated largely as a result of considerations of trade advantage.

Trading contacts, which had picked up at the local level in the latter half of 1985, expanded further in 1986, largely as a result of the Lao policy of economic decentralisation, which left it up to individual provinces to raise whatever foreign currency they could. On the government-to-government level increased trade was facilitated in 1987 by an agreement over direct transhipment of goods via Thailand, and by Bangkok's decision to reduce the number of categories of strategic goods that could not be sold to Laos without licence from 273 to 61, and then to 30 only. [39] But trade brought its own conflicts, as Lao military officers and provincial officials negotiated with their Thai opposite numbers and with sharp businessmen intent on exploiting new trading opportunities. It was reportedly one of these minor differences over logging operations in a disputed border area that led to the full-scale fighting between opposing armies that broke out in November 1987.[40]

The origins of the incident were soon lost sight of as fighting flared. But what was to have been an incisive Thai military operation to push Lao forces out of the disputed area soon deteriorated into a stalemate as the Lao clung desperately to their positions atop Hill 1428. With losses of 103 dead and 602 wounded and one F-5E fighter and one

0V-10 prop jet shot down at a cost of some US$80 million, as against estimated Lao casualties of 340 dead and 257 wounded,[41] the Thai agreed to a ceasefire arranged by Kriangsak after two visits to Vientiane. Talks between delegations from the respective foreign ministries subsequently foundered on differences of interpretation of the Franco–Siamese Treaty of 1907, which delineated the border, but the ceasefire continued to hold.

What is significant about this most recent serious incident between Laos and Thailand is its aftermath. Instead of retreating into sullen isolation, the two sides seem to have undergone a conversion: better to trade than fight. So while relations officially remain strained, commercial contacts of various kinds have begun to flourish. Lao–Thai friendship markets have sprung up along the border. Thai businessmen have been welcomed in Vientiane for the first time to partake in small joint-venture industrial projects. There is talk of large-scale Thai investments in commercial property and tourism. New timber extraction contracts are being negotiated. So why the sudden turn about?

Various suggestions have been put forward. The word in Vientiane among some diplomats is that the Lao 'victory' in holding off superior Thai forces has provided the national self-confidence necessary for Laos to treat with Thailand on a basis of some equality. A more plausible explanation is that certain Lao leaders have seized an opportunity that was never previously available. Foremost among these is General Sisavat Keobounphan, the Commander-in-Chief of the Lao army who negotiated the ceasefire with his Thai opposite number, General Chavalit Yongchaiyudh, and, as concurrently mayor of Vientiane, has made use of his high-level Thai contacts to promote trade and investment in the city. The opportunity to do this arose through the convergence of a number of factors – Sisavat and the Lao military's standing following their 'victory', realisation that the Vietnamese way to socialism had proved an economic disaster, and the need in the light of attempts to solve the 'Kampuchean problem' to build bridges to Bangkok. Together these have brought about an extraordinary, if still fragile, change in Lao–Thai relations – a change which once again advances Laos' national interests while at the same time conforming with current Vietnamese priorities.

Two further developments which occurred in 1988 deserve mention as illustrating the LPDR's determination to extend its 'multiform relations, particularly with the capitalist world. Laos welcomed the first French government minister to visit the country since 1975. This cleared the way for a subsequent mission to reach agreement on the outstanding debt Laos owes France (two-thirds cancelled, one-third paid off through a low interest loan). The way was thus opened for a rapid resumption of French aid, and for private French investment in Laos.[42] New initiatives were also taken with respect to Japan. Lao Foreign Minister Phoune Sipaseut paid his first official visit to Tokyo and the Japanese responded with increased economic assistance. A Japanese parliamentary delegation that later visited Vientiane promised a doubling of Japanese aid to Laos to around US$15 million annually within 5 years.[43] Meanwhile Laos continued to enjoy friendly relations with both Sweden and Australia.

CONCLUDING ASSESSMENT

In a study of Lao foreign policy undertaken at the end of 1985, I suggested that the decade since 1975 could be divided into three periods – from 1975 to the Vietnamese occupation of Kampuchea early in 1979, when Laos attempted to pursue a middle way between contending communist states; from 1979 to 1983, when Lao foreign policy was closely identified with that of Vietnam; and from 1983 to 1985, when tentative moves to steer a more independent course were taking place.[44] From 1986 to 1988 this last tendency became more pronounced. Both China and the United States have responded to Lao readiness to improve relations within the restraints imposed by the Vietnamese 'special relationship'. The Lao tactic of improving relations at the local level while at the same time maintaining rhetorical support for broader Indochinese (especially Vietnamese) interests, which proved so effective in the case of China, has been extended to Thailand. Denunciation of Thai policy (especially as formulated by the Ministry of Foreign Affairs) continues, though more subdued, even as commercial, cultural, and even military contacts blosssom.

Thus the logic of Lao foreign policy remains what it has always been – to ensure through the cultivation of friendly relations with all neighbouring states and as many potential aid-providing states as possible the security and continued economic development of the LPDR, all within the constraints imposed by the 'special relationship' with Vietnam. The Lao have become adept at doing one thing (pursuing friendly relations at the local level) while saying another (proclaiming their solidarity with Vietnam) – both with the full knowledge of the Vietnamese. The relationship with Vietnam still remains intact, if somewhat weakened as a result of the weakness of Vietnam itself, for the very good reason that developments which further Lao national interests serve to create conditions which Hanoi believes to be in the interests of all three Indochinese states – and of Vietnam in particular. What remains to be seen is the extent to which Lao national interests are able to predominate in the event that these are considered by Vietnamese leaders to conflict with those of Vietnam. When this last occurred in 1978–9, Vientiane was forced to toe the Hanoi line. If the present trend continues, and Laos succeeds in establishing close and friendly relations with all her neighbours and the major aid-donating states, the Vietnamese may meet with rather more resistance in bending the Lao to their will in the future – the 'special relationship' notwithstanding.

Notes

1. Statement of the First Summit Conference of the Three Countries of Indochina (Laos, Kampuchea, Vietnam), Vientiane 22–3 February 1983 (Phnom Penh, Ministry of Foreign Affairs, 1983).
2. Kaysone Phomvihan (1980) *La Revolution Lao* (Moscow: Editions du Progrès) pp. 203–8.
3. As Kaysone put it in an interview with Radio Moscow. Transcript in *Khaosan Pathet Lao* (KPL) *News Bulletin* 3 October 1988.
4. Cf. Geoffrey C. Gunn, 'Foreign Relations of the Lao People's Democratic Republic: The Ideological Imperative', *Asian Survey*, 20, 1980, pp. 990–1007.
5. Ky Son, 'The Special Vietnam-Laos Relationship Under Various Monarchies and during the Anti-French Resistance', *Vietnam Courier*, 16, no. 7, July 980, pp. 10–13.
6. The name Phomvihan was taken to emphasise the Lao side of his ancestry. It is a Buddhist technical term not otherwise used as a surname in Laos. Cf. Arthur C. Dommen (1985) *Laos: Keystone of Indochina* (Boulter, Colorado: Westview Press), p. 109.
7. For the text, see Martin Stuart-Fox (1987) *Vietnam in Laos: Hanoi's Model for Kampuchea* (Claremont, Calif.: The Keck Center for International Strategic Studies, Essays on Strategy and Diplomacy, no. 8, appendix 2.
8. On Vietnamese military assistance to Laos, see Carlyle A. Thayer, 'Laos and Vietnam: The Anatomy of a "Special Relationship", in Martin Stuart-Fox (ed.) (1982) *Contemporary Laos: Studies in the Politics and Society of the Lao{People's Democratic Republic* (St Lucia, Queensland: University of Queensland Press), pp. 255–7.
9. Foreign Broadcasts Information Service *(FBIS)*, Daily Reports for Asia and the Pacific, 8 November 1985.
10. On these frontier negotiations, see Martin Stuart-Fox (1986) *Laos: Politics, Economics and Society* (London: Frances Pinter), pp. 176–7.
11. The most recent such meeting was in Phnom Penh in July 1988.
12. For an examination of how the relationship functions in practice, see Martin Stuart-Fox, *Vietnam in Laos, op.cit.* A recent study of the relationsip is provided

by Joseph J. Zasloff, 'Vietnam and Laos: The Special Relationship'. Paper prepared for the Conference on Indochina Relationships, held by the Institute for Foreign Affairs, US Department of State, March 1987.

13. Kaysone Phomvihan, 'Thirty Years of the LPRP's Struggle for National Independence and Socialism', *Tap Chi Cong San*, March 1985. Translated in *FBIS*, 27 March 1985.
14. See Martin Stuart-Fox, *Laos: Politics, Economics and Society, op.cit.*, pp. 81–4.
15. Cf. Martin Stuart-Fox, 'National Defence and Internal Security in Laos', in Martin Stuart-Fox (ed.), *Contemporary Laos, op. cit.*, pp. 230–1.
16. *The Nation* (Bangkok), 15 May 1988.
17. I have stressed this positive aspect previously. Cf. Martin Stuart-Fox, *Laos: Politics, Economics and Society, op.cit.*, p. 201.
18. For a detailed examination of these events, see Martin Stuart-Fox, 'Laos: The Vietnamese Connection', in Leo Suryadinata (ed.) (1980) *Southeast Asian Affairs 1980* (Singapore: Institute of Southeast Asian Studies), pp. 191–209.
19. This period is examined in Martin Stuart-Fox, 'Laos in China's Anti-Vietnam Strategy', *Asia Pacific Community,* no. 11 1981, pp. 83–104.
20. Cf. Department of Press and Information of the Ministry of Foreign Affairs of Democratic Kampuchea, *Black Paper* (Phnom Penh, September 1978).
21. For the text of this agreement, see Martin Stuart-Fox, *Vietnam in Laos, op.cit.*, appendix 3.
22. It was already significant that in the booklet published in Moscow to commemorate the tenth anniversary of the founding of the LPDR, no mention was made of the Lao–Vietnamese 'special relationship' in the chapter on foreign policy. See Youri Mikheev (1985) *Les debuts du socialisme au Laos* (Moscow: Editions de l'Agence de presse Novosti).
23. *FBIS*, 8 November 1985.
24. This is an estimate of military expenditure plus approximate cost of equipment averaged out over a 10-year period. Cf. *The Military Balance 1986-1987* (London: The International Institute of Strategic Studies, 1986) where foreign military assistance for 1983 was estimated at US$125 million (p. 161).
25. Marcel Barang, 'Perestroika in the Vientiane Style', *South*, July 1988.
26. *Indochina Chronology*, 8, no. 1, Jan–March 1988, p. 13.
27. *Ibid.*
28. Cf. Sophie Quinn-Judge, 'A bear hug for ASEAN', *Far Eastern Economic Review*, 3 March 1988.
29. Cf. Nayan Chanda, 'A Troubled Friendship', *Far Eastern Economic Review*, 9 June 1988.
30. *Indochina Chronology*, 8, no. 1, Jan–March 1988, p. 13.
31. Few foreign observers accepted the reality of this so-called 'Lanna' division. Cf. MacAlister Brown and Joseph P. Zasloff (1986) *Apprentice Revolutionaries: The Communist Movement in Laos, 1930-1985* (Stanford: Hoover Institution Press), p. 185.
32. Martin Stuart-Fox, *Laos: Politics, Economics and Society, op.cit.*, p. 188.
33. *Indochina Chronology*, 5, no. 4, Oct.–Dec. 1986, p. 11.
34. *Indochina Quarterly*, 6, no. 4, Oct.–Dec. 1987, p. 13.
35. *The Nation*, Bangkok, 25 May 1988.
36. Cf. Martin Stuart-Fox, 'The Kampuchean Problem: Time for Realism', *World Review*, 27, no. 2, June 1988, pp. 56–72.
37. Cf. the collection of papers in Donald H. McMillan (ed.) (August 1988) *Conflict Resolution in Kampuchea* (Brisbane, Queensland: Centre for the Study of Australian–Asian Relations).
38. For these opposing positions, see Pheuiphanh Ngaosyvathn, 'Thai–Lao Relations: A Lao View', *Asian Survey*, 25, 1985, pp. 1242–59; and Sarasin Viraphol, 'Reflections on Lao–Thai Relations', *Asian Survey*, 25, 1985, pp. 1260–78.

39. Cf. Charles A. Joiner, 'Laos in 1987: New Economic Management Confronts the Bureaucracy', *Asian Survey*, 28 1988, pp. 95–104.
40. *The Nation's Midyear Review*, Bangkok, June 1988, p. 102.
41.   *Ibid.*, p. 101.
42. Economic Intelligence Unit, Laos, no 3, 1988, p. 21.
43. *The Nation*, Bangkok, 29 March and 2 April 1988. *FBIS*, 30 June 1988.
44. Martin Stuart-Fox, *Laos: Politics, Economics and Society, op.cit.*, p. 197.

8 Relations between Laos and Thailand, 1988
Ambassador Saly Khamsy

and

Comment on the LPDR Statement
Counsellor Pradap Pibulsonggram

RELATIONS BETWEEN LAOS AND THAILAND, 1988

Ambassador Saly Khamsy

I am particularly grateful to the Center for the Study of Foreign Affairs, Foreign Service Institute, for organising this symposium at a very opportune moment when my country is facing a threat of territorial encroachment perpetrated by one of its immediate neighbours, namely Thailand. I would like to talk on the foreign policy of the Lao PDR (People's Democratic Republic) in general, with a focus on Lao–Thai relations and, to some extent, Lao–American relations.

The relations between Lao and Thai peoples have been since time immemorial those between neighbours and brothers. The two peoples have been bound by blood ties and, by their ethnic affinities, are very close to each other in culture, language, customs, habits, and religion.

On this basis Lao–Thai relations should have developed harmoniously. However, over recent decades and quite recently they have developed in a way contrary to the wishes of the two peoples, and to the general trend of solving all contention between nations by peaceful means, which is prevalent everywhere in the world today.

The main cause of such a situation is the revival of a Pan-Thai policy by some elements within the Thai ruling circle.

As everybody knows, the Lao PDR is a small country of about $3\frac{1}{2}$ million inhabitants. Since its founding on 2 December 1975 the Lao PDR has been pursuing a policy of peace, friendship, and mutually advantageous cooperation with all countries, regardless of their different socieconomic systems, in particular with its immediate neighbours, including Thailand. The Lao PDR needs peace in order to devote all its efforts to the task of national reconstruction. Aware as we are of the benefit of this policy of peace and good neighbourly relations, the Lao government has not ceased to pursue this policy with Thailand with the aim of making our frontier with that country one of peace and friendship in the interest of both the Lao and the Thai peoples.

Untiring efforts made by the Lao government in this regard, widely supported by peace-loving world opinion, including that in Thailand itself, have been able to reach some agreements, founding thereby the juridical basis for good neighbourly relations between the two countries. Trade and transit agreements were signed in June 1978 by the two governments, following an agreement to establish a commercial air link.

Two Lao–Thai joint communiqués were signed by the Lao Chairman of the Council of Ministers Kaysone and the then Thai Prime Minister Kriangsak on 6 January and 4 April 1979, in Vientiane and Bangkok. These communiqués provided for the implementation of peace and security along the common border of more than 1,700 km, so that the people living on both sides could devote themselves peacefully to the activities of their daily life, such as fishing, cultivation on the river banks and the islands, travel, and transportation. Joint Committees for Border Contacts were established by the two sides at a local and national level, with the task of preventing or resolving, in a friendly way, all misunderstandings and conflicts likely to occur along the common border, in the spirit of non-interference in the internal affairs of the other side and respect for national sovereignty and reciprocal interests.

But, in practice, implementation of these agreements is facing many obstacles. On our side the Lao government is practising a policy of peace and good neighbourly relations, and is striving patiently and by all means to achieve them. On the other hand, it should be noted that in Thailand there are some elements in the ruling circle whose attitude is unfriendly, hostile, and even aggressive towards the Lao People's Democratic Republic. They continue to perpetrate a secret war, mainly psychological, of spying and of sabotage against Laos, aimed at creating there a climate of permanent insecurity in order to weaken us economically and to sow division among various social strata and ethnic groups. Examples of sabotage and plundering committed along the Mekong river are numerous, including attacks on and looting of our transport boats, the theft of buffaloes and oxen, and destruction of our crops.

Parallel to the above-mentioned activities, the method of armed provocation and aggression adopted against our country became more acute than ever when, in June 1984, three Lao villages of Sayaboury province were attacked and occupied by regular troops of the Thai Army. A final and just solution has not yet been found to the problem of sovereignty over these three villages, and despite the fact that the case was brought to the UN Security Council in October 1984, there was a further tragic occurrence in June 1987 in the area of Na Bo Noy commune, Botene district, in the same Lao province of Sayaboury. The Thai side dispatched its troops into this area with a view to occupying it, and to protecting a private Thai company engaged in illegally cutting and sending valuable Lao wood to Thailand. More than once the Lao local border patrols issued warnings to the offenders, who were caught red-handed. But the Thai side did not pay heed to the warnings and to our proposals for talks aimed at peacefully solving the problem, which led to armed clashes. Thereafter the Thai side reinforced its armed forces in this area, and unilaterally declared that the river (a tributary of the main river) is the border between the two countries, contrary to the provisions of the Protocol annexed to the Franco–Siamese Treaty of 23 March 1907, which stipulates unambiguously that the main river, not its tributary, constitutes the frontier between the two countries.

Since then the Thai side has chosen to aggravate the situation by unleashing large-scale attacks against Lao positions. From the beginning of December 1987 they resorted to numerous air raids and heavy artillery fire. They even used shells filled with chemical and phosphorous substances, and fragmentation bombs, against our positions. The Lao government has urged the Thai side, more than once, to hold talks with a view to settling the situation peacefully. But the Thai side has refused to comply with our legitimate request. Finally, through the initiative of the Lao Chairman of the Council of ministers Kaysone and his contact with the Thai Prime Minister, a ceasefire agreement was reached on 17 February 1988 by the Lao and

Thai military delegations, at the end of their first round of talks held in Bangkok. A second round of talks was held later in Vientiane, at the end of which both sides agreed to extend the ceasefire and the agreement on withdrawal of troops until a just political solution could be found.

In the following two rounds of political negotiations, which were held in a friendly atmosphere, alternatively in Bangkok and in Vientiane, the Thai side chose to stick to its initial position by claiming that the main river tributary is the boundary line, while the Lao side consistently relied on the provisions of the protocol annexed to the Franco–Siamese treaty of 1907, as stated above. The attitude of the Thai side demonstrated their intention to prolong negotiations and delay the solution to the border contention in this area, with the aim of continuing to encroach upon Lao territory. Hence the negotiations failed to respond to the aspirations and expectations of the peoples from both countries, as well as public opinion in the region and the world.

It is our firm conviction that, in order to succeed, the talks should be conducted in a constructive manner and that relevant legal documents such as the Franco–Siamese Treaty of 1907 and its protocol should be taken as the basis for solving the dispute. The Lao PDR has consistently taken the position that it intends to settle this border dispute by peaceful negotiations. The governmental delegation of the Lao PDR stands ready to go to Bangkok at any time to continue the negotiations, aimed at finding a just and equitable solution, in the interest of the longstanding and eternal friendship between the brotherly Lao and Thai peoples, and peace and security in Southeast Asia and in the world.

In the case of the United States, which is on the other side of the globe, Laos has never infringed the honour or interests of this country and its people. The Lao people and its government have had nothing against the American people, at any time. Laos has always respected the most fundamental principles of international relations, and expects the same from other countries.

In the humanitarian area the Lao government and people have in the past cooperated with the US government on many occasions, in particular in February 1985 and February 1986 in searching for and excavating the remains of US soldiers missing during the war against Laos. We are now, together with the US, conducting the third joint excavation of a plane crash site in the southern part of the country. All these unilateral and joint excavations show Lao goodwill and the desire to give practical help. In this connection I would like to emphasise once again that the Lao government and people have never been prejudiced against the United States, and that the settlement of humanitarian questions must be carried out in a spirit of reciprocation.

The Lao government and people greatly sympathise with the families and next-of-kin of the US soldiers missing during the war in Laos. At the same time the Lao government and people are concerned with the families of tens of thousands of fallen and handicapped Lao citizens who suffered as a result of the war. They are also concerned with the population in some areas of the country, who continue to daily suffer from the war – for example, from unexploded bombs. Therefore the Lao people wish to see equal humanity on the part of the US side in this respect.

So, in brief, we have nothing against the United States and the Americans, who are a great peace- and justice-loving people. We are looking forward to cooperating more and more with the US side in the settlement of our mutual humanitarian issues, including the MIAs. We are looking forward also to improving and normalising relations with the USA on the basis of the principle of mutual respect of independence, sovereignty, territorial integrity and non-interference in the internal affairs of each other.

COMMENT ON THE LPDR STATEMENT

Counsellor Pradap Pibulsonggram

I must admit that I was disappointed with the statement from the Laotian Representative, who portrayed Thailand as a country that harbours ill will towards Laos. Thailand is a peace-loving country. The current border dispute between Thailand and Laos was cited by the Laotian representatives to demonstrate that my country is a trouble-maker. Since the matter has been raised, I feel it necessary to give you a Thai point of view, so that readers will have a balanced and accurate perception of the situation:

1 The Thai–Lao border dispute needs to be addressed on the basis of the treaty of 1907 as a whole, as well as its Protocol and relevant maps. A resolution of such a problem cannot be based merely on a

certain part of the treaty, as put forth by the Laotian representatives.

2 The Thai government has called for setting up of a Thai–Lao joint committee to deal with the boundary, since there are some forty-two points that still pose potential problems for our two countries, because the borderline is unclear.

3 Resolution of the border problem should be settled through negotiations. Thailand pursues a policy of good neighbourliness and wishes to resolve any dispute with Laos through peaceful means. Regrettably, during the initial phase of the dispute, Laos chose instead to resort to force, causing unnecessary loss of life on both sides. We welcomed the positive trend that developed later on; both sides have now engaged in peaceful settlement, and have already undertaken two rounds of negotiations. At present we are waiting for Laos to send a delegation to Bangkok for the third round.

Thailand and Laos have a close cultural affinity. We have a longstanding record of close friendship. The Royal Thai government wishes to strengthen our bilateral relations even more. Trade currently is significant, and we want to see it expanded further. Thailand is a transit country for the external trade of landlocked Laos. Our two countries are also working closely under the UNDP-sponsored Mekong Project. We should try to work together to promote closer cooperation in all fields of endeavour for the mutual benefit of our two peoples.

Dialogue between the two countries is still ongoing, and the governments of Laos and Thailand are in touch on the matter. The new government in Bangkok will continue to try to reach a mutually satisfactory resolution of the border problem.

9 Laotian Refugees in Thailand: The Thai and US Response, 1975 to 1988
W. Courtland Robinson

INTRODUCTION

In three decades of civil and international conflict in Laos three-quarters of a million people were left homeless, their fields and villages overrun in the deadly territorial struggles between royalist, communist and neutralist armies, or blasted by an American air war that dropped more than 2 million tons of bombs on Laos, making it, on a per capita basis, the most heavily bombed nation in history.[1] Many of the refugees did not wait for the official end to leave the country, and by 2 December 1975, when the Lao People's Democratic Republic was established, more than 54,000 people already had fled into neighbouring Thailand.[2] In the years following, the refugee flows from Laos have ebbed and surged but never stopped. More than 375,000 have entered Thailand since 1975, fully 10 per cent of the population of Laos. Of these, the international community has resettled about 250,000 with the United States taking 75 per cent of this total, and another 50,000 are estimated to have settled surreptitiously in Thailand.[3] At the end of 1988 about 77,000 Laotians[4] were living in four refugee camps close to the Thai–Lao border. Only about 3,000 have chosen to repatriate voluntarily through a UN-sponsored programme, although between 15,000 and 17,000 are thought to have gone home on their own.

Thailand has played reluctant host to more than 1 million refugees from Cambodia, Laos, and Vietnam since communist governments came to power in those countries in 1975. Its asylum policies over the years have vacillated from hardline restrictionism to an open door and, moreover, have been applied differentially to various nationalities and ethnicities. But it is generally true that, since the Geneva Conference on Indochinese Refugees in July 1979, Thailand has been willing to serve as a country of temporary asylum for Indochinese refugees, in return for which the Western industrialised nations, led by the United States, have pledged to provide financial support and resettlement commitments.[5]

That reciprocal understanding suffered perhaps its most fundamental challenge in January 1988, when Thailand declared that Vietnamese boat refugees were no longer welcome and established a naval blockade to interdict boats and turn them back out to sea. One Thai official said, 'it is necessary to prevent the influx not only of the Indochinese immigrants, but also of other nationals because they can endanger our national security and create social problems'.[6] Thailand's immediate concern was a tripling of Vietnamese arrival rates from 1986 to 1987, the result, in part, of well-organised smuggling operations that brought at least 7,500 people out of Vietnam in 1987 by way of an overland route through Cambodia to the port city of Kompong Som and thence to Thailand's east coast by boat.

Thailand's longstanding ambivalence over the Indochinese refugee presence has come to a head. Foreign policy interests favour continued leniency, but domestic pressures call for increased control of the borders. The government wants refugees to leave Thailand, and sees resettlement overseas as the best alternative for those now in the country, but officials are wary that the opportunity for settlement in the West plays a significant part in encouraging further outflows.

Meanwhile the United States' long time partners in resettlement – principally France, Canada, Australia and the United Kingdom – show growing reluctance to commit to more Indochinese admissions. Even in America, where more than 800,000 Indochinese now make their homes, the issue of refugee admission numbers from Southeast Asia each year provokes deeper polarity in Congress and the Administration, as the programme's supporters and detractors engage in ever more heated debate.

The history of lowland Lao refugees in Thailand is marked by periodic, indeed almost cyclical, surges in arrivals, followed by more restrictive policies – pushbacks, humane deterrence, border screening – which initially depress arrival rates but, in turn, give way to increasing leniency and a corresponding upswing in new arrivals. The arrival patterns for hill-tribe refugees, primarily Hmong, are more erratic, but reflect some of the same trends.

Also significant is the way in which the rise and fall of international resettlement numbers have both affected, and been affected by, Thai asylum policies.

THE INITIAL EXODUS FROM LAOS

It is hardly surprising that the Hmong were the first to leave Laos in the face of a communist victory. More than 44,000 had fled into Thailand by the end of 1975. One faction of this hill-tribe group had aligned itself first with colonial French interests and later with the Royal Lao government (RLG) against the communist Pathet Lao and its ally, the Vietminh.[7] In 1961 American military advisers to the RLG contacted a Hmong general, Vang Pao, to persuade him to set up a line of defence in Xieng Khouang Province against advancing Pathet Lao troops. Thus began the CIA-financed training of the Hmong 'secret army', or 'armée clandestine', which grew to 9,000 by mid-1961 and peaked at nearly 40,000 in 1967. Hmong losses during the war were catastrophic: between 1963 and 1971 18,000 to 20,000 were killed in combat.[8] Untold thousands of civilians died in the flight from the battle zones, as the Hmong fled their mountain strongholds to the malaria-ridden lowlands. The Hmong population in Laos was estimated at about 300,000 in 1970.[9] By 1973 close to 120,000 Hmong were refugees within Laos, the great majority in Xieng Khouang. [10]

In spring 1975 it became clear to the Hmong and their American backers that the war was lost. With Pathet Lao and Vietnamese troops massing for a major assault, on 15 May, Gen. Vang Pao, along with perhaps 3,000 other Hmong, was airlifted from Long Tieng to safety in Thailand. About 60,000 Hmong fled south to establish a new base in the Phu Bia massif, while thousands more fought their way to the Mekong River and crossed to Thailand.[11]

Cooper suggests that the threat of starvation provided the Hmong with another compelling reason for mass departure. Not only had the long war removed large areas from cultivation through bombing and chemical defoliation, but also

a great many Hmong families came to rely increasingly on food drops by aircraft, handouts in the population centers, or the soldier's pay earned by adult males. Most estimates of the number of Hmong on some form of 'welfare' during this period total over one hundred thousand... When, in 1975, the alternative means of livelihood came to an abrupt end, tens of thousands of Hmong found themselves abruptly face to face not only with the fear of the enemy's revenge but also with a situation of accumulated resource scarcity... Had they remained in Laos, it is difficult to see how they could have avoided large-scale famine.[12]

In addition to the Hmong another 10,000 highlanders of other ethnicities – primarily Tai Dam, Nung and Mien – sought refuge in Thailand in 1975. The Tai Dam and Nung, who numbered about 2,000, had originally left Vietnam after the 1954 Geneva Accords and were simply continuing to run from their old enemies, the Vietminh. In July and August several thousand Mien crossed into Thailand from the provinces of Luang Prabang and Sayaboury.[13]

The lowlanders, or ethnic Lao, did not leave the country nearly so precipitately as the Hmong, although by the year's end just over 10,000 had crossed into Thailand. Larger outflows were triggered in late 1975 and early 1976, when the new regime rounded up 10,000 to 15,000 former RLG military and police officers, government officials, and others suspected of royalist sympathies, and transported them to remote 're-education' camps to the northeast and southeast, where their socialist transformation was to be achieved through enforced attendance at political 'seminars' and collective manual labour.[14]

In May 1976 the LPDR rounded up about 1,300 of Vientiane's 'prostitutes, addicts, gamblers, hippies, thieves and lost children' and took them to 're-education centers for social evils' near the Nam Ngum Dam.[15] Lao arrivals in Thailand averaged 18,500 annually in 1976 and 1977.

The Thai Response

By early 1975 Thailand had established twenty-one temporary camps along its Lao and Cambodian borders to accommodate the influx of Indochinese. In July of that year the Royal Thai government signed an agreement with the UN High Commissioner for Refugees (UNHCR), under which Thailand continued to provide temporary assistance to the refugees – food, shelter, clothing and medical care – and UNHCR sought international contributions of cash, materials, equipment and services.[16]

By October there were nearly 50,000 Laotian refugees in camps dotting the border provinces from Chiang Rai in the north to Ubon in the northeast. The largest camps were near Nan (14,000 Hmong and Lao), Nong Khai (14,500 Lao, Hmong and Tai Dam), and Khon Kaen (12,600 Hmong). Ubon, one of the very first Laotian camps, housed only 500 Lao in late 1975. Three years later, it would swell to 38,000.[17]

Since the beginning of the Indochinese refugee influx, Thailand has officially characterised the arrivals as *phu opayop* or 'displaced persons', such a person being defined by regulations first issued in 1954 as someone 'who escapes from dangers due to an uprising, fighting or war, and enters in breach of the Immigration Act'.[18] Muntarbhorn notes that 'in principle, therefore, all displaced persons are prima facie illegal immigrants' and, as such, are subject to imprisonment, fines and expulsion.[19] Indeed the Thai government made clear as early as August 1975 that its immigration laws applied equally to Indochinese.[20] Thailand is not signatory to the 1951 Geneva Convention relating to the status of refugees and the 1967 Protocol, which define a refugee as any person who

owing to well-founded fear of being persecuted for reasons of race, religion, nationality, membership of a particular social group or political opinion, is outside the country of his nationality and is unable or, owing to such fear, is unwilling to avail himself of the protection of that country; or, who, not having a nationality and being outside the country of his former habitual residence is unable or, owing to such fear, is unwilling to return to it.[21]

Negative government statements, temporary detention by border police, fines, and even occasional pushbacks of incoming refugees at the Mekong River border did little to deter initial arrivals, so Thailand ultimately relented and, from 1975 to 1977, Laotian refugees enjoyed virtually unimpeded access to UNHCR camps. In addition to coordinating international contributions to refugee programmes UNHCR carried out its traditional mandate of protecting refugees while it undertook to search for one of three 'durable solutions' local integration, resettlement overseas, and voluntary repatriation.

The US Response

In the hectic days and weeks before Saigon fell to communist forces on 30 April 1975 the US government helped to evacuate nearly 130,000 Vietnamese. Virtually all of them were resettled in the United States under the parole authority of the Attorney General, which enabled him, 'for emergent reasons or for reasons deemed strictly in the public interest', to admit individuals or groups into the country without regard to the numerical limitations set in the Immigration and Nationality Act.[22] US criteria for the admission of Indochinese refugees were based on close family ties in the United States, previous employment by the US government, and close association with the US government.[23]

In August 1975 the Attorney General, in consultation with the Department of State and with Congress, authorised the admission of the first group of Laotian refugees, totalling 3,466 people, under the 'Lao Parole Program'. Less than a year later, in May 1976, the US government instituted the 'Extended Parole Program', which allowed for the resettlement of an additional 11,000 land refugees, mostly Laotians, but including also a small number of Cambodians and Vietnamese.

The United States clearly was acting out of a sense of obligation to its wartime allies in offering resettlement to former government and military officials and their families. The Hmong, however, speak of a more fundamental commitment made to them as a people. One Hmong phrased the American 'contract' as: 'You help us fight for your country, and if you can't win, we will take you with us and will help you live'. A Hmong resettlement study concluded that, 'Though there are several versions of the "Promise", there can be no doubt that assurances were made to support the Hmong during the war, and to provide assistance in the event Laos was lost'.[24]

By the middle of 1976 UNHCR was persuaded that the best course for the Laotian refugees was either local integration in Thailand or voluntary repatriation. When the US Ambassador to Thailand called Cesare Berta, the UNHCR regional representative, to inform him of the second parole programme for Laotians, Berta reportedly said, 'This is a catastrophe. This is disastrous'.[25] UNHCR at that time was active inside Laos with the relocation of the hundreds of thousands of people displaced by the war, and feared that the prospect of large-scale overseas resettlement would draw many over the border.

Laotians continued to cross the border, and on 22 July 1977 the Thai government and UNHCR signed an agreement stating, 'It is recognized that a distinction must be made between persons who qualify as being within the competence of UNHCR and those who leave their country of nationality or habitual residence for reasons of personal convenience, for example, economic migrants, or persons who are not bona fide refugees'.[26] To sort out such distinctions, Thailand asked the UNHCR for assistance in developing procedural guidelines to implement a screening programme for new arrivals. US officials in Bangkok reportedly protested and the idea was not long pursued.[27] In August another Indochinese parole programme was authorised for 15,000 people, and admissions criteria were further liberalised to include individuals without previous ties to the United States but who had not been offered resettlement by any other country and who presented 'compelling humanitarian reasons'.[28] Parole of another 7,000 was authorized in January 1978. By that point, the United States had admitted 4,752 Hmong and other hill-tribe people, and 5,949 Lao.

The Lao Surge

In 1978 lowland Lao arrivals in Thailand jumped to 48,781, nearly three times the number for the previous year and far the largest annual total before or since. The reasons for this surge are varied. Many certainly feared the possibility of re-education camp. Van-es-Beeck cites a litany of other reasons for flight, including alarm at the degree of Vietnamese control, the disorganisation of the public service, the poor state of economy, and the 'petty controls of a suspicious administration ...limitations on freedom of movement and on the sale of produce, the introduction of pricing, agriculture taxes, the obligation of civil servants to cultivate a cooperative garden and to attend political seminars, and the disappearance of benefits deriving from Lao contacts with the West'.[29]

Zasloff has noted the 'widespread discontent' in the Mekong River Valley at government efforts to collectivise agriculture. As one refugee put it, 'People feel that the fields and buffalo don't belong to them but to the community. They grow poorer'. An Asian Development Bank report in 1979 stated that 17 per cent of the rural population were in farming cooperatives.[30]

Food shortages also contributed to the refugee flow. Several years of serious drought had created a grain deficit estimated at 112,975 tons in March 1978. The shortages were exacerbated by production disincentives such as a stiff agricultural tax and rapid collectivisation.[31]

It is impossible to calculate how many Lao would not have left their country if no overseas resettlement opportunities had been available. Even without such prospects, Thailand had its attractions. It was just across the Mekong River, after all, linguistically and culturally compatible, with a better economy and a (relatively) stable government. This is not to disparage the fear and desperation that forced so many to leave their homeland. It is to point out, nonetheless, that the patterns of Lao movement into Thailand closely follow the fluctuations in the asylum policies of Thailand as they offered, or withheld, access to resettlement.

Hmong and other hill-tribe migrations, on the other hand, showed little of the same patterns. After the initial influx of 45,000 in 1975, hill-tribe refugee movements tailed off, averaging just over 6,000 per year from 1976 to 1978. But in 1979 arrivals in Thailand rose again dramatically to 24,000. LPDR and Vietnamese forces had continued their attacks on Hmong resistance efforts in the Phou Bia and Phou Ta Mao mountains in 1976–8. The French newspaper *Le Monde* reported in 1978 that 7,000 Hmong had been killed in Laos since 1975. Vang Pao has cited a vastly higher figure of 95,000 Hmong dead during the same period. Chemical poisoning, he claims, killed 50,000, while another 45,000 died 'from starvation and disease or were shot trying to escape to Thailand'.[32]

Additional factors contributing to the continued Hmong exodus included acute shortages of medicine, strict food rationing, rice tax, low agricultural productivity, arbitrary arrests, labour conscription, and work collectivisation.[33]

DETERRENCE AND CONSOLIDATION

The spring and summer of 1979 witnessed an explosion of refugees from Indochina. The Vietnamese invasion of Cambodia and the outbreak of a violent border war between China and Vietnam triggered massive flows into Thailand, Malaysia, Indonesia, the Philippines and Hong Kong. Nearly 60,000 Vietnamese arrived in first-asylum countries in June alone, and the total refugee population in the region climbed above half a million. At the Geneva Conference on Indochinese Refugees in July 1979 worldwide resettlement pledges totalled 260,000. President Carter announced that the United

States, for its part, would admit 168,000 Indochinese for the year, a rate of 14,000 people every month.

By the end of 1979 a total of 146,619 Indochinese had been moved from Thailand to resettle overseas, almost half of those in 1979 alone. But Thailand's refugee population stood at 271,582, including 135,744 Cambodians, 126,537 Laotians, and 9,301 Vietnamese. Clearly resettlement alone would not solve the problem, and Thailand was growing impatient. 'The influx of displaced persons into Thailand has affected our economic, political, and national security sectors', said the Ministry of Interior (MOI) in September 1979, and proceeded to count the ways: refugees were a financial burden, they disrupted the local economy, they damaged national resources, they created discontentment among the people, they made Thailand lose credibility with its neighbours, they distracted local officials from serving Thai citizens, they provoked hostile activity between Thailand and neighbouring countries, and they might be engaged in spying and subversive activity. 'We do not have an open-door policy', MOI stated. 'As a matter of record, our borders are closed. Displaced persons who enter our country do so illegally.'[34]

In March 1980 the Thai and Lao governments initiated a programme of voluntarily repatriation for refugees in cooperation with UNHCR, but only 193 Lao chose to return in the first year. In 1981 279 Lao and 261 highlanders returned to Laos, and in 1982 the numbers of Lao and hill-tribe repatriates climbed modestly to 791 and 278 respectively. That, as it turned out, was to be the highwater mark for the programme. As of January 1988, a total of 3,136 Laotians, including 890 hill-tribe people, have voluntarily returned home via this programme, although it is believed that for every 'official' repatriate, four return on their own.[35]

Humane Deterrence

International resettlement continued to move large numbers of Laotians out of Thailand through 1980–1, and camp populations slowly were beginning to decline. The United States admitted more than 27,000 hill-tribe and 31,000 Lao in 1980, its largest ever annual total for Laotian refugees. Thai officials remained concerned that camp conditions, coupled with availability of overseas resettlement, were creating too much of a lure. In January 1981 Thailand instituted a policy of 'humane deterrence' for Laotian refugees, especially the lowland Lao. A new camp, Nakhon Phanom or Na Pho, was opened on 1 January and all newly arriving Lao were placed there, without access to resettlement. Moreover a more austere level of services was established, 'intended to maintain existing refugees at a living standard below that of Thai citizens'.[36] Refugees lived in block-style housing, five persons to a room, twenty rooms to a house. Rations were 'survival-level', and international aid agencies were prohibited in camp.[37]

US refugee officials generally approved of these new measures, though not without misgivings. In August 1981 a special refugee advisory panel commissioned by the State Department and headed by Marshall Green filed its report on the Indochinese refugee programme:

> The prospect of an ongoing, substantial exodus strongly underlines the urgency for humane measures to deter the flow of increasing numbers of refugees whose reasons for fleeing derive more from normal migration motives than from fear of persecution. Certain deterrents, such as austere camps, sealing of borders, or keeping people in holding centers or refugee camps for long periods of time, are not attractive prospects. Yet these and other mea-sures...must be considered.[38]

The US refugee programme in Southeast Asia was under intense scrutiny and pressure to scale back in 1981. More than 500,000 Indochinese had resettled in hundreds of communities all across America, thousands more were arriving every month, and the resettlement system seemed strained to breaking. Refugee welfare dependency rates were at 67 per cent, and local service providers felt overwhelmed and underinformed as to who these new Americans were and what they needed. Restrictionist attitudes had been rein-forced by the influx of 130,000 Cubans during the Mariel boatlift in the spring and summer of 1980, as well as by thousands of Haitian boat people fleeing political oppression and poverty.

In addition the United States had passed a major new Refugee Act in March 1980 which, among other things, had redefined refugee status to bring it in line with the UNHCR definition. Gone were the old geographical and ideological restrictions that limited refugee status to someone fleeing a communist country or the Middle East. But gone, too, was the system of ad hoc parole programmes. Instead Congress and the Administration were to consult before each fiscal year on the numbers of refugees to be admitted. The new Act also gave the Attorney General responsibility for determining refugee admissibility, a responsibility that was, in turn, delegated to the Immigration and Naturalisation Service (INS), within the Department of Justice.

Not long after the new act was passed INS began to insist that Indochinese applicants for refugee admission must undergo case-by-case processing, and were no longer entitled to 'blanket' refugee status as a group. The State Department argued otherwise and, through vigorous lobbying at the cabinet level, was able to postpone case-by-case determinations at least until 30 September 1981, the end of the fiscal year, but the contest was far from over.[39]

The Green report sought a middle ground in this debate. 'It is imperative that the refugee, as defined, remain a distinctive category of person', the report said, though it expressed the view that 'as far as the Indochinese refugees are concerned, it is proper to maintain the current presumption that all those who have fled to date and are available for resettlement are refugees within the meaning of the Refugee Act'. The report suggested, however, that some distinctions might need to be made in the future. Vietnamese, it said, 'are entitled to refugee status. The same conclusion was reached as to the Hmong people of the Laotian highlands. The Panel was less certain of the validity of this conclusion as to Lao lowlanders...the majority of people now fleeing seemed to be primarily motivated by a desire to improve their basic living conditions'.[40]

Following the imposition of humane deterrence policies, Lao arrivals in Thailand fell dramatically, from 29,000 in 1980 to 16,400 in 1981, then to 3,200 in 1982. Hill-tribe arrivals showed a corresponding decline from 14,800 in 1980 to just 1,800 in 1982. Lest this decrease be ascribed solely to Thailand's deterrence policies, it should be noted that during this same period the LPDR began to moderate the pace of collectivisation, relax tax regulations, and release some of the re–education camp detainees.[41]

Consolidation

As Laotian arrivals decreased, Thai authorities undertook a consolidation and ethnic 'homogenisation' of the Laotian camps. During 1982 three hill-tribe camps – Chiang Khong, Chiang Kham, and Sob Tang – were officially closed, and their populations moved to Ban Nam Yao. The lowland Lao camps, Ubon and Nong Khai, were also closed, with the Hmong in Nong Khai moving to Ban Vinai and the Lao to Na Pho.

Opened in December 1975 to accommodate the initial exodus of Hmong from Xieng Khouang, Ban Vinai is located 12 kilometres from the Mekong River separating Laos and Thailand. The camp maintained a population of around 11,000 until 1979, when a large influx from Laos nearly tripled that figure. The population increased again in 1982, with the movement of 11,000 Hmong from Nong Khai, and in 1983 when 8,000 highlanders were relocated from Ban Nam Yao. By June 1984 Ban Vinai was 90 per cent Hmong, with a population of 44,000.

First-time visitors to Ban Vinai are struck by the absence of barbed-wire fences and prominent sentry outposts. The road in from the main gate is lined with dozens of small shops selling brightly coloured *pa ndau* quilts and story-cloths. Ban Vinai has an open, settled look to it, more like a village than a refugee camp. In fact it does have one of the highest living standards of any refugee camp in Southeast Asia, one that compares favourably in some ways to life outside the camp in Thailand's poverty-stricken northeast.

A 1986 survey of the camp suggested, however, that rural comparisons are misleading; a more apt analogy might be Bangkok's infamous Klong Toey slum:

> Like other poor urban communities, Ban Vinai has problems of inadequate health, overcrowding, welfare dependency, unemployment, substance abuse, prostitution, and anomie (suicide, abandonment, loneliness). Furthermore, like other rural migrants to the city, Ban Vinai refugees are adjusting to life in a densely populated area, and from the life of a cultivator to the schedule and complexity of an urban environment. As refugees, however, they face the additional stresses of living in at best a temporary haven.[42]

The haven the Hmong had found was not nearly temporary enough to suit some Thai officials, and they watched with alarm as Hmong resettlement to the United States plummeted from 27,000 in 1980 to 3,800 in 1981, and remained at that level through 1986. These numbers were scarcely offsetting the Ban Vinai birth rate of 5.4 per cent, to say nothing of new arrivals from Laos.[43] Despite declining refugee admissions ceilings in the United States, the door was still open for the Hmong. They simply chose not to step through.

There were several reasons for this reluctance to move. First, Vang Pao and other resistance leaders were concerned that large-scale resettlement of Hmong was depleting both the supply and the resolve of their fighters, and reportedly sent a message to Ban Vinai that people were to stay put. One former military commander under Vang Pao said, 'I stay [in Ban Vinai] I have power. In the U.S., I have free decision, independence, but no power'.[44] Even freedom seemed circumscribed in the United States as word filtered back to the camp of the resettlement 'horror stories': welfare rates broaching 100 per cent in several Hmong communities, death that came in the middle of the night to seemingly healthy young men, families cooped up in crowded tenement housing, no jobs, no land to farm, no place, it seemed, for the Hmong. Ban Vinai looked better all the time, with its guaranteed shelter, food, security, and health care. And for increasing numbers of Hmong, it was the only home they had ever known.

When Thai officials reopened Chiang Kham as a humane deterrence facility in May 1983, little more than 1 year after the camp had closed, it was not to deter new arrivals – only 1,800 highlanders entered Thailand in 1982 – so much as to press Ban Vinai residents either to seek resettlement or go back to Laos. Ban Vinai was closed to all new arrivals. Those who tried to enter the camp clandestinely were rounded up and packed off to Chiang Kham, with its barbed wire, minimal services and no opportunity for resettlement.

Oddly enough, at the very time Thailand was tightening its policies for hill-tribe refugee groups, it was relaxing them for lowland Lao. Both the UNHCR and, to a greater extent, the US Embassy had been pressing Thailand for access to some of the priority cases in Na Pho: former military officers and re–education camp prisoners, as well as families that had been split by the new deterrence policies. Fathers who had reached Thailand before the new policies took hold, for example, and had been cleared for admission to the United States, refused to leave without their wives and children, who had followed them out and were now stuck in Na Pho. In mid-1983 Thailand allowed resettlement interviews for several thousand of such cases in Na Pho. In 1984 lowland Lao arrivals totalled 14,600, more than triple the previous year. Factors inside Laos that contributed to this surge included the levying of a new tax and beginning of a new military conscription. A 1985 Senate report noted that there were 5,000 to 6,000 single men in Na Pho, ranging in age from 15 to 25, but concluded that the initiation of resettlement processing in the camp was the 'primary cause' for the new wave of Lao arrivals in 1984. 'The pull factor created by the U.S. refugee resettlement program simply cannot be underestimated.'[45] By the middle of 1985 Na Pho held 38,000 people. Partly to relieve the intense overcrowding, international resettlement commitments for lowland Lao rose from 4,800 in 1985 to 11,600 in 1986.

Resettlement interviewing eventually was made available to some of the Hmong and other hill-tribe groups in Chiang Kham in 1985. The United States took 750 from Chiang Kham that year, and in 1986 the Thai Ministry of the Interior informed the embassies of the resettlement countries that they were free to interview anyone in Chiang Kham, Na Pho and Sikhiu, a humane deterrence camp for boat Vietnamese.[46]

More than 18,000 Laotians crossed into Thailand in 1984, and Laotian camp populations climbed to 80,000. Alarmed at this new influx and acting presumably on directives from Bangkok, local border officials began to turn away asylum-seekers early in 1985. A fact-finding team from the US Committee for Refugees, a private refugee advocacy group, visited fifteen immigration and police stations along the Thai–Lao border in June 1985 and found that local officals 'freely explained that new arrivals were routinely pushed back'. The team found that 'significant numbers' of pushbacks had occurred, that 'the greatest impact had been on the Hmong', and noted an 'immediate and substantial' drop in arrivals.[47] US Embassy figures, for example, recorded 11,418 Laotian arrivals in Nong Khai province in 1984, with monthly arrivals for the last 3 months of the year rising from 1,100 to 1,400 to 1,700. In January 1985 arrivals tallied only 406, dropped to zero the next month, and totalled only 34 from March to June. For all of 1985 hill-tribe arrivals were only 943, down from 3,600 the previous year.

Under pressure from the international community to find an alternative to pushbacks that might still deter Laotian migration, Thailand settled, for the second time, on the idea of a screening programme.

THE LAOTIAN BORDER SCREENING PROGRAMME

On 1 July 1985 Thailand, with the cooperation of UNHCR and the support of the US Embassy, implemented a border screening programme for Laotian asylum-seekers. Three hundred MOI officials were enrolled in a short training course on interviewing. According to a 1985 MOI internal document, screening questions were to focus on residence, place of birth, education, occupation, economic status, family composition, political activity, criminal record, and reasons for fleeing to Thailand. 'Those who are refugees' initially included three categories:

1 former officials, military, or police during the pre-LPDR period;
2 persons who used to work in embassies, international organisations, foreign firms during the pre-LPDR period;
3 persons who participated in political and social movements against the communist governments.

'Those who are illegal immigrants' included:

1 persons who claim dissatisfaction with the new regime, owing to tax collection, forced labour or the draft;
2 persons who desire to have a place for business because of their dissatisfaction with the LPDR economic system;
3 persons influenced by others, especially Lao hill tribes;
4 persons who claim relatives in Thailand or a third country

As far as can be ascertained, these lists were never made public.

Thailand's stated screening criteria for refugee status now include a fourth category for persons who have relatives in a third country. The inclusion of this last category suggests that Thailand has been willing to screen in only those people with a reasonable chance of resettlement, and seeks to screen out all the rest. As one senior Thai official put it, 'If they are not refugees for other countries, they are not refugees for Thailand either'.[48]

The screening process theoretically has three stages. Cases are bought to one of nine MOI district committee officers for an interview, which UNHCR legal advisers can attend as observers. If the case is screened in, it is then sent to the MOI provincial committee or the provincial governor for confirmation. Once confirmed, those who are screened in are sent to either Ban Vinai or Na Pho, depending on their ethnicity. If the case is rejected, UNHCR is given an opportunity to appeal before the screened-out individuals are placed in a detention centre pending repatriation to Laos.[49]

In December 1985 UNHCR reported the screening of 2,064 Laotians, of whom 1,055 people had been approved, 593 rejected, and 416 put on hold pending further proof. By the end of 1986, 18 months after screening had begun, a total of 7,021 people had been interviewed, with 4,665 approved, 1,822 rejected, and 440 pending. The number of interviews was substantial, and the 66 per cent approval rate exceeded many expectations; but it became clear that there was a problem developing: hardly any Hmong were getting screened, and evidence suggested that pushbacks, primarily of Hmong, were re-emerging as a common practice. A UNHCR internal document reported pushbacks of 362 people in 1986.

Thailand denied that the pushbacks were anything more than local aberrations and insisted that the Hmong were purposely circumventing the screening programme and entering, instead, through organised smuggling rings. 'It's a vicious circle', admitted a UNHCR legal officer in Bangkok. 'The Hmong are sneaking into Thailand because they feel they might be pushed back to Laos if they make their presence known. And because the Hmong are still sneaking in, pushbacks are more likely to take place.'[50]

The circle turned more vicious still in 1987, as Thai authorities barred close to 1,300 Hmong near Nam Pun, a remote border area in Nan province, from seeking asylum and assistance in Thailand. Months went by without access to adequate food and medical care, despite appeals by UNHCR and international aid organisations. In Ban Vinai, on 15 March, local Thai officials removed thirty-eight Hmong from camp and returned them to Laos. The action prompted a swift and strong protest from the United States. 'We are protesting this action to the Thai government as a serious breach of human rights', a State Department spokeman said. 'We view this incident as possibly the most serious instance of forced repatriation from Thailand since 1979', when nearly 40,000 Cambodians were forced back across the Thai–Cambodian border. Two days after the first incident, ninety-seven Hmong were apprehended trying to enter Ban Vinai and repatriated.[51]

Thai government statements reiterated the policy that 'armed resistance groups who attempt to cross the border into Thailand are denied entry' and that 'those who come across with the assistance of organised smuggling rings are apprehended as illegal immigrants'. The Nam Pun group was in the first category, Thai officials maintained, and the Ban Vinai group was in the second.

Later in the year Thai policy on the Hmong softened, influenced by a redoubled US effort that resettled 8,400 highlanders, the third largest number ever to be resettled in a single year. Thai officials agreed to admit the Nam Pun group into the screening process, and to do the same for an estimated 10,000 unregistered Hmong living in and around Ban Vinai. From December 1987 to January 1988 9,610 Hmong in Ban Vinai were moved to Chiang Kham for screening. As of March, 3,581 of the Ban Vinai transfers had been interviewed and 98 per cent had been screened in. By April 1,700 Hmong had been moved from Nam Pun to Ban Nam Yao for screening.

Access to the screening process for new arrivals, highland and lowland, was more difficult than ever before in 1988. From January to March only about 500 Laotian new arrivals were screened at the border provinces. Some pushbacks did occur but, more frequently, district officials refused to interview the newcomers for fear that doing so could invite accusations of collaboration in the smuggling rings.

By the end of 1988 the border screening programme was in a state of almost total collapse. Lack of access has certainly been the most serious flaw, but rampant extortion and bribery have also impeached the credibility of the screening decisions. Refugees have reported paying amounts ranging from 2,000 to 36,000 Baht(US80–1,500), some simply to enter the process, others to obtain a favourable decision or to be transferred to a UNHCR camp.

A final difficulty has been the reluctance of the LPDR to take back any of the screened-out people, despite a tentative agreement reached with UNHCR to do so. With close to 2,500 people rejected by the screening process and waiting in crowded detention centres, only forty-four had actually been returned to Laos as of December 1988.

THE SITUATION TODAY

The Laotian refugee situation in Thailand today is an intricate mix of convoluted, even contradictory, trends and signals. The screening programme seems to have failed, though perhaps not irreparably. Voluntary repatriation, at least for lowland Lao, has enjoyed a limited success, though it is far more problematic for the Hmong. Local integration has never been tried on more than a token scale.

Resettlement, for its part, has served a critical protection function in maintaining relatively open borders, but has inadvertantly contributed to larger outflows of Laotian asylum-seekers. With continued refugee flows, pushbacks, tragically, also continue, and tensions run high along the border.

Amid all this, one statistic stands out. Of the 77,000 Laotian refugees in Thailand, more than 60 per cent have been in camps for over 4 years. There is no simple way to unravel such a knot; indeed only by a proliferation of alternatives, of many answers, will any solutions be found.

Repatriation

The fact that only about 17,000 people may have returned to Laos in the last 13 years is hardly an encouraging sign for the future. For repatriation ever to work on a larger scale, it must be both safer and more advantageous than prolonged stay in a refugee camp. Information from UNHCR is sketchy on the status of returnees, but there have been no solid reports of government reprisals. To assist with initial reintegration, UNHCR provides every returnee with a resettlement kit, which includes such items as cloth, mats, sewing kits, kitchen utensils, and occasionally tools necessary to resume a former occupation. Rice is also provided for the first 6 to 12 months.

Since 1980 UNHCR has also invested more than $2.5 million in development projects in eight different provinces where returnees have settled. Typical projects have included the construction of schools, rural dispensaries and irrigation systems, as well as the provision of technical assistance and vocational training.[52]

Expansion of such development initiatives, particularly in the provinces immediately bordering Thailand, could only improve the prospects of repatriation. Thailand in particular should be encouraged to invest in Mekong River area development as one way of easing tensions along the border.

To the extent that repatriation has worked at all, however, it has worked for the lowland Lao. For the Hmong ever to return in large numbers to Laos would probably first require a more overtly political settlement. The scapegoating and rejection that the Hmong now encounter on both sides of the Mekong, aggravated certainly by continued resistance activity, remain a serious human rights concern and pose one of the most intractable dilemmas confronting Thai–Lao relations.

Local Integration

Of all the roads not taken in the Indochinese refugee programme, perhaps the most tantalising is that of local integration, which has never amounted to more than a token gesture in the Laotian refugee context. Some have argued that this is the fault of a massive international resettlement effort that quickly sapped any interest Thailand or the refugees might have had in such an idea. One Senate report in 1978 stated that the Thai government 'has always recognized the need for some local settlement, and has agreed, in principle, with the UNHCR's proposals for the local settlement of refugees; the only question is timing'.[53] The report mentioned one estimate for an integrated rural development project for up to 50,000 refugees and costing $30 million per year over a 3 to 4 year period.

Optimal timing for such a venture presumably awaited a lull or, better yet, a cessation in refugee flows, since, the report continued, 'rightly or wrongly, the Thais have feared that moving on a program of local settlement would simply encourage a heavier influx'. Arrival rates have been down since 1982, but that can hardly be called a lull, and, Thailand no doubt would insist, such a circumstance has been achieved only through more restrictive asylum policies.

Others argue that Thailand never seriously considered local settlement on a large scale. A 1979 MOI document did speak encouragingly of using UNHCR funds for such self-help projects as cultivating family-centred gardens, raising livestock, and developing handicrafts and other cottage industries. But it also said, 'Some high ranking foreign officers have suggested displaced persons be permitted to resettle in Thailand. Someone has even offered to make U.S. $2 million available to begin such a program. Thailand neither asks for nor wants money – we want the displaced persons out of our country'.[54]

Aside from the estimated 50,000 or so Laotians who have unofficially settled in Thailand in the last 13 years, the only successful local integration project is Ban Sob Kok village, where about 600 ethnic Htin and Hmong were allowed to settle after their release from Ban Nam Yao in 1984. With seed money of less than $40,000, a voluntary agency named the Ockenden Venture launched the project, which became self-sufficient within 2 or 3 years, thanks to a wide array of initiatives, including diversification of crops, soil protection, fishponds, handicraft industries, health care and hygiene, and primary education.[55] There are also 1,799 hill-tribe people in Ban Nam Yao awaiting settlement of their claims to Thai citizenship.

Resettlement

Since 1982 the United States has steadily reduced its refugee admissions ceilings for Southeast Asia, although the Laotian percentage of the Indochinese total has gradually increased, from 9 per cent in 1982 to 40 per cent in 1987. As numbers decreased, from 73,500 in fiscal year 1982 to 40,000 in 1987, restrictions multiplied. On 21 April 1982 the United States announced that, as of 30 April, refugees entering asylum countries would need to demonstrate a close US link in order to be considered for resettlement. In the parlance of refugee processing this eliminated Priority-6, which comprises people 'with no immediate relatives already in the United States, no history of employment with the U.S. government or U.S.-based organizations, and no connections with the U.S.-supported, pre-April 1975 governments of the Indochinese countries'.[56]

In August 1983 the INS published its *Worldwide Guidelines for Overseas Refugee Processing,* primarily in response to a presidential directive calling upon the Attorney General to 'determine whether there are categories of persons who, under the Refugee Act of 1980, share common characteristics that identify them as targets of persecution in a particular country'.[57] The intent of this directive clearly was to find a compromise between the proponents of 'blanket' refugee eligibility for all who fled Indochina, and those who favoured case by case interviewing for everyone. For individuals from Laos the INS established the following categories: former officials of the Royal Lao Government; former members of the Royal Lao Military; persons required to undergo re–education, or who were imprisoned because they were considered politically or socially undesirable; persons formerly or presently employed by US or Western institutions, or persons educated in the West; Hmong; and accompanying family members of anyone falling into these categories.[58]

From June 1983 to June 1987 INS approval rates for the Hmong held constant at 99 per cent, while Lao approval rates averaged 77 per cent but dropped for periods of time to 50 or 60 per cent. By comparison, Vietnamese rates averaged 89 per cent during the same period, while Cambodian approval rates were the lowest of all the groups at 70 per cent.

More than 8,400 Hmong resettled in the United States in 1987, and more than 10,000 in 1988. In 1986 Hmong attitudes shifted in favour of resettlement, and by the middle of the year more than 10,000 Hmong had signed a list expressing interest in going to the United States.[59] This disposition may be shifting back to neutral again, although the younger generation still tends to lean toward resettle-ment. 'At the moment, we're just managing to meet our quotas', said an official with the Joint Voluntary Agency (JVA) in Thailand, which prescreens and prepares refugee cases for interviewing by INS; 'I've got cases on my books where they've said they'll maybe go in 1989 or 1990 or just "next time, next time". They get pressure from their elders who don't want to make the move or they've heard reports from relatives that life isn't so easy abroad'.[60]

International resettlement should continue to be provided to the Hmong who seek it, but more care should be taken that they are not coerced in the process. There is little question that Thai pushbacks of the Hmong have been coupled with pressure on the United States to admit larger numbers, which raises very real fears that resettlement is being manipulated to, in effect, reward inhumane practices. It is also important for Thailand to come to terms with the fact that it has become a regional haven for hill-tribe people, not only from Laos but from Burma as well. More than 25,000 highland refugees from Burma, predominately Karen, have fled into Thailand to escape recurring conflicts with the Burmese government. Recently the Thai government has stepped up efforts to repatriate some of these groups. On 18 September 1987, for example, officials in Chiang Rai province began a 10-day operation to push back 1,800 people of the Lisu and Akha ethnic groups.[61]

Thailand, it should be noted, often has demonstrated considerable concern and innovation in dealing with most of its nearly 400,000 hill tribe people, 50,000 of whom are Hmong.[62] Some of these development-oriented approaches could be well applied in the case of the Laotian Hmong, rather than exclusively relying upon heavy-handed immigration enforcement.

Despite Na Pho's official designation as an austere, closed camp, the reality is somewhat more benign. The population is down to about 19,000, so overcrowding has eased considerably. The camp has a 'relatively intact and coherent social structure' and, with the restrictions on international voluntary agency activity, residents have assumed greater responsibility for services, particularly in the areas of education and social services. Relations with the Thai camp officials and local villagers are some of the best in Thailand. Residents have permission on a limited basis to go outside the camp, even to take part-time work.[63]

Na Pho is, at heart, still a refugee camp, however, and most of the people would prefer resettlement. Former re-education camp pri-soners and their families should continue to have priority in US admissions. But the patterns of previous Lao movement into Thailand suggest that any steps taken to modify current resettlement restrictions in order to move the 6,800 'longstayers' in Na Pho might simply trigger increased inflows, thereby compounding the problem rather than resolving it. Rather the international community should encourage and support Thailand to expand self-sufficiency projects in Na Pho, until such time as camp residents can be integrated locally or return home.

The United States should also expand its dialogue with Laos on the issue of establishing normal immigration channels for both Hmong and lowland Lao. In return for progress on this issue increased

Table 9.1 Laotian refugee movement to and resettlement from Thailand

	Arrivals	HILL-TRIBE Resettlement		Camp population
		Worldwide	US only	
1975	44,659	454	450	44,205
1976	7,266	4,593	4,250	46,878
1977	3,873	2,418	52	48,270
1978	8,013	5,424	3,873	50,859
1979	23,943	12,328	11,301	61,474
1980	14,801	28,927	27,247	53,866
1981	4,356	4,437	3,789	56,054
1982	1,816	3,003	2,511	52,918
1983	2,920	1,414	1,162	47,343
1984	3,627	2,401	2,299	54,748
1985	943	2,330	2,250	56,238
1986	4,448*	4,349	4,304	59,476
1987	759	8,636	8,400	54,095
1988	11,715**	9,635	9,370	58,314
TOTAL	132,863	87,273	77,185	

*This figure includes about 4,300 highlanders rounded up in Thailand, especially Kamphaeng Phet Province, in mid-1986 and placed in Chiang Kham camp.

**1988 statistics are through 30 September. The arrival figure includes about 9,800 Hmong who had been living in Ban Vinai without registration and, as such, had not been counted previously. They were moved to Chiang Kham. Also included is a group of 1,400 Hmong who had been living on the border near Nam Pun for over 1 year and were moved to Ban Nam Yao and then to Phanat Nikhom.

Table 9.1 continued

	Arrivals	LAO Resettlement		Camp population
		Worldwide	US only	
1975	10,195	1,019	62	9,086
1976	19,499	11,221	5,613	17,364
1977	18,070	4,739	274	30,695
1978	48,781	10,436	5,821	69,050
1979	22,045	26,032	16,125	65,063
1980	28,967	46,286	31,854	50,730
1981	16,377	21,822	16,688	33,337
1982	3,203	6,285	4,386	23,137
1983	4,571	5,712	4,421	20,697
1984	14,616	6,677	4,452	27,346
1985	13,344	4,797	3,665	37,019
1986	2,911	11,602	9,422	26,342
1987	2,672	9,643	7,860	20,889
1988	1,409	4,060	2,543	19,004
TOTAL	206,660	170,331	113,186	

Source: UN High Commissioner for Refugees.

economic aid should be forthcoming. As one observer put it, 'One humanitarian consideration is surely to widen the range of choice for the potential refugee, including that of not leaving'.[64]

Table 9.1 illustrates the movement of Lao and hill-tribe refugees.

Notes

1. Arnold R. Isaacs (1984) *Without Honor: Defeat in Vietnam and Cambodia* (New York: Vintage Books, 1984), pp. 161–2. See also Joseph J. Zasloff, 'The Economy of the New Laos, Part 1: The Political Context', American Universities Field Staff Reports, No. 44, 1981, p.2.
2. Except where otherwise noted, all refugee arrival, resettlement and repatriation figures, as well as camp populations, are from the UN High Commissioner for Refugees (UNHCR).
3. See US Department of State (1983) *Country Reports on the World Refugee Situation: Report to the Congress for Fiscal Year 1987* (Washington, DC), p. 49.

4. In this chapter the term 'Laotian' refers to the political designation of current and former nationals of Laos, while the term 'Lao' is reserved for members of the lowland Lao ethnic group as distinct from highland or midland Lao.
5. See Gil Loescher and John A. Scanland (1986) *Calculated Kindness: Refugees and America's Half-Open Door, 1945–Present* (New York: The Free Press), pp. 144–6.
6. Cited in Court Robinson, 'Vietnamese Refugees in Thailand Face First Asylum Crisis', *Refugee Report*, Vol. IX, No. 2, 26 February 1988, p. 3.
7. Gary Y. Lee, 'Minority Policies and the Hmong', in Martin Stuart-Fox (ed.) (1982), *Contemporary Laos, Studies in the Politics and Society of the Lao People's Democratic Republic*, (St. Lucia, Queensland: University of Queensland Press), p. 202.
8. Isaacs, *op.cit*, p. 169.
9. Yang Dao, 'Why did the Hmong Leave Laos', Bruce T. Downing and Douglas P. Olney (eds) (1981) *The Hmong in the West* (Minneapolis: University of Minnesota), p. 3.
10. Lee, *op.cit.*, p. 203.
11. Christopher Robbins (1987) *The Ravens: The Man Who Flew in America's Secret War in Laos* (New York: Crown Publishers, Inc), pp. 333–7.
12. Robert Cooper, 'The Hmong of Laos in', Glenn L. Hendericks, Bruce T. Downing, and Amos S. Deinard (eds) (1986) *The Hmong in Transition* (New York: Center for Migration Studies).
13. Bernard J.Van-es-Beeck, 'Refugees from Laos: 1975–1979', in Stuart-Fox, *op.cit.*, pp. 324–5. Non-Hmong Hilltribes people continued to leave Laos but their population in Thai camps never exceeded 13,500. As of July 1988, there were 7,704 non-Hmong highlanders in Thailand, including 3,629 Mien.
14. Amnesty International (1985) *Background Paper on the Democratic People's Republic of Laos Describing Current Amnesty International Concerns* (London), pp. 1–2.
15. Cited in Zasloff, 'Politics in the New Laos,' Part II: The Party, Political "Re-education", and Vietnamese Influence', *AUFS Reports* No. 34, 1981, p. 4.
16. Ministry of the Interior, Operation Center for Displaced Persons in Thailand (1979) *The Unfair Burden: Displaced Persons from Indochina in Thailand* (Bangkok), pp. 1-3.
17. US Congress, House Committee on the Judiciary, Subcommittee on Immigration, Citizenship and International Law (1976) *Refugees from Indochina: Hearings before the Subcommittee* (Washington, DC: US Government Printing Office), p. 726.
18. Cited in Vitit Muntarbhorn, 'Refugees: Law and National Policy Concerning Displaced Persons and Illegal Immigrants in Thailand', unpublished manuscript, p. 7.
19. *Ibid.*, p. 7.
20. US Congress, Senate Committee on the Judiciary, Subcommittee on Immigration and Refugee Policy (1982) *Refugee Problems in Southeast Asia: 1981: Staff Report...97th Congress, 2nd Session* (Washington, DC: US Government Printing Office).
21. Office of the United Nations High Commissioner for Refugees (1979) *Collection of International Instruments Concerning Refugees* (Geneva) p. 10.
22. US Congress, Senate Committee on the Judiciary (1978) *Humanitarian Problems of Southeast Asia, 197–8: A Study Mission Report...95th Congress, 2nd Session* (Washington, DC: U.S. Government Printing Office), p. 23.
23. US General Accounting Office (1979) *The Indochinese Exodus: A Humanitarian Dilemma: Report to the Congress by the Comptroller General of the United States* (Washington DC: US Government Printing Office), pp. 50–1.

24. Department of Health and Human Services, Office of Refugee Resettlement (April 1985) *The Hmong Resettlement Study*, Vol. 1, Final Report, p. 18.
25. Loescher and Scanlan, *op.cit.*, p. 127.
26. US Congress, *Humanitarian Problems in Southeast Asia: 1977–78, op.cit.*, p. A.
27. Astri Suhrke, 'A New Look At America's Refugee Policy', *Indochina Issues*, September 1980. Thailand's Ministry of the Interior on 17 August 1977 instructed the east coast and border provinces to comply with a new cabinet-approved 'prevention and expulsion policy', under which 'aliens who fled into Thai territory and lived near the border should be immediately sent back by the authorities who spot them'. This policy has been inconsistently applied but occasionally has been invoked to defend particular pushback incidents.
28. Loescher and Scanlan, *op.cit.*, p. 127.
29. Van-es-Beeck, *op.cit.*, p. 327.
30. Zasloff, 'The Economy of the New Laos, Part II: Plans and Performance', AUFS Reports, No. 45, 1981, p. 3.
31. See Nayan Chanda, 'Food: Drought-Hit Laos Asks for More', *Far Eastern Economic Review*, 3 March 1978.
32. In J. Hamilton-Merritt, 'Poison Gas War in Laos', *Readers Digest*, October 1980. p. 37.
33. Lee, *op.cit.*, pp. 211–12.
34. MOI, *The Unfair Burden, op.cit.*, pp. 13–21.
35. Murray Heibert, 'Flexible Policies Spark Tenuous Recovery', *Indochina Issues*, May 1983.
36. James A. Hafner, 'Lowland Lao and Hmong Refugees in Thailand: The Plight of Those Left Behind', *Disasters,* Vol. 9, No. 2, 1985. p. 83.
37. Marilyn Lacey (1987) 'A Case Study in International Refugee Policy: Lowland Lao Refugees', *People in Upheaval* (New York: Center for Migration Studies), p. 24.
38. The *Indochinese Refugee Situation*, better known as the Green Report, is included in US Congress, *Refugee Problems in SEA: 1981, op.cit* p. 49.
39. See Loescher and Scanlan, *op.cit.*, pp. 197–206.
40. US Congress, *Refugee Problems in Southeast Asia, op.cit.*, p. 53.
41. Jacqui Chagnon and Roger Rumph, 'Lao-Americans: A New Constituency', *Southeast Asia Chronicle*, No. 85, August, 1982, p. 21.
42. Catholic Office for Emergency Relief and Refugees (1986) *Report of Survey of Refugee and Problems in Ban Vinai Refugee Camp, Thailand, 1985–1986* (Bangkok), p. 3.
43. Hafner, *op.cit.*, p. 89.
44. David Moffat and Wendy Walker, 'I Stay, I Have Power', *Boston Globe*, 17 March 1985.
45. US Congress, Senate Committee on the Judiciary, Subcommittee on Immigration and Refugee Policy (1985) *U.S. Refugee Program in SEA: 1985...99th Congress, 1st Session* (Washington, DC: US Government Printing Office), p. 15.
46. Krisdaporn Singhaseni, 'The Northernmost Camp', *Refugee*, May 1986, p. 17.
47. Josephe Cerquone (1986) *Refugees from Laos: In Harm's Way* (Washington, DC: US Committee for Refugees), p. 12.
48. In Jeff Crisp, 'Two-way Traffic Across the Mekong,' *Refugees*, September 1987, p. 30.
49. Refugees International, unpublished field notes, March 1987.
50. In Crisp, *op.cit.*, p. 30.
51. In Barbara Crossette, 'Thais Pressing Ouster of the Laotians', *New York Times*, 19 March 1987.
52. Crisp, *op.cit.*, p. 28.
53. US Congress, *Humanitarian Problems of South Asia, 1977-78, op.cit.*, p. 16.

54. MOI, *The Unfair Burden, op.cit.,* p. 25.
55. Thomas Luke (March 1988) *Integration of Refugees in Host Countries,* p. 30.
56. State Department cable, 21 April 1982.
57. National Security Decision Directive Number 93, 13 May 1983.
58. Department of Justice, Immigration and Naturalization Service (August 1983) *Worldwide Guidelines for Overseas Refugee Processing,* pp. 30-32.
59. See Donald A. Ranard, 'The Last Bus', *Atlantic,* October 1987.
60. Cited in Julia Wilkinson, 'Letter from Ban Vinai', *Far Eastern Economic Review,* 24 March 1988.
61. See Court Robinson (1988) 'Refugees in Thailand', *World Refugee Survey: 1987 in Review* (Washington, DC: US Committee for Refugees), pp. 52–3.
62. Alan G. Wright '*A Never Ending Refugee Camp: The Explosive Birth Rate in Ban Vinai*' (Bangkok, 1986), p. 9.
63. Lance Clark, field notes on a visit to Na Pho.
64. Cited in Suhrke, *op.cit.,* p.7.

Part V
US Policy towards Laos in Historical Perspective

10 Lao Nationalism and American Policy, 1954–9

Arthur J. Dommen

This chapter examines American policy in Laos from the Geneva settlement of 1954 to the early months of 1959, as described in recently declassified diplomatic correspondence between the Department of State and the American Embassy in Vientiane. While the broad outlines of the American failure in Laos are known, this new evidence reveals to what extent American policy worked at cross-purposes to Lao nationalism in this early period of American involvement.

In particular the re-evaluation that took place in the wake of American failure to prevent the formation of the first coalition government in Laos and American opposition to Prince Souvanna Phouma's continuing as prime minister after the 1958 supplementary elections to the National Assembly were decisions fraught with consequences for the survival of an independent non-Communist Laos. The American evasion of the challenge to Laotian sovereignty posed by the North Vietnamese action in occupying an area of Tchepone District in Savannakhet Province in December 1958 seemed conclusive proof of the contradictory nature of American policy towards the royal government.

HISTORICAL BACKGROUND

Laos has been an identifiable state since early in its history. If we leave aside the twenty-three kings from the perhaps legendary Koun Lo to Fa Ngum, the coronation of the latter in 1353 as King of Lan Xang marks the advent of the Lao nation, as Lao historians profess to see it from the nomenclature in use at the time. This nation subsequently fell on many vicissitudes, but exists to the present day.

The establishment of the French protectorate in the nineteenth century over the kingdom of Luang Prabang did not subvert the institutions of that monarchy. On the contrary, the burning issues of the day had to do with the relationship between the monarch and the rest of what the French called, loosely, Laos. On the exterior administrative convenience was served by the attachment on occasion of this or that province to the Luang Prabang kingdom, or an adjustment of the borders with Vietnam or Cambodia. But the main impact of the French presence was to put an end to the centuries of warfare in which Laos had been the victim of more powerful neighbours, centuries which had been the crucible of Lao nationalism.

The King of Luang Prabang remained the incarnation of the Laotian state. Even during the turbulent events of 1945, with the formation of the Lao Issara government in Vientiane, the Lao were ambivalent about the question of the monarchy's future. Prince Phetsarath himself, even after being stripped of his title of viceroy, did nothing to break his bond of personal loyalty to King Sisavang Vong. He saw the pro-republican agitation as being largely instigated by the Vietminh agents who accompanied Prince Souphanouvong, his half-brother, back to Laos from Vietnam. Finally Lao nationalism seemed to have come into its own with the promulgation of the constitution of 1947, which at last gave legal status to the unification of all of Laos. The Lao Issara, who had fled across the Mekong into Thailand, were offered amnesty and returned, except for those few who joined Ho Chi Minh and provided a thin but useful cover for the Vietminh in their invasions of Laos in 1953 and 1954.

The Pathet Lao (as these last were called) were to move into the provinces of Sam Neua and Phong Saly 'pending a political settlement' under the terms of article 14 of the Agreement on the Cessation of Hostilities in Laos at Geneva on 20 July 1954. In a unilateral statement to the conference the Royal Lao Government (RLG) pledged 'to take the necessary measures to integrate all citizens, without discrimination, into the national community and to guarantee them the enjoyment of the rights and freedoms for which the Constitution of the Kingdom provides'.[1] The exact conditions for the clearly intended integration of the Pathet Lao (PL) were left to further negotiation between the parties concerned. The RLG, however, made no commitments in response to North Vietnamese Foreign Minister Pham Van Dong's thinly veiled suggestions of a coalition in Laos.[2] Unlike Vietnam, Laos was not partitioned, and the sovereignty exercised by a sole government was recognised universally.

The United States viewed the French withdrawal from Indochina as an inevitability, and took some satisfaction from the fact that the

former Associated States were launched on their course as independent kingdoms and states. The preservation of this independence was
uppermost in the minds of policymakers in Washington. The means
to use in assisting Laos in this aim were to form the subject matter of
much of the dialogue between American diplomats in Washington
and Vientiane in the post-Geneva years.

A WEB OF CONTRADICTIONS

Broadly stated, American policy in this period was to see that Laos
was 'not allowed to go behind the Iron Curtain', in words penned by
Secretary of State John Foster Dulles during the Geneva Conference.[3] Implementing this policy, however, proved more difficult
than would seem to have been strictly necessary in view of the
Department's recognition of Laos' strategic position in Indochina.
This is so on at least three major counts:

First, and most costly in its consequences, the American disregard
for China as a major actor in Indochina was a mistake. Chou En-lai
had approached Foreign Secretary Anthony Eden of Britain at
Geneva to tell him, in terms that strongly suggested China was
prepared to act as a guarantor of the settlement, that China would
recognise the kingdoms of Laos and Cambodia so long as they did not
allow military bases on their soil:

> It really looks as if the Chinese may want a settlement in Laos and
> Cambodia: Chou went so far as to say that the Vietminh would
> respect the unity and independence of Laos and Cambodia and
> that the Chinese would recognise the Royal Governments, who
> might be members of the French Union, provided they could be
> left as free countries without American or other bases.[4]

In August 1956 Chou warmly welcomed Souvanna Phouma on an
official visit to Peking. American diplomacy strove to discourage
contacts between Vientiane, on the one hand, and Peking and Hanoi
indiscriminately, on the other. A neutral Laos did not hold the same
strategic importance for Peking as it did for Hanoi, preoccupied with
the reunification of Vietnam. For Hanoi, whose leaders had ambitions of revolution in both Laos and Cambodia dating back to the
1930s, it was doubly important in 1954–9 to try to make Laos 'neutral'
on Hanoi's side, and its main instrument for doing this was the PL.[5]

Secondly, Washington's failure to extend to the Lao leaders credible guarantees of Laos' territorial integrity in the event of invasion from China or North Vietnam, in response to repeated requests for such guarantees, complicated the task of the nationalists in obtaining recognition of their neutrality by their more powerful neighbours, particularly North Vietnam.

Thirdly, American actions aimed at preventing coalition deliberately made integrating the PL a more hazardous course for the RLG. This had the twofold consequence that it seemed to many Lao nationalists that the United States was actually opposing the territorial unity of Laos except as it might be effected through force, and that the PL kept open the option of resuming armed resistance. In this they enjoyed the full backing of Hanoi (so far as is known), a course of action that would have been precluded had integration been completed in accordance with the hopes entertained by successive governments in Vientiane.

Eventually, the American purpose of ensuring the survival of an independent non-Communist Laos failed. With the admitted benefit of hindsight, it seems clear that the reasons have much to do with ideology and mistaken analogies with European situations.[6] American policy became ensnared in a web of contradictions. Instead of taking a forthright stand in support of Lao nationalism, the United States succeeded only in weakening the very leaders in Vientiane who offered what was perhaps the most feasible course, politically and militarily, for eliminating the threat posed by the PL–North Vietnamese alliance. Consequently, this threat continued to grow.

THE BEGINNING OF AMERICAN AID

The American military aid programme in Laos developed out of the so-called pentalateral agreements of 1950 and 1951 among the United States, France, and the Associated States of Vietnam, Laos, and Cambodia.[7] Article 6 of the Geneva agreement prohibited the introduction of foreign military personnel into Laos, except for a French training mission. Furthermore, in a unilateral declaration, the RLG renounced participation in any military alliance. Therefore, as early as 5 August 1954, the Office of the Army Chief of Staff warned the Military Assistance Advisory Group (MAAG) in Saigon that a preliminary analysis of the agreement 'indicates major problems in implementing future United States policy in Indochina'. MAAG personnel were instructed to exercise caution in discussions with officials of France and the Associated States.[8]

The fact that Laos had not up to that point formally requested military aid from the United States was a matter of some relief to the State Department. On 18 August Dulles wrote to Defence Secretary Charles E. Wilson that, in considering military aid to the Associated States, 'the case of Laos may be set aside', since Laos had to look to France 'for aid in training and other purposes',[9]

By October, however, the situation had changed. The RLG had made a request for direct US military aid, bypassing the French. Also, and perhaps more importantly, American officials were impressed with the seriousness of France's expressed intention to withdraw all but a token presence from Indochina, a situation the Americans saw as threatening to create a vacuum in Laos, particularly in view of repeated warnings from the American Minister in Vientiane, Charles W. Yost, that the PL–Viet Minh were consolidating their positions in Sam Neua and Phong Saly. By October the Laotian Minister in Washington was pressing the Department's Office of Philippine and Southeast Asian Affairs to know what had happened to his government's request for direct US military aid.[10]

The Joint Chiefs of Staff, meanwhile, in accordance with their previous analysis, had omitted Laos entirely from their planning for military aid programmes in Indochina.[11] When pressed by Dulles on the question of a programme in Laos, Wilson replied:

> The Joint Chiefs of staff have reviewed Minister Yost's recommendations and consider that, from a military point of view, they cannot recommend the provision of Mutual Defense Assistance Program support of Laotian forces over which the United States, under the terms of the Geneva Accords, would have no control.[12]

Dulles, however, was determined not to allow US policy in Laos to be held hostage by a technical restriction in the accords. If American military personnel were not allowed in Laos, then American civilians would have to do the job of keeping Laotians trained in the use of American military equipment and in accounting for its disposition to the satisfaction of the Defense Department. And the place to find such qualified personnel was among the rosters of retired military personnel. This was the origin of the 'civilian' military assistance group in the Embassy in Vientiane known as the Programs Evaluation Office (PEO). On 31 October Deputy Under Secretary Robert

Murphy was able to write to Gordon Gray, Assistant Secretary of Defense, as follows:

> The Department of State is exceedingly pleased that the Department of Defense accepts responsibility for payment of all expenses, including those of administrative support, connected with maintenance of the civilian supervisory group. The remaining obstacle to recruitment and dispatch of personnel urgently required for adequate supervision of large-scale United States military asssistance has thus been removed.[13]

The PEO was activated on 13 December 1955. Pay of the Lao armed forces generated a flood of kip, the Laotian currency, necessitating a programme to import goods concurrently to sop up the kip and prevent runaway inflation.

The immediate object of American military aid – hardware and pay – was to allow the royal forces (ANL), whose strength was put at 23,500, to cope with the threat posed by the PL, estimated in 1955 at 5,000 men organised in ten battalions. In the view of the American military attaché in Vientiane, this aid was intended to give the ANL a 'capacity for harrassing guerrilla-type action and not in terms of resisting a direct assault by a superior force'.[14] Much less was there any belief among American officials in either Vientiane or Washington that the ANL would be capable of defending Laos in the event of an invasion from China or North Vietnam.

To prepare for this last contingency, the Laotian leaders sought explicit guarantees from the United States that in the event of such an invasion the United States would come to their aid with its own or allied forces. The manner in which such requests were handled will be made plain in a following section. For the moment, we turn our attention to the Laotians' efforts to achieve the political settlement they had spoken of at Geneva.

AMERICAN POLICY AND NEGOTIATIONS WITH THE PATHET LAO

As Washington confronted the dilemma of continuing PL control over Sam Neua and Phong Saly, Yost was prepared, in effect, to write off these two provinces. 'Our first objective should be to assist the Lao Government to maintain its authority over ten provinces not occupied by Pathets', he advised the Department.[15] This advice seriously underestimated the Laotian leaders' determination to assert the RLG's sovereignty over Sam Neua and Phong Saly. Thus, almost from the very start, American policy was at loggerheads with that of the RLG leaders over the question of the two provinces.

On 3 December 1954 Yost delivered the first of what would be many homilies on the subject of the adverse attitude of the US government toward any move to include the PL in a coalition government. His warning to Foreign Minister Phoui Sananikone coincided with the RLG's opening moves to negotiate with the PL. 'I also said very earnestly', Yost reported, 'I was sure my government would feel obliged to reconsider the entire question of aid to Laos if Communists should participate in Lao Government.'[16] The warning was backed up by high officials of the Department's Office of Philippine and Southeast Asian Affairs.[17]

But the hopes of an early and fruitful outcome of negotiations with the PL entertained by Prime Minister Katay D. Sasorith and his cabinet were soon dashed. A series of meetings, facilitated by the International Control Commission (ICC), saw the PL make more and stiffer conditions for a peaceful settlement with each passing day. Fighting broke out and escalated as the RLG tried to enforce its writ in Sam Neua and Phong Saly.

It remained for Prince Souvanna Phouma, Phetsarath's younger brother, who had been prime minister during the Geneva Conference, to carry through the lengthy process of negotiating the integration of the PL. For this task, he believed, he had an advantage over others, in that the nominal PL leader, Prince Souphanouvong, was his half-brother and not, he thought, a communist.

In the speech he made when presenting his government to the National Assembly on 20 March 1956 Souvanna Phouma called the settlement of the PL problem 'preoccupation number one' and 'the gravest and most urgent' question before the country.[18] In fact serious negotiations did not get under way until August.

THE AMERICAN POSITION HARDENS

Faced with the imminence, and then the fact, of the negotiations between the RLG and the PL succeeding, Washington reacted sharply, instructing the American Ambassador, J. Graham Parsons, to renew previous warnings to the Laotian leaders, and undertaking a review of options available to counter what was now described as 'the current adverse trend in Laos'.[19] 'Our objective remains to contain, reduce, and eventually eliminate Communist influence', a Department policy memorandum said.[20]

To achieve this objective, the memorandum listed a number of assets to American policy, among which was Laos' 'total dependence upon outside aid, which at present is principally American, for survival as a politically independent state'.[21] Liabilities, on the other hand, included 'dim appreciation of Communist objectives and estimation of the Pathet Lao as nationalists', and 'Prime Minister Souvanna's vanity, weakness of character, and supreme faith that he can control the Chinese Communists, the Viet Minh, and the Pathet Lao'.[22] The memorandum stated displeasure that 'our expressions of "serious concern" have too obviously not been taken seriously by the Lao', and suggested the time might come when 'we may wish to disengage or threaten to disengage'.[23] No immediate action was to be taken, however.

In spite of repeated American admonitions, Souvanna Phouma pursued his negotiations with the PL. On 31 October an agreement for cessation of hostilities was signed.[24] On 2 November another agreement for the implementation of a policy of peace and neutrality was signed.[25] On 24 December an agreement was signed on measures to guarantee civic rights and non-discrimination to former PL and to integrate PL cadres.[26] This was followed on December 28 by the issuance of a joint communiqué on remaining matters to be negotiated.[27]

As the agreements reached in the negotiations became known (and the PL was assiduous in propagating them to the population), American opposition had the effect of making the PL look more and more like nationalists, while doing nothing to strengthen Souvanna Phouma's hand. In other words, two 'liabilities' were made even more damaging to American interests. On the other hand, the 'asset' that Laos depended almost entirely on American aid was to be turned before long into a liability as well.

A State Department memorandum dated 7 November 1956, titled 'Preventive Action in Laos', expressed alarm at the prospect the RLG would make concessions on the key issues of integration of the PL, administration of the northern provinces, general elections with PL participation, and PL membership in the government. The memorandum stated in part: 'Something must be done now to stop, if possible, the unfavorable trend in Laos. CIA agrees with our assessment that the situation is deteriorating and that negotiations with the Pathet Lao are being handled in a naive and slipshod manner'.[28]

The memorandum contained a recommendation that 'We make our position known in advance in terms responsible Lao authorities can understand. We should tell them that we may be obliged to reappraise our policy toward Laos, including the possible suspension of aid, if they take certain steps'.[29] Instructions to this effect were dispatched to Ambassador Parsons, who delivered the warning in writing to Souvanna Phouma on November 13. In response to Souvanna Phouma's plea for American support, the Department expressed its satisfaction that the prime minister 'was clearly worried by our letter of November 13'.[30] 'On November 22 we instructed the Ambassador to inform Souvanna that the U.S. was unable to respond favorably to the Prime Minister's appeal for support since it considered the entrance of Communists into the Lao Cabinet would threaten Lao independence'.[31]

LAOTIAN REQUEST FOR SECURITY GUARANTEES

The protracted negotiations with the PL and continued propaganda on behalf of the PL by Radio Hanoi had done nothing to lessen the sense of insecurity the Laotian nationalists felt at not having an explicit guarantee of support from the United States in the event of an invasion of their country. As early as May 1956 Yost had reported that Crown Prince Savang Vatthana and Prince Souvanna Phouma had raised with him and other American officials 'with increasing insistence during recent months' their desire for more concrete assurances as to the aid Laos could expect in the event of an invasion from Communist countries.[32] In response to continued prodding on the subject, and in anticipation of Souvanna Phouma's visits to Peking and Hanoi, the Department prepared a personal message from Dulles to the Crown Prince in terms stressing the immense forces commanded by the United States and its SEATO allies, especially in the air and on the sea, and stating that the Chinese and North Vietnamese communists were fully aware that these forces 'would be used in the case of aggression'.[33] The message was delivered to Savang on 8 June.

In its review of 4 September 1956, setting out assets and liabilities, the Department listed assurance of 'military protection in the event of Communist aggression' as a priority need to support Laotian independence and retard Laotian neutralism.[34] Savang's visit to Washington that month gave the Department an opportunity to make the assurances direct. A Department memo quoted President Ngo Dinh Diem of South Vietnam, who did not hold a very high opinion of the Laotian leaders' firmness against the communists, as saying that 'the most important step the United States could take to improve the situation' in Laos would be to give the RLG such assurances.[35] Nevertheless, as the communist bloc moved toward detente in the wake of the Twentieth Congress of the Soviet Communist Party, American policymakers grew increasingly uneasy about what they perceived to be Laos' vulnerability to persuasion-cum-subversion, and focused their attention on this possibility rather than on that of an invasion.

SOUVANNA PHOUMA'S POSITION

Souvanna Phouma's position was based on the premise that national unity was the priority objective. As he stated in an information note that constitutes the fullest account available of his thinking in early 1957 at the start of another round of negotiations with the PL, 'It is intolerable to remain any longer in a situation where two provinces of the Kingdom are amputated territorially and demographically'.[36]

But his reasons for continuing the negotiations went beyond this priority. The PL was tightening its hold, militarily and politically, on the two provinces. The RLG was not ignorant of the fact that the PL owed their origins to the Vietnamese communists, or that they were attempting to carry out subversion throughout the kingdom. The RLG had created a special service, the Information, Documentation and Socio-Political Action Service (SIDASP), to meet this threat. The RLG would go far, however, in the search for a solution other than by military force. This was not subject to criticism or blame from any outsider: the matter concerned a difference among Laotians.

The RLG was convinced that not all the PL leaders were communists, but included many who, for various reasons, had joined an organisation encadred by communists. The best, and indeed the only, means of making it possible for them to escape the communists was to include them as a minority in the government. It was necessary in the negotiations not to allow the communists to make these people fail. It had therefore been necessary to make concessions. The RLG knew it was running a great risk. It had decided to make the effort nonetheless because it was certain of success, of attaining territorial integrity, and, after the elimination of the communists, of having a government that would be in a position to impose constitutionality and the sovereignty of the state.

With respect to foreign countries, Souvanna Phouma's note said that the RLG's good neighbourly relations with North Vietnam and China were intended frankly to isolate the PL. He did not rely only on assurances of good behaviour from Hanoi and Peking, but, in dealing with his government, they made it difficult to support the PL in anti-government subversion.[37]

There was no denying the fact that Souvanna Phouma was more pro-Western than pro-communist. The 2 November 1956 agreement on a neutral foreign policy contained a secret protocol not to establish diplomatic relations with Communist China and North Vietnam in the immediate future.[38] And even American officials admitted that at the time he visited Peking and Hanoi in 1956 he urged the Crown Prince to visit the United States for the balancing effect such a visit would have.[39]

In February 1957 the negotiations resumed, with the return of Prince Souphanouvong to the capital. On 21 February an agreement on modalities for holding elections was signed.[40] In a broadcast appeal for national unity on 8 April Souvanna Phouma chided his critics for producing no constructive solution and defended the continuation of the negotiations as the only alternative to civil war or the abandonment of the two provinces.[41] His fellow citizens apparently heeded his reasoning and supported the negotiations. In a crucial vote in the National Assembly on 29 May 1957 a question, 'Is the Assembly satisfied with past agreements signed between the Royal Government and the Pathet Lao?', was approved by a show of hands without any opposition, while a second question, 'Is the Assembly satisfied with the implementation of these agreements already signed?', was disapproved unanimously.

A third vote, this one secret, on the question, 'Does the Assembly want the government to carry on with the policies outlined by the Prime Minister?', resulted in eleven votes for the government and thirteen votes against.[42] The government resigned.

In the event Souvanna Phouma was probably not reluctant to resign. He had brought the negotiations with the PL along quite a distance, and the Assembly showed itself pleased with the results achieved. Agreement with the PL on the key issues surrounding the setting up of a coalition was still ahead, with the PL holding on to their 'temporary' administration of the two provinces. Although the fighting had stopped for the moment, the situation could turn sour very quickly. Moreover, another factor influenced Souvanna Phouma's thinking. By resigning at the end of May he avoided having actual negotiations with the communists injected into the annual Congressional debate over the aid appropriation for Laos.

By now the American aid programme had grown to such massive proportions (the programme ranked first in the world in per capita terms) that the abuses it generated had begun to attract the attention of a critical Congress, in spite of official attempts to keep news stories of corruption out of the American press. As Ambassador Parsons noted to the Laotians, the Congressional and public economy drive directed at the budget, and especially the Military Support Program (MSP), was a new factor on the US side that rendered the outcome of any necessary reappraisal of US policy in Laos much more doubtful. 'Should appropriation hearings coincide with disastrous RLG accommodation to Communists, outcome for Laos aid program predictable.'[43]

A Department telegram advised the Embassy:

> Executive Branch has difficulty each year defending Laos program because of striking disparity between population and aid request figures but has thus far been able to justify relatively large expenditure as sum needed (in view Laos' extreme lack own resources) assist this vulnerable country maintain its independence. If, however, at moment when Congress already seeking means reduce U.S. foreign aid outlay Lao take Communists into government, Congress could only assume Laos not doing utmost preserve its independence.[44]

Threatened Congressional scrutiny of the aid programme in Laos provided ammunition for those in Washington who favoured using the threat of an aid cutoff to prevent the formation of a coalition government. The threat lost some of its credibility, however, because of the ill-timed actions of other members of the country team. The PEO, for example, was preparing to expand its presence in Laos and the Defense Department was asking the Embassy to rent six additional houses in the capital. Parsons warned: 'Conclusion may be drawn U.S. intends keep on no matter what RLG–PL deal'.[45]

As a new mood of optimism blossomed in Vientiane in May 1957, the usefulness of the 13 November 1956 letter from Parsons to Souvanna Phouma was cast in doubt. As Parsons advised the Department:

Were I to reiterate flatly at this stage policy set forth November 13 letter ...it would merely lend credence to reports which some of our friends are not above peddling, that United States more interested in keeping couple Pathet Lao (commies) out of government than in helping Laos with settlement of its national problem. I doubt even United Kingdom Ambassador would find it possible to support us in such attitude. We would thus be alone, with diminished chances of influencing evolution of affairs here.[46]

The Department as a result began to backtrack on the link between the 13 November letter and an aid cutoff. As a memorandum of June 28 to Dulles put it:

We may thus soon be faced once again with the necessity to take a position on coalition. We need not now decide publicly on our stand in a completely hypothetical situation, but we should privately be prepared to be flexible if a strong anti-Communist becomes Prime Minister. Ambassador Parsons shares this view. We may wish at some future time *tacitly* to accept coalition (that is, we would not reduce or withdraw our aid) if 1) the Pathet Lao were integrated into the National Army under an adequate control system, 2) the Government's administration were actually restored in the two provinces, and 3) the Government was in such command of the situation that Pathet Lao entry into the Cabinet did not represent a material increase in Communist subversive potential because their ability to manoeuvre under the foregoing conditions would be so thoroughly circumscribed. We would not, however, openly shift our policy on coalition, if at all, until the Pathet Lao had fulfilled the foregoing conditions. We have succeeded in preventing disastrous developments under Souvanna by standing firm against coalition and do not wish to lose ground by a premature or unnecessary change.[47]

THE ADVENT OF THE COALITION

The cabinet crisis provoked by Souvanna Phouma's resignation in May finally came to an end in August when the King again invited Souvanna Phouma to make a new attempt at forming a government. The vote was favourable. In his investiture speech on 8 August Souvanna Phouma reiterated that the re-establishment of territorial unity through the settlement of the PL problem was the top priority.[48] Once again Ambassador Parsons sought by all means to delay the negotiations, questioning the concessions the RLG was preparing to make and arguing the unenforceability of the commitments made by the PL. Souvanna Phouma remained unconvinced by Parsons' arguments, saying in effect that achievement of the final goal was worth some risk-taking. Parsons, in turn, was unconvinced by Souvanna Phouma's counter-arguments.

Although the United States was now on record as being against the entry of the PL into the government, either before or after elections, the Embassy was preparing to predicate an actual American continuation of aid on how the Laotian implementation worked out step by step. Ambassador Parsons spelled out these steps in a telegram to the Department:

> Continuance of United States attitude would be reviewed upon completion of each step and would depend on our determination of following questions:
>
> (Step One) Whether military and administrative control of two provinces has in fact passed completely into hands of RLG. Our findings would be based on our own investigations, on the spot.
>
> (Step Two) Whether integration of ex-PL cadres (administrative and military) has been carried out in a manner safeguarding integrity and security of RLG and ANL.
>
> (Step Three) Whether the Neo Lao Hak Sat, or any other successor to PL, was in fact an independent political party, free from foreign domination, and loyal to constitution and crown.
>
> (Step Four) Whether the ex-PL or any other candidates advanced by Neo Leo Hak Sat for ministerial appointments in accordance constitutional procedures are themselves independent and without subversive or disloyal intentions or connections.
>
> (Finally), as our attitude dependent on future circumstances as outlined no need and in fact undesirable attempt define position more precisely now.[49]

In spite of Foreign Minister Phoui Sananikone's assurances to US officials during a visit to Washington in October that a coalition was still a long way off, [50] the negotiations in Vientiane began to move rapidly that month. Parsons was later to blame the rapidity with which the final agreements were concluded on the fact that Souvanna Phouma no longer felt the restraining hand of Phoui, but it is far more likely that Souvanna Phouma took advantage of Parsons' absence accompanying Phoui to speed up the negotiations. At all events the American Embassy was taken aback; an Embassy officer noted 'some remarkable concessions on part of PL'.[51] The RLG at the same time was receiving indications of low morale among PL troops, [52] and Souphanouvong and the PL leaders may have felt under pressure to conclude the deal that was being offered them rapidly.

Officials in Washington at this time were sufficiently alarmed at the course of events to start bringing up references to the experience of Czechoslovakia with a coalition government containing communists.[53] These comparisons, however, when relayed to Souvanna Phouma, reportedly made little impression.[54] Ambassador to South Vietnam, Elbridge Durbrow, described to Souvanna Phouma a talk Ambassador W. Averell Harriman had had with Eduard Beneš about coalition government and referred to the suicide of Foreign Minister Jan Masaryk in March 1948 following the Communist coup.[55]

On 22 October there was final agreement on re-establishment of the royal administration over the two provinces and integration of PL cadres. The agreements reaffirmed the full sovereignty of the RLG over the two provinces, provided for a government of national union to be presented to the National Assembly for investiture, and supplementary elections to the National Assembly to be held 4 months later.[56] Yet another warning from Washington to the effect that the United States would 'closely examine each step in execution in order to ascertain whether RLG remaining in effective control situation and defending position recognized at Geneva'[57] fell on deaf ears. The only concession Souvanna Phouma was willing to make was to hold up public announcement of the agreements until after Parsons' return to Vientiane.

A joint communiqué signed by Souvanna Phouma and Souphanouvong on 2 November announced the agreements.[58] The agreements on modalities of implementing them were signed on 12 November.[59] As the first concrete step, Souphanouvong in a symbolic ceremony on 18 November formally returned to the royal authority in the person of the Crown Prince the administration of the two provinces, together with all the troops, civil servants, and war materials belonging to the PL. On the afternoon of the same day the National Assembly approved by unanimous vote the national union government, which included Souphanouvong as Minister of Plan, Reconstruction and Urbanism and Phoumi Vongvichit as Minister of Cults and Fine Arts.

In spite of pleas to Ambassador Parsons to give the RLG 1 or 2 months in which to demonstrate that the agreements with the NLHS were working according to plan,[60] Parsons cabled the Department his recommendations for an interim policy pending the re-evaluation in Washington. He urged that in the meantime American military and economic aid not be reduced, while not permitting the RLG to assume that aid would continue regardless of performance.[61] The Department cabled its concurrence in Parsons' recommendations the next day, noting that the last point would present a major difficulty.[62]

Delay was no longer possible, however. On 23 November Parsons handed Souvanna Phouma the official notification that the re-evaluation of American policy which had been impending since the letter of 13 November 1956 was now at hand.[63] Fearing an abrupt cutoff of aid in reaction to the coalition, Canada, Australia, France and Britain all urged a continuation of American aid to Laos.[64]

In a letter to the ICC on 26 November Souvanna Phouma stated that the agreements constituted a preliminary political settlement as envisaged in article 14 of the Geneva Agreement and that the activities of the ICC were therefore nearing an end.[65] Only the elections remained to complete the mission of the ICC.

In preparation for contesting the elections, the PL had formed the Lao Patriotic Front (Neo Lao Hak Sat – NLHS) under the chairmanship of Prince Souphanouvong in January 1956. This front, like the PL itself, was under the control of the still secret Lao Communist Party.[66] The statutes of the NLHS, as amended on 20 September 1957, were accepted as legal by the Ministry of Interior in Vientiane. The NLHS opened its Vientiane office on 26 November. Ambassador Parsons forwarded a copy of the NLHS statutes to the Department on 2 December.[67]

NLHS propaganda was aimed at enlisting the widest possible support from the population. To avoid alienating voters, the NLHS made no public mention either of its communist direction or of its links, through the party, with Hanoi. The NLHS banked heavily on the popularity of its leader, Souphanouvong. But substantive issues like the corruption associated with American aid played into the hands of the NLHS propagandists. The Embassy officers travelling in the provinces reported the concern of local RLG officials that no serious effort was being made to counter the NLHS propaganda. The view that American aid, in spite of its large amount, was hardly visible outside Vientiane was widespread, and even the Crown Prince mentioned it in his conversations with the Ambassador.[68] In July 1957 the Embassy quoted opinion in the capital as saying that if elections were held tomorrow, NLHS sympathisers would get into the National Assembly.[69] Another advantage enjoyed by the NLHS was the discipline of its cadres, proven over the years of hard living in the northern provinces; by December the Embassy was describing the NLHS as the 'best organized political party in the country'.[70]

As long as the traditional nationalist parties held a monopoly of electoral politics in Laos, the Embassy was inclined to accept whatever balance the elections produced in the National Assembly, although Bong Souvannavong, with his demands that Laos accept Chinese economic aid and other manifestations of 'neutralism', tried the Embassy's patience at times. The sudden entry of the NLHS on to the electoral scene, and the prospect of a 'definitive test'[71] with the old-line politicians, forced the Embassy into a more active role. It therefore lobbied hard for a merger of Phoui's Independents and Katay's Progressives. Since the electoral law provided each voter with as many votes as there were seats in the voter's province, rival parties had an obvious interest in limiting the number of candidates they presented. For a time it seemed as if agreement to this effect had been reached and the old-line parties would support each other's candidates. But in the end no such agreement prevailed.

The mood in Vientiane as the coalition assumed office was upbeat, nevertheless. Reassured by Souvanna Phouma's statement to the National Assembly that no party, including the NLHS, would be allowed to engage in subversive propaganda against the government, such as inciting the population to disobey the authorities, and that those who carried arms after implementation of the agreements would be considered rebels and treated accordingly,[72] the Laotians were willing to give the NLHS a chance to show its goodwill. Souphanouvong himself assured the Assembly that the PL wanted to implement '100 percent' the agreements. In case there were still Laotians who did not rally to the government and continued to agitate within the kingdom, they should be considered as non-PL, and the PL agreed to collaborate with the RLG in fighting against such people.[73] The date for supplementary elections was set at 4 May; a total of twenty-one seats were to be contested.

On 8 December in the little town of Sam Neua, composed of about fifty thatched houses and ten masonry houses, many of them still showing damage from the fighting, and in the presence of ICC observers and of some fifty PL soldiers and 200 civilian spectators who provided applause, authority over the province was ceremonially transferred to the RLG. Prince Souphanouvong spoke first, followed by Col. Singkapo Chounlamany. Then Prince Souvanna Phouma spoke. The next day, in a simple ceremony lasting 15 minutes, the new governor of the province was installed.[74] Similar ceremonies were held in Phong Saly a few days later.

The Embassy reported that reoccupation of the two provinces by the ANL up to the borders of China and North Vietnam had gone off without incident. Integration of PL troops was begun, with 6,129 men reporting for processing and over 3,500 weapons being turned in by 31 January 1958.[75] More ominously, certain PL units were reported by a French observer in Laos to have crossed the border into North Vietnam, taking their arms with them.[76]

In an effort to reassure friendly powers that Laos was not going communist as a result of these activities, Souvanna Phouma embarked on visits to a number of countries early in 1958. In Washington American officials were prepared to adopt a correct, but reserved, attitude toward the prime minister, in view of the imminent re-evaluation of American policy. 'To avoid having the discussion bog down in fruitless argument on the character of the PL', a briefing paper for Dulles suggested, 'it would be better to bypass the point by stating that dissidents, whether Communist or non-Communist, are inimical to Souvanna's aims of fostering nationalism and true unity for the progress and prosperity of Laos'.[77] Also it was considered advisable to remind Souvanna Phouma of the historical examples of Czechoslovakia and Hungary.

No headway was made, however, on another matter that had become a point of contention between Washington and Vientiane. The Department was seeking reform of the way American economic aid was administered. Under the system in force, the dollar exchange needed to finance imports under licence was purchased from the National Bank at the official exchange rate of 35:1, even though the kip were almost invariably acquired at a third of that price. The tendency not only of merchants, but also of civil servants and of army officers, to take advantage of what the Embassy described as 'the unparalleled opportunities for profiteering' by this system was causing a sharp decline in public morality.[78] In some instances the goods were not even crossing the border into Laos, but were being resold in Thailand, thereby nullifying the purpose of the aid. But since reform of the system implied devaluation of the kip, the RLG demurred. Nevertheless American officials now set a deadline of the end of June for the beginning of negotiations on the issue.

The problem was that the date for the elections was drawing near. Meanwhile the integration of the PL had hit a snag. Under the November agreement the whole process was meant to be completed within 60 days of the formation of the coalition. However, the PL demanded the acceptance by the ANL of 112 officers, 191 non-commissioned officers, and 95 corporals. The RLG offered to accept the normal complement of two battalions plus some senior staff, totalling 36 officers, 154 non-commissioned officers, and 208 corporals, later raising this to 43 officers and 171 non-commissioned officers. This dispute was not resolved, and thus integration was effectively stalled.

The United States, having previously informed the RLG of stringent limitations on the number of PL it was prepared to see taken into ANL ranks, could not very well have urged the RLG to make further concessions to resolve this issue. The United States in fact made it clear that it had an interest in not seeing the PL integrated into the ANL.

On 11 March the Embassy reported that, since the United States refused to fund the ANL unless some form of escrow agreement could be negotiated with the RLG for the dollars sold to the National Bank, only ANL officers and some enlisted men had so far been paid:

> Delay in paying ANL and police had created malaise in government circles and members government claim U.S. is playing into hands of dissatisfied elements with leftist opposition reaping benefits. Economic aid program is also being seriously hampered and work on certain projects has been temporarily halted.[79]

Another telegram reported that in view of possible development of anti-American sentiment in the ANL because of the held-up pay, two end-use observer teams presently in the field would remain in Vientiane on their return and no new teams would be sent out as a precaution.[80]

It was not until mid-April that the scheduled March and April ANL funds were released to the RLG.[81] By then the United States was represented in Vientiane by a new ambassador, Horace H. Smith. Parsons, however, continued to exert a powerful influence on American policy towards Laos in his new capacity of Deputy Assistant Secretary of State for Far Eastern Affairs.

THE 1958 ELECTIONS

The results of the 4 May supplementary elections are shown in Table 10.1. They came as a shock to many, although the explanation is simple. A combination of skilful propaganda on issues of real substance; discontent among soldiers and civil servants over the pay issue, with many soldiers voting for NLHS candidates;[82] and vote-splitting among the non-NLHS nationalist parties; redounded to the benefit of the NLHS. This last factor allowed the NLHS, for example, to capture one of two seats in Thakhek with barely one-quarter of the total vote, and three of four seats in Luang Prabang with less than one-half the total vote. Immediately after the elections NLHS propaganda began demanding the holding of general elections.

In Washington the Department now demanded the formation of a 'broadly based conservative cabinet excluding NLHS'.[83] Congressional and public reaction to the election results and allegations of waste in the aid programme, it told the Embassy, made it difficult to justify continued aid to Laos. Unless the non-NLHS nationalists formed some kind of common front, there was no sound basis on which to argue that continued aid would produce a different result from heretofore. Citing a telegram from the Embassy in Saigon, the Department said, 'We agree with Vietnamese that Souvanna should if possible be eliminated as candidate Prime Minister'.[84]

SOUVANNA PHOUMA'S DOWNFALL

In difficulties in Vientiane, Souvanna Phouma was under pressure on three fronts in the midst of a growing cabinet crisis. Politically he had to deal now with demands being made by a new grouping of middle-level civil servants for the most part calling itself the Committee for the Defence of National Interests. This grouping, which was

Table 10.1 Results of the 4 May 1958 supplementary elections

Province	Number of candidates			Number of votes			Seats won
	NLHS and allies	Nationalists	Other	NLHS and allies	Nationalists	Other	
Nam Tha	1	6	0	4,642	22,054		1 Nationalist
Luang Prabang	4	8	1	113,302	106,898	19,709	3 NLHS & allies; 1 independent
Thakhek	2	6	2	30,975	58,592	29,665	1 NLHS & allies; 1 independent
Phong Saly	1	4	0	10,000	9,216	2,925	1 NLHS & allies
Vientiane	2	7	2	58,430	73,465	17,760	2 NLHS & allies
Sam Neua	1	2	0	20,780	31,347		1 NLHS & allies
Xieng Khouang	1	1	0	13,561	31,620		1 Nationalist
Saravane	2	3	3	53,222	43,579		2 NLHS & allies
Attopeu	1	1	1	1,968	20,696		1 independent
Pakse	2	8	4	71,921	65,703	19,864	2 NLHS & allies
Savannakhet	3	6	12	65,646	74,868	164,831	1 Nationalist; 1 NLHS & allies; 1 Non-inscribed
Sayaboury	1	2	4	5,005	11,016	22,841	1 Non-inscribed

formed in June, claimed to stand for sweeping administrative reforms and a strongly anti-communist policy.[85] The encouragement that the CDNI may have received in this their initial foray into Laotian parliamentary politics, and the sources of financial backing they could count on – these were not people who commanded any wealth of their own – are not clear from a reading of the diplomatic correspondence available up to now. Their newspaper, printed on glossy paper unlike anything seen heretofore on the Laotian scene, bespoke of their resources. The advent of the CDNI forced Souvanna Phouma to accommodate their political demands as far as he could in view of the fact that they did not hold seats in the National Assembly, and he tailored the draft of his investiture speech to a strongly anti-communist tone.[86]

Militarily, while benefiting from the ceasefire he had negotiated with the PL, Souvanna Phouma had to bear in mind the continued intransigence of the PL on the integration issue. Since his position had been that the 4 May elections fulfilled the last of the obligations Laos had incurred at the Geneva Conference, the ICC had adjourned *sine die*. Souvanna Phouma had considered the presence of the ICC as an outside interference in the process of settlement among the Lao that he had sought to achieve. But the disappearance of the ICC, over vehement objections from Hanoi, meant one possible safeguard less as the test of the workability of the negotiated agreements approached. Moreover the Americans were now actively exploring ways for upgrading the effectiveness of military aid to the ANL. Ambassador Smith had already approved in May an increase in the personnel of the PEO.[87] Thought was also being given to the possibility of transforming the PEO into a MAAG along the lines of the MAAG in South Vietnam.[88] Political considerations dictated caution, however, in the State Department's view.

On the economic front negotiations with Souvanna Phouma's government over financial reforms had still not resumed, with the result that the aid appropriation for Laos for fiscal year 1959 was held up. On this issue Washington had assumed full control, relegating the Embassy to the status of a reporter in transmitting the RLG position.[89] This question was to drag on without resolution into October.

Smith was sensitive to Lao susceptibilities on all three of these interrelated issues. On 2 August he cabled the Department that he did not consider it wise to try to force Souvanna Phouma 'to mold cabinet more closely in accordance with our desires'. Smith harboured doubts about the young, untried men of the CDNI, and about the extent of the support they would muster among the civil service and the army if the time came for that. 'I continue to consider', he went on, 'that any effort at a military coup at this time would almost certainly play into Communist hands and hasten or make truly inevitable the day of Communist control of this country.' He added: 'The two northern provinces might again split off in open rebellion and in the other ten provinces with aid and "volunteers" from the Viet Minh, all but the few central points covered by the 300 paratroopers and such additional ANL units as are effectively armed, supplied and trained might be openly taken over by the NLHS. If the ICC returned it might even find evidence after such debacle leading it to conclude that the NLHS has the support of the majority of the population'.[90]

The next day Smith cabled the Department that Phoui Sananikone blamed the cabinet crisis on the CDNI and its exaggerated demands for a share of power. Phoui also had gained the impression, Smith said, that internal decisions among the CDNI 'candidates' for cabinet posts were being dictated not by Souvanna Phouma but by their predicted acceptability as negotiators with Washington over pending questions; he had asked Smith to drop a word in the right places if this were not the case. Two days later, with the cabinet crisis still not resolved, Smith asked the Department bluntly:

> Under these circumstances it important to know whether it is really U.S. policy to in any way encourage young elements to refuse to participate this government in belief it is U.S. intention, unless CDNI gets at least one or two more young people into a legally invested government, to support the CDNI and ANL in establishing, by methods of at least doubtful constitutionality but more probably inevitably requiring an outright coup, a government composed entirely or clearly controlled by these young men ... I hope that wording first sentence final paragraph of DEPTEL 168 [Department Telegram No. 168] does not indicate that we intend encourage younger elements to attempt coup at this time rather than enter government as suggested by Souvanna.[91]

The Department immediately cabled Smith assurances that it did not imply that 'we intend encourage younger elements attempt coup at this time rather than enter government as now suggested by Souvanna'.[92] Nevertheless, considering the pressures mounted by

CDNI, the discussions of upgrading the training of the ANL, and the imminence of negotiations with Washington for resuming normal aid flows on which the government depended, it is difficult to avoid the impression that officials in Washington, having failed in their attempt to prevent a coalition, set about to sabotage the coalition and to ensure the downfall of Souvanna Phouma even when the latter adopted a staunchly anti-communist stance. In doing this they seem to have been prepared to accept consequences that Smith may only have guessed at with his sensitivity to the situation.

After several more days of fruitless discussions Souvanna Phouma realised at last that it was futile to go on trying to meet the CDNI's insatiable appetite for a share of power, and gave up trying to form a new government. He was named ambassador to France. The new government, when it eventually took office on 18 August, was headed by Phoui.

THE TCHEPONE INCIDENT

This was the situation that prevailed when Laos came face to face with the gravest threat to its territorial integrity and sovereignty since 1954. In December 1958 North Vietnamese security forces occupied a string of small hamlets in the eastern part of Tchepone District in Savannakhet Province. These troops, whose action had been unprovoked by the Lao side, raised the North Vietnamese flag and made it clear they were there to stay.

In response to the vigorous protests against their action raised by Phoui's government, Hanoi claimed that the area in question was called the Canton of Huong Lap and historically been under Vietnamese jurisdiction. Huong Lap, Hanoi said, was part of Vietnam. No map in support of this claim was produced, however. The RLG, on the other hand, published an information note giving the history of the demarcation of the border in that area by the French Residents in Laos and Annam, respectively, in March 1914, and proving indisputably that the area occupied was on the Laos side of the line.[93]

The August cabinet crisis had provoked fresh requests from the Crown Prince for American guarantees in the event of aggression, to which the Department responded by repeating the personal message Dulles had sent the Crown Prince on 8 June 1956.[94] Now, however, the Crown Prince approached the US Ambassador with a new sense of urgency. He was urging Phoui to convene a special session of the

National Assembly to discuss the situation, and it would help if the country knew where the United States stood. (The special session resulted in special powers being voted Phoui for the space of 1 year.)[95]

In an initial set of instructions to Ambassador Smith the Department, in a telegram approved by Parsons, advised that the RLG's informing the United Nations Secretary General of the border situation constituted the 'most effective measure that can be taken although additional recourse to UN or perhaps SEATO should be explored if situation deteriorates further. Meanwhile, consider it important RLG not appear hasty or nervous in reacting to Vietnamese Communist military and diplomatic pressure'.[96] Parsons also rebuffed a French initiative, made through the British Embassy in Washington, to hold tripartite talks on the Laos crisis.[97]

The Department meanwhile had improvised a reply to the Crown Prince's latest request, but it was so hedged that it could hardly have reassured a friendly government or a head of state, especially of a state facing a violation of its border. After some delay Smith succeeded in delivering this reply to the Crown Prince. Its substantive portion read: 'Department wishes reassure RLG continued U.S. support heretofore but in view imprecise nature demarcation Lao frontier with North Vietnam and complex history border problems this area considers it impracticable either U.S. or SEATO undertake specific frontier guarantee'.[98]

Smith recorded what happened after the message was delivered:

> The Crown Prince asked if the message from the Secretary of State were simply oral or whether it would subsequently be presented in writing. I replied that it was intended as an oral reply to an oral inquiry by His Royal Highness.
>
> The Crown Prince then very politely and moderately expressed his dissatisfaction with the terms of the Department's reply: America, he said, is of the opinion that the Lao borders are not precisely enough delimited to permit a guarantee of frontiers, whereas the Lao view is that the maps establishing those borders are precise and definite, that there is no doubt as to the exactitude of the borders. However, with respect to any outbreak of hostilities, the RLG does not question the right of the Department or of the Pentagon to decide whether or not the U.S. should intervene. He has no criticism of U.S. policy; he believes that the U.S. is a great friend of Laos and he reaffirms that there will be no change in the Lao attitude toward the U.S.[99]

The Crown Prince in his dignified reply was correct on the matter of the exactitude of Laos' border with Vietnam, and the Department was incorrect. As might easily have been verified in Washington, the Tchepone-Est sheet of the French 1/100,000 map of French Indochina shows that the border runs to the east of the area occupied by North Vietnamese troops, and thus the area was clearly in Laos and not subject to imprecision as to who had sovereignty. Moreover, since this map had been used by the French and Viet Minh military negotiators at Geneva and at the Truong Gia ceasefire talks as a basis for drawing the Demilitarized Zone between North and South Vietnam, the North Vietnamese were in effect choosing this particular moment to effect a change in the border unilaterally and with force of arms. The Department's contention therefore that the border was 'imprecise' was entirely fatuous.

Not even the NLHS deputies in the National Assembly accepted the North Vietnamese claim in public, or even tried to contend that the border was 'imprecise'. As Souphanouvong told the National Assembly in the debate over Phoui's request for special powers, maps of different dates are not alike and thus produce misunderstandings; he argued therefore that the border problem should be settled through negotiations.[100] To the Lao nationalists, their borders were sacred, the symbol of sovereignty and independence. Souvanna Phouma himself had negotiated long and hard with the North Vietnamese over conflicting claims to a small territory in the Nong Het area. A joint border commission had been set up to try, without success, to resolve the dispute. It is hardly surprising that the Lao reacted so strongly to the North Vietnamese aggression against their country in Tchepone.

In point of fact the Department probably had other motives on this occasion for its evasion of the Crown Prince's request for guarantees. There had occurred a potentially dangerous military confrontation in the Taiwan Strait in August between the Chinese Communists and Nationalists. Alarms had been raised in various capitals that the United States might be dragged into war on behalf of its ally. The Department therefore was not eager to have a fresh confrontation on its hands over rival claims to an obscure border area in Indochina.

CONCLUSIONS

There is no doubt that the American policy after the Geneva Conference aimed at preserving the independence of Laos. The doubt occurs regarding the consistency of this aim with the realities of Laos, and, given these realities, the workability of the means used to achieve the aim.

American policymakers repeatedly defined independence to exclude the PL. Yet the PL, and its political arm the NLHS, were a reality that had to be dealt with, as the 1958 elections showed. The RLG leaders showed a strong sense of reality in negotiating with the PL, so the failure of the United States to achieve its aim cannot simply be blamed on some deficiency on the part of the RLG. The situation the RLG was left with after Geneva may have had its special, peculiar features. But it was the United States that misunderstood them, not the RLG.

If, in offering the NLHS positions in the government, the RLG was demonstrating to the US Congress that it was not 'doing its utmost' to protect the independence of Laos, it was opting to end the guerrilla war which had gone on more or less continuously since 1954. This was a noble aim. It was a moral aim. It made sense politically and militarily. For the United States to have encouraged a continuation of the guerrilla war, particularly when it was not prepared to send in its own forces, would have been immoral. For Souvanna Phouma therefore, 'doing its utmost' meant taking the large risks consequent upon negotiating agreements with the PL that were known to be difficult to implement and verify. American support for his efforts would have made these risks more bearable, and perhaps even reduced them.

Independence also meant territorial sovereignty. Souvanna Phouma was not prepared, as Yost was, to accept the separation of the two northern provinces indefinitely and base his policy on the remaining ten provinces in non-communist nationalist hands. The alternative of enforcing territorial sovereignty by continuing the war against the PL was quite clearly beyond the capability of the ANL. The basic tactical reality in Laos in 1958 remained, as it had been in 1954, that an army, even one equipped with modern weapons, fighting a guerrilla war against an enemy possessing secure sanctuary across the North Vietnamese border could not achieve a satisfactory outcome. The United States was in a position to make known a guarantee of the territorial sovereignty of Laos, yet it repeatedly eluded requests for such a guarantee, even when they came from the Crown Prince, whose traditional position placed him above politics.

The situation in Laos in 1954–9 was different from the situation in Czechoslovakia in 1948, which American policymakers kept referring to as a likely precedent. The Czechoslovak government had seen its allies Britain and France subscribe to the dismemberment of its territory in 1938, leading President Beneš to resign in protest, a chapter in Czechoslovak history that left a legacy of distrust of the West. In 1948 Czechoslovakia felt once again isolated from the West, subject this time to pressures from the Soviet Union. Laos, on the other hand, enjoyed universal good will as a newly decolonised country aspiring to neutrality, and, more important perhaps, having a strong Western presence in the form of the French military training mission and the large American aid programme. No foreign country, with the exception of North Vietnam, had territorial ambitions in Laos in 1954–9. There is no evidence that either the Soviets or the Chinese were prepared to support territorial designs on a genuinely neutral Laos.

It is true, on the other hand, that the communists within the NLHS were interested in pursuing power, like the Czechoslovak communists in 1948. They could not achieve this without the cooperation of the nationalists, whom they deliberately included in the NLHS as part of a united front strategy. The nationalists in the NLHS were not prepared to see the dismemberment of Laos for the benefit of any foreign country, or even to support a foreign country's claim to a relatively unimportant piece of Laotian territory, as Souphanouvong's statement in the National Assembly at the time of the Tchepone incident makes clear.

Hanoi's objective in Laos was just as clear as Washington's, but its means were used to better advantage. The number one objective was to prevent at all cost a split between the communists and the nationalists in the NLHS. Such a split would have been disastrous for its revolutionary goals. Hanoi succeeded in attaining this objective; up to the very moment of seizure of power in 1975, the communist direction of the NLHS, as indeed the existence of the Lao Communist Party, was kept a secret.

It is worth speculating about what Hanoi's position would have been if Souvanna Phouma had been enabled to implement his coalition policy fully. While the PL was able to thwart the ICC in its neutral observer role in the areas under PL control, the situation would have been less favourable had the PL been obliged to give up its areas of exclusive control and allow the RLG and resident diplomats in Laos to travel freely at the behest of the ministries in Vientiane. With its base areas no longer secure, the PL would have been forced to decide whether to play the coalition game in a frankly nationalist manner, or withdraw to Hanoi to await more favourable circumstances. Hanoi would probably have advised the Laotian left, as it was advising the Cambodian left at the time, to go along with the role of a loyal opposition. No one need have been hoodwinked by this: Sihanouk certainly was not. In the capital the Laotian communists would have been subject to police surveillance. Hanoi would have been helpless to shield them. Those who withdrew to Hanoi, on the other hand, would have been without a popular base in Laos from which to operate. Moreover Hanoi's decision about waging war in South Vietnam would have been vastly complicated.

American policy toward Souvanna Phouma's governments in 1954–9 virtually ensured the perpetuation of Hanoi's control over the whole of the NLHS front, precisely the situation Souvanna Phouma saw the necessity of avoiding by means of internal politics and external diplomacy. On both scores he encountered American opposition. After 1958 American and North Vietnamese interests coincided to an increasing degree in seeing the coalition experiment in Laos fail, as North Vietnam became dependent on Laos for its logistical operations in South Vietnam.

Notes

1. The texts of the Agreement on the Cessation of Hostilities in Laos and the RLG's unilateral declarations are in Department of State (1981) *Foreign Relations of the United States 1952-1954*, Vol. XVI, *The Geneva Conference* (Washington: GPO), pp. 1521–30 and 1542–44.
2. *Ibid.*, p. 1214.
3. Handwritten note by Dulles to Assistant Secretary of State for Far Eastern Affairs, Walter S. Robertson, 18 June 1954. This and all subsequent notes, memoranda, and telegrams cited here are in the National Archives, Washington, DC, Department of State Central Files, Boxes 3362–74, and Records of the Bureau of Far Eastern Affairs.
4. James Cable (1986) *The Geneva Conference of 1954 on Indochina* (New York: St. Martin's Press), p. 97.
5. China's preoccupation in 1957–9 with Mao Tse-tung's disastrous Great Leap Forward would probably have severely limited Peking's ability to influence diplomacy in Indochina. The point is, American policymakers failed to perceive that Peking's interests in Laos did not coincide with those of Hanoi, and thus that Peking's help might be enlisted, through indirect diplomacy such as the Warsaw ambassadorial talks, to preserve an independent state in Laos.
6. Several of those influential in setting American policy in Laos had previously served in European diplomatic posts.
7. Russell H. Fifield (1958) *The Diplomacy of Southeast Asia: 1945–1958* (New York: Harber & Brothers), p. 361.

272 *Lao Nationalism and American Policy, 1954–9*

8. Telegram from Department of the Army/Office of the Army Chief of Staff to Chief MAAG (Indochina) Saigon, 5 August 1954.
9. Dulles letter to Wilson, 18 August 1954.
10. Memorandum of Conversation by Paul J. Sturm, 13 October 1954.
11. Memorandum by Kenneth T. Young, Jr., 30 November 1954.
12. Wilson letter to Dulles, 16 February 1955.
13. Murphy letter to Gray, 31 October 1955.
14. Embassy to State, Telegram No. 1022, 31 December 1957.
15. Embassy to State, Telegram No. 437, 12 October 1955.
16. Embassy to State, Telegram No. 158, 3 December 1954.
17. Memorandum of Conversation between Robert E. Hoey and Ourot Souvanna-vong, Laotian Minister to Washington, 6 December 1954.
18. Third Interim Report of the International Commission for Supervision and Control in Laos, Cmnd. 314 (London: HMSO, 1957), p. 53.
19. Memorandum from Young to Robertson and William J. Sebald, 4 September 1956.
20. *Ibid.*
21. *Ibid.*
22. *Ibid.*
23. *Ibid.*
24. Third Interim Report, *op. cit.*, pp. 57–9.
25. *Ibid.*, pp. 60–1.
26. *Ibid.*, pp. 62–6.
27. *Ibid.*, pp. 66–7.
28. Memorandum from Young to Robertson, 7 November 1956.
29. *Ibid.*
30. Memorandum from Sebald to the Acting Secretary, 23 November 1956.
31. *Ibid.*
32. Memorandum from Yost to Young and Robertson, 28 May 1956.
33. Memorandum from Robertson to Under Secretary of State Herbert J. Hoover, 7 June 1956.
34. Memorandum from Young to Robertson and Sebald, 4 September 1956.
35. Memorandum from Young to Robertson, 21 September 1956.
36. 'Note d'Information, Présidence du Conseil', undated but minuted by Howard P. Jones, 18 February 1957, with the comment that 'none of the ideas in it are new'. Translated from the French by the author.
37. *Ibid.* Translated from the French and paraphrased by the author.
38. Embassy to State, Telegram No. 706, 3 November 1956.
39. Memorandum from Young to Robertson, 17 August 1956.
40. Third Interim Report, *op. cit.*, pp. 68–76.
41. Embassy to State, Telegram No. 1741, 13 April 1957.
42. Embassy Despatch No. 251, Enclosure 1, p. 9, 4 June 1957.
43. American Embassy, Bangkok, to State, Telegram No. 3445, 20 May 1957.
44. State to Embassy, 23 May 1957.
45. Embassy to State, Telegram No. 1101, 11 January 1957.
46. Embassy to State, Telegram No. 2077, 6 June 1957.
47. Memorandum from Robertson to the Secretary, 26 June 1957. Italics in original.
48. Fourth Interim Report of the International Commission for Supervision and Control in Laos, Cmnd. 541 (London: HMSO, 1958), pp. 37–51.
49. Embassy to State, Telegram No. 2077, 6 June 1957.
50. Memorandum of Conversation by Patricia M. Byrne, 7 October 1957.
51. Embassy to State, Telegram No. 598, 17 October 1957.
52. *Ibid.*

53. State to Embassy, 11 October 1957. The US position on integration of PL troops had been set forth in a secret aide-mémoire handed to Souvanna Phouma on 6 November 1956.
54. Embassy to State, Telegram No. 654, 24 October 1957.
55. Embassy to State, Telegram No. 998, 13 December 1958. No date was given, but the conversation may have occurred in November or December 1943.
56. Embassy to State, Telegram No. 646, 23 October 1957.
57. State to Embassy, Telegram No. 422, 23 October 1957.
58. Fourth Interim Report, *op. cit.*, pp. 57–9.
59. *Ibid.*, pp. 59–67
60. Embassy to State, Telegrams Nos. 714, 2 November 1957, and 870, 24 November 1957.
61. Embassy to State, Telegram No. 849, 20 November 1957.
62. State to Embassy, Telegram No. 571, 21 November 1957.
63. Embassy to State, Telegram No. 871, 24 November 1957.
64. State to Embassy, Telegram No. 571, 21 November 1957.
65. Fourth Interim Report, *op. cit.*, pp. 69–71.
66. On the relationship between the front and the party, see MacAlister Brown and Joseph J. Zasloff (1986) *Apprentice Revolutionaries: The Communist Movement in Laos, 1930–1985* (Stanford: Hoover Institution Press), pp. 58–60.
67. Embassy No. 76, 2 December 1957.
68. Embassy to State, Telegram No. 998, 13 December 1957.
69. Embassy to State, Telegram No. 158, 30 July 1957.
70. Embassy to State, Telegram No. 928, 4 December 1957.
71. Embassy to State, Telegram No. 849, 20 November 1957.
72. Embassy to State, Telegram No. 855, 21 November 1957.
73. *Ibid.*
74. Embassy Despatch No. 82, 13 December 1957. This consisted of the report of USIS photographer Ta Trung Chanh, who noted the absence from the ceremony of Kaysone Phomvihan, who as 'General Kaysone' was reputed to be the *éminence grise* of the PL, and not yet officially identified as the secretary-general of the Lao Communist Party.
75. Embassy to State, Telegram No. 1270, 31 January 1958. Details of the agreement under which the coalition was established are reported in Embassy to State, Telegram No. 646, 23 October 1957.
76. Jean Deuve (1984) *Le Royaume du Laos 1949–1965* (Paris: Ecole Française d'Extrême Orient), p. 101.
77. Memorandum from Robertson to Secretary, 11 January 1958.
78. Embassy Despatch No. 81, 9 December 1957.
79. Embassy to State, Telegram No. 1521, 11 March 1958.
80. Embassy to State, Telegram No. 1607, 25 March 1958.
81. Embassy to State, Telegram No. 1718, 12 April 1958.
82. Deuve, *op. cit.*, p. 110.
83. State to Embassy, Telegram No. 1420, 26 May 1958.
84. *Ibid.*
85. Embassy Despatch No. 178, 19 June 1958.
86. Embassy to State, Telegram No. 219, 1 August 1958.
87. Embassy to State, Telegram No. 2016, 27 May 1958.
88. Memorandum from Byrne to Maurer, 29 January 1958.
89. Embassy to State, Telegram No. 2156, 17 June 1958.
90. Embassy to State, Telegram No. 229, 2 August 1958.
91. Embassy to State, Telegram No. 252, 5 August 1958.
92. State to Embassy, Telegram No. No. 184, 6 August 1958.

274 *Lao Nationalism and American Policy, 1954–9*

93. For a history of the area and a map, see Arthur J. Dommen (1971) *Conflict in Laos: The Politics of Neutralization* (New York: Praeger), rev. ed., pp. 338–51.
94. State to Embassy, Telegram No. 185, 5 August 1958.
95. The text of the motion approving special powers for Phoui is reported in Embassy to State, Telegram No. 1241, 14 January 1959.
96. State to Embassy, Telegram No. 919, 30 January 1959.
97. Memorandum of Conversation by Thomas J. Corcoran, 8 January 1959.
98. State to Embassy, Telegram No. 1030, 20 February 1959. This telegram was cleared by Parsons, among others.
99. Memorandum of Conversation by Ambassador Horace H. Smith, 24 March 1959.
100. Embassy to State, Telegram No. 1239, 14 January 1959.

11 The United States and Laos, 1962–5

Leonard Unger

In order to understand United States actions in Laos during my assignment there as Ambassador, from 1962 to 1965, we have to look back into the political atmosphere of the 1950s when some of the US–Soviet cooperation of wartime and of the early post-1945 years had given way to doubts, then suspicions, then grave distrust and hostility. There was the war in Korea; the takeover of the mainland of China by Mao Tse-tung and his communist forces; the bloody war in Indochina which left Vietnam split into two hostile halves at the 17th parallel; the insurgencies, usually communist-supported, in Malaysia, the Philippines, Burma, Indonesia and elsewhere; the spread under US pressures and leadership of mutual security treaties (SEATO, ANZUS, etc.); and the reluctant acceptance of a world divided into two hostile camps.

In Southeast Asia the French had been driven out of Indochina by 1954 and three successor states set up – Cambodia, Laos and Vietnam. Vietnam had been divided, presumably temporarily, into a communist north and western-oriented South. It became the theatre of a bloody north–south struggle which inevitably brought in also its smaller, less populous and weaker neighbours to the west, Cambodia and Laos. It was in an effort to forestall that involvement and to remove Laos from the developing international struggle that in July 1962 the neutrality of Laos was reaffirmed in the Geneva Accords, including a Declaration on the Neutrality of Laos and the Protocol of that declaration. These were signed and adopted in Geneva at that time by thirteen communist and non-communist countries.

Some of those provisions are fundamental to this history, but first we need to recall some further pertinent background. At the end of French rule in Indochina in 1954, during the negotiation of the earlier Geneva Accords creating Cambodia and Laos as independent states, the vulnerability of those fragile, newly revived nations was recognised. Provisions were formulated to secure international recognition of their neutral status and to try to assure their immunity from the mounting atmosphere of East–West tension. In a world sharply divided then between the communist and the Free World those arrangements for Indochina were promptly followed by the conclusion of a western-oriented eight-nation multilateral mutual defence treaty under US leadership. This accord, the Southeast Asia Treaty, and its implementing organisation (SEATO), were intended to provide security assurances for the Asian partners, i.e. the Philippines (already tied to the US in a bilateral Treaty), Thailand and Pakistan, which then had an eastern wing, now Bangladesh. Indochina was not directly involved but its nations (Laos, Cambodia and South Vietnam but not including North Vietnam) were loosely associated as 'protocol states'.

There were optimistic expectations initially that identification of Laos as 'neutral' in the 1954 Accords would make it possible for the newly independent, small and underdeveloped nation to live in peace and devote its energies to modernisation. Rather early on these hopes were seen to be unrealistic, given the sharp political divisions then rapidly emerging in Southeast Asia. In an article written for *Current History* in December 1972 Arthur Dommen summed up the hostile relationships with which it was obliged to contend:

> It would be hard to find two nations that trusted each other less than North Vietnam and the United States after 1954. The two came face to face in Laos long before they did in Vietnam. Hanoi, with its principal interest in the struggle for unification with South Vietnam, had to keep its lines open to the south through Laos. Thus, while both sides in the conflict were talking in terms of Laos, they actually meant South Vietnam. Laos was caught in the middle... Can it be regarded merely as coincidence that the Lao crisis of the summer of 1959 broke out just at the moment when the fortunes of the Vietnamese Communist Party in South Vietnam had sunk to their lowest ebb under the crippling effect of the Diem government's policy measures? I think not. Hanoi needed to have secure use of the mountain trails through Laos, if not for the present, at least for the future, in the event aid to the compatriots of the South became necessary.

It soon became clear that without some strong international intervention to guarantee that such a formula would be respected, Laos would soon again become a battleground.

Accusations as to who was responsible for the failure of the 1954 formula would contribute little to this discussion. In spite of its projected neutrality, Laos found itself involved in the increasingly sharp political split that was occurring in Indochina and Southeast Asia in general. Centre to right-wing governments, usually under influence from Thailand and the West, were generally in office in the 1950s and charges were made that Lao territory was used for raids on North Vietnam, and perhaps neighbouring Chinese, Burmese and Cambodian territories as well. During those early Cold War years there was a disposition in Washington to divide the world into the 'wes' and 'theys'; neutrality was regarded by many with great suspicion – as a cover for sympathy and even collaboration with the enemy, then defined as the communist world. It was not many years before, that the communist armies had pushed Chiang Kai-shek and his Nationalist Government off the mainland, to take refuge on Taiwan, and France's pull-out of Indochina had left a vigorous Communist government in the northern half of Vietnam.

Then an important shift in policy – foreign as well as domestic – took place in the United States as the new Kennedy Administration took over from Eisenhower early in 1960 and ended the predominant role of Secretary of State, John Foster Dulles. A moderate Secretary of State, Dean Rusk, was now serving his president; like Dulles, he had a strong taste for international affairs but with doubts about the wisdom of at least some of the Dulles-sponsored mutual security treaties, especially perhaps the SEATO Treaty.

Also serving the president, sometimes with an independent mandate, was Averell Harriman. He had served Franklin Roosevelt in a number of delicate situations and returned to a more active role in foreign affairs when the Kennedy administration took over.

Many influential Americans questioned the wisdom of such extensive US involvement in East Asian affairs, apprehensive about the precipitation of 'another Korea'. Many questioned how much the United States could accomplish in a divided Vietnam, and apprehensions were expressed lest the US bog down in another 'quagmire', as had the French in their Indochina War. With this in mind, Harriman saw Laos, as well as Cambodia, as buffer states, providing a 'cordon sanitaire' between Thailand and Vietnam, and he sought to achieve their internationally recognised neutrality through the negotiation of a new set of Geneva Accords. The statute for the neutrality of Laos

was negotiated in Geneva, the Conference co-chaired by Britain and
the Soviet Union, and completed on 21 July 1962. Harriman developed a good working relationship with Pushkin, his Soviet opposite
number, and was persuaded that Pushkin could and would see to a
loyal execution of the accords on the communist side; unfortunately
Pushkin died soon after the Geneva meeting had adjourned.

At the same time, according to Dommen, 'when the United States
Air Force technicians examined aerial photographs of convoys of
trucks and armaments crossing from North Vietnam into Laos in the
autumn of 1962 and shipped the evidence back to Washington, they
were astonished that President Kennedy took no action'. While it had
been hoped that the neutralisation of Laos would terminate the
possibility of its territory being used as a route of passage from North
to South Vietnam, as time went on this became in fact the central
problem, as Hanoi did not respect Laos' neutrality and did make
maximum use of Lao territory for the passage of men and material
into South Vietnam to pursue its aggression there. In his recent book,
The Key to Failure, Norman Hannah puts forward the thesis that the
war in Vietnam was unwinnable as long as Laos and Cambodia were
available as safe routes of passage southward for the men and
material from North Vietnam. His discussion of the Laos aspects of
that episode seems to me complete and accurate. It reflects the
agonised judgements that had to be made almost daily in trying to
navigate between the Charybdis of an impotent neutrality and the
Scylla of trying to block the traffic on the 'Ho Chi Minh Trail'.

Prince Souvanna Phouma was undoubtedly well aware of what was
taking place along his long eastern frontier with the two Vietnams,
and if he had any doubts, I was putting the evidence before him
rather frequently. The first such instance, as I now recall, was in the
late spring of 1963, when I showed him photographs of a truck
convoy coming over a pass from North Vietnam into Laos and
headed southward. There was no credible explanation except that
this convoy was on its way through Laos to supply North Vietnamese
forces – or their allies – in the war against South Vietnam. This
would constitute a violation of Laos' sovereignty in any case, but *a
fortiori* since the recently adopted accords forbade 'the introduction
of foreign military personnel' as well as 'the use of Laotian territory
to interfere in the internal affairs of another country'.

In various ways – some known to me and some not – Souvanna
sought to block this traffic, but in such a way that Laos would not find
itself sucked into the Vietnam maelstrom, and that its hard-fought-

for neutrality would not, in the larger context, be abandoned or jeopardised.

An automatic Lao government reaction to any such evidence of North Vietnamese cheating on the Geneva Accords was to put the matter before the International Control Commission, which had been reconstituted as part of the setting up of the tripartite government in the spring of 1962. Initially its Chairman was Avtar Singh, and its two other members were a Pole, Marek Thee, and a Canadian, Paul Brifle. The chairmen of the various ICCs in Indochina, Laos included, were intentionally from a declared neutral background; in my experience this almost always meant an Indian representative. And this usually meant ambiguous action by the chairman, who was usually careful not to point any finger too clearly.

There was a period during my time in Laos, however, when India's relations with China had deteriorated seriously over frontier disputes along their common boundary in the Himalayas. The United States, still far from having made up its differences with the People's Republic of China, was pleased to be able to take up some cases of charged violations of the Laos Accords, committed either by the PRC direct, or by North Vietnam which – in those days – was a friend of the PRC. In that period of perhaps 18 months it was possible to persuade the Indian chairman to make an objective study of complaints, from both right-wing and neutralist sources, and oblige the North Vietnamese (and sometimes the Chinese) to pay more attention to the international agreements on Laos than they had previously been prepared to do.

It would be false, however, to suggest that in this way any serious obstacle was presented to North Vietnam's almost unhindered use of the Ho Chi Minh Trail. What could have been done to inhibit such traffic has been carefully presented in Norman Hannah's and Arthur Dommen's books and in other such studies. Our assignment in Vientiane was to do whatever was feasible to carry out the provisions of the 1962 Geneva Accords and to avoid a renewal of warfare in Laos.

As time passed, however, the abuse of Lao territory by the North Vietnamese and the increasingly grave threat this posed for South Vietnam precipitated some counteraction. As Arthur Dommen points out, 'by the summer of 1964, American jets were in action over Laos, hitting North Vietnamese anti-aircraft gun emplacements and supply convoys on the Ho Chi Minh Trail'. It became the task of the US Ambassador to review projected missions to eliminate those which would be too sensitive politically and to press for those with maximum effectiveness. Also conflict with the policies of importance to PM Souvanna were to be avoided, given the very delicate international posture he needed to preserve.

Thus my central task remained one of supporting in every way possible the tripartite government and its leader. History is often well illustrated and enriched by the occasional anecdote, and there is one of mine out of my Laos experience which bears on this point. On or about 19 April 1964 I attended a meeting of US Ambassadors in Southeast Asia, held in Saigon and chaired by the Secretary of State, Dean Rusk. Not long after it opened I received disturbing, then alarming messages from my Deputy in Vientiane, Philip Chadbourn: Prince Souvanna Phouma had been taken prisoner and put under house arrest by General Kouprasith and his right-wing forces! The general was expected in the near future also to convoke the National Assembly and propose that it adopt resolutions which would wipe the statutes clean of the provisions of the Geneva Accords of 1962, and establish a government which, whatever its token neutralist participation, would be run by the right-wing forces of Prince Boun Oum and General Phoumi Nosavan. Needless to say it would have no communist participation and would mean the end of the neutral solution worked out in Geneva in 1962.

I arrived back in Vientiane on the first plane I could commandeer in Saigon. Phil Chadbourn fortunately had managed to frustrate what appeared to be Kouprasith's plan to prevent my landing. On the ground we learned that Prime Minister Souvanna was at home and my first stop was there. Right-wing soldiers were on guard, blocking my access to his compound, but I noticed, as did Souvanna, that adjacent to his compound there was a close, parallel driveway and I had my driver drive up that to get as close as possible to Souvanna's home. He came out on his balcony and I leaned over the fence and we had a conversation intended to assure him of continuing US support of his coalition government and to try to forestall his resignation. (The French Ambassador injected a *bon mot*, remarking as Souvanna and I shouted back and forth, fence to balcony to fence, 'Ah, voilà, la diplomatie à la Romeo et Juliette').

My next stop was the National Assembly, where Kouprasith came from the Assembly floor for a quick conversation in which I gave him the unequivocal message that US support – moral, financial and legal – was for the tripartite solution and for the government of Prince Souvanna Phouma. Moreover he could expect nothing from the United States if he persisted in his effort to push aside the Souvanna government and seek to install a right-wing regime. Most of my ambassadorial colleagues supported this démarche in essentially the same terms.

Fortunately for our immediate purposes Kouprasith concluded that he had little choice but to back down, and so the 'Geneva Solution' was put back on the track. Unfortunately it was secure only until 1975, when the fate of the non-communist government was sealed in Laos as well as in Vietnam. Regrettably there was no Soviet ambassador at that time willing to step in and save the coalition government from extinction – and save many persons from extinction as well.

As already noted, the new Geneva Accords of 1962 on Laos were intended to usher in a new era in which Laos would be lifted out of the East–West test and be enabled to function on the world scene as a truly neutral nation. The Geneva Accords were the principal internationally-endorsed instruments to make this status explicit and to sketch out a regime which would reinforce the neutral status. Prince Souvanna Phouma was the embodiment of this governmental neutrality. The head of state of Laos at this time was the King, Sawaeng Wattana, and technically the US Ambassador, like all other ambassadors, was accredited to him. The royal seat in Laos was not in the administrative/governmental capital, Vientiane, but some 250 miles north across extremely rugged country, in Luang Prabang.

On various state occasions the government leaders and the diplomatic corps were ferried up by air to the royal capital where His Majesty would meet RLG leaders in the newly formed tripartite government. On such occasions His Majesty (in spite of some private reservations about the real intentions of the Pathet Lao) would seek to use his authority and influence to assure that the tripartite solution would function as smoothly as possible.

On the first such gathering in the palace in Luang Prabang after the Geneva Accords had come into effect the three leaders of the improbable new coalition were instructed by His Majesty to sit together on an oversized ottoman – oversized it had to be to accommodate the Princes Souvanna Phouma, Souphanouvong and (especially) Boun Oum. In the presence of government leaders, the diplomatic corps and some press His Majesty made clear his loyalty to the Geneva Accords and explicitly instructed the three leaders of the coalition government to discharge their responsibilities so that the objectives of the new accords (a neutral, peaceful and secure Laos) would be realised. (His Majesty was deposed many years later once the Pathet Lao were securely in control of the government; his son the Crown Prince was reportedly killed and the King himself, after several years of miserable existence in Sam Neua, died essentially in exile in his own country).

In an earlier, happier period, when the new coalition government had just begun to function, His Majesty was invited by President Kennedy to visit the United States. I was asked to accompany the royal party, which included leaders from the government's three parties, and our visit began in the White House; there the King of Laos and his chief ministers were received by the President and high US officials. This provided an effective opportunity for President Kennedy to tell the visitors (including the Pathet Lao leaders) that the United States gave its full support to the Geneva solution for Laos. Moreover the United States was ready to help Laos with its economic and other problems so that, along with assistance from other sources, the problems of the past might be alleviated. It was also made clear that, as we understood, all parties of the Royal Lao Government also supported this solution and the leadership of Prince Souvanna. Significant glances passed back and forth between Souvanna and the right-wing leader present, General Phoumi Nosavan, and his Pathet Lao counterpart, Phoumi Vongvichit. The only glitsch in this visit which I recall was Phoumi Vongvichit's pique at not having been invited to participate in a visit to the CIA.

(A special pleasure for me on that occasion – not part of the official programme – was a visit to the National Geographic where His Majesty had learned that a new World Atlas was in preparation. We two geographers had the pleasure of inspecting the draft page which covered Laos, and His Majesty, carefully inspecting his Kingdom on paper, pointed out a minor improvement or two which he invited the National Geographic to consider.)

The highlands of Laos are inhabited by a remarkable variety of hill people from many ethnic backgrounds, and with differing languages, customs and levels of sophistication and prosperity. One of the larger and more important groups, especially from a political and military point of view during the period under consideration, were the Meo (as we knew them then) or the Hmong (as they are known today). Under the leadership of their General Vang Pao the great majority of the Hmong had supported the Sananikone government and other earlier governments of a conservative political complexion and had rather close links with Thailand and some US intelligence officials.

Also they played an important role in resisting the Pathet Lao efforts to take control of their strategic highland areas.

One of my first tasks on taking up my duties in Vientiane was to convey friendly messages to General Vang Pao as well as to explain the US government's determination to support the new coalition under Prince Souvanna. To accomplish this I made a point early on to fly to Long Tieng, high up on the plateau, where Vang Pao had his headquarters, and we had a friendly and successful meeting. Specifically I assured him of continuing US support, assuming, as he confirmed, that he shared our objective of supporting Prince Souvanna in his efforts to build a successful coalition government and a peaceful prosperous Laos.

Vang Pao and I have been in touch intermittently over the years that have followed; it is to be regretted that such a dynamic, sharp, hard-working person, devoted to his country and to his highland people, should have been obliged to leave behind his homeland and his countrymen. In fact many of them have also been forced to leave their homes and live a frustrating existence in exile, in the United States and elsewhere. The press has carried stories of unhappy Lao/Meo/Hmong refugees resettled in a completely alien environment (e.g. Orange Co., California), where strange surroundings and unfamiliar work and language problems have taken their toll, especially among the men.

Vang Pao and I had one opportunity to recall the old days in Vientiane and Long Tieng, when, as I was conducting a seminar on Southeast Asia at Harvard's Kennedy School, I persuaded him to come from his residence, then in Montana, to give my students a first-hand account of the situations he faced and the role he had played. On the same occasion he met the large colony of Meo who had settled in the Boston area, many of whom appear to have been successful in building a new life there.

Another military and politically important figure from the epoch in Laos was the feisty, independent-minded little Royal Lao Army officer who had been responsible for upsetting the earlier conservative government of Phoui Sananikone and opening the way for Prince Souvanna's coalition several years earlier, Captain Kong Le. It was he who vigorously backed Prince Souvanna with a pledge to bring to Laos a more honest rule, with more consideration for the average person. In spite of the indignation he inspired – especially among right-wing individuals who had been Laos' power-brokers for many years after the departure of the French – Kong Le caught the popular fancy, especially of those persuaded that some social and economic reforms were essential in Laos.

He explained in our first meeting that he saw Prince Souvanna as a leader who could generate the reforms the country needed. Around 1960 he had led a revolt which separated several thousand men from the Royal Lao Government's military forces – primarily army – and enlisted them in support of Souvanna Phouma. I will not attempt to rehearse the complicated history that followed those events, but suffice it to say that it was the military support provided by Captain Kong Le which was an important factor in Souvanna Phouma's taking on or holding his leadership of the government of Laos at one or two critical junctures.

When I took up my ambassadorial duties in Vientiane in the summer of 1962, I recognised that a considerable gap of distrust and suspicion had to be closed between Kong Le and the new US Ambassador, given some of the American policies in the preceding period. So I flew from Vientiane to the Plain of Jars (a plateau northeast of Vientiane where many of the Neutralist and some of the Pathet Lao forces were installed) to get acquainted. As expected, I found Kong Le there (exercising on the parallel bars!). We hit it off well – as far as I could ascertain – and we both saw the value of our cooperation in working toward the goal we shared of Souvanna Phouma's making a success of his new coalition government and of a neutral Laos, divorced from the military struggles of its neighbours.

In the last days of 1964 we departed Laos, and I returned to the State Department to chair the Interdepartmental Working Group on Vietnam, and other tasks relating to the deepening crisis over Indochina. By then it seemed clear that, with the escalating struggle in Vietnam, the crucial importance of the Ho Chi Minh Trail through Laos to North Vietnam if it was to continue its aggression against South Vietnam and Kampuchea, and the mounting determination of the US to prevent a communist victory in Vietnam and Kampuchea, isolating Laos as an island of peace in Southeast Asia was a hopeless ambition. Subsequently destruction was visited on Laos, especially in the area adjoining Vietnam. Finally all hope for neutrality was brought to an end when two Pathet Lao leaders, Nouhak and Kaysone, who in my days in Laos had given orders from Sam Neua or Hanoi, saw no further need for concealment and in 1975 moved to Vientiane to take charge quite openly.

Now that many formerly hostile relationships have been relaxed one can hope that some of the spirit of the 1962 Geneva Accords can be recaptured in Laos.

12 The Chinese Road in Northwest Laos 1961–73: an American Perspective

G. McMurtrie Godley and
Jinny St Goar

IMPACT OF THE ROAD

Any road in a mountainous jungle region is important as an avenue of transportation and communication, but the road the Chinese built in northwest Laos during the 1960s was never simply that. This artery was particularly laden with strategic and tactical considerations. The diplomacy related to the road could have led to explosive actions, and was always revealing of the players' motivations.

For Americans in Laos, where so much evidence of enemy activity disappeared under the triple canopy jungle or was washed away by heavy monsoon rains, a hard-top road was visible. People could photograph it, count the workers, map its progress, and argue about its intended purposes and the larger implications. In the American view this road was the pathway to spread the communist revolution into Thailand, forming a red circle around Indochina. There was a historical angle to this perspective: the primary catalyst to the US presence in Southeast Asia in the 1950s had been the fear of the Chinese sweeping through Laos, Thailand, Malaya, and on into the Indonesian archipelago. In the 1960s the arm that could push down a row of dominoes seemed then to be stretching out to do just that.

For the Chinese the road was perhaps a stab at breaking out of their 'encirclement', a term they used frequently to describe their circumstances in the late 1950s. After the Korean War and the Indochinese settlement with the French in 1954, the Chinese were hemmed in by the SEATO alliance on their southern flank, and South Korea and Taiwan on the east. As the decade progressed and China's relations with the Soviets deteriorated, the circle of hostile forces was completed on all sides. While Americans suffered from the

Map 3 The Chinese Road in Northwest Laos, 1961–73

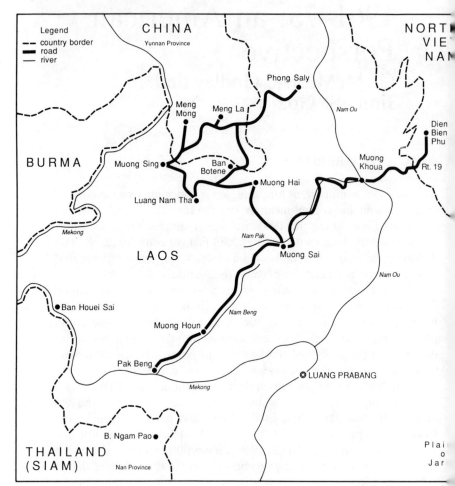

Map prepared by Mia

Yalu River syndrome – fearing the Chinese Army would rush across any of its borders to attack, as it had at the border with North Korea, the Chinese feared an American assault on insecure borders. This fear was given additional plausibility during the 1950s as the US built up its military presence in Thailand.

For any interested party, the road raised issues of domestic politics that were tangled with international themes. But perhaps because of geographic proximity to China and the relative openness of their governments (relative to the Chinese, that is), this seemed even more true for the Laotians and the Thais. The Laotians were the least inclined to frame discussions of the road in terms of the Cold War debate, having had a long history of tributary relations with Peking and being located immediately at China's border; the Thais were perhaps most inclined, as their military (and their economy in general) was benefiting most from the American expenditures that were spurred on by Cold War apprehensions.

However, the 1960s and the early 1970s marked a transition from Cold War politics in international relations to realignment, or detente. The Chinese road offers a useful device for tracking this change, as it was the subject of intense scrutiny during those years.

The genesis of this road was a visit Prime Minister Prince Souvanna Phouma paid to Peking in April 1961, when he was negotiating the ceasefire that led to the 1962 Geneva Accords. Souvanna, the leader of the centrist faction in Laos, asked Chinese Premier Chou En-lai to develop a road from China's Yunnan Province into Laos. An official of Souvanna's neutral Royal Lao Government signed the formal agreement for the road with a Chinese representative in January 1962. The Chinese were to build a road from Meng La in southern Yunnan eastward to Phong Saly town.

What would Prime Minister Souvanna Phouma have had in mind in asking the Chinese to do their road-building in this particular location? Phong Saly province had North Vietnam to the east and China to the north and west. However the Nam Ou (Ou River), a tributary flowing into the Mekong just north of Luang Prabang, joins the province politically and culturally to the Mekong valley. Under the terms of the 1954 Geneva Agreement, Phong Saly had been one of the two provinces to which the Pathet Lao were assigned as regroupment areas at the specific request of Chinese Premier Chou En-lai.[1] But the Laotian communists and their North Vietnamese advisers were not as entrenched in Phong Saly as in the other regroupment area, Sam Neua province, and in Xieng Khouang province. For all that it was designated as a region for the Pathet Lao to gather their troops, Phong Saly province remained loyal to Prince Souvanna Phouma and his brand of neutralism. By requesting the road-building there, the prime minister was enlisting the Chinese perhaps as a hedge, especially if it should turn out that the Chinese and the Vietnamese were not always such close allies.

In the larger international arena Prince Souvanna Phouma was attempting to establish his neutralist credentials. He had been bitterly disappointed by American efforts in the late 1950s to sabotage Laotian neutrality and to tilt any coalition government toward the West. In early 1961 Souvanna was just returning from self-imposed exile in Cambodia, where he had fled when the American-backed right-wing forces of General Phoumi Nosavan had marched toward Vientiane. While Souvanna had been planning his next move in Phnom Penh, the Soviets had staged their largest airlift since World War II to the combined Pathet Lao and neutralist forces on the Plain of Jars, where they were opposing General Phoumi. The neutralist prime minister's visit to Peking and his request for the Chinese road into Laos were evidently intended, in part, to counterbalance this heavy Soviet influence in Laos. In addition to visiting Peking in April 1961, Souvanna Phouma also stopped in Hanoi.

As for the Chinese interest in building the road, they would have had several reasons for wanting to consolidate their control in southern Yunnan and expand their presence in Laos. Foremost was their worry about units of the Kuomintang Army that had retreated after the communist victory in 1949 to this general area. In March and April 1961 reports of KMT troop movements circulated: perhaps as many as 5,000 soldiers had come from Burma to Laos and Thailand. These KMT regulars were still supported from Taiwan, a clear proxy for the US. It was even speculated at the time that Americans were moving the KMT around in an effort to pressure the Soviets to negotiate over Laos, betraying American ignorance of the developing Sino–Soviet split.[2]

The KMT aside, the Chinese communists were still concerned about the local populace in southern Yunnan, an area that was traditionally uncertain as to its loyalty to the central government in Peking. Ethnic minorities, distinct from the Chinese Han majority, inhabited the region. The Lu of Meng La had considered their principality – the Sip Song Pan Na, or Twelve Rice Fields – to be quasi-independent of the Chinese central government, paying taxes (or 'tribute' under the Chinese Empire) to Peking but otherwise having the limited contact that distance ensured. The road from Meng La would be a graphic display of the central government's interest and authority; and, once built, it would be an aid to controlling the area.

In all likelihood the Chinese had a strategic purpose too for this road from Meng La to Phong Saly town. In the 1950s they had focused first on the roads of southern Yunnan near the Burmese and North Vietnamese borders. Then, in 1958–9, the Chinese had worked on roads near the Lao border, and farther west along the Indian border. During these same years they had helped the North Vietnamese build some roads in northwestern North Vietnam. The Meng La/Phong Saly segment would be yet another spoke in this web.

By chance April 1961 was an important month for American relations with Laos. US military advisers, eager to expand their role, were pressing to come out from under their thin cover of wearing civilian garb; they had been covert out of deference to Laotian neutrality and because the French were the only foreign military presence permitted under the 1954 Geneva Agreement.[3] The Chinese had insisted most strenuously on this arrangement, with the thought that the French presence would preclude any American bases. No doubt the Chinese had become increasingly uneasy about the growing American military presence in Laos. Then the Bay of Pigs fiasco occurred.

During the week that the American-supported invasion of Cuba was foundering on the coral reefs, newly elected President Kennedy was deciding what to do about Laos. First he agreed to the Pentagon's request to put US military men in Laos into uniforms. Although Roger Hilsman, then the director of State's Bureau of Intelligence and Research later attributed this decision to the need to stand tough against the communists somewhere in the world after such a failure in Cuba,[4] it was largely coincidental that the change should have occurred so shortly after the Bay of Pigs. While taking this symbolic action, Kennedy resisted the tougher advice of the former vice-president, Richard M. Nixon, to commit American air power in Laos.

Nixon later recalled Kennedy's comments: 'I just don't think we ought to get involved in Laos, particularly where we might find ourselves fighting millions of Chinese troops in the jungles. In any event, I don't see how we can make any move in Laos which is 5,000 miles away, if we don't make a move in Cuba, which is only 90 miles away'.[5]

Kennedy was searching for an appropriate response to the war in Laos, which continued to smoulder, even after a ceasefire was reached in May 1961. Most of the Washington bureaucracy switched gears during this time to support Kennedy's view that Laos was no place for a military engagement against the Chinese, or the Russians, and that the country should be genuinely neutralised. Ambassador-at-large W. Averell Harriman met Prince Souvanna Phouma, was very taken with him personally, and became convinced of the prince's suitability and efficacy as the leader of a neutral Laos. In mid-May representatives of fourteen countries convened at Geneva to negotiate a Laotian settlement. But the gears were grinding at the Pentagon, where military men were not so quick to give up their goal of a fortified, pro-Western Laos. With Thai acquiescence, supplies and material still flowed to the rightist general, Phoumi Nosavan, who was related to the Thai Prime Minister Sarit. By late 1961 General Phoumi was concentrating his efforts in northwest Laos.

General Phoumi moved troops in force to a base at the town of Luang Nam Tha in an area some 50 kilometres south of the Chinese road. This was but one of several places where the general was trying to stir up some military action, as he feared the negotiations in Geneva would strengthen the Pathet Lao unduly. General Phoumi's intent was to galvanise the Thais against the communist threat, and to shake the American belief in neutralism. From Luang Nam Tha, moving east and south as well as northward from the Beng Valley, he launched a 'probe' against an enemy camp at Muong Sai, alleging there were Chinese soldiers in addition to the Pathet Lao and North Vietnamese.[6]

Phoumi's largely fabricated reports succeeded in frightening the Thais enough to move troops north to protect their upper north eastern border. But Americans were set on a neutral solution for Laos as the only practical course of action, and patience was running thin with the general's antics. In February 1962 Ambassador Harriman fired General Phoumi's closest American military adviser in Laos, Jack Hazey; and in March Secretary of State Rusk reassured the Thais with a commitment in writing that the US would come to their aid if ever an enemy – be it Chinese, Vietnamese or Laotian – were threatening. Soon after that General Phoumi's image as a military leader was further tarnished when his troops fled from Luang Nam Tha in total disarray after a slight provocation.

Even with this hapless outcome, given its conviction that Thai security depended on Laos, the US was willing to move about 10,000 ground and air force troops into Thailand as insurance against a communist drive on General Phoumi's heels.[7] Some of the American soldiers were dispatched as far north as Udorn; their presence served the additional purpose of encouraging the communists to put an end to delays and ceasefire violations and to settle the negotiations.

The region of north-northwest Laos continued to be the object of much politicking after the signing of the Geneva Accords (July 1962). Prime Minister Prince Souvanna Phouma sent none other than General Phoumi Nosavan to Peking to confirm the road-building agreement. Prince Souvanna chose the right-wing general to signal that he would not double-cross the US with respect to the Chinese, for all his determination to bring to Laos the substance as well as the form of neutralism.

But General Phoumi added a curious twist to this mission. A member of the Laotian delegation to Peking later recalled the rightist general had tried to ingratiate himself with Chou En-lai by meeting privately to work out an agreement that probably remained unwritten. In this consultation Phoumi reportedly asked that the Chinese road be extended to Luang Nam Tha, the town that his troops had abandoned in panic at the thought of a Chinese invasion only 7 months earlier. Radio Peking announced Phoumi's agreement to Chinese aid in the form of road-building not only to Luang Nam Tha but also as far as Ban Houei Sai, on the Mekong River opposite Thailand. Confusion persisted. Prince Souvanna subsequently claimed General Phoumi had merely proposed the Nam Tha extension. Furthermore the prime minister had no recollection of any discussion of the Ban Houei Sai segment; in any event the Royal Lao Government had never approved anything more than the Meng La/Phong Saly road.

The Chinese put as many as 10,000 labourers to work building the road to Phong Saly town in 1962–3. Chinese armed sentries guarded construction sites. But for all this labour and attention, the road itself was a relatively simple dirt and gravel strip of laterite, the red clay soil found all over northern Laos. This portion was completed and formally turned over to the Royal Lao Government at a ceremony in Phong Saly town on 25 May 1963. According to Laotian government officials, all the road–builders were then withdrawn to China, with the possible exception of maintenance crews.

By this time Phong Saly province was well on its way to becoming a Chinese preserve. The Chinese consulate in Phong Saly town was formidable; it had the the region's only electrical generator. General

Khammouane Boupha, the local warlord, was increasingly difficult to contact for both Americans, with whom he had worked closely in the late 1950s, and representatives of the Laotian government. It appeared that General Khammouane, a practical man, was making a separate peace with the Chinese.

After May 1963 the Chinese denied all news reports about their continued road-building activity. But by mid-November 1964 they were building laterite roads south and west of Meng La, from the Yunnanese town of Meng Mong to Muong Sing[8] and Luang Nam Tha in Laos. There was little information on the work force but it was smaller than the crew that had built the Meng La/Phong Saly segment. Once these roads were completed to Muong Sing and Luang Nam Tha about a year later, the Chinese slackened off for several years.

Circumstances were changing rapidly in Southeast Asia. Under the Geneva Agreements for Laos, the Pathet Lao were no longer confined to their two provinces for regroupment; they had participated in the coalition government for less than a year, and then withdrawn from Vientiane in opposition to the government. By late 1963 the Royal Lao Government forces – the neutralists had now joined the rightists and their American supporters – were pitted against the Pathet Lao and their North Vietnamese sponsors (with, of course, support from the Chinese and the Russians) on the Plain of Jars and the Khammouane Plateau. In the latter arena General Phoumi Nosavan's offensive was widely interpreted as his effort to 'regain face' after the debacle at Luang Nam Tha the previous year.[9] The military encounters on the Plain were sparked by dissension and tensions among the neutralists, exacerbated by the Pathet Lao, who were trying to lure neutralists into their camp. The Laotian coalition that had been carefully constructed in 1962 had disintegrated to a point of outright confrontation, and factions in the neutralist middle chose sides to the right or left.

During these months the North Vietnamese had moved closer to the Chinese as the Sino–Soviet split had intensified. Before World War II Ho Chi Minh had spent time in both China and the Soviet Union, but now the struggle for South Vietnam was looking like a protracted one directed by rural guerrillas, in short a Maoist strategy.[10] Moreover the Russians' agreement with the Americans to the Nuclear Test Ban Treaty in July 1963 had weakened their position as leader of the fight against the capitalist camp, to say nothing of their role as co-chairman of the Laos negotiations. Having opted for detente and the role of peacemaker, Khruschev proposed an international conference on Laos in July 1964 – a proposal that did not sit well with the Chinese or the North Vietnamese.

Perhaps Ho Chi Minh caught wind of the fact that Khrushchev's hold on power was becoming tenuous in the summer of 1964.[11] Just after the Tonkin Gulf incident in early August, North Vietnam's tilt toward Peking began to right itself as the Vietnamese communists reassessed Moscow's utility.[12] The Soviets would be important as a source of military hardware, for which the North Vietnamese need became all the more pressing as the Americans were poised for entry into the war for South Vietnam.

All this manouevring within the communist bloc was relevant to the Chinese road in Laos in that a central concern was supplies and the road was a link in that network. The Chinese were refusing the Soviets both an air corridor to North Vietnam and landing rights at bases in southern China to serve North Vietnam. The Chinese mistrusted Soviet intentions and were angling for primacy as the patron of the North Vietnamese and the Pathet Lao. The infrastructure was a means to that end.

By 1967 information came to light about North Vietnamese/ Chinese logistics west of the Nam Ou that further confirmed the Chinese control of the region around the road.[13] This pattern was probably established after the pause in road-building in Laos in 1965. In any event the system relied on Chinese-built roads[14] as follows. Annual requests for supplies for Laos went first to the Northwest (North Vietnam) Military Region headquarters at Son La. The North Vietnamese operating in northwest Laos sent their requests directly to this office, while the Pathet Lao appeals went to the central headquarters in Sam Neua, to be bundled with the wish-lists from all six provinces of northern Laos before being forwarded to Son La.[15] The chain proceeded from Son La to Hanoi to China.

Both Vietnamese and Laotians picked up their goods – arms, ammunition, basic food staples, footware, blankets and mosquito nets – in Kunming, Yunnan. The allotments remained separate, with the Laotians receiving additional commodities that were then sold to civilians, including groceries, agricultural tools and cloth. The Vietnamese brought all their supplies through the Laotian town of Muong Sing at the Chinese border to store in Luang Nam Tha for use by their forces in northwestern Laos.[16] The Pathet Lao had no such central warehouse, but the sale of the civilian commodities must have

remained under their control, as proceeds financed Laotian communists' administrative expenses. The Chinese were underwriting their
Laotian allies in both military and political functions.

After a $2\frac{1}{2}$ year hiatus in Chinese road-building in northwest Laos,
American intelligence picked up the first evidence of Chinese troops
along the road. Throughout the summer rainy season of 1968 Chinese
contruction crews with heavy equipment built a link between the
Meng La/Phong Saly road and the Laotian town of Ban Botene – a
paved road. South from there the hard-top split: one branch led to
Luang Nam Tha, and the other went east toward Muong Hai, then
south to Muong Sai, a town on the Nam Pak, which flowed north into
the Nam Ou. The Chinese advised the people of Ban Botene to build
air-raid shelters, and in October nine anti-aircraft guns appeared near
the town.

In November Prime Minister Souvanna Phouma told Americans in
Vientiane he was frightened and worried, and reported the Soviets'
reaction. At mention of the Chinese road, the Soviet ambassador
shrugged, then bemoaned the Chinese as unpredictable and irrespon-
sible. Souvanna estimated the number of Chinese road-workers at
5,000.

American intelligence on the road ranged from high-altitude photo
surveillance to some rudimentary techniques, for example, estimat-
ing the number of Chinese workers at a camp by the number of
volleyball courts. Several networks fed information from people on
the ground. CIA-trained teams of local Laotians patrolled regularly,
counting workers, noting machinery and marking progress. Beginning in 1963 the US Agency for International Development had set up
medical dispensaries with Laotian staff throughout the country;
inevitably the medics heard the regional news as patients came from
surrounding towns. Similarly the grapevine of villagers travelling to
market towns carried accounts of unusual events. These less formal
sources were no less carefully monitored, but all intelligence-
gathering is vulnerable to human foibles. Every so often, just when
the system appeared fail-safe, with all its double-checks, it would
become apparent that a road-watch team had eaten its rations,
enjoyed a walk in the hills, and completely fabricated its reports.

Because the renewed road-building in the rainy season of 1968
occurred about the same time as the start of the Paris Peace Talks
between North Vietnamese and US negotiators, Americans mulled
over the idea that Peking might be preparing for an Indochinese
settlement that did not suit its fancy. In May the Chinese had been

open about their displeasure with Hanoi's willingness to talk. It later became evident that the Chinese had moved a construction force to Laos from North Vietnam after the partial halt to American bombing there in March 1968 – crews that had been in North Vietnam repairing damage from the American bombs.[17]

Shortly, Prince Souvanna Phouma explained his strategy for dealing with the road for the next several months. He cautioned the US Air Force to be most careful not to attack inadvertently. USAF activity over Laos had been building up gradually since 1964, with a boost since the partial halt over North Vietnam, thanks to the availability of planes; at this time the USAF was flying approximately fifty sorties a day over northern Laos. Souvanna's admonition was premised on the unwritten agreement that Phoumi Nosavan had reached in Peking in late 1962; perhaps there was enough substance for this to serve the Chinese as a legitimate pretext for retaliation if they could claim the agreement had been violated. Whether the Chinese had grounds for their actions, the prime minister deferred any reaction until he could ascertain their intentions. Maybe the Chinese were worried by recent North Vietnamese road-building in Phong Saly province, he speculated. The Vietnamese were then upgrading what was known as Route 19, south and west from Dien Bien Phu toward the Nam Ou.

Souvanna Phouma was quick to remind those calculating a response to the road of the 800 million Chinese citizens who were willing to avenge any perceived wrong. An unfortunate incident in December 1968 reinforced this point. A plaque from the People's Republic's embassy in Vientiane disappeared. The PRC *chargé d'affaires* protested; he demanded to know who the Laotians considered themselves to permit such an insult to the great Chinese, who could send down 10,000 troops – that would be enough – and expunge Laos from the map. The threat to use the People's Liberation Army was highly unusual. This same Chinese diplomat continued to feign ignorance of any compatriots building any roads in Laos since the portion completed in 1963.

In early 1969 the Chinese road turned north from Muong Sai, heading only toward Route 19 and Dien Bien Phu. Chinese intentions were a greater mystery than western intelligence could divine. Even Souvanna was at a loss.

An old trail led south from Muong Sai into the Beng Valley, through which the Beng River flowed south into the Mekong. This trail, which could be upgraded to a road, ended at the town of Pak

Beng at the mouth of the Beng, where the Mekong runs a scant 25 kilometres from the Lao–Thai border. The corner of Thailand due south of Pak Beng, northeast Nan province, was home to Thai dissidents, against whom Bangkok had staged sporadic military actions throughout the 1960s. Because of the proximity of this sensitive region to Pak Beng, the Thais became more nervous, and vocal, about Chinese intentions in northwest Laos when, after periodic mortar attacks, Pathet Lao and North Vietnamese forces moved into Pak Beng in early April 1969.

The history of the Thai insurgency warrants a brief digression, as it goes a long way toward explaining the Thai reaction to the Chinese road, and the pressure the Thais exerted on Americans and Laotians with respect to the road.[18]

Traditionally the northern Thai principalities that centred around the towns of Chieng Mai, Lamphang, Nan and Cheing Rai had closer relations with the Laotian principality of Luang Prabang than with Bangkok. The French colonialists knew nothing of these links across the Mekong when, in the late nineteenth century, they wrested from the Siamese the collection of fiefdoms they called Laos. The connections remained, and, by inference, so did the distance some northern Thais felt from their central government. The region is as mountainous as northwest Laos, and as much of an ethnic patchwork.

Bangkok tried more actively to make its presence felt in the far north from the 1950s. One of the first issues raised was whether to grant Thai citizenship to highland tribal people. Thai-dwelling Hmong, one of these tribal peoples, had migrated south from China more recently than the Hmong of Laos, and retained family ties with Hmong remaining in China as well as linguistic similarities. At about the same time, Thai Hmong were recruited from Nan, Chieng Rai and Petchabun provinces to serve with the Pathet Lao in Laos.[19] The communist recruiters promised to re-establish a Hmong king, harking back to the glory days of the Hmong kingdom in China about 1,500 years earlier. Would the Hmong and other highland tribal people of the north, many with their roots in China, be loyal to Bangkok? The Thai central government wondered about that.

In late 1966 and early 1967 there were reports of people leaving northern Thailand for military training at the Hoa Binh military academy in North Vietnam. The Thai Border Patrol Police started asking for identification papers at the northern borders, and shortly the authorities had their first bona fide communist prisoner with a telling background. A Sino–Thai, he had been born in Bangkok, had returned to China for schooling and had been recruited there by the Chinese Foreign Ministry in 1964. This young communist had spent some time near Hanoi, and then did on-the-job training in Laos.[20] He seemed to confirm all Bangkok's worst fears.

The Thai army reacted to this and other incidents by launching a campaign to move highland villagers down to the lowlands where they could be monitored more easily. Any who refused were labelled 'communists', and in some cases were then attacked with napalm. This gross overreaction was checked, but even as late as March 1969 the widely respected Thai King Bhumipol was prompted to speak out against army tactics that were still creating 'red Meos'.[21]

To some extent the Thai army used the Chinese road in Laos to add to the claims about the threat of communist aggression in the north – fuel to fire the Thai domestic debate about how to handle insurgency. And because the US contributed heavily to the Thai military budget – the figure ranged from 25 per cent to 33 per cent in 1965–9 – Americans were necessarily drawn into the discussion.[22]

This is not to make light of Thais' unease about security in the north. Not only did they have hard evidence of the insurgency, but the Communist Party of Thailand's 'Office No. 30' and the 'Anti-American School 31' were both located near the Laotian town of Muong Sai. In April 1969 the friendly evacuation of Pak Beng and the advance of Chinese road-building portended more expeditious overland routes between China, North Vietnam, and the insurgents' area of northern Thailand.

While Souvanna was worried too about the Chinese intentions, the Thais irritated him. They were stirring up trouble, with some grounds but exaggerated claims. Any fighting around the road would start on Laotian soil, with Laotian lives on the line. At this point Souvanna was reluctant to challenge the People's Republic on its violations of both Laotian territory and the 1962 Geneva Agreement unless a large power was willing to back him up. The prime minister was taking soundings on the depth of his American support.

AMBASSADOR GODLEY IN LAOS

This was the situation by July 1969 when I arrived in Vientiane as the American Ambassador. The Chinese were progressing steadily south through the Beng Valley while all others observed. As long as the Chinese purposes remained obscure, and as long as Souvanna believed a shred of legitimacy covering the Chinese road-building could be construed from General Phoumi's ambiguous conversations in Peking in 1962, Washington was wary of taking any action. Moreover, if the Chinese *chargé*'s protests over the missing plaque in Vientiane and his threat of the People's Liberation Army invading Laos were any clues to how they might react to objections about the road, then only the most foolhardy would tread heavily. The Chinese had sent their army to trounce the Indians when President Nehru denounced their road-building in the disputed Sino–Indian border area in 1962. The parallel with Laos was clear. And the Chinese might be more vigorous in their response to Laos, it being a small state and a former Chinese tributary.

But only a few months later the Sino–Indian dispute seemed more like an argument for action than restraint. By this logic the Indians had made the mistake of waiting too long before they protested, allowing the problem to get out of hand.

In addition Prime Minister Souvanna Phouma was changing his position; though still unwilling to put objections to the road in writing to the Chinese, he was under pressure from several sides to take some action against the road. For all the exasperation they might provoke, the Thais had good access to Souvanna's ear; they were providing trainers for the Laotian forces both in Laos and Thailand, two artillery battalions, air bases for USAF planes flying over Laos and numerous other contributions to the Royal Laotian Government's defence effort. The Thais had close links to the Laotian right wing. The Laotian king in Luang Prabang was also pressuring Souvanna for a move against the road. His Majesty was more immediately threatened by reason of proximity; the road was heading for the Mekong at a point about 150 kilometres by flat river from Luang Prabang. Once the king weighed in for a military solution, Souvanna could no longer hold out.

In mid-December 1969 we in the American Embassy in Vientiane made our first pitch to Washington for military action against the road. Our suggestion was to limit harassment to visible but harmless overflights and a blocking force of Laotian guerrillas. The idea was to draw the line while Laotian diplomats discreetly approached their Chinese and Russian counterparts. Keeping these moves quiet would allow the Chinese the opportunity of backing off, whereas public pressure would run the risk of locking each side into irreconcilable positions.

Public pressure was already building. Just before the embassy staff had submitted our proposal for low-keyed action to Washington.

Souvanna had given his first interview about the road. Talking to a reporter for the *Bangkok Post*, the prime minister said the recent construction by the Chinese in the Beng Valley was not covered by the 1962 agreement.

Some of my colleagues in Washington squirmed: they had hoped Souvanna would limit his commentary to private rather than public channels. However, Prince Souvanna Phouma was in a tough spot in domestic politics. His cabinet members were all abuzz about a report by Senator Mansfield with a passing reference to the lack of concern among Laotian officials about the Chinese road. The right wing, often synonymous with the armed forces, was irate. The rightist Minister of Foreign Affairs, Khamphan Panya, went so far as to suggest that with Americans wishing for peace in Vietnam, perhaps we were planning to throw Laos to the Chinese. General Ouane Rattikone, commander-in-chief of the Royal Lao Army, told American embassy officals that he feared Souvanna would not be tough enough in dealing with the Chinese. In Vientiane we surmised that Souvanna's comments to the *Bangkok Post* had been directed as much at the Laotian rightists as at the Chinese.

The US had to be careful not to close down too many of Prince Souvanna Phouma's options so as to avoid isolating him from his right-wing support. Nonetheless the military proposal was offered to Washington with reservations: we felt obliged to support Souvanna, but were not perturbed when Washington took the role of nay-sayer. At the front line we were fearful of the massive Chinese army; the Yalu River syndrome was a great chastener.

The US was not in a particularly strong position to object to Souvanna's using the press to manage his domestic debate. (Frankly I preferred he sound off to the press rather than personally to me.) In October the *New York Times* had published a small story headlined 'China Road Force in Laos at 20,000: Asian sources say link to Muong Sai is completed'. Although the story was attributed only to unnamed 'Asian diplomatic sources', some American had given at least an oblique go-ahead. The sources based their claims on information derived from aerial photos shown by American officials; no American would comment, but none would challenge the story either.[23]

The timing of this story was too fortuitous to have been simple chance. In the preceding month American press attention to Laos had increased markedly, with the Vientiane press corps swelling from its usual three or four to some twenty. The Laotian Hmong general, Vang Pao, had just retaken the Plain of Jars, the first time the Royal

Lao government had occupied this strategic territory since 1964. For his victory the general had relied on American air power both to move his troops and to bomb the enemy. This had certainly happened before, although never resulting in such a dramatic success. In addition the US Congress was planning hearings about the extent of American commitment to Laos later that month. The sub-text to the *New York Times* story about the Chinese road was: we may be violating the spirit of the 1962 Geneva Agreement (only at the request of the Laotian government and with no American ground troops), but, in addition to those North Vietnamese Army regulars whom General Vang Pao has just defeated on the Plain of Jars, look at the Chinese.

By this time the road was an open secret. But Washington was prepared to take action against it only if the Laotians put their objections in writing to the Chinese, and gave the Chinese a chance to respond. The Laotian king, the head of state in this constitutional monarchy, could send a protocolary note to thank the Chinese for the road, indicating the Laotians considered the project complete.

The suggestion seemed far-fetched to me. To my knowledge the king had never signed a policy statement. He had never taken the lead on a controversial issue, being loath to expose himself to criticism from any quarter. In this case he had an easy out. We were informed that the king's thinking ran along the following lines: since the Pathet Lao claimed they were building the road (a Pathet Lao spokesman had recently tried to pass off this ruse), then why not bomb it as the Royal Lao Air Force or the USAF would any bona fide Pathet Lao installation?

Souvanna too was agitating for military measures, but he was still willing to try diplomatic moves. He would talk to the Soviet and British ambassadors, whose countries had co-chaired the 1962 Geneva Conference and had a continuing responsibility, in theory, for Laotian neutrality. However, the Soviets were typically wary of their role as international peacemaker in Laos; it impinged on their more valued role as leaders of the communist world, which was in danger of being ceded to the Chinese. The British had little clout and even less interest in roiling the already troubled waters in Southeast Asia. They offered the brave advice that the Laotians file a protest, a slight diplomatic escalation from the protocolary note that Washington had proposed.

My colleagues in Washington had put forth this suggestion perhaps in the interests of a stalemate. In Vientiane we knew only a bit of the story, but enough to be aware that Washington's agenda with Peking had higher priorities than Sino–Lao relations. For all the years when there were no direct contacts in Peking or Washington, American and Chinese diplomats had held intermittent talks in Warsaw, where the PRC had an embassy, as did the US. Communication was circuitous and discreet but nonetheless taking place.

President Richard Nixon had taken office in January 1969 with some new ideas about how the US should deal with China. In 1967, writing in *Foreign Affairs*, he had hinted at the need to open relations with the People's Republic, since it was, after all, the colossus of the Orient. During his presidential campaign in 1968 Nixon repeatedly claimed to have a 'secret plan' to end the war in Vietnam. He refused to outline it and suffered a fair bit of ridicule for discretion that could just as easily have been hiding a void. In fact he was hoping for diplomatic relations with the Chinese and improved relations with the Soviets. Nixon believed both large enemies would see a benefit to better relations with the US – at least as a counterweight to the other's improving friendship with America, a tricky play on trilateralism. Abetted by his globalist adviser, Henry Kissinger, Nixon expected that both communist powers would then pressure North Vietnam to leave South Vietnam under the American umbrella.

This reasoning was too clever by half. In fact the syllogism played into the pitfall that the State Department is supposed to war against – ignorance of local conditions, in this case North Vietnam's tenaciousness in its drive to gain control of South Vietnam. With hindsight it appears Nixon and Kissinger overestimated the intention of either the Soviets or the Chinese to influence the North Vietnamese, and policymakers neglected the element of US weakness. Chairman Mao understood from Vietnam the shortcomings of American power; US military might alone was not insurance of victory. Judging by the lack of response to the Chinese road in Laos, Mao could have deduced that the Americans were beginning to recognise the limited utility of military power in such circumstances.

With luck, the Chinese were developing an interest in drawing closer to the United States for their own reasons, leaving aside the growing American appreciation for political versus military strength. However, the Chinese approach was not premised on the power alignments that Richard Nixon perceived; rather the Chinese were becoming increasingly fearful of their neighbour to the north, the Soviet Union. Spooked by the Soviet invasion of Czechoslavakia in August 1968, the Chinese realised the Brezhnev Doctrine of limited sovereignty for satellite communist states could just as easily apply to them. This apprehension had a geographic focus too: the Sino-Soviet border had long been disputed, dating back to the era of the tsars' expansionist drives into Chinese-claimed northern territories. In March 1969 tensions erupted, and for the next several months incidents spread from the border between the Chinese province of Heilongjiang (the northern region of the area formerly known as Manchuria) and Soviet Siberia as far west as China's Sinkiang and Soviet Kazakhstan.

On 11 December 1969 a move of diplomatic protocol with historic ramifications took place. The American Ambassador to Poland was invited to enter the Chinese mission in Warsaw by the front door.

Would the US then provide the wherewithal to its Laotian allies for an operation against the Chinese road in Laos? As the Chinese pushed farther south towards the Mekong, the Thais agitated more vociferously in favour of a blocking action, as did the Laotians – the King and Souvanna included.

By this stage discussions of the Chinese road were increasingly framed in terms of the politics of American disengagement from Southeast Asia. President Nixon had announced the first troop withdrawals from South Vietnam in June 1969, effective by the end of August. During the summer the Thais agreed to start talks about gradually sending home the 48,000 Americans stationed there. By the autumn Nixon's respite from the pressures of the anti-war movement had expired, and America's Southeast Asian allies worried about how speedily responsive the US would be to domestic dissent. In early December the *New York Times* reported the US was spending $1 billion to support a single Thai division in South Vietnam; the Thais were so angered by this publicity and foolish overstatement that they threatened to withdraw from the SEATO alliance. In one breath the Thais berated American inability to keep a secret, compounding the sin with an irresponsible press corps, and in the next they fretted about the Chinese in the Beng Valley.

A week after the fuss about subsidies for the Thai troops in South Vietnam, the 'Voice of the People of Thailand' announced the first 'liberated village' in a broadcast from Peking. That village, Ngam Pao, nestled in the mountains of Thailand's northeastern Nan Province, due south of the Chinese line of advance through Laos.

For all the fears about taking on the Chinese, American officials in Vientiane worried that passivity might encourage the Thais or the Laotians to act unilaterally. On the other hand, inaction could persuade the Laotians they had no choice but to accommodate their communist neighbours at the expense of Lao–American relations.[24] So in formulating plans for the dry season that was just beginning, embassy staff scaled down the first proposal for military action. Operation Snake Eyes would be limited to a wider programme than usual of intelligence gathering by CIA-trained Laotian guerrillas along the Chinese road.

Betraying our ambivalence about the prospect of taking on the Chinese, however, our proposal included the counter-arguments. Any probe would not deter the Chinese, as the earlier proposal for blocking would have. In addition, the enemy could always reinforce its positions, thanks to the fine road leading to wherever we chose to harass. A Lao–American military failure along the Chinese road would then bolster the enemy's morale; they would conclude that while we were willing to support the Laotians in combat with the North Vietnamese, we were unwilling to put our all behind a fight that might lead to a confrontation with the awesome numbers of the Chinese People's Liberation Army. On the domestic political scene in Laos the US would run the risk of strengthening the hand of the right, those who wished to replace Souvanna. If the operation failed, the Laotian military would blame the US, which could in turn affect the higher American priority – Laotian acquiescence to the fight against the North Vietnamese along the Ho Chi Minh Trail. The US had no interest in aggression against the Chinese, but also could not go too far in restraining the Laotians for fear of undermining an ally's faith in American support.

In the first week of January 1970 two Laotian T-28s strayed just within range of the Chinese anti-aircraft guns. Responding to fire, one pilot dropped a bomb that knocked the leaves off some trees, revealing about fifteen parked trucks. The Laotians could not restrain themselves, and they flew away only after ten trucks were ablaze.

The Chinese could hardly object. Since they continued to deny any knowledge of the road's existence, let alone protective anti-aircraft guns, any protest would only blow their cover. The Laotian military appeared to be satisfied, and perhaps unwilling to push their luck. Souvanna was angry with the pilots but realised he was getting out of a sticky situation with minimal damage; a few weeks later he coyly told the press the Chinese road was, like the Ho Chi Minh Trail, 'not for tourism'. The Thais continued to watch the road with high anxiety, raising or lowering the decibel level of their agitation as other factors impinged. Americans remained riveted to photo intelligence reports and the like, engaging in endless discussions of what might be done next.

President Nixon had approved a small blocking action by US-financed Laotian forces in the Beng Valley by mid-January, but this approval was contingent on the Laotians making a public statement to the Chinese, a change of style from the previous prerequisite of private but official notice. Prime Minister Souvanna Phouma's passing commentary to the press was not directed to the Chinese, and so it did not count. The king inquired periodically when he could expect military action against the road, and it was becoming clear the US had backed itself into an unfortunate position with respect to the Laotian government.

It was widely known around Vientiane that American stipulations were forestalling any move against the road. The Soviets and the Poles rarely failed to remind Laotian officals of this limit to American support. The Soviets even went so far as to suggest the 'mysterious' pattern of American bombing could indicate that Laos was a site of Sino–American collusion.[25] The impression that Americans were dictating the Laotians' response (or lack thereof) to a foreign incursion served neither American nor Laotian purposes. Therefore I did my best to get Washington to set a deadline: if the Chinese advanced south of Muong Houn, say, would the US help stop them with military measures?

I sent that message to Washington in mid-March 1970, an unforgettable time for the convergence of events that pushed the Chinese road off anyone's list of hottest trouble spots in the region. On 17 March the North Vietnamese and their Pathet Lao allies were threatening General Vang Pao's headquarters southeast of the Plain of Jars; civilians were evacuated from the neighbouring town, leaving a 200-bed hospital to be set on fire by the enemy. The following day Cambodian Prime Minister Norodom Sihanouk was ousted in a coup by his top advisers, General Lon Nol and Prince Sirik Matak. The subsequent South Vietnamese and American invasion of Cambodia, targeting North Vietnamese and Vietcong sanctuaries, relegated the Chinese road in Laos to back-burner status for several months.

In June 1970, as the Chinese started clearing their path south of Muong Houn, the American Embassy in Vientiane revived the proposal to Washington of small-scale guerrilla harassment, this time with air support from the Royal Thai Air Force. (We chose not to recommend USAF jets in the interest of downplaying the proposed confrontation, and the Laotian Air Force had only T-28s, which were vulnerable to the Chinese 57 mm anti-aircraft guns.) But the chance for Washington's approval was lost. Those at the State Department who had argued against the Cambodian invasion on the grounds that it would precipitate an unduly strong domestic reaction had strengthened their hand when just such a reaction occurred. Moreover, unlike the Cambodian sanctuaries, the military gains in attacking the Chinese road would not be justifiable in terms of speeding the withdrawal of American troops from South Vietnam. Moreover, for the first time, Sino–American talks in Warsaw were cited as an additional reason for restraint. By late September, after a joint State–Defense review, the answer was definitive and final: no US-supported action against the road. While the US could not tell the Laotians what to do with assets under their control, their T-28s were supplied by the US and the supply was running out.

Major changes were afoot in Sino–American relations. Apart from the Warsaw talks, both sides started dropping hints of interest in better relations. Chairman Mao had his picture taken with American journalist Edgar Snow on 1 October, the PRC's National Day, while Nixon said casually he would like to visit China.[26] Unbeknown to anyone in State, in a message hand-delivered through the Pakistanis in early December, Premier Chou En-lai invited Nixon to send a representative to Peking. Concurrently American military brass in Saigon were planning an invasion of central Laos, an effort to cut the Ho Chi Minh Trail that would inadvertently test China's faith in our sincere desire for better relations.[27]

In January 1971 fire control radar installations first appeared along the Chinese road in northwest Laos. China was preparing for the worst.

Much as the US feared the prospect of an invasion by untold numbers of Chinese infantry, China's leaders worried about their vulnerability to an American attack.[28] The groundwork for the operation into Laos (Lam Son 719) started in early January. American forces were not to enter Laos, but, in this preparatory phase, they worked on the portion of the east-west road, Route 9, that runs thorough northern South Vietnam. Route 9 crosses Laos too, running just south of the 17th parallel. Given the North Vietnamese level of preparedness once the combat phase of Lam Son 719 started, they probably had picked up intelligence about the planned operation before then; and there is little doubt the North Vietnamese informed their Chinese allies.

On 8 February South Vietnamese troops, supported by American air power and artillery, crossed the border into Laos. Washington had reason to believe that China was worried about the possible use of tactical nuclear weapons as part of Lam Son 719.[29] To allay this fear, in his 17 February press conference on the operation President Nixon explicitly ruled out the use of tactical nuclear weapons. He also specified that the operation was not directed against China. Nevertheless by late February as many as twenty-five fire control radar vans were stationed along the Chinese road in northwest Laos to support the anti-aircraft guns and to relay information to Kunming – in effect an early warning system.

In early March Premier Chou En-lai went to Hanoi to reassure the North Vietnamese of China's support in general and to increase military aid in response to the South Vietnamese attack on the Ho Chi Minh Trail in south-central Laos. No doubt Nixon, Kissinger and their few associates who knew about Chou's invitation were holding their breath. For those not in the know, Chou's comments in Hanoi were notable for linking the security of North Vietnam to that of the People's Republic, the first such close identification in several years.[30]

However, Lam Son 719 was probably most important to the Chinese in underscoring the American commitment to withdraw from Vietnam, a lesson that even those who were unapprised of the Chou–Nixon correspondence could draw. The operation was a disaster. This was evident as early as mid-March, and the last South Vietnamese Army troops were withdrawn from Laotian soil on 9 April. The most enduring images from the effort were pictures of South Vietnamese soldiers clinging to American helicopter runners in their desperate attempt to get away and American forces in South Vietnam did not try to remedy the debacle.[31]

The Chinese could not have hoped for a more favourable outcome. Had the South Vietnamese troops succeeded, China would have had to come to Hanoi's aid. If the US had mounted a salvage operation, the credibility of America's gradual withdrawal from South Vietnam[32] would have been damaged.

But the Chinese were hedging their bets. In April 1971 they brought more anti-aircraft guns into Northwest Laos, grouping them around the most southerly point along their two-lane black-top, Muong Houn; and they added even more sophisticated radar equipment. With some 2,000 additional anti-aircraft personnel, the Chinese air defence force in Laos was up to 6,000 or 7,000, and about

16,000 Chinese in all were engaged in working on the road through the Beng Valley, according to intelligence at the time. It looked as if the Chinese feared a surprise air attack by Americans based in Thailand.[33]

That same month in Japan, the Chinese invited the American ping-pong team to visit China, the start of 'ping-pong diplomacy'.[34]

In late April, while the Chinese renewed work on northern legs of the road in northwest Laos (between Ban Botene and Muong Sai, and southwest toward Luang Nam Tha), some Laotian officials welcomed the apparent thaw in Sino–American relations. Oddly enough, when two USAF planes accidentally bombed the Chinese road, the incidents elicited no reaction.[35] The errors were successfully hushed up, and the Laotians continued to wax eloquent about their own desires for friendship with the Chinese. Prime Minister Souvanna Phouma went so far as to tell *New York Times* reporter Henry Kamm that the Lao people were of Chinese origin, and the Chinese were the only neighbours that had never attacked Laos. The Laotians were eager for peace.

A new mystery to the road construction then appeared. Since early 1971 the road from Muong Sai toward Dien Bien Phu had stopped at Muong Khoua on the west bank of the Nam Ou. By mid-year it seemed safe to conclude the bridge that would connect the Chinese roads directly to northwestern North Vietnam simply would not be built. Either the Chinese were reluctant to give the North Vietnamese too easy access to the Chinese sphere of influence in Laos, or the North Vietnamese were refusing the Chinese a direct route into northwestern North Vietnam.

In July 1971 the wheels of change spun a full revolution. President Nixon announced that Kissinger's secret trip to Peking had paved the way for a presidential visit, the start of normalising relations.

I was as surprised as any other American at the speed of radical shifts in power alignments. However, the Laotians were several steps ahead, already engaged in discussions about sending an ambassador to Peking. Souvanna had not anticipated Kissinger's trip, but his reaction was completely favourable; his rightist foreign minister described the news as 'a perfumed bombshell'. Later that summer, when the rains were horrendous in Laos, the Chinese chargé offered the first small aid package, a little money to combat the floods.

The Chinese continued to send mixed messages through Laos. In March 1972, just after Nixon and Chou had issued their historic joint communiqué from Shanghai, the first Chinese infantry regiment moved into the Muong Sai area of northwest Laos; and road-workers were completing the segment to Pak Beng, a sophisticated operation, with bulldozers, graders, and cement mixers. For several months, about this time, Laotian and Thai forces in Sayaboury Province lost an average of one man a day (killed or wounded) to Chinese-made plastic mines. Also attributable to the road were newly evident North Vietnamese advisers. From all reports, these cadres were supporting the Thai insurgents.

By late 1972, as Kissinger announced that 'peace is at hand' between Hanoi and Washington, it was no time to take on the Chinese. I had stopped raising the issue of the road with Laotians several months earlier. Even so I made one last effort to solicit Washington's approval for the Laotians and the Thai to draw a line beyond which the Chinese could only advance with force. The recommendation was not approved, as the issue was moot; it was entirely up to the Laotians and their Thai allies.

The US still had not much more of an idea what the Chinese were up to in northwest Laos than when they had started building the road. The American position had evolved gradually from cautious belligerence to withdrawing from Southeast Asia and opening relations with the People's Republic. The road had provided a useful point of reference for gauging the interests of allies, the Laotians and the Thais. But as for China, this erstwhile enemy's unavowed activities left more questions than answers.

Were the Chinese trying to strengthen their access to Phong Saly Province or exert control over their troubled southern border – or both? Were they showing the North Vietnamese what useful allies they could be in supplying the Pathet Lao? Were they carving a sphere of influence to limit North Vietnam's hegemony in Indonchina? Was the road a logistical hedge against attack from Thailand? Or was it more a funnel for support to the Thai insurgents? Was the road a place to signal the North Vietnamese or the Pathet Lao that a Sino–American thaw did not mean abandonment by the Chinese? Why was the bridge across the Nam Ou at Muong Khoua – a bridge that would have completed the road to Dien Bien Phu – never built?

These unanswered questions remain a sobering reminder of how limited American understanding of the region was then. But through the even partial explanations supplied at the time, and the additional questions these provoked, insights were gained; particularly revealing were the spectrum of responses from the US and from the Laotians and the Thais. Perhaps some historians will be able to shed fuller light on China's motives behind events surrounding their road in northwest Laos.

POSTSCRIPT

After the Pathet Lao took power in December 1975, they permitted the Chinese to continue road-building in northwest Laos as far south and east as Luang Prabang. Chinese influence predominated in this corner of Laos, marked by the unusal presence of economic and cultural missions in Oudomsai province, the region encompassing Muong Sai and the Beng Valley. No other foreign country was represented by consulates outside Vientiane; even Soviet advisers were kept out of northwest Laos.[36]

Relations between communist China and Laos started to deteriorate in 1977, when the Laotians signed their 25-year treaty of friendship with the Vietnamese, who were tilting more toward Moscow and stepping up pressure on their indigenous Chinese population. Initially the Laotians maintained a certain distance from the developing Sino–Vietnamese rancour. In April 1978 they staged a ceremony with some pageantry to thank the People's Republic for the roads in the northwest, a ploy that had been repeatedly urged on the former Royal Laotian Government as a signal that the roads were considered complete. In acknowledgement the Chinese withdrew 10,000 road workers, then reintroduced 5,000.[37] By late 1978 the Lao asked and the Chinese agreed to close their offices in Oudomsai. Before leaving, the Chinese bulldozed their buildings in Oudomsai town.

After the Vietnamese invaded Cambodia in December 1978 and the Chinese Army responded to teach the Vietnamese a 'lesson' in February 1979, reports of Chinese troops massing at the Laotian border circulated. The Chinese denied these allegations, referring to 'pressure' that forced the Laotians to make such charges; in fact the reports had come from Vietnamese and Soviet sources. The Vientiane government asked the Chinese to stop their road-building while extending 'profound thanks' for the effort.[38] Although both the Chinese and the Laotians were 'clearly reluctant actors',[39] each obliged to acrimonious exchanges by their respective relations with the Vietnamese and the Soviets, the rhetoric heated up.

By May 1979 the Chinese were harbouring Laotian resistance fighters in the Lao Socialist Party, whose goal was to liberate the country from Vietnamese influence. In June the Vientiane government reduced the Chinese diplomatic representation to twelve, led by a chargé d'affaires (the same level accorded the US). During these months the Laotians closed a re-education camp in the far north and walked all inmates south to Attopeu province. Apparently the Lao authorities were concerned the Chinese would not only invade but also take advantage of this concentration of anti-government manpower.[40]

Sino-Lao relations have since taken a turn for the better, in part thanks to the warming of Sino–Soviet relations. The Laotians greeted Soviet General Secretary Gorbachev's July 1986 Vladivostok speech with enthusiasm for the Sino-Soviet thaw he inaugurated. The Lao then announced their desire to resume ambassadorial-level relations with the Chinese, provided the Chinese stopped supporting anti-government elements in the northwest.[41] Two years later, in May 1988, the ambassadors, Phoungsavath Boupha and Liang Feng,[42] were named.

Notes

1. George McT. Kahin (1986) *Intervention: How America became involved in Vietnam* (New York: Alfred A. Knopf), footnote 71 (to text p.59), p. 451 cites: Francois Joyaux (1979) *La Chine et le Reglement du premier Conflit d'Indochine* (Paris: Publications de la Sorbonne), p. 231, for Chou's request that Pathet Lao regroupment areas abut China as well as Vietnam.
2. Arthur Dommen (1971) *Conflict in Laos: The Politics of Neutralization* (New York: Praeger), p. 193.

   American recognition of the Sino–Soviet split was sporadic. On the one hand, in negotiating the 1962 Geneva Agreement the US assumed that the Russians would be able to rein in the Chinese in Laos. On the other hand, the US certainly would not have entered into those negotiations had detente with the Russians, launched in 1959 when Khrushchev visited President Eisenhower at Camp David, not progressed. Since American's warming relations with the Soviets were one of the most irksome points of friction between the Chinese and the Soviets, and since this thaw and the resulting dilution of bipolarism contributed to American willingness to entertain the solution of neutrality for Laos, one can hardly argue that the US was categorically blind to the Sino–Soviet split.

   For a first-rate discussion of these dynamics, see Donald Zagoria (1967) *Vietnam Triangle: Moscow, Peking, Hanoi* (New York: Western Pub. Co. Inc.), 1967.
3. The US had not signed the 1954 Geneva Agreement, and therefore refused to be bound by its terms.

   American military advisers, the White Star teams, arrived in Laos under the auspices of the civilian Program Evaluation Office, starting in July 1959. When planners had proposed this particular training program, they were somewhat surprised at its acceptance, but later heard that the French had okayed the White Stars on the assumption the Laotians would refuse them; but the Laotians too had agreed to the advent of these American military teams, assuming the French would veto the program. See 'Case Study of US Counterinsurgency Operations in Laos, 1955–1962' (U) by Ben R. Baldwin, Richard D. Burke, Richard P. Joyce, Chrystal M. O'Hagan, M. Wanda Porterfield, Robert H. Williams, William Woodworth, Roswell B. Wing (Chair) (Research Analysis Corp., McLean VA, Operational Logistics Division, Technical Memorandum RAC T-435, September 1964), p. A15.

The change in question in 1961 was to transform the PEO into a uniformed Military Assistance Advisory Group.

4. Roger Hilsman (1967) *To Move a Nation: The Politics of Foreign Policy in the Administration of John F. Kennedy* (New York: Doubleday & Co), p. 134. Hilsman suggests there had been no thought to changing the civilian-clad military men in Laos into uniforms until the Bay of Pigs occurred days before this decision. That was not the case; the request for military uniforms in Laos had been submitted months earlier. But who is to say that Kennedy would have okayed military garb in Laos at the time, had it not been for the Cuba disaster?

5. Richard M. Nixon, 'Cuba, Castro and John F. Kennedy', *Readers Digest*, November 1964.

6. Hugh Toye (1968) *Laos: Buffer State or Battleground* (London: Oxford University Press), pp. 179–85.

7. Some of these troops were deployed for long-since-planned SEATO manoeuvres. However this deployment became the occasion for establishing a larger American military bureaucracy: a Military Assistance Command for Thailand (MAC-THAI). See the transcript of hearings before the Senate Foreign Relations Subcommittee on Security Agreements and Commitments Abroad: Thailand, November 10, 1969, pp. 614–15 (referred to hereafter as 'Thai hearings'.).

8. The Yunnanese town might be Meng Mang. Muong Sing was an important regional market town because of its salt wells.

9. At this point General Phoumi was benefiting from what was referred to as 'Cabinet Special Militaire', an organisation that was outside the Ministry of Defence and was used by Americans as a funnel for military aid.

10. This does not undercut the interpretation that both Souvanna Phouma and Phoumi Nosavan might have thought they could play off the Sino–Vietnamese antagonism. That hostility was traditional – Ho Chi Minh preferred the French to the Chinese as occupiers immediately after World War II, with this explanation: 'Better to sniff a bit of French shit briefly than eat Chinese shit for the rest of our lives' – and the papering over during the revolutionary period has proven to be thin.

11. Khrushchev was ousted in October 1964, in large measure, according to Zagoria, *op. cit.*, p. 43, because of Hanoi's leaning toward Peking in the Sino–Soviet conflict.

12. The timing of this change tempts the following speculation: it happened to coincide with China's resuming work on the road. Although no hard evidence exists, it seems logical the Chinese were quick to help the Laotians in an effort to counterbalance the North Vietnamese tilt toward Moscow. Granted Laos, and particularly northwest Laos, was a small sideshow to the larger struggle in Vietnam; nonetheless the road provided a foothold for the Chinese.

13. The workings of the logistics systems were revealed by two North Vietnamese Army defectors in Laos: Captain Mai Dai Hap, who came to Laos in February 1964 and defected in December 1966; and Ngo Van Dam, a medical student who headed the Nam Tha provincial medical services from October 1966 until he

312   *The Chinese Road in Northwest Laos 1961–73*

defected in May 1967. They were among some fifty defectors and prisoners of war, both North Vietnamese and Pathet Lao, whom Paul Langer and Joseph Zasloff interviewed in 1967. See their monograph, *Revolution in Laos: The North Vietnamese and the Pathet Laos*, Memorandum RM-5935-ARPA (Santa Monica: Rand Corp.), September 1969, pp. 161–3, 222.

14. North Vietnamese advisers were also in touch with their headquarters in Son La by 15-watt radio. Langer and Zasloff, *op. cit.*, p. 149, cite reports 'at least once a month… every three months, they send a broader summary… in unusual circumstances, they may… consult immediately…' In other words, the logistics system did not have to rely exclusively on roads.

15. *Ibid.*, pp. 147–8. At this stage the North Vietnamese had 'volunteer forces' in each Laotian province – two or three companies of 100–125 men – as well as 'mobile forces', who were called up from North Vietnam as needed. And for the most part, each Lao People's Liberation Army (the military arm of the Pathet Lao) battalion had two North Vietnamese advisers – one military, the other political.

16. It seems probable that there were similar storage facilities in Phong Saly province, and in the western half of Luang Prabang province, that the communists even then called 'Udomsai'. And it would have been logical for the Vietnamese portion of Chinese-supplied goods for these provinces to have gone from the Chinese town of Meng La, for example, directly to Phong Saly town.

17. Interestingly enough, these Chinese road crews had been part of a rather substantial movement of troops into North Vietnam in mid-1965, apparently in reaction to the advent of US ground troops to South Vietnam; by December 1965 some 35,000 Chinese anti-aircraft personnel, railroad engineering crews as well as the road crews, and supply units were active in North Vietnam. Evidently their purpose was to warn the American and South Vietnamese military about the prospects they would face in invading North Vietnam, as some hawks advocated then. For a fuller discussion, see Allen (1975) *The Chinese Calculus of Deterrence* (Ann Arbor: University of Michigan Press).

18. The Communist Party of Thailand Central Committee decided in 1960 to adopt a rural Maoist strategy that would be directed out of four regional branches: north, northeast, central and south. Even though the Thai government worried about the Chinese connections to all regions, only the north is of interest here because of its proximity to the Chinese road in northwest Laos. Nonetheless it is worth bearing in mind that so many Chinese have immigrated to Thailand over the past 200 years – with a large group moving from southern China to Bangkok in the 1930s and 1940s – that by some estimates the population of the capital city is now 50 per cent ethnic Chinese *(Far Eastern Economic Review*, 18 February 1988, pp. 44–8). It was not unusual for Chinese born in Thailand to return to China for a 'proper education' – see the example of the Sino-Thai prisoner captured in 1967 cited in the text below.

19. Jeffrey Race, 'The War in Northern Thailand', *Modern Asian Studies*, vol.8, 1, 1974, p. 92, cites 'a considerable number of Meo tribesmen (perhaps 400), who were recruited in 1957–9, and then left Laos in 1962, 'Meo' referring to the Hmong people.

20. *Ibid.*, p. 97.

21. *Ibid.*, p. 105. The King used the name often used for Hmong at the time – 'Meo'. About this time the Hmong let outsiders know this name is derogatory, meaning 'savage'.

22. 'Thai hearings', *op.cit.*, p. 634, cites figures for US military assistance (MAP/MASF) and as a percentage of the Royal Thai Government defence budget (only the Ministry of Defence, not including police and paramilitary, which would have raised the American percentage significantly): 1965: 24.40; 1966: 28.10; 1967: 31.13; 1968: 32.56; 1969: 28.65.

23. *New York Times*, 16 October 1969, p. 13.
24. One important determinant of US actions was fear that the Laotians would decide their American alliance was no longer worth their allowing the US to bomb the North Vietnamese along the Ho Chi Minh Trail, as mentioned in the text below. Inaction against the Chinese road was thus invoked as a reason for military actions elsewhere in Laos. For example, when General Vang Pao was being pushed off the Plain of Jars in late December and early January, serious consideration was given to the first use of B-52s in northern Laos; Kissinger and Nixon had been eager to use these bombers since July 1969. Kissinger had been pushing the embassy staff in Vientiane to find plausible military targets for the B-52s. A few targets were proffered in January–February 1970; however, the rationale rested heavily on the psychological benefits of the weapon – for one, to demonstrate American resolve to the Laotian allies while hesitating to confront the Chinese.
25. I. Andronov, a frequent Soviet commentator on Laos, wrote a column to this effect in *Novoye Vremya*, 19 March 1970. The US Embassy staff was not above poking fun of the Soviet flight patterns around the road; to avoid the Chinese anti-aircraft guns, Soviet planes always made a wide detour.
26. Henry A. Kissinger (1979) *White House Years* (Boston: Little Brown), p. 699. According to Kissinger, no American was acute enough to pick up Mao's message. Nixon commented on China in passing during an interview with *Time* magazine primarily about the crisis in Jordan.
27. Nixon and Kissinger received Premier Chou's invitation on 8 December 1970; planning for Lam Son 719 started in Saigon the same day.
28. See, for example, the conversation between Chinese Vice Foreign Minister Ch'iao Kuan-hua and a northern European ambassador, recounted in Ross Terrill (1971) *800,000,000: The Real China* (Boston: Atlantic-Little, Brown), p. 146. Some time between March and December 1971 the European queried the Chinese: hadn't Washington assured Peking the goals in Lam Son 719 were 'limited'? Replied Dr Ch'iao: 'We can never be sure.' He recalled the self-unleashing of General MacArthur on the Chinese-Korean border while Truman protested the 'limited' nature of the US's Korean operation. 'We were fairly confident of Nixon's limited intentions in Laos, but not sure some general wouldn't take it into his head to provoke China, or cover failure with a drastic escalation'.
29. *Ibid*, p. 145. Australian journalist Terrill wrote that he heard rumours as early as January 1971 of China's worries about nuclear weapons associated with the American/South Vietnamese build–up along the DMZ.
30. Reactions to Chou's speech and the joint PRC/DRV communiqué at the end of his visit offer a classic example of differing emphases, though not mutually exclusive. Chinese Vice Foreign Minister Ch'iao Kuan-hua explained in same conversation with the European diplomat, cited above in note [28], that the Chinese fear of some unauthorised American general leading the charge from Lam Son 719 to the Chinese border, 'can be discerned between the lines' of Chou's speech (Terrill, *op.cit.*, p. 146).
    In his memoirs, Kissinger writes, '...Chou En-lai during a visit to Hanoi... stayed clear of any personal invective against Nixon or threat of Chinese intervention', *op. cit.*, p. 707.
31. In December 1969 the US Senate had passed the Cooper–Church amendment to the Defense Appropriations bill, prohibiting the introduction of American ground troops to Laos or Thailand. To make an exception for Lam Son 719 would have required reopening the debate in Congress, a move the Nixon Administration was not prepared to make without any assurance of success.
32. Lam Son 719 was touted as a test for the policy of Vietnamisation; as American troops from South Vietnam withdrew, the South Vietnamese Army was to take

over the fight. In addition to the credibility of the policy being at stake, the larger issue for the Chinese was whether we were as good as our word. Moreover the US withdrawal from Vietnam was closely linked to improving Sino–American relations. One of the opening gestures on Nixon's part had been his two-point statement to De Gaulle in March 1969: the new president intended to get his country out of Vietnam, and to improve relations with the People's Republic. As the Chinese observed Nixon taking steps toward the former, his intentions on the latter gained credence.

33. The road and its air defences could well have been an issue in Chinese domestic politics. At this time there were probably some bruising internal debates; by September 1971 several top military leaders had dropped out of sight, including Lin Piao, who had been Minister of Defence, Vice Chairman of the Politburo, and Mao's designated successor. The world later learned Lin Piao and others had died in a military plane crash in Mongolia on 12 September.

34. Chou En-lai finally replied to Nixon's December 1970 acceptance of an invitation. Kissinger speculates as to the reasons for Chou's delay, citing first Lam Son 719 (*White House Years, op. cit.*, p. 714). The anti-aircraft guns and personnel introduced along the road in Laos during January and February 1971 would further confirm that speculation.

35. These bombings occurred on 5 May and 14 May in response to Chinese anti-aircraft fire near Muong Khoua, perhaps far enough north to keep the incidents out of any limelight.

36. C.L. Chiou, 'China's Policy towards Laos: Politics of Neutralisation', in Martin Stuart-Fox (ed.) (1982) *Contemporary Laos* (St Lucia, Queensland: University of Queensland Press), pp. 291–305, passim.

37. *Ibid.*, p. 299, Chiou footnotes, *Far Eastern Economic Review*, 16 June 1978.

38. *Ibid.*, p. 300, Chiou cites Martin Stuart-Fox, 'Laos: The Vietnamese Connection', in *Southeast Asian Affairs 1980*, Leo Suryadinata (ed.) (Singapore: Institute for Southeast Asian Studies/Heinemann, 1980), p. 198.

   A curious irony: the charges of Chinese troops massing for an invasion of Laos reminds one of the Yalu River syndrome of the 1950s and 1960s.

39. *Ibid.*, p. 301.

40. First-hand reports of the 'Long March' came out of Laos with a flood of refugees in 1980–1.

41. China's aid to other regional dissidents had been cut off earlier in somewhat parallel negotiations: in 1979, as a pre-condition for allowing Chinese support to pass through their territory to the anti-Vietnamese Cambodians, the Thais had secured China's promise to end aid to the Communist Party of Thailand.

   About the same time, the Laotian communist government threw the CPT out of their Lao sanctuaries because of the CPT's pro-Chinese sympathies. And the CPT lost their camps within Cambodia. By the early 1980s the Thai army had run such a successful amnesty programme for CPT members that the organisation is now almost entirely defunct.

42. Ambassador Phoungsavath Boupha is related to General Khammouane Boupha of Phong Saly, recently LPDR Deputy Minister of Agriculture, Irrigations and Cooperatives.

13 US–Lao Relations, 1988

David Floyd Lambertson

In 1982 both the Lao and US governments agreed to try to improve their bilateral relationship through concrete steps on each side. For the United States the principal standard of measurement is progress on the POW/MIA question, which remains a matter of very high priority for the US government. I think there has been progress. That this relationship will continue to develop is certainly our hope, and we want to continue working with the Lao government toward that end.

The US agenda for its relationship with Laos includes three prominent issues, the first of those being the POW/MIA question. Now under way is a joint excavation of a crash site, which will last a week or more, the third such joint excavation that has taken place. We are very pleased that it is happening, and we hope that it is the harbinger of additional joint activities. We also note that the Lao government has undertaken two unilateral crash site excavations and returned the remains to the US government. These excavations are difficult undertakings in Laos because of the terrain and the passage of time since the crashes took place. We want this progress to continue and want to continue working with the Lao government to maintain it.

The second prominent issue is narcotics. Laos is emerging as a major producer and major source of illicit opium and marijuana. There is increasing evidence of involvement by Lao government officials and the military. The US government believes the Lao government should do more to attack this problem as part of its responsibility in an international effort to combat what is obviously an international scourge. Any country with a narcotics problem, whether it is the United States or Laos, is in a very real sense a victim country. All of us have to work together to get out of this very serious situation.

We would like to see more efforts by the Lao government. We note that there is an UNFDAC project which looks as if it will be implemented. We have offered bilateral assistance for a narcotics control project. Vientiane has not yet responded. I note that it has been said that Vientiane's view is that this is something that should await a more general improvement in the bilateral relationship. From our point of view, undertaking this joint project would itself represent important progress toward an improved relationship that both countries want.

The narcotics issue is one of intense public and political interest in the US and will be a major campaign issue. It has been pointed out that the Lao government has taken a sincere approach to this question. I trust that this is so and hope that we will see a steadily increasing pattern of cooperation on this issue. We are prepared to work with the Lao government bilaterally or in support of multilateral efforts to control the problem in Laos and to contribute to a reduction of the problem worldwide.

Finally a third prominent issue in the US–Lao bilateral relationship from our point of view is the refugee question. The United States has an historic and broad concern for the welfare of refugees, certainly including refugees along the Laotian–Thai border. In particular the US government hopes for effective implementation of the UNHCR–sponsored screening programme in Thailand and strongly opposes pushbacks of refugees from Thailand. Most disturbing are the reports of the mistreatment of refugees when they are returned to Laos. US officials are urging Bangkok and Vientiane to work out an acceptable programme for the repatriation of screened-out Lao. We think the screening programme is very important and we hope it can be expanded and made to work as it should.

Another issue that is often raised in US–Lao relations is the question of the Lao resistance. There are a number of groups attempting to disrupt and even overthrow the government of Laos. Suffice it to say that the US recognises the LPDR and does not provide support to any of those resistance groups nor do we encourage private Americans to take part in those kinds of activities. Congress lifted its ban on aid to Laos in 1985, but sentiment remains strong in the Congress against providing formal economic assistance, due mainly to the question of progress on POW/MIAs and reports of increased narcotics production. Those are the things that affect the atmosphere, affect perceptions, and affect sentiment.

Nevertheless the United States recognises Lao humanitarian concerns and has agreed to work within our capabilities to respond to those concerns. We provided emergency assistance to Laos in the form of funds to combat dengue fever outbreaks in 1985 and 1987, and emergency donations of rice in 1984 and again in 1987. The US has also offered to train Laotian personnel in the disposal of unexploded ordnance remaining from the Indochina War. We have not been taken up on that offer but it is one that is on the table.

In general the bilateral relationship between Laos and the United States has matured in recent years. We are able to talk about issues much more candidly and we have made some progress. There is still room for a lot more progress and for mutual education. An area we need to expand is the narcotics issue. Here too there has been progress. A year ago it was impossible for us to talk to Laotian government officials about this issue. It was regarded as too sensitive and something that we simply could not raise or, if we did, we got no response. Now we are able to discuss these issues, even with very senior officials of the Laotian government. This reflects a recognition on the part of the Laotian government that a problem does exist and that Laos must be part of an international solution. This is a reflection of a positive and forward looking approach on the part of the Laotian government.

We anticipate that the implementation of the New Economic Management Mechanism in Laos should stimulate economic activity, heighten interaction across the Mekong River, and, on a broader scale, contribute to the integration of Laos into the international community. Increased economic ties inevitably will be coupled with better understanding of other issues and will result in a steadily increasing Laotian voice in international relations.

As Laos continues to move in this direction, I am confident that the US–Laotian bilateral relationship will improve. It will develop on the basis of mutual respect for the sovereignty, the independence, and the interests of each partner – as Ambassador Saly outlined in his contribution.

So I look forward to a steady development of our bilateral relationship. From our point of view it must be premised on progress on these very key issues with the POW/MIA question at the top. I might simply reiterate that we are very pleased with the joint excavation now under way, and we are hopeful that we will have more of the same in the months ahead.

Appendices

Appendices

Appendix A
Department of State Report to Congress*

INTRODUCTION

This report by the Department of State, prepared in consultation with the Department of Justice (including the Drug Enforcement Administration), the Department of the Treasury (including U.S. Customs Service), the Department of Defense, the Agency for International Development, and the Central Intelligence Agency, is submitted pursuant to Section 2013 of the Anti---Drug Abuse Act of 1986 (P.L. 99–570). This is the third semiannual report which Congress requires on official involvement in narcotics trafficking by governments and senior officials; crimes in which U.S. drug enforcement agents have been victims; and the issue of 'hot pursuit.' The report concerns the 24 major producing and major transit countries identified in accord with Sec. 481(h) of the Foreign Assistance Act (the Act).

For purposes of this third report, the agencies consulted were asked to review earlier country-by-country findings in the INCSR and the previous 2013 report; and report appropriate changes, if any. These findings are provided in the appendix. To facilitate review of the findings in this latest report, the country summaries draw upon the 1988 INCSR for information on narcotics-related corruption in each of the 24 major countries.

The report's preparation presents a number of problems to the narcotics control community, including the requirement for a separate Presidential certification process (distinct from the process established under Sec. 481[h] of the Act), the lack of any legislative history to guide interpretation and application of the language, and the requirement for disclosures of information that the narcotics control community maintains only in investigatory and intelligence files.

THE REQUIREMENTS

Section 2013 of the Anti-Drug Abuse Act of 1986 (P.L. 99–570), requires that, not later than six months after enactment and every six months thereafter, the President prepare and transmit to Congress a report on official involvement in narcotics trafficking and other topics. The responsibility for making certifications pursuant to this report has been delegated to the Secretary of State.

---

*Section 2013, PL99–570 Reports and Restrictions concerning certain countries, 1 May 1988.

Appendix A

SPECIAL REPORT

Certification Under Section 481(h), FAA

On March 1, President Reagan gave Laos a national interest certification, citing a failure on the part of the government to cooperate fully with the U.S. on narcotics control, or to take adequate steps of its own, but finding that there are vital national interests which would be placed at risk should certification be denied.

The President's decision was to grant a national interest certification under Sec. 481(h), with an understanding that the certification issue would be revisited May 1, to assess promised progress on the POW/MIA issue, specifically pledges of cooperation in early 1988 on joint excavations of crash sites, and to consider progress, if any, on narcotics control.

At that time, it was said that, given the high national priority assigned to the POW/MIA issue by President Reagan, progress on this issue would be viewed as the principal measure of Lao sincerity in fulfilling its expressed desire for better relations with the U.S.

The expectation was that any site excavations would occur in March and April, the dry season. The Department of State was advised April 8 of an official LPDR proposal for a joint site excavation at the end of April. A U.S. military team is now excavating a crash site in southern Laos. This excavation is considered to have met the MIA/POW conditions of the national interest certification.

However, as reported under Subsection (a)(1)(A), the U.S. continues to obtain information on the involvement of Lao Government officials in narcotics trafficking. Despite information indicating the extensive involvement of Lao government and military officials in the narcotics trade, it is encouraging to note that some senior officials have reportedly acknowledged to Western diplomats their country's narcotics problem. In February 1988, the Lao Government agreed in principle to accept its first narcotics control project, to be funded by the United Nations Fund for Drug Abuse Control. An UNFDAC project formulation team met in Vientiane at the end of April to discuss technical aspects of the project's implementation.

Appendix B
State Department Report to Congress on: Narcotics in Laos, 1988

A.1. STATUS OF ILLICIT NARCOTICS PRODUCTION & TRAFFICKING

Cultivation of illicit opium and marijuana, and production of heroin have increased significantly over the past two years in the Lao People's Democratic Republic (LPDR). Prospects for a reversal in that trend over the coming year are doubtful. Estimates of the opium crop range between 150-300 metric tons for 1987, most of which is grown by the Hmong hill-tribes in northern Laos. Opium cultivation is deeply embedded in Hmong culture, and provides the economic mainstay for these traditional mountain peoples. Marijuana is cultivated largely along the Mekong river by lowland Lao, and smuggled across to Thailand.

The increase in cultivation, production (including heroin refining), and trafficking of illicit drugs in this country can be attributed in large part to the lure of relatively high profits for one of the world's poorest countries. Also, the relative success of eradication efforts carried out by the Governments of Thailand and Burma has compelled traffickers in the Golden Triangle to shift more of their activities to Laos. There have been many reports that Lao officials, particularly those in the military and at the provincial level, have been involved in narcotics production and trafficking. U.S. officials are especially concerned by reports linking the mountain area's development corps and the army to drug trafficking. Reports of their involvement increased in 1987. The United States and other governments are also concerned by repeated reports of the establishment of heroin refineries in Laos as well as by increases in production of opium and marijuana.

The Lao government has not focused on the elimination of narcotics production and trafficking as a national priority. The government declares that there is no abuse of illicit drugs in Lao society, except among older Hmong. Consequently, there has been no public campaign against the evils of trafficking and production, and the government does not appear to have any plans to eradicate opium poppies or marijuana. In addition, the rugged terrain, sparse population and woefully inadequate infrastructure of Laos makes central control difficult, especially in the Golden Triangle area.

Despite lack of cooperation on narcotics control, Laos was certified in 1987 on grounds of national interest based on Lao government agreements to cooperate further on the POW/MIA issue and on embryonic consultations on narcotics control between the two governments. Our discussions on narcotics with the LPDR are continuing. In February 1988, the LPDR turned over remains thought to be of missing Americans; they have also agreed to one or more joint excavations within the next several months.

Lao currency is nonconvertible, and there are no reports of narcotics-related money laundering.

A.2. ACCOMPLISHMENTS IN 1987

Lao officials have demonstrated an increased willingness to discuss narcotics problems, particularly when compared to a former attitude which refused to acknowledge drug abuse and trafficking as anything other than an external problem. The Lao were exposed to the full range of international sentiment on the issue at the United Nations-sponsored International Conference on Drug Abuse and Illicit Trafficking (ICDAIT) in Vienna in June 1987. At that time, Lao Vice Foreign Minister Soubanh stated: "The problems of abuse and illicit trafficking in drugs have taken on alarming proportions and caused disastrous social consequences in many countries. The Lao delegation shares the concerns of the international community faced with this situation." The Lao expressed similar sentiments in a letter from Acting President Phoumi to President Reagan in February 1987. Another step in persuading the Lao of the seriousness of narcotics problems was the visit in April of Secretary Aziz Bahi of the International Narcotics Control Board (INCB). His was the first INCB visit since the establishment of the LPDR in 1975. As one consequence of his visit, the Lao government will receive a mission from United Nations Fund for Drug Abuse Control (UNFDAC) in February 1988.

The United States offered to finance a program of crop substitution and narcotics control training during talks held in Vientiane last August. The Lao government has not accepted that offer, but neither has it rejected it. In a joint communique issued at the conclusion of the talks the Lao and U.S. governments stated: "On the subject of narcotics, both sides recognized the seriousness of the problem and reaffirmed their intention to contribute to the international effort to combat it".

The Lao government continues its efforts to persuade Hmong tribesmen to resettle in lowland areas and take up cultivation of crops other than opium. This policy is designed not only to reduce the cultivation of opium, but to halt the environmentally disastrous consequences of slash-and-burn agriculture. How successful the policy has been is open to question. United Nations funds have been used to establish a pilot village for dislocated Hmong, which so far has proven more successful than anything attempted by aid donors in the past. The bulk of the Hmong, however, remain attached to their traditional way of life which includes the growing of opium.

Finally, international pressure on the Lao government has produced at least a shifting of lowland marijuana cultivation away from the banks of the Mekong. Whether fields have been moved from points openly visible from Thailand to others less obvious is uncertain. It is certain, however, that marijuana is no longer grown on the outskirts of the capital city.

A.3. PLANS, PROGRAMS AND TIMETABLES

Given this situation, it is not possible to predict when or what the government of the LPDR will do about narcotics eradication or crop control. It is clear that international pressure, particularly from bilateral and multilateral lending agencies and from the U.N. system, will be key to encouraging Lao efforts. The results of the February 1988 UNFDAC visit will provide a benchmark against which policy and actions can be judged. The Lao government is unable to fund either suppression or crop substitution efforts on its own. Assistance and encouragement from abroad are central to any results.

A.4. ADEQUACY OF LEGAL AND LAW ENFORCEMENT MEASURES

The LPDR suspended the constitution and codes of law when it came to power twelve years ago. There are, at the moment, no narcotics control laws. Unpublished regulations call for the confiscation of illicit narcotics and the arrest, fining and imprisonment of traffickers. By these regulations, the Lao government claims to have banned production and sale of opium for private gain, but permits opium sales to communist bloc countries for licit processing. There are no known prohibitions against cultivating, selling or consuming marijuana which, in fact, has been used as a traditional condiment in local cooking. Reportedly, some traffickers have been arrested and punished since 1975, but details are not available.

There are persistent rumors that a constitution and legal codes are in preparation and may be promulgated in 1988. Until these are made public, there is no way to judge their adequacy in the narcotics control field.

B.1. NATURE OF ILLICIT DRUG PRODUCTION

Opium production is a vital part of hilltribe culture and economy and has been so for over 150 years. During the French colonial period (1893-1953) poppy cultivation was favored and, indeed, taxed by the French Administration. Cultivation and trafficking flourished during the twenty years of civil strife between 1953 and 1975, and by the early 1970's the trade in heroin, marijuana and other narcotics was heavy. Drug abuse in the urban areas along the Mekong was rife and apparent in Vientiane and Savannakhet, the country's largest cities.

Following the revolution in 1975 both cultivation and trafficking declined steeply but has increased in the last two to three years. The new Lao government arrested drug addicts, prostitutes, alcoholics and other "social undesirables" and confined them in rehabilitation centers north of Vientiane. These centers reportedly still exist.

B.2. FACTORS AFFECTING PRODUCTION

Tradition, geography, a lack of basic infrastructure and grinding poverty combine to favour illicit narcotics production. Opium is the most readily grown and saleable crop in the country's mountainous, undeveloped and largely lawless northern uplands. The small size of opium bricks and their high value make them ideal for mule or human transportation out of the roadless hills. Currently, no other crop provides as much income for the

Hmong and other hilltribes. Previous opposition by these peoples to the central government would cause it to act cautiously in trying to suppress their only cash crop.

Marijuana can be grown throughout the country, and, again, there is no other crop which provides the peasant farmer as much return for his labor.

Overall, wages are miniscule and make it difficult even for government employees to make ends meet. The lure of quick money, often aided by the supply of marijuana seedlings to the cultivator, and the involvement of local police and military officials, combine to provide powerful incentives.

Moreover, narcotics control, suppression and eradication efforts in neighboring Burma and Thailand have attracted powerful, armed traffickers to Laos. Provincial autonomy, unique among communist states – and a product both of history and the lack of roads and communications – assists these organizations in making inroads among Lao farmers and officials. It is fair to say that the significant increases in production that have been reported over the past three years are partially attributable to drug control successes elsewhere.

Since there is no public outcry over the dangers of drug abuse, and only nascent realization on the part of some Lao government officials of the dangers attendant on widespread trafficking, there has been no concerted effort to deal with the problem. The increasing concern over illicit narcotics in the Soviet Union and Vietnam may translate into greater effort in Laos. But that effort is still to come. It will require considerable infusions of training, technical assistance and financial help when it does.

B.3. MAXIMUM ACHIEVABLE REDUCTIONS

Prospects are dubious for any reduction in illicit drug production in 1988. The Lao government has not formulated plans to eradicate, which would draw internal opposition as long as opium and cannabis provide the current level of profits in this cash-poor country and as long as there is little pressure from the international community. Laos has not yet acknowledged large scale cultivation of opium poppy and marijuana within its territory, and has yet to formulate plans for either eradicating illicit crops or interdicting shipments of illicit drugs transitting its territory. Lao expressions of concern over the world narcotics problem may lay the groundwork for future cooperation, provided the international community continues to press Vientiane and is willing to provide financial and technical support

B.1 Statistical Tables

Data Tables

Year	*1986–87*	*1985–86*
Opium: (range)		
Cultivated (ha)	16,130–46,775	16,130–46,775
Eradicated (ha)	—	—

Harvested (ha)	16,130–46,775	16,130–46,775
Yield (mt)	150– 300	100– 290
Consumed	unk	unk
Seized	unk	unk
Exported	unk	unk
Available for Refining	unk	unk
Loss factor	unk	unk
Year	*1986–87*	*19856–86*
Heroin:		
Produced	unk	unk
Seized in country	unk	unk
Consumed in country	unk	unk
Exported to USA	unk	unk
Exported elsewhere	unk	unk
Marijuana:		
Cultivated (ha)	unk	unk
Eradicated (ha)	—	—
Harvested (ha)	unk	unk
Yield	unk	unk

Appendix C
Human Rights in Laos, 1988: Report to US Congress prepared by Department of State

The Lao People's Democratic Republic (LPDR) is a totalitarian, one-party, Communist state. The Lao People's Revolutionary Party (LPRP) is the source of all political authority in the country, and the party's leadership imposes broad and arbitrary controls.

The LPRP came to power in 1975 after a protracted and bitter insurgency, supported by North Vietnam, whose military political and economic assistance during that conflict was invaluable to it. Vietnamese influence, codified in a 25-year Treaty of Friendship and Cooperation signed in 1977, continues to be pervasive. The leaders of both Lao and Vietnamese Communist parties have been comrades in arms and colleagues in government for over three decades; hence they share many ideological, political, and economic perceptions. In addition, Vietnam stations between 40,000 and 50,000 troops in Laos to guarantee the security of the regime. Laos also receives large amounts of economic, technical, and military assistance from the Soviet Union. The Government constantly proclaims its indissoluble link to Vietnam and Cambodia as a loyal member of the Indochina group of nations and of the 'Socialist community of states.'

Nonetheless, unlike every other Socialist state, the LPDR has no constitution and no published code of law. The individual is subject to the arbitrary control of the State and the LPRP. No national elections have been held since the establishment of the regime. A constitution is reportedly in draft, but there has been no announcement yet about its promulgation.

Laos' approximately 3.6 million ethnically diverse people, scattered thinly over difficult terrain about the size of Oregon, have no common national history and share few traditions. National institutions are weak. The policies of the LPRP, particularly in its first 5 years, as well as very difficult economic conditions in general, have driven about 325,000 Lao into exile since 1975. Among those refugees were most of the educated elite; hence the LPDR has a shortage of teachers, administrators, and technicians in all fields. This has made the task of development – and Laos is one of the poorest countries in the world – more difficult than ever. There appears to be little enthusiastic support for the regime.

Several armed Lao resistance groups, supported financially from abroad, continue their activities along the Lao–Thai border and in selected areas inside Laos. Although the regime cites these groups as a menace to its safety and security, in fact they pose no serious threat to it.

Human rights violations continued in 1987, although, on the basis of the limited information available, the number of reported violations may have decreased since the formation of the LPDR in 1975. However, the limited availability of information makes it difficult to confirm such a trend. Re-education camps, the regime's preferred instrument for inducing obedience, continued to decline in population and an undetermined number of camps have been closed. Some former camp prisoners have been permitted to obtain passports and exit visas and have been able to travel overseas.

Economic reforms in the past year have introduced a greater choice of consumer goods and greater freedom to associate for profit. Provinces have been encouraged to engage in direct trade with foreign commercial concerns in certain economic fields. This, coupled with traditional provincial autonomy (a historical consequence of rugged topography and poor transportation and communications) has meant a slight but noticeable brightening of daily life in many parts of the country.

RESPECT FOR HUMAN RIGHTS

Section 1   Respect for the Integrity of the Person, Including Freedom from:
(a) Political Killing
There have been reports that Lao government and Vietnamese patrols have fatally shot persons fleeing from Laos as well as those entering the country illegally. In those instances in which the LPDR confirms such incidents, it generally claims that the persons were smugglers or suspected members of the Lao resistance.

An unknown number of people are killed annually in combined Lao/Vietnamese military operations against resistance forces. Many of the insurgents appear to be former Royal Lao Army troops and Hmong tribesmen. Both sides are reported to use brutal tactics, with the antigovernment forces attempting assassination and ambush of Lao, Vietnamese, and other Communist military and civilian personnel. There are also recurrent reports of attacks by bandit groups in isolated or interior areas on vehicles bearing government officials and on civilian buses. Official policy calls for the execution of resistance leaders, but no such executions were reported in 1987.

In mid-March international attention focused on a press story of three Hmong (a Lao highland minority) groups who were pushed back from Thailand and reportedly suffered casualties after their forced return. Similar reports surfaced in November. The government has denied such casualties, but international organization representatives have thus far not been allowed to contact these groups to verify their safety. The Lao Government has denied knowledge of these incidents.

(b) Disappearance
There were numerous cases of secret arrest and removal of persons to re-education camps in the first years of the current regime. In the last several years reports of disappearances have decreased, however.

(c) Torture and Other Cruel, Inhuman, or Degrading Treatment or Punishment
A relatively small number of 're–education' prisoners continue to be held in harsh conditions. Former prisoners have reported that punishment for misbehavior could include brutal public beatings, shackling, deprivation of food, and sometimes, for those who tried to escape, torture with electric shocks or execution. Some inmates have died from malnutrition. Government officials have publicly denied reports of mistreatment of persons in re-education camps.

(d) Arbitrary Arrest, Detention, Exile, or Forced Labor
The Government continues to maintain a number of 're–education' camps, or 'seminar camps', in which persons who served the previous government, or who have offended the current one, are imprisoned. Accurate figures for camp populations are not available, but rough estimates are that 2,000 persons are still detained.

Since 1979 conditions in most of the camps have improved noticeably, and a number of the camps have been reported closed.

Most detainees now live in a kind of internal exile with severe restrictions on their freedom of movement. Generally, these conditions are no worse than those of poor Lao living in the countryside. Many reportedly have been assigned to collective farms or construction units inside their former camps. Some are on probation or cannot obtain necessary travel documents. Others who have lost property and families are reported to have chosen to remain in areas near the camps to begin new lives.

In 1987 government officials claimed, as they had in 1985, that nearly all soldiers and officials sent to the camps in 1975–76 had been released and that 'only a few' remained in detention. The accuracy of that statement cannot be verified. There are accounts, however, that groups of camp detainees were released in late December 1986–January 1987, in February, and again in May–June. Release of some categories of detainees appears to have become more regular over the past year.

Those accused of hostility to the regime or of what the Government calls 'socially undesirable habits', such as prostitution, drug abuse, idleness, and 'wrong thought,' are sent to 'rehabilitation' centers, usually without trial. Most of these persons have been allowed to return to their homes after periods ranging from a few months to several years of hard labor, political indoctrination, and admission of guilt.

(e) Denial of Fair Public Trial
No code of law exists in Laos, and there is no guarantee of due process. The Government has promulgated interim rules and regulations for the arrest and trial of those accused of specific crimes, including armed resistance to the Government. Although the regulations allow an accused person to make a statement presenting his side of the case, they provide no real opportunity for the accused to defend himself and do not permit bail or use of an attorney. Rather, the Government has issued instructions on how to investigate, prosecute, and punish wrongdoers. These instructions are applied capriciously and inconsistently. People can be arrested on the unsupported

accusations of others and detained while the accusations are being investigated, without being informed of the charges or of the identity of the person making the accusations. Investigations often take a long time unless family members and friends take a strong interest in the case. Government officials and their families easily can influence the judgments reached. There is some provision for appeal, although important political cases tried by 'people's courts' are without an appeals process. Death sentences must be approved by the Council of Ministers. Lao regulations call for judgment to be given in public. This often amounts to a public announcement of the sentence and not a public trial.

(f) Arbitrary Interference with Privacy, Family, Home, or Correspondence
Search and seizure are authorized by the security bureaux themselves rather than by an impartial judicial authority, and government regulations, which are not always followed, provide little protection for the persons affected. International and domestic mail is selectively opened on a routine basis. Mail from China and non-Communist countries is particularly suspect. Telephone calls frequently are monitored. Privately owned land may not be sold but may be inherited. Houses, appliances, and other private property can be sold only with difficulty in most cases, since the possession of large amounts of cash in this poor country draws immediate government suspicion. Inheritances cannot be passed on to relatives who have left the country as refugees and acquired another nationality.

The Government makes no attempt to stop Lao from listening to foreign radio stations such as the Voice of America, nor from setting up antennas to bring in Thai television from across the Mekong River. The state security apparatus monitors family life extensively through a system of neighborhood wardens and informers.

Section 2 Respect for Civil Liberties, Including:

(a) Freedom of Speech and Press
Public expression of opposition to the Government is not permitted, and persons who indulge in such activity have been jailed. Newspapers and the state radio are subservient to the LPRP and to the Government, reflecting only their views. Ordinary Lao citizens may not import foreign news magazines or books; censorship is strict. Academic freedom does not exist.

(b) Freedom of Peaceful Assembly and Association
The Government controls all meetings and, except for religious, athletic, and communal events, organizes them. Individuals do not have the right to join together to promote nonregime-sponsored activities nor to protest government policies. All associations – such as those for youth, women, workers, and a 'peace organization' – are government-controlled and authorized 'mass organizations.' These are organized to exercise government control and disseminate government policy. All professional groups are organized by the party, and their leadership is ordinarily drawn from party ranks. Lao associations are permitted to maintain relations with like-minded politically

acceptable organizations in other countries, particularly those in Communist countries. Ordinary Lao citizens are permitted association or contact with foreigners only in unusual circumstances, usually involving their work.

Trade unions are organized as 'mass organizations' of the party without the right to engage in collective bargaining. They have no real influence in determining working conditions.

(c) Freedom of Religion

Nearly all Lao are Buddhists or, in the case of most highland groups, animists. In official statements, the Government has recognized the right of the people to free exercise of religious belief as well as the contributions religion can make to the development of the country.

Many Lao believe, however, that the Government is engaged in a long-term effort to subvert the role of religion because it considers the maintenance of temples and the activities of monks nonproductive and because it objects to an active group with an independent system of beliefs. This effort includes carefully controlling the education of young monks and compelling the Buddhist clergy to propagate elements of Marxist-Leninist doctrine. Further, since 1975, the Government has periodically taken over Buddhist and Christian places of worship for use as government schools, offices, and fire and police stations, as well as for political indoctrination centers and warehouses. Nonetheless, since the Third Party Congress in 1982, the Government has eased its stand on Buddhism. While it has not, so far as is known, contributed to the restoration of temples and religious institutions, it has not opposed efforts of the faithful to do so.

Monks remain the only social group still entitled to special honorific terms of address, which even high party and government officals continue to use. Buddhist clergy are prominently featured at important state and party functions. Religious festivals are permitted to take place without hindrance. Young people regularly enter into religious orders for short periods.

Links may be maintained with coreligionists and religious associations in other countries only in cases approved by the Government, usually involving other Communist countries. Most traditional links to Thai Buddhists have been severed. Missionaries are not formally banned from entering Laos to proselytize, but in most cases they are denied permission. Many top party officials still participate in religious ceremonies, but members of the military are forbidden even to have Buddhist funerals.

Roman Catholics and Protestants are permitted to worship, but the activities of their churches are closely observed. Vatican officials visited Laos in 1987 to meet with the Bishop of Vientiane, as well as with local church and government officals. However, the Government did not permit the Bishop of Vientiane to travel to Bangkok to meet with Pope John Paul II when he visited southeast Asia last year. Attendance at Christian services continues to require discretion. Since 1975 Christians have not been permitted to operate schools, seminaries, or associations.

The Goverent takes steps including the use of media to persuade highland minority groups to abandon their 'old fashioned' animist beliefs.

(d) Freedom of Movement Within the Country, Foreign Travel, Emigration, and Repatriation

Lao citizens must obtain permission from the authorities for all internal travel of any distance and in all cases when crossing provincial boundaries. Non-Lao residents in Vientiane must in principle obtain permission to travel outside it, and in practice, except for nationals of a very few countries, such permission is rarely granted. A curfew is enforced intermittently in the capital and other major cities. Its rules change from time to time, often without notice. Government officials have cited threats of 'disorders' created by 'reactionary elements' as the reason for the restrictions.

Foreign travel is permitted for officials, students in government-approved programs, and some others who have access to foreign exchange. Few Lao are permitted to study or train in non-Communist countries, even at their own expense. Exit visas, which are required, are not easy to obtain, but restrictions have been eased over the past 2 years. For pensioners, the elderly in general, and those with hard currency, it seems less difficult to obtain exit visas than in the past, and the number of travelers to the West and to the United States has increased sharply – although the absolute numbers are still small. Border crossing permits are available for those with business in Thailand. The number of permits increased in 1987 in keeping with the opening of additional border trade locations and the reduction in the number of items restricted by the Thai Government for trade with Laos. The permits are not, however, granted automatically and may be denied for political or personal reasons.

The Government states that those wishing to emigrate may do so. In practice, however, legal emigration is rarely authorized for ethnic Lao. To guard against emigration, those permitted to travel must often leave their families behind as a guarantee of their return. Since 1975 over 325,000 Lao have registered as refugees in Thailand. An unknown number have crossed the border and simply settled with kindred ethnic groups.

Some of those fleeing are fired upon and killed by Lao or Vietnamese border patrols as they attempt to cross the Mekong River. Government authorities have imprisoned many Lao seeking to leave the country illegally.

The Lao and Thai Governments have agreed to take back, on a case-by-case basis, those of their respective citizens who have illegally crossed into the other country and now wish to return home. Since May 1980, when agreement was reached with Thailand and the United Nations High Commissioner for Refugees (UNHCR) on a voluntary repatriation program, over 3,000 Lao voluntarily have returned to Laos under the auspices of the UNHCR. Those accepted for return receive several days of political indoctrination and then are released to return to their homes, where they are placed under the control of the village authorities. The UNHCR provides basic necessities for the returnees and monitors their treatment and living conditions thereafter. There appears to be no official harassment or maltreatment of these voluntary returnees, and UNHCR officials have not been prevented from visiting them. In addition, perhaps as many as 10,000 persons have repatriated themselves without official involvement.

The Lao Government also has agreed in principle to take back Lao in Thailand whom the Thai have determined do not meet requirements for refugee status. Although procedures for the return of these 'screened-out' Lao were worked out between the two countries in late 1986, it was not until October 1987 that the first small group of Lao was repatriated. A second, larger group returned in December.

Section 3 Respect for Political Rights: The Right of Citizens to Change Their Government

Laos is ruled by a small elite of the LPRP, the sole party. There is neither freedom to participate in politics outside the party nor popular choice of policies or officials. After the Communists gained power in 1975, but before the establishment of the present regime in December of that year, local elections were held in which voters chose from a list of candidates selected by the party. Reportedly, those local officials not only constituted the National Council of People's Representatives, which proclaimed the LPDR but also chose the Supreme People's Assembly, although the latter process was not publicized. There have been no national elections. A few 'by-elections' have been organized to replace representatives who have died or been transferred. Citizens are not free to change their system of government.

Section 4 Governmental Attitude Regarding International and Nongovernmental Investigation of Alleged Violations of Human Rights

Laos does not cooperate generally with private international organizations interested in human rights. However, it does occasionally permit visits by officials of international human rights organizations if the purpose of the visit is not specifically related to allegations of human rights violations. In mid-1986 Amnesty International wrote to government officials concerning allegations that Laotian forces had killed 35 Lao refugees in Thailand, including women and children, as punishment for leaving Laos and suspected involvement in armed opposition activities. In response, the Government provided Amnesty International with an official statement denying responsibility for the incident.

Section 5 Discrimination Based on Race, Sex, Religion, Language, or Social Status

Traditionally, women in Lao society have been subservient to men and often discouraged from obtaining an education. Today the active, government-controlled Lao Women's Federation has as one of its stated goals the achievement of rights for women 'equal' to those of men. The Government claims that a higher percentage of women make up the school population now than before 1975, and that women are being encouraged to assume a greater role in economic and state-controlled political activity.

Approximately half of the population in Laos is ethnic Lao, also called 'lowland Lao;' 20 percent are tribal Thai; 15 percent are Phoutheung (or Kha); and another 15 percent are other highland groups (Hmong, Yao and others). The Government is attempting to integrate these groups and overcome traditional antagonisms between lowland Lao and minority groups.

The Hmong are split on clan lines. Many were strongly anti-Communist; others sided with the Communist Pathet Lao and the Vietnamese. The Government is repressive toward all groups that fought against it, especially those continuing to resist its authority by force. The Hmong tried to defend some of their tribal areas after 1975, and some continue to support anti-LPDR resistance groups. Vietnamese and Lao armed forces conduct military operations against both resistance groups, the minority-based ones in the north and the resistance forces from lowland Lao groups, mainly in southern Laos.

The Government wants to resettle in the lowlands some ethnic minorities who now inhabit mountainous areas. After resettlement they would be under closer government control and engage in settled agricultural production rather than destructive slash-and-burn techniques. For this purpose, the Government has reportedly relied on a voluntary program based on material inducements. The situation for local ethnic Chinese has been marked by government suspicion and surveillance in the period after 1979 when Sino–Lao relations deteriorated seriously. These relations appear to be improving. At the September 1987 meeting of the Front for National Construction, state and party leaders called for cooperation with and from the Chinese (and south Asian) merchant communities. A majority of the Chinese community departed in the post-1975 period, largely for economic reasons. Those who remain have maintained Chinese schools in Vientiane and Savannakhet and Chinese associations in several provincial capitals.

CONDITIONS OF LABOUR

Laos has set neither minimum wage, maximum workweek, nor safety or health standards for the workers in its almost entirely rural and agricultural economy. Public wages in particular remain extremely low. Workweeks typically are under 48 hours, with some exceptions, such as during urgent road-building or construction projects. Workplace conditions are not systematically exploitative, but they sometimes fail to protect workers adequately against sickness or accident. Work permits customarily are not issued to persons under age 18, although children frequently work with their parents in traditional occupations such as farming and shopkeeping.

Appendix D
Amnesty International Report on Laos, 1988

Hundreds of political prisoners were freed in a series of large-scale releases but hundreds of others, including many prisoners of conscience, remained for a twelfth year in detention without trial or restricted for 're-education'. A number of other people detained more recently for alleged anti-government activities also reportedly remained in prison. On at least two occasions Laotians who had crossed the border seeking asylum in Thailand were said to have been forcibly returned by the Thai authorities and immediately detained without trial in Laos. At least six other Laotians were allegedly killed by security forces in Laos after they were forcibly returned from Thailand

No official figures were available but unofficial estimates suggested that at least several hundred people arrested in 1975 were still detained without trial or restricted for 're-education'. They had been taken into custody as the Provisional Government of National Union was replaced by the forces which proclaimed the Democratic People's Republic of Laos. The detainees were held in various provinces, including Houa Phanh and Xieng Khouang in the northeast, Attapeu in the south and Savannakhet in central Laos. They were not permitted to return to their homes despite government claims that 're-education' was abolished in the early 1980s.

Large-scale releases, particularly from the northeast and the south, began in December 1986. In Houa Phanh province, for example, at least 300 people were reportedly released from restriction between January and June, leaving approximately 400 detainees in the Houa Phanh restriction sites at Sop Pan, Sop Long and Houay Cha. Additional releases from Houa Phanh and other provinces reportedly took place in March, May and August.

Those released during 1987 included a number of prisoners of conscience: Viboun Abhay, a former civil servant and member of the National Consultative Council; Khamkhing Souvanlasy, a former director of education in the Education Ministry; Pane Rassavong, a former general planning commissioner, and Tiao Sisouphanouvong, a former Director of Civil Aviation. Amont other political prisoners said to be released were Toulong Lyfoung, a former public prosecutor; Phao Southi, a former colonel in the Royal Lao Armed Forces: Souvat Boulom, former Secretary General of the National Assembly, and Khamsay Kiattavong, a former army officer. At least 13 former members of the armed forces who had been restricted in Attapeu province since 1975 were among others also reportedly released from Attapeu province in 1987.

At least two long-term detainees were reported to have died from natural causes during 1987. They were Ounheuanh Sinbandith, a former police director in the Ministry of Interior who reportedly died on 2 March from heart disease, and Samlith Ratsaphong, a prisoner of conscience and former information director in the Ministry of Information who reportedly died at the age of 62 from heart disease in Houa Phanh hospital. Information was also received last year about the deaths of other long-term detainees which had occurred in previous years as a result of old age or inadequate medical treatment.

There was new information about seven possible prisoners of conscience detained without trial for several years at Nong Pat Prison, which was established in the early 1980s in the Thoulakhom district of Vientiane province to hold prisoners from northern and central provinces. The seven prisoners were reportedly arrested in the late 1970s and early 1980s for offences ranging from 'attempting to escape re-education' to 'involvement in political agitation' and 'improper contact' with people living abroad. Apparently no formal charges were brought against them and they were not tried. Several of them were reportedly tortured or ill-treated while interrogated during prolonged in-communicado detention.

In September at least four people were reported to have been arrested and detained without trial when they were forcibly returned to Laos from Thailand. They had apparently crossed the Mekong River to seek asylum in Thailand soon after their release from 're-education', which had followed 12 years of detention without trial.

Two months later allegations were received that at least six Laotians of Hmong ethnic origin had been executed extrajudicially by Laotian security forces on 20 November. The victims were reportedly the men in a group of 15 men, women and children who had crossed the border earlier that month to seek asylum in Thailand. They had been forcibly returned to Laos by the Thai authorities.

Amnesty International continued in 1987 to inform the government of its concern about the detention without trial or restriction of people held since 1975. The organization pressed for a full review of their cases and the release of those not brought to trial on specific charges. In June Amnesty International publicly welcomed the reported releases but urged that elderly and ailing prisoners be given special consideration for release.

Amnesty International also investigated the cases of the seven detainees held at Nong Pat Prison and called for their release or prompt and fair trial on recognizably criminal charges. Amnesty International also urged the authorities to investigate reports that they had been tortured or ill-treated during interrogation.

Index

160; development of 29–38;
social programme 159–80;
international communist
support for 188; Treaty of
Friendship with Vietnam
191–4. *See also* coalition;
Communist Party; constitution;
Ho Chi Minh Trail; neutrality;
United States; Vietnam
Lao People's Revolutionary
Party 7, 33, 44, 47–9, 52, 56;
change of direction 84–6;
social programme 159–61, 174
Lao Soung 4, 136, 143, 144
Lao-Tai 134
Lao Theung 4, 136–8, 143, 144,
153
Laos: historical background 243–5
legal system 8, 13–14, 23, 124,
325, 328
Lenin, New Economic Policy
of 33, 85, 86, 99–100, 106,
109
Leum Insisiengmay 54
Liang Feng 310
life expectancy 68, 169, 170
literacy 4, 27–8, 75, 139, 142,
148–50, 159, 161–3
livestock production 18, 19, 70, 72
logs 70, 98; exports of 112, 114,
115. *See also* timber
Loven people 134
Lu 134
Luang Prabang 4, 134, 136, 142,
243–4, 281
Luther, Hans 121–2

Maichantan Sengmani 10
maize 70, 134
malaria 71, 169–71
Malaysia, refugees to 222
malnutrition 71, 142
managerial employment and
skills 21, 22, 76, 98, 175
Mao Tse-Tung 305
marijuana 315, 323–7
market economy: movement
towards 33, 77, 85, 103, 104;
theories of 88–9

marketing, reforms in 72
Marxism-Leninism 5, 7, 15, 31,
32, 139, 191–2
Masaryk, Jan 257
maternal health 169, 177
measles 169, 171
mechanisation in agriculture 94
medical personnel 82, 166, 170,
172, 175
Mekong basin projects 17, 67,
214, 232
Meng La, Chinese road from
287–9
Mennonites, aid from 17
'Meo' people 133, 134, 140, 153,
282–3
Mien highlanders 218
Military Assistance Advisory
Group 246–7, 264
minerals 17, 35, 67, 115–17
mining 19, 71, 92, 156, 192
minorities: protection of 159, 160;
illiteracy among 161, 163. *See
also* ethnic groups
monarchy 4, 5, 21, 43, 48, 56,
133, 243–4
monetisation 68, 78–9, 111
Mongolia 25, 81
Mon-Khmer people 4, 134, 136
Moreland, Bob 84
mortality rate 169, 170
Muntarbhorn, Vitit 219
Muong Koua Muong 146–8
Murphy, Robert 247–8

Nam Ngum power station 18, 74,
92, 114–15
Nam Tha, siege of 46, 51
Nam Theum power station 74, 81
narcotics 315–17, 321–7
National Assembly 13, 48, 53
national interests in economic
planning 121–3
National Political Consultative
Council 48, 52, 53
nationalism in Laos 243–71
Neo Lao Issara 138, 148
Neo Lao Haksat: founded 44;
success in elections 44, 262;

private enterprise 33, 34, 67, 74, 78, 97–100, 106–8
privilege 8, 59
production, relations of 15, 106, 160, 161, 188
Programs Evaluation Office 247–8, 254, 264
project finance 81–2
provincial government 78
Provisional Government of National Union 48–50, 52, 53, 57–9
public service employment 110–11. *See also* bureaucracy
pushbacks of refugees 219, 228, 230–32, 235, 316, 329

Quakers, aid from 17, 153

racism 153–6, 334
rattan 115
raw materials, shortages of 91, 92
Reagan, Ronald 201
re-education camps 6, 21, 22, 32, 48, 91, 145, 218, 221, 225, 227, 235, 329
refugee camps 215, 218, 219, 223–31, 235
refugees: displaced by civil war 90, 147; after communist seizure of power 21, 28, 30–32, 143, 188; in Thailand 215–37, 316, 333. *See also* asylum; displaced persons; UN High Commission for Refugees
regional economic cooperation 121–4
Reich, Robert B. 88
religions 159, 160, 332. *See also* Buddhism
repatriation of refugees 215, 220, 223, 229–32, 316, 333
resettlement of minorities 152–3
resettlement of refugees 215–17, 222–8, 232–6
rice production 16, 30, 32, 70, 75, 79, 91, 92, 94, 102, 113, 134, 142, 147–8, 151

river transport 74–5
roads 4, 16–19, 24, 74, 96, 151, 152, 192; Chinese, in northwest Laos 285–310
Robinson, W. Courtland xi, xvi, 215–37
Rowley, Kelvin 84
Royal Lao Army 45, 46, 48, 140, 255, 260, 261. *See also* Pathet Lao
Royal Lao Government: adherents 6, 14, 217, 234; in coalition 44–7, 53, 244, 246; neglect of education, health and minorities 141, 161, 168; renunciation of military alliances 246; negotiations with Pathet Lao 249–57, 260; dependence on US military aid 247–52
Rumania 41, 121
rural development projects 81–2
Rusk, Dean 277, 280, 290

St Goar, Jinn xi, xvii, 285–310
Sali Vongkhamsao 8, 10, 12, 104, 110, 113, 125
Saly Khamsy x, xvi, 209–14, 317
Sam Neua province: base for Pathet Lao 57, 138–9, 159, 244, 247–9, 287; question of sovereignty over 250, 253–8, 260, 269
Saman Vignaket 10
sanitation 150, 169–71
Sarit 290
Savang Vatthana 251, 252
Savannaket 45, 107
Save the Children Fund 17
Sawaeng Wattana 281, 282
schools 139, 141, 149, 162–4, 232
scientific and technical revolution 15, 160
screening of refugees 228–31, 316, 333–4
'self-reliance' 95, 121, 123
self-sufficiency in food 16, 30, 32, 75, 76, 93, 94, 96, 99, 142
services sector of economy 90, 92